How the East Was Won

How did upstart outsiders forge vast new empires in early modern Asia, laying the foundations for today's modern mega-states of India and China? In *How the East Was Won*, Andrew Phillips reveals the crucial parallels uniting the Mughal Empire, the Qing Dynasty and the British Raj. Vastly outnumbered and stigmatised as parvenus, the Mughals and Manchus pioneered similar strategies of cultural statecraft, first to build the multicultural coalitions necessary for conquest, and then to bind the indigenous collaborators needed to subsequently uphold imperial rule. The English East India Company later adapted the same 'define and conquer' and 'define and rule' strategies to carve out the West's biggest colonial empire in Asia. Refuting existing accounts of the 'rise of the West', this book foregrounds the profoundly imitative rather than innovative character of Western colonialism to advance a new explanation of how universal empires arise and endure.

Andrew Phillips is an Associate Professor at the School of Political Science and International Studies at the University of Queensland. His books include *War, Religion and Empire: The Transformation of International Orders* (Cambridge University Press, 2011) and *International Order in Diversity: War, Trade and Rule in the Indian Ocean* (co-authored with J. C. Sharman, Cambridge University Press, 2015).

LSE INTERNATIONAL STUDIES

Series Editors

George Lawson (Lead Editor)
Department of International Relations, London School of Economics

Kirsten Ainley
Department of International Relations, London School of Economics

Ayça Çubukçu
Department of Sociology, London School of Economics

Stephen Humphreys
Department of Law, London School of Economics

This series, published in association with the Centre for International Studies at the London School of Economics, is centred on three main themes. First, the series is oriented around work that is transdisciplinary, which challenges disciplinary conventions and develops arguments that cannot be grasped within existing disciplines. It will include work combining a wide range of fields, including international relations, international law, political theory, history, sociology and ethics. Second, it comprises books that contain an overtly international or transnational dimension, but not necessarily focused simply within the discipline of International Relations. Finally, the series will publish books that use scholarly inquiry as a means of addressing pressing political concerns. Books in the series may be predominantly theoretical, or predominantly empirical, but all will say something of significance about political issues that exceed national boundaries.

Previous books in the series:

The World Imagined: Collective Beliefs and Political Order in the Sinocentric, Islamic and Southeast Asian International Societies Hendrik Spruyt

Socioeconomic Justice: International Intervention and Transition in Post-war Bosnia and Herzegovina Daniela Lai

Culture and Order in World Politics Andrew Phillips and Christian Reus-Smit (eds.)

On Cultural Diversity: International Theory in a World of Difference Christian Reus-Smit

How the East Was Won

*Barbarian Conquerors, Universal Conquest
and the Making of Modern Asia*

Andrew Phillips

University of Queensland

CAMBRIDGE
UNIVERSITY PRESS

CAMBRIDGE
UNIVERSITY PRESS

University Printing House, Cambridge CB2 8BS, United Kingdom

One Liberty Plaza, 20th Floor, New York, NY 10006, USA

477 Williamstown Road, Port Melbourne, VIC 3207, Australia

314–321, 3rd Floor, Plot 3, Splendor Forum, Jasola District Centre, New Delhi – 110025, India

103 Penang Road, #05–06/07, Visioncrest Commercial, Singapore 238467

Cambridge University Press is part of the University of Cambridge.

It furthers the University's mission by disseminating knowledge in the pursuit of education, learning, and research at the highest international levels of excellence.

www.cambridge.org
Information on this title: www.cambridge.org/9781107120976
DOI: 10.1017/9781316343272

© Cambridge University Press 2021

First published 2021

A catalogue record for this publication is available from the British Library.

Library of Congress Cataloging-in-Publication Data
Names: Phillips, Andrew, 1977– author.
Title: How the East was won : barbarian conquerors, universal conquest and the making of modern Asia / Andrew Phillips, University of Queensland.
Description: Cambridge ; New York, NY : Cambridge University Press, 2021. | Series: LSE International Studies | Includes bibliographical references and index.
Identifiers: LCCN 2021026790 (print) | LCCN 2021026791 (ebook) | ISBN 9781107120976 (hardback) | ISBN 9781107546714 (paperback) | ISBN 9781316343272 (ebook)
Subjects: LCSH: Colonies – Asia. | East and West. | Imperialism. | Asia – Foreign relations – Europe. | Europe – Foreign relations – Asia. | Mogul Empire – Politics and government. | China – Politics and government – 1644–1912. | India – Politics and government – 1765–1947. | BISAC: POLITICAL SCIENCE / International Relations / General
Classification: LCC DS33.4.E85 P45 2021 (print) | LCC DS33.4.E85 (ebook) | DDC 950/.3–dc23
LC record available at https://lccn.loc.gov/2021026790
LC ebook record available at https://lccn.loc.gov/2021026791

ISBN 978-1-107-12097-6 Hardback
ISBN 978-1-107-54671-4 Paperback

This book is dedicated to my parents

And to my Brisbane family

Daniel Celm, Sophie Devitt and Joseph and Juliet Celm

Contents

Maps

Preface and Acknowledgements

This book reflects my enduring interest in empires in general, and more particularly my fascination with Asia's historical empires, and their foremost present-day legatees, India and the People's Republic of China. Current commentaries on global politics often fixate on the decline of a Western-dominated international order, and the corresponding resurgence of Asian Great Powers. Without denying the significance of these trends, this book arose from my dissatisfaction with narratives that presume as prologue an elongated era of Western global domination, one that is only now ending with China and India's Phoenix-like revival. Instead, history shows us that the West's age of dominance in Asia was briefer than many recall, and also critically dependent on diverse coalitions of indigenous allies at every stage of infiltration, conquest and consolidation. Western modes of conquest and colonial governance were hardly unique. Instead, they built heavily on Asian precedents, with Mughal and Qing empire-builders pioneering the same logic of conquest by customization that later also under-girded the Western moment of dominance in Asia. Finally, the contemporary megastates of India and China are hardly the modern avatars of ancient 'civilizational' states. Instead, they are the far more recent products of 'barbarian' conquest, their gargantuan dimensions and geopolitical heft owing much to the cultural statecraft of the very same 'foreign' conquerors that modern nationalists now routinely revile.

The surprising parallels between Asian and Western empire-building inspired me to write a book that I hope will interest two different audiences: International Relations (IR) scholars, and a broader readership interested in world history.

The IR community is my original intellectual tribe, and this book contributes to an ongoing debate among IR scholars about how international hierarchies arise and endure in world politics. Despite a wave of incredibly exciting recent scholarship focusing on Asia's historical international relations, much of the field still presumes that instances of universal conquest are rare, with the ambitions of would-be hegemons most often checked by balancing coalitions of rival Great Powers. Though this narrative may accurately capture the last five centuries of European history, it is a poor fit with the same time frame in South and East Asia, where 'barbarian' minority conquest dynasties were frequently successful in establishing universal dominion over regional orders. Accordingly, this book aims to redress this disconnect between IR theory and the historical record, by offering a comprehensive explanation of the recurrent rise of 'barbarian' conquerors in regions that have historically been the world's most enduring concentrations of population, wealth and power.

For readers interested in the larger question of the 'rise of the West' in world history, I hope to offer a provocation, by systematically situating the Western ascendancy within its larger Eurasian context. In doing so, I do not seek to diminish the immense violence and exploitation that characterized Western colonial expansion. I do however aim to dislodge a persistent Western exceptionalism that conceives the modern world as one originating from an initial European epicentre, and that correspondingly overstates Western agency in the construction of the global order. Instead, drawing critically but appreciatively from the work of both area specialists and global historians, I offer here a polycentric account of early modernity that was critically shaped by both European and non-European empire-builders. This polycentric vision more accurately captures Asia's past – while the interweaving of Western and non-Western agency also better anticipates both Asia and the world's likely long-term future.

I have been working on this manuscript for a long time, and I appreciate the forbearance of Cambridge University Press, as well as the inspiration and intellectual generosity of my friends and colleagues, over the course of the book's gestation. I owe special thanks to Christian Reus-Smit and the brilliant team of contributors we worked with in producing *Culture and Order in World Politics*.[1] Exploring the intersection of cultural diversity and international order with such an amazing interdisciplinary team helped hugely in refining my thinking on the cultural statecraft that helped shape Asia's early modern empires, significantly impacting this book's theoretical architecture. Likewise, I remain immensely grateful to Jason Sharman for his wonderful friendship and intellectual comradeship. Concurrent with this book, Jason and I co-wrote *Outsourcing Empire: How Company-States Made the Modern World*, and our thinking on the centrality of company-states as vanguards of early modern globalization

---

[1] A. Phillips and C. Reus-Smit (eds.), *Culture and Order in World Politics* (Cambridge: Cambridge University Press, 2020).

significantly shaped my understanding of the dynamics of Western infiltration into South and East Asia.[2] I am also extremely appreciative both to Julian Go and George Lawson, and to Janice Bially-Mattern and Ayşe Zarakol, for giving me the opportunity to road-test early versions of the book's argument elsewhere.[3]

In writing this book, I have been immensely grateful for the opportunity to receive constructive and stimulating criticism from interlocutors at a variety of different meetings and institutions. I thank audiences at University of Cambridge, Griffith University, the University of Leeds, the London School of Economics, the Norwegian Institute of International Affairs and the University of Queensland (UQ) for their feedback. Thanks also to Daniel Nexon as discussant for his feedback on a paper-length version of the argument presented at the 57th Annual International Studies Association Meeting, and also to fellow panel participants. I owe a special thanks to the participants at UQ's regular St Lucy's History and Theory reading group and to my magnificent colleagues at UQ's School of Political Science and International Studies. Thanks also to Sebastian Kaempf and Matt McDonald as fellow members of the Woollongabba Writers' Collective, for their incisive intellectual critiques, good humour and relentless sledging.

More broadly, I have benefited in immense and incalculable ways from conversations and correspondence with the amazing community of scholars that form the Historical International Relations Section of the International Studies Association. More tangibly, a huge thanks to Jonathan Haslam at Cambridge University Press for his unstinting support and endless patience as this project took shape, as well as to anonymous reviewers for their feedback on various incarnations of this work. I would also like to thank George Lawson, Kirsten Ainley, Ayça Çubukçu and Stephen Humphreys for including this book within the LSE International Studies series. Thanks also to Kye Allen for his meticulous research assistance, and to my incredibly professional indexer Dave Prout. Thanks also to my terrific copy editor, Alice Stoakley, and to Catherine Smith, Raghavi Govindane and the rest of the amazing team at Cambridge University Press for helping to bring this book to fruition.

---

[2] A. Phillips and J. C. Sharman, *Outsourcing Empire: How company-states made the modern world* (Princeton: Princeton University Press, 2020).

[3] A. Phillips, 'Asian incorporation and the collusive dynamics of Western "expansion" in the early modern world' in J. Go and G. Lawson (eds.), *Global Historical Sociology* (Cambridge: Cambridge University Press, 2017), pp. 182–98; A. Phillips, 'Making empires: Hierarchy, conquest and customization' in A. Zarakol (ed.), *Hierarchies in World Politics* (Cambridge: Cambridge University Press, 2017), pp. 43–65.

I also acknowledge the Australian Research Council for crucial financial support through Discovery Early Career Research Council grant DE130100644.

Finally, as always, I thank my mother and father for their love and support, as well as my Brisbane family – Daniel Celm and Sophie Devitt, and Joseph and Juliet Celm.

Introduction

[The] art of ruling native races is a thing of infinite variety not amenable to standardization.[1]

Empires are 'untidy things'.[2] Today's sovereign state monoculture, which fastidiously parcels political authority into territorially exclusive and juridically equal national states, is an anomaly. Historically, it has been empires rather than sovereign state systems that have more often organized life between political communities. These empires have moreover not generally gelled around a single hierarchy, with suzerains enfolding culturally and structurally similar satellites like a set of *Matrioshka* dolls. Instead, they have typically been messy multicultural conglomerates, with the centre tied to its vassals via a thicket of customized compacts.

Traditionally devoted to studying sovereign states dwelling in anarchy, International Relations (IR) scholars are now paying far greater attention to understanding international hierarchies.[3] Pioneering analyses of historical East Asia have been especially influential in kindling this interest.[4] In particular, the contrast between Western sovereign anarchy and Sino-centric

---

[1] British colonial official, cited in C. Newbury, *Patrons, Clients, and Empire: Chieftaincy and over-rule in Asia, Africa, and the Pacific* (Oxford: Oxford University Press, 2003), p. 73.

[2] A. Baker, 'Divided sovereignty: Empire and nation in the making of modern Britain', *International Politics*, 46(6) (2009), 693.

[3] See for example A. Zarakol (ed.), *Hierarchies in World Politics* (Cambridge: Cambridge University Press, 2017). See also J. M. Hobson and J. C. Sharman, 'The enduring place of hierarchy in world politics: Tracing the social logics of hierarchy and political change', *European Journal of International Relations*, 11(1) (2005), 63–98; J. M. Hobson, 'The twin self-delusions of IR: Why "hierarchy" and not "anarchy" is the core concept of IR', *Millennium: Journal of International Studies*, 42(3) (2014), 557–75; and D. A. Lake, *Hierarchy in International Relations* (Ithaca: Cornell University Press, 2009).

[4] See for example V. T.-B. Hui, *War and State Formation in Ancient China and Early Modern Europe* (Cambridge: Cambridge University Press, 2005); D. C. Kang, 'Hierarchy and legitimacy in international systems: The tribute system in early modern East Asia', *Security Studies*, 19(4) (2010), 591–622; S. D. Krasner, 'Organized hypocrisy in nineteenth-century East Asia', *International Relations of the Asia-Pacific*, 1(2) (2001), 173–97; S. H. Park, 'Changing definitions of sovereignty in nineteenth-century East Asia: Japan and Korea between China and the West', *Journal of East Asian Studies*, 13(2) (2013), 281–307.

hierarchy has helpfully unsettled IR's earlier Eurocentrism. At the same time, however, it has also dangerously distorted the way that we think about international orders' comparative evolution. East-West tales of difference and divergence blind us to the *crucial similarities* that united Western and Asian imperial projects in South and East Asia, the world's two most populous regions, from the sixteenth through to the twentieth centuries.

At home, Western Europeans may have haltingly evolved towards sovereign anarchy following the Peace of Westphalia.[5] But as Europeans meanwhile insinuated their way into Asia, they were forced to conform to elaborate systems for managing cultural difference laid down by Mughal and Manchu conquerors, who had themselves only recently consolidated their rule. Later, when the English East India Company (EIC) pivoted from trade to conquest, it moreover confronted remarkably similar challenges to its Mughal and Manchu predecessors, in establishing, consolidating and legitimizing minority rule over indigenous majorities.

The Mughal, Qing and British empires together transformed early modern Asia. In each instance, demographically tiny and culturally marginalized raiders and traders from Asia's steppe, forest and sea frontiers 'rolled up' pre-existing international systems, eventually winning dominion in their respective regions through universal conquest.[6] Notwithstanding their differences, and regardless of whether they were ruled by Asians or Westerners, these empires were built on customization – not standardization. Frontier conquerors won regional primacy not by replacing local cultures, but by remixing them to reshape local identities and curate new constituencies for empire. Equally, conquerors did not import the institutions of imperial rule wholesale, but instead typically fashioned them from existing local practices and resources. Finally, once entrenched in power empire builders in all instances improvised incorporative diversity regimes, understood as elaborate systems to organize cultural diversity in ways conducive to the stabilization and legitimation of their rule.

How and why did vast multicultural empires emerge as the dominant systems for organizing international politics in early modern Asia? How

---

[5] Although for important revisionist takes on the significance of the Peace of Westphalia for European political development, see D. H. Nexon, *The Struggle for Power in Early Modern Europe: Religious conflict, dynastic empires, and international change* (Princeton: Princeton University Press, 2009); A. Osiander, *Before the State: Systemic political change in the West from the Greeks to the French Revolution* (Oxford: Oxford University Press, 2008); and B. Teschke. *The Myth of 1648: Class, geopolitics, and the making of modern international relations* (London: Verso, 2003).

[6] The terminology of system 'roll-up' is taken from D. K. Nedal and D. H. Nexon, 'Anarchy and authority: International structure, the balance of power, and hierarchy', *Journal of Global Security Studies*, 4(2) (2019), 170.

did Asian and Western minority conquest elites subsequently govern imperial orders in South and East Asia? And how did these empires adapt to potentially fatal challenges to their legitimacy following their post-conquest consolidation? These are the three questions that drive this inquiry.

My motives in writing this book are both theoretical and historical. Theoretically, this book advances our understanding of the nature and workings of hierarchy in world politics through a comparative examination of three of the world's largest imperial international orders – the Mughal Empire (c. 1526–1858), the Qing Empire (c. 1644–1912), and the British Raj (c. 1765–1947). Current debates on international hierarchy have conceived hierarchies as arising from either asymmetries in material power;[7] through the negotiation of incomplete contracts between dominant and subordinate actors;[8] or through the production of cultural hegemony, where superordinate agents use their superior communicative prowess to generate forms of cultural and symbolic capital that then entrench their supremacy over weaker actors.[9]

Conversely, this book develops a new perspective on empires' emergence and reproduction, drawing from the literature on the historical sociology of empires, and also from recent constructivist scholarship theorizing the nexus between cultural diversity and international order.[10] I argue that to establish empires over vast and culturally heterogeneous regions, minority conquest elites must first build a broad conquest coalition of allies extending far beyond their immediate retinue. Following the initial wave of conquest, conquest elites must then bind indigenous collaborators to nascent imperial hierarchies, as well as block the emergence of potential anti-imperial coalitions among their subject populations.

---

[7] R. Gilpin, *War and Change in World Politics* (Cambridge: Cambridge University Press, 1981); I. Wallerstein, *The Capitalist World-Economy: Essays by Immanuel Wallerstein* (Cambridge: Cambridge University Press, 1979).

[8] A. Cooley and H. Spruyt, *Contracting States: Sovereignty transfers in international relations* (Princeton: Princeton University Press, 2009); Lake, *Hierarchy in International Relations*.

[9] I draw the idea of asymmetries of communicative and cultural prowess from J. Bially-Mattern, personal correspondence, 10 October 2013. For recent examples, see S. E. Goddard, 'When right makes might: How Prussia overturned the European balance of power', *International Security*, 33(3) (2008-9), 110–42; J. Go, 'Global fields and imperial forms: Field theory and the British and American empires', *Sociological Theory*, 26(3) (2008), 201–29.

[10] See for example J. MacKay, 'Legitimation strategies in international hierarchies', *International Studies Quarterly*, 63(3) (2019), 717–25; J. Mulich, 'Transformation at the margins: Imperial expansion and systemic change in world politics', *Review of International Studies*, 44(4) (2019), 694–716; and Nedal and Nexon, 'Anarchy and authority'.

Building conquest coalitions, binding indigenous collaborators to post-conquest hierarchies, and blocking the prospective formation of anti-imperial coalitions formed the main imperatives of imperial statecraft in early modern Asia. Each entailed profound interventions to reconfigure target populations' cultural identities in ways that would support both conquest and alien rule. The importance of 'divide and rule' strategies for maintaining empires is already broadly known. I argue in this book, however, that early modern empire builders' interventions were constitutive of actors' identities from the earliest stages of conquest, and remained integral to empires' subsequent maintenance. 'Define and conquer'[11] strategies helped curate constituencies for conquest in the initial stages of imperial emergence and expansion, making universal dominion possible. 'Define and rule'[12] strategies – crystallized in diversity regimes tethering authorized forms of cultural difference to imperial authority structures – then cemented collaborators' ties to the imperial centre, and were critical to empires' subsequent legitimation and survival.

Rather than seeking to airbrush empires' essential untidiness and heterogeneity, then, this book foregrounds it, seeing in empires' irrepressible irregularity and cultural diversity a key feature of their constitution, as well as a major source of their adaptability and resilience.[13] I develop this framework from a comparison of three supposedly very different empires, one ostensibly Western (the British Raj), and the other two undeniably Asian (the Mughal and Qing empires). This comparison advances the book's historical contribution – explaining how the West came to dominate far larger and historically wealthier societies in South and East Asia from the late eighteenth through early twentieth centuries.

The question of 'rise of the West' remains one of the social sciences' defining questions. Accounts stressing Western exceptionalism, processes of uneven and combined development, and imperialists' harnessing of indigenous 'networks of domination' have done much to help us understand how Western Europeans briefly succeeded in suborning far

[11] I take this term from P. K. Crossley, 'Making Mongols' in P. K. Crossley, H. F. Sui and D. S. Sutton (eds.), *Empire at the Margins: Culture, ethnicity, and frontier in early modern China* (Berkeley: University of California Press, 2006), p. 72.

[12] I take this term from M. Mamdani, *Define and Rule: Native as political identity* (Cambridge, MA: Harvard University Press, 2012).

[13] In this regard, my argument echoes Karen Barkey's analysis of the Ottoman Empire, who identified a source of the empire's longevity in its 'inherently flexible' structure and maintained that the Ottoman centre's interest in leveraging the Empire's endemic diversity (rather than trying to efface it) helped to assure the empire's resilience in the face otherwise seemingly insuperable governance challenges over centuries of apparent 'decline'. See generally K. Barkey, *Empire of Difference: The Ottomans in comparative perspective* (Cambridge: Cambridge University Press, 2008).

more populous societies in South and later East Asia.[14] But in confining their analyses to Western imperialism, existing explanations obscure the scale, success and resilience of Asian empire-building projects that first predated and then proceeded in parallel with Western expansion. They also overlook the profound similarities in the strategies and practices Westerners and their Asian counterparts both pursued in building and maintaining their empires. Finally, these omissions distort our recollection of the true nature and magnitude of British hegemony in Asia in the nineteenth and early twentieth centuries. Within South Asia and the broader Indian Ocean littoral, this hegemony rested on a wafer-thin patina of Western modernity stretched over an empire that remained tightly anchored in indigenous collaborative networks.[15] And in East Asia, following the Second Opium War and Britain's adoption of a Cooperative Policy, Britain's relationship with the 'Manchu Raj' was more symbiotic than antagonistic. There, the British worked with the Manchus to maintain a hybrid East Asian order that only began its definite transition to a sovereign state system following the Sino-Japanese war, and the Qing Dynasty's subsequent slow-motion unravelling.[16]

Just as John Hobson has masterfully demonstrated the hybrid origins of the 'Oriental West', then, my purpose here in re-examining the rise of the West in Asia is similarly revisionist.[17] In abjuring conventional approaches in favour of an analysis of Western and Asian empires' co-evolution, I relativize the Western ascendancy, reframing the puzzle from a Eurocentric consideration of 'the rise of the West' to a more hemispheric focus on 'how the East was won'. In mounting this challenge, I do not deny the tectonic force of the 'global transformations' that catapulted the West to collective world dominion in the nineteenth century.[18] But I do contest conventional 'vanguardist' narratives of the Western

---

[14] See for example W. H. McNeill, *The Pursuit of Power: Technology, armed force and society since AD 1000* (Chicago: Chicago University Press, 1982); G. Parker, *The Military Revolution: Military innovation and the rise of the West, 1500–1800* (Cambridge: Cambridge University Press, 1996); J. Hobson, *The Eastern Origins of Western Civilization* (Cambridge: Cambridge University Press, 2004); K. Pomeranz, *The Great Divergence: China, Europe, and the making of the modern world economy* (Princeton: Princeton University Press, 2000); P. MacDonald, *Networks of Domination: The social foundations of peripheral conquest in international politics* (Oxford: Oxford University Press, 2014).

[15] See for example J. Onley, 'The Raj reconsidered: British India's informal empire and spheres of influence in Asia and Africa', *Asian Affairs*, 40(1) (2009), 44–62.

[16] J. K. Fairbank, 'Synarchy under the treaties' in J. K. Fairbank (ed.), *Chinese Thought and Institutions* (Chicago: Chicago University Press, 1957), pp. 204–31.

[17] Hobson, *The Eastern Origins of Western Civilization*, p. 36.

[18] B. Buzan and G. Lawson, *The Global Transformation: History, modernity and the making of international relations* (Cambridge: Cambridge University Press, 2015).

ascendancy in Asia.[19] Customization remained the mainstay of Western empire-building in Asia both before and after the supposedly transformative triad of industrialization, rational state-building and the spread of ideologies of progress ramified throughout the world in the nineteenth century. Western hegemony in Asia came later than many assume, built off the foundations laid by Asian predecessors and counterparts, and was neither as deep nor as exclusively Western as both scholars and popular commentators all too commonly assume.

This revisionism matters fundamentally for our understanding of contemporary transformations now reshaping world politics in the wake of China and India's Great Power (re)-emergence. Large sections of the Western commentariat today remain fixated on the rise of non-Western Great Powers and the potential impact of this power shift on global order. These debates reflect a more general anxiety that the world that Western dominance created may now be on the cusp of dissolution.[20] Against this presumption of exclusive Western authorship, however, an innovative wave of revisionist scholarship has powerfully demonstrated that today's global order bears the mark of significant non-Western innovations dating back to the post-1945 period.[21]

This book endorses this revisionism, but extends it back in time to the early modern era, to demonstrate the hybrid and collaborative foundations of the empires – both Western and Asian – that defined international order in South and East Asia from the sixteenth through to the early twentieth centuries. Parsing out the processes through which the Mughal, Manchu and British empires emerged gives us a better foundation for understanding how past Asian orders have been reconfigured in the face of tectonically disruptive power transitions. But this study also aims to correct an outdated historiography that artificially elongates the epoch of Western hegemony in Asia, and in so doing exaggerates the novelty of the supposed 'return' of Asian agency coincident with Asian Great Powers' contemporary resurgence.

Finally, I must note this study's scope and limits. This book examines three ostensibly very different empires to foreground their underlying

---

[19] B. Buzan, 'Culture and international society', *International Affairs*, 86(1) (2010), 2.

[20] The literature on this topic is voluminous. See for example M. Jacques, *When China Rules the World: The end of the western world and the birth of a new global order* (London: Penguin, 2012); R. Meredith, *The Elephant and the Dragon: The rise of India and China and what it means for all of us* (New York: W. W. Norton, 2008).

[21] A. Acharya, *The End of American World Order* (London: Polity, 2014); E. Helleiner, *Forgotten Foundations of Bretton Woods: International development and the making of the postwar order* (Ithaca: Cornell University Press, 2014); C. Reus-Smit, *Individual Rights and the Making of the International System* (Cambridge: Cambridge University Press, 2013).

similarities, and so better understand how universal conquest was possible in the very distinct historical context of early modern Asia. Though my focus is restricted to the Mughal, Manchu and British empires, the book's stress on customization as the foundation of empires' rise and reproduction is by no means limited to these cases, as I illustrate below in passing references to other major empires, including Tsarist Russia and the Ottoman Empire.

Nevertheless, my aim is not to advance a general theory of empire. The logic of customization provides one – but only one – pathway to empire. In other contexts, notably European settler colonialism in the New World and Nazi imperialism in the twentieth century, empires spread by standardization, not customization. This entailed the attempted obliteration of cultural diversity through assimilation or extermination, rather than conquest elites' attempts to co-opt this diversity via incorporative ideologies of rule.[22] Explaining why either customization or standardization predominates in empire builders' strategies is itself a vitally important question. But for now I set this task aside for the more discrete challenge of explaining how the logic of customization defined empires' development in early modern South and East Asia.

The Argument

Defining Key Terms

Already I have introduced terms that demand definition. The first of these is hierarchy. I follow John Hobson and Jason Sharman's definition of hierarchy as referring to 'a relationship between two (or more) actors, whereby one is entitled to command and the other is obligated to obey, and this relationship is recognized as right and legitimate by each'.[23] This incorporation of notions of right and legitimacy into my understanding of hierarchy is undertaken advisedly, for it would seem incongruous with the coercion and exploitation characteristic of historic empires. I do not intend to sanitize the immense violence and oppression that empires typically exemplify. Rather, I simply seek to stress that hierarchies (of which empires are a special form) rest on fundamentally social bargains between superordinate and subordinate actors, which cannot properly be

---

[22] See, for example, generally R. Horsman, *Race and Manifest Destiny: The origins of American Anglo-Saxonism* (Cambridge, MA: Harvard University Press, 1981); T. Todorov, *The Conquest of America: The question of the other* (Norman: University of Oklahoma Press, 1984). On the Third Reich as an exterminationist empire, see M. Mazower, *Hitler's Empire: How the Nazis ruled Europe* (New York: Penguin, 2008).

[23] Hobson and Sharman, 'The enduring place of hierarchy in world politics', 69–70.

understood absent the conceptions of legitimacy through which they are constituted, contested and occasionally transformed.

Most scholarship on international hierarchy has naturally focused on variants of hierarchy within today's sovereign state monoculture.[24] These instances of international hierarchy are muted by the norms of universal juridical equality that infuse today's global order. Conversely, for most of history, international hierarchies have emerged in highly inegalitarian cultural contexts, taking the form of empires. I understand empires as hierarchical systems of rule between formally unequal political communities. Unlike sovereign state systems, where authority is formally distributed among a community of independent sovereign states, political power in empires flows from a single apex, and cascades downwards to encompass a broad range of polities subordinate to the imperial core. Likewise, in contrast to the universalistic rights-based regimes that define modern nation-states, empires rest on 'regimes of unequal entitlement',[25] in which actors advance their goals not by appealing to universal rights, but through recourse to the special privileges granted them by imperial superiors. Occasionally likened to a 'rim-less wheel',[26] empires tie vassals to the centre through 'particular, distinct compacts',[27] while minimizing the scope for exchange (be it military, cultural or commercial) between these vassals.

Finally, this book studies empires within the context of the broader international orders they help constitute. I follow Reus-Smit's definition of international orders as 'systemic configurations of political authority, comprised of multiple units, organized according to some principle of differentiation: sovereignty, suzerainty, empire, or some combination'.[28] More specifically, imperial international orders are defined as hierarchical systems of political authority that centre on territorial empires, but additionally encompass a penumbra of surrounding partially autonomous polities over which the imperial centre successfully claims suzerainty.

---

[24] See for example I. Clark, *The Hierarchy of States: Reform and resistance in the international order* (Cambridge: Cambridge University Press, 1989); T. Dunne, 'Society and hierarchy in international relations', *International Relations*, 17(3) (2003), 303–20; and E. Goh, *The Struggle for Order: Hegemony, hierarchy, and transition in post-Cold War East Asia* (Oxford: Oxford University Press, 2013). See again also Cooley and Spruyt, *Contracting States*; Lake, *Hierarchy in International Relations*.

[25] C. Reus-Smit, 'Struggles for individual rights and the expansion of the international system', *International Organization*, 65(2) (2011), 214.

[26] A. J. Motyl, *Imperial Ends: The decay, collapse, and revival of empires* (New York: Columbia University Press, 2013), pp. 121–2.

[27] C. Tilly, 'How empires end' in K. Barkey and M. von Hagen (eds.), *After Empire: Multiethnic societies and nation-building* (Boulder: Westview, 1997), p. 3.

[28] C. Reus-Smit, *On Cultural Diversity: International theory in a world of difference* (Cambridge: Cambridge University Press, 2018), p. 189.

Thus, for example, the Sinosphere centred on the Qing Empire, but extended also to neighbouring vassals, such as Korea and Vietnam, that nevertheless enjoyed highly levels of autonomy under the umbrella of Qing suzerainty.[29] Likewise, the British Raj encompassed not merely British India, but also a ganglia of partially autonomous dependencies in the Persian Gulf, East Africa and maritime Southeast Asia, which the British also successfully incorporated into their empire over the nineteenth century.[30]

Traditionally, international relations scholars have coded imperial international orders as tributary or suzerain state systems.[31] In preferring the term imperial international orders, I aim to avoid the confining language of tributary or suzerain state systems, which anachronistically attribute a statist character to polity forms that typically varied widely in their internal constitutions. Though this distinction might seem pedantic, it is crucial to foregrounding the great heterogeneity of polities that comprise imperial international orders, and the corresponding diversity of the customized compacts tying these polities to the imperial centre.

The Puzzle and the Argument Previewed: Minority Conquest in Early Modern Asia

This book explains how imperial international orders first emerge, how they are governed, and how they then either succeed or fail in adapting to challenges to their legitimacy. I focus on three minority conquest empires in early modern Asia that arose from seemingly inauspicious circumstances. In each case, formerly stigmatized cultural outsiders took over existing regional systems populated by indigenous majorities that hugely outnumbered them. The conquerors did so without enjoying either decisive military-technological or epidemiological advantages over locals. Conquered regions were moreover wealthy and well-armed (at least by early modern standards), and possessed lettered elites that considered themselves privileged legatees of 'civilization' and had historically often disdained foreign merchants and warriors. Vastly outnumbered, culturally stigmatized and mostly out-gunned, Mughal, Manchu and British conquest elites should have remained marginal irritants, confined to the geographic edges of the regions they ultimately enveloped. Instead, each conquered on a subcontinental scale, rolling up local international

---

[29] Kang, 'Hierarchy and legitimacy in international systems'.
[30] Onley, 'The Raj reconsidered'. See also S. Bose, *A Hundred Horizons: The Indian Ocean in the age of global empire* (Cambridge, MA: Harvard University Press, 2009).
[31] See for example Krasner, 'Organized hypocrisy in nineteenth-century East Asia', 173–97; and M. Wight, *Systems of States* (Leicester: Leicester University Press, 1977).

systems and incorporating defeated polities into new empires of immense size, sophistication and reach. How was this possible?

The short answer to this puzzle is collaboration. 'Barbarians' won because they enticed locals to bandwagon as allies within broad-based multicultural coalitions, on a scale sufficient to compensate for the conquerors' initial numerical inferiority. Once they had overwhelmed remaining indigenous resistance, triumphant conquest elites then entrenched their rule by enlisting local intermediaries as key partners in imperial projects, relying mainly on them to administer the empire, and to defend it from both internal rebellion and external predation.

The prominence of collaboration in my argument will be unsurprising to students of empire. What distinguishes my position is the primary emphasis I accord to the organization of cultural diversity in empires' emergence and consolidation. In the conquest phase of empire, barbarians achieved victory through 'define and conquer' strategies. These entailed cultivating constituencies for empire within target polities, through the curation of new forms of collective identity that eased indigenous bandwagoning with barbarian would-be empire builders. Subsequently, imperial conquest elites then consolidated their power through 'define and rule' strategies. These strategies crystallized in their mature form in imperial diversity regimes, which legitimized alien rule by organizing cultural difference in such a way as to bind intermediaries to the imperial centre, while pre-emptively blocking the potential emergence of anti-imperial coalitions. Following their consolidation, imperial diversity regimes then simultaneously empowered and constrained conquest elites. Undeniably, diversity regimes enabled conquest elites both to encompass the multicultural patrimonies already under their sway, as well as offering pathways for further conquest. But they also locked in conquest elites to a particular model of governance that proved immensely difficult to change without the danger of alienating local intermediaries, with potentially fatal consequences for imperial rule.

Having offered a précis of the book's central argument, I now schematically outline its components in greater detail.

The Argument I: Define and Conquer – Customization and the Emergence of Empires

Define and conquer strategies were indispensable to minority conquerors in organizing and mobilizing the coalitions needed to conquer on a grand scale. Empires formed in early modern Asia not primarily from cultural and institutional imposition, but through empire builders' creative corruption and appropriation of indigenous cultural resources and institutions to construct new hierarchies. I call this process customization, to stress empires' emergence through conquerors' ad hoc refashioning of local cultural resources, and their parallel reassembly of indigenous institutions and practices to advance imperial ends.

Customization is an analogue to localization, a concept derived from Southeast Asian historiography that initially referred to the process by which local rulers imported and creatively adapted foreign cultural elements in order to bolster their legitimacy and power.[32] Conversely, customization refers to foreigners' appropriation of indigenous cultural idioms to legitimize their participation in local political systems. Not confined to the cultural domain, customization extends to institutional reassembly, entailing empire builders' refashioning of existing indigenous institutions and practices to radically new ends.

In early modern Asia, incorporation through customization predominated over obliteration as the primary means through which both Asian and Western empires were forged. *Western and Asian modes of imperialism were more similar than they were different – each employed similar practices of customization to win dominance over indigenous majorities.* The reasons for this lay in part with congruent conceptions of political authority prevalent across early modern Eurasia. Both European and Asian conquerors conceived sovereignty as divisible, and endorsed practices of legal pluralism that reflected incorporative over assimilative strategies of imperial rule.[33] These ideational predilections in turn reflected functional imperatives, specifically the need to rule primarily through local intermediaries, owing to the extremely limited governance capacities of early modern polities. Prior to revolutionary increases in their capacities for direct territorial administration in the nineteenth century, Western and Asian polities both relied primarily on patrimonial systems of indirect rule to uphold their authority.[34] Consequently, imperial expansion required would-be conquerors to harness the governance capacities already inhering in indigenous institutions and practices to maintain their rule. Whether it was Mughal or British imperialists relying on Indian *munshis* to help

---

[32] O. W. Wolters, *History, Culture, and Region in Southeast Asian Perspectives* (Singapore: SEAP Publications, 1999), p. 55.

[33] See generally L. Benton, *Law and Colonial Cultures: Legal regimes in world history, 1400–1900* (Cambridge: Cambridge University Press, 2002). See also S. P. Dolan and D. Heirbaut, "'A patchwork of accommodations": Reflections on European legal hybridity and jurisdictional complexity' in S. P. Dolan and D. Heirbaut (eds.), *The Laws' Many Bodies, c.1600–1900* (Berlin: Duncker and Humblot, 2015), 9–34.

[34] D. W. Allen, *The Institutional Revolution: Measurement and the economic emergence of the modern world* (Chicago: University of Chicago Press, 2011); C. S. Maier, *Leviathan 2.0: Inventing modern statehood* (Cambridge, MA: Harvard University Press, 2014), chapter 1.

administer the Indian subcontinent, or Manchu overlords depending on the Confucian literati to maintain order, empire builders succeeded to the extent that they exploited and adapted indigenous governance capacities to the imperatives of empire.

Asian and Western empires bore family resemblances from the earliest phases of conquest precisely because of the common barriers to imperial entry that frontier empire builders encountered, and the comparable imperatives entailed in negotiating these barriers. Asian and Western empire builders likewise enjoyed similar opportunities for conquest, and contrived parallel solutions – in define and conquer strategies – to make good on these opportunities.

Turning first to barriers and imperatives, Asian and Western empire builders confronted similar challenges arising from cultural difference and demographic insignificance. Undeniably, the barbarian stigma operated with varying potency across my cases, being most constraining for the Manchus, least limiting for the Mughals and operating with intermediate intensity for the British. These variations aside, empire builders in all three cases faced meaningful cultural barriers to conquest. The tiny numbers of Mughal, Manchu and British relative to indigenous majorities further seemed to constrain them militarily, and so stymie any imperial ambitions.

To cross the threshold from being marginal predators to contenders for universal domination, empire builders had to lower the cultural barriers to conquest. They also had to entice sufficient numbers of locals to bandwagon with them to make the formation of a multicultural conquest coalition possible. As I argue in Chapter 2 ('The Eurasian Transformation'), the peculiar conditions of early modern Eurasia provided novel opportunities to meet these imperatives. Already, steppe, forest and sea traders and raiders possessed asymmetric military advantages in cavalry and blue water naval warfare, which had historically enabled frontier predation. These asymmetric military advantages proved an essential starting point – but only a starting-point – for universal conquest. As well as these advantages, frontier predators also perversely benefited from the growing commercial and cultural sophistication of Eurasia's key sedentary power centres from the late medieval period. Growing elite appetites for exotic luxuries potentially conferred immense arbitrage opportunities for militarized long-distance traders. This potentially enabled them to build up significant war chests off the back of trading superprofits that could later be leveraged to buy up indigenous allies. The growth of ostensibly cosmopolitan 'civilizing projects' in Eurasia's sedentary power centres meanwhile ironically provided frontier predators with potentially valuable tools of legitimation, provided they could repurpose them in ways that neutralized the barbarian stigma while facilitating local acceptance of foreign suzerainty.

These structural opportunities made frontier empire-building possible. But define and conquer strategies proved the necessary expedient to fully realise these opportunities. In each of my cases, conquest elites curated new constituencies for empire through sustained efforts to reshape indigenous collective identities in conformity with the needs of their nascent empires. In both South and Northeast Asia, local warlords and warrior communities provided the latent raw material from which conquest coalitions could potentially be forged. To achieve this outcome, however, empire builders needed to reshape indigenous subjectivities, both to make these constituencies more 'legible' and controllable, but also to orient key indigenous intermediaries towards affiliation with conquest elites.

Diverse practices of customization proved pivotal to successful define and conquer strategies. Certainly, the promise of material rewards (either regular pay or a share in the booty harvested from initial conquest) provided an essential glue for early modern conquest coalitions. But Mughal, Manchu and British conquest elites equally cannibalized existing indigenous sources of cultural capital and remixed them to ensure the long-term loyalty of their retinues. The specific practices entailed in define and conquer strategies included widespread religious and cultural patronage; the imagination and institutionalization of real and fictive kinship ties linking foreign conquest elites with local protégés; the appropriation and repurposing of longstanding traditions of military entrepreneurship; and the absorption and adaptation of indigenous rituals of incorporation to yoke intermediaries to emergent hierarchies. Together, these practices remade local identities, enabling bandwagoning for universal conquest, and catapulting minority conquest elites from the margins to positions of hegemonic dominance.

The Argument II: Define and Rule – Diversity Regimes and Imperial Governance

Define and conquer strategies underpinned the first burst of conquest inaugurating new empires. But the practices that made up these strategies were highly protean, consisting of ad hoc expedients geared to the immediate goal of cobbling together viable conquest coalitions. Conversely, consolidating minority rule demanded systematic efforts to bind local intermediaries to the imperial centre over the longer term. This shift from define and conquer to define and rule strategies entailed the widespread codification and institutionalization of cultural difference to support the legitimation of imperial authority. In their mature form, these practices of codification and institutionalization crystalized as diversity regimes, understood as 'systems of norms and practices that simultaneously configure authority and construct [cultural] diversity'.[35]

As Chris Reus-Smit and I have argued elsewhere, diversity regimes fulfil a generic function within international orders in tethering authorized forms of cultural difference to the legitimation of political authority.[36] Within empires ruled by minority conquest elites, diversity regimes fulfilled this imperative in three ways. First, they helped to differentiate minority conquerors from conquered populations, investing them with a separate and distinct identity warranting their right to rule. Second, they interpellated indigenous identities to foster collaborators' identification with the imperial centre; facilitate their subordinate integration into imperial hierarchies; and foreclose the possibility of constituent communities seceding from the empire. Third, imperial diversity regimes also curated indigenous collective identities to inhibit cooperation between different constituent communities. This forestalled the emergence of anti-imperial coalitions, again helping to uphold minority rule and keep the empire intact.

The empires I consider in this book all adopted incorporative rather than assimilative diversity regimes. Each for the most part celebrated cultural diversity, rather than trying to sublimate or obliterate it. This commitment to incorporation over assimilation was of course relative rather than absolute, and varied widely across time and space. Empire builders occasionally deviated from incorporative to assimilative approaches to managing cultural diversity, often with disastrous consequences for the legitimacy of the prevailing order. And a system-wide commitment to incorporation over obliteration occasionally faltered at these empires' far-flung frontiers, where strategies of coercive cultural assimilation – in one instance even escalating to genocide – occasionally held sway.[37]

These caveats aside, incorporative diversity regimes were equally indispensable to consolidating Mughal, Manchu and British rule. Conquest elites in all cases faced the same imperatives. They needed to differentiate themselves from locals; justify their suzerain status; encourage indigenous

---

[35] C. Reus-Smit, 'Cultural diversity and international order', *International Organization*, 71 (4) (2017), 876.

[36] Phillips and Reus-Smit (eds.), *Culture and Order in World Politics*.

[37] On the genocidal character of the Qing Dynasty's campaign against the Zunghars, see M. Levene, 'Empires, native peoples, and genocide' in D. Moses (ed.), *Empire, Colony, Genocide: Conquest, occupation, and subaltern resistance in world history* (New York: Berghahn Books, 2008), p. 188.

identification and collaboration with the empire; and minimize the pro-
spects of local collaborators either seceding or forming anti-imperial
coalitions. Each pursued define and rule strategies, harnessing and repurposing local cultural and institutional resources, to achieve these aims.
This customization of indigenous cultures and institutions to legitimate
imperial orders finally yielded distinctive diversity regimes in each case.

The mature Mughal Empire settled on a diversity regime marked by
syncretic incorporation. Within this framework, the emperor derived his
legitimacy from his ability to secure 'peace for all' (universal reconciliation) through the exercise of his semi-divine charisma. In practice,
incorporation centred on efforts to acculturate the empire's heterogeneous cultural elites into an imperial court culture characterized by
pervasive (primarily religious) syncretism. The emperor and his court –
the pivot of the Mughal diversity regime – did not seek to segregate the
empire's diverse communities into frozen reified fragments. Nor, however, did Mughal court culture aim to absorb and eliminate cultural
difference between its constituents. Instead, the Mughals thrived through
syncretism. They celebrated cultural differences between imperial constituencies, by sponsoring a courtly culture that promiscuously encouraged cross-pollination and the emergence of hybrid identities. This
diluted the pull of more parochial loyalties, mitigated the risks of sectarianism, and dampened centrifugal pressures that might otherwise have
destroyed the empire.

The Manchus by contrast embraced *segregated incorporation* as the
mainstay of their diversity regime. This regime emphasized the centrality
of what we would now label ethnicity in demarcating the boundaries of
collective identity within the empire. Like its Mughal counterpart, the
Manchu diversity regime was profoundly emperor-centric, and the
imperial court likewise served as the principal site for acculturating ruling
elites. But in place of the Mughal court's syncretism, the Qing emperor
'[controlled] cultures by incarnating them'.[38] That is, the Qing emperor
served as chameleon-in-chief, engaging diverse imperial constituencies
through different customized idioms of rule that remained strictly siloed
and separated from one another. Alongside this emperor-centric legitimation strategy, the empire also developed distinct modes of imperial
governance to manage its different constituencies. This was most evident
for example in the Manchus' continued reliance on the Confucian
scholar-gentry and the imperial bureaucracy to run the Sinic core, versus
their development of a court for the administration of the outer provinces

---

[38] P. K. Crossley, *A Translucent Mirror: History and identity in Qing imperial ideology*
(Berkeley: University of California Press, 1999), p. 221.

(the Lifan Yuan) to govern their ganglia of dependencies on the steppe frontier.

The British Raj finally persisted for much of its existence on a diversity regime characterised by *ecumenical incorporation*. The British placed great store on the significance of religious affiliation as a primary axis of cultural difference within their empire. However, unlike the Mughals, the British did not resort to cultural syncretism as part of their define and rule repertoire, except on a localized and limited basis. Nor did the British seek to invest their rule with a semi-divine aura. Instead, Britain's imperial mission centred initially on the need to restore a supposedly pristine Hindu 'civilization' to its former glory following an era of 'foreign' Mughal domination. This narrative saw religious divisions, especially among Muslims and Hindus, as South Asia's primary axis of cultural difference. It furthermore presumed a mode of imperial governance built on the necessity of upholding an inter-communal peace, based on scrupulous (mis)recognition of distinct Hindu and Muslim religious and legal cultures that should perpetually remain separate.

The varied diversity regimes – Mughal syncretism, Qing segregation and British ecumenicism– of course capture only part of a more complex reality. In truth, empire builders pragmatically pursued a multitude of practices to mould cultural difference in the service of imperial legitimation. These practices frequently transgressed the boundaries of the ideal-typical models sketched above, and so are advanced advisedly. Above all, the trichotomy of syncretic, segregated and ecumenical diversity regimes is intended as a simplifying device that foregrounds the key features of the empires under review, and clarifies their main parallels and contrasts. A more granular account exclusively focused on any one of these polities in isolation might accord greater weight to regional variations in the define and rule strategies that empire builders deployed in different parts of their realm. Alternatively, it might stress variations in define and rule strategies developed at different points in the arc of empires' evolution, perhaps accenting the impact of individual emperors' contrasting ideological preferences on the organization of cultural difference.

I am mindful of the historical importance of these geographical and temporal differences, and engage them throughout the book where necessary to better understand individual empires' specific developmental trajectories. Nevertheless, my main goal is a comparative one, simply being to highlight the dominant tendencies of these empires' respective diversity regimes, and to illustrate the bounded variation that existed in the define and rule strategies empire builders each adopted to consolidate imperial international orders in the wake of universal conquest.

The Argument III: Legitimation Challenges and Imperial Resilience During the Global Transformation

This book is mainly concerned with explaining the dynamics of universal conquest and post-conquest consolidation. Nevertheless, it also encompasses themes of crisis, adaptation and resilience, albeit as a secondary focus.

An important argument in IR stresses the transformative impact of the 'global transformation' – a nineteenth-century confluence of industrialization, rational state-building and the spread of ideologies of progress – that together reshaped international orders in the nineteenth century.[39] Without denying the importance of the global transformation, I maintain that the legacies of an earlier era of universal conquest powerfully constrained imperial elites' efforts at modernization in both South and East Asia.

Hostage to a historical outlook that privileges the rise of the West via international society's coercive expansion, IR scholars have neglected the parallel crises of empire that Britons and Manchus both faced in the mid-nineteenth century, as well as similarities in their adaptations to these crises. Conversely, in this book's final empirical chapter, I explore the interlinked crisis of empire that almost toppled both British India and the Qing Empire, and that catalysed conservative (and for a period, highly effective) renovations in their respective diversity regimes.

Driven by economic interest, religious conviction and a commitment to a particularly expansive form of transformational liberalism, British imperial elites in the Company Raj pushed for India's coercive modernization from the 1830s, while simultaneously agitating for the Qing Empire's forced opening to increased trade and diplomatic contact with the West. This aggressive attempt to transform both the British Raj and the Qing Empire deviated significantly from the define and rule and divide and rule practices and accompanying diversity regimes that had formerly supported both orders. Within British India, an Anglicist project to modernize India abraded sharply against the established regime of ecumenical incorporation, alienating critically important indigenous intermediaries while likewise exposing the increasingly threadbare fiction of the EIC's continued nominal subservience to the Mughal Emperor. This revisionism culminated in a local backlash – in the form of the Indian Mutiny – that nearly extinguished British power in South Asia. In East Asia, meanwhile, foreign (mainly British) efforts to bypass Qing restrictions on trade and diplomatic contact inadvertently helped unsettle the

[39] Buzan and Lawson, *The Global Transformation*.

empire's system of segregated incorporation. This helped to catalyse a wave of internal rebellions in both the empire's Sinic core and its heterogeneous borderlands, at one point threatening the Qing Empire's continued survival.

Though these crises nearly destroyed both the British and Qing imperial orders, both instead proved remarkably resilient. Empire builders in both instances preserved themselves in power through conservative renovations of existing diversity regimes. This was purchased at the price of British retrenchment of liberal transformative ambitions, intensified dependency on indigenous intermediaries in British India and a post-Opium Wars partnership of sorts between the British and Qing empires that persisted down to the 1890s.

In the British Raj, the Mutiny forced the British to largely abandon earlier efforts to modernize and standardize subject societies. Instead, a post-rebellion *modus vivendi* saw colonial authorities explicitly empower client rulers through a refined and extended system of 'indirect rule' that would later spread throughout the empire, shaping British imperial governance for the remainder of the empire's existence. Likewise, the British recalibrated their legitimation strategies to again privilege conservative religious intermediaries.[40] Imperial ideology henceforth stressed an understanding of India as a mere 'geographic expression'[41] composed of immutably different and antagonistic peoples that only the British could pacify. An overhaul of the empire's strategy of imperial recruitment – away from high-caste Hindus and towards 'martial races' on the empire's north-western frontiers – completed what amounted to a highly conservative renovation of the Raj's imperial hierarchy.

The renovation of the British Raj roughly coincided with equally extensive adaptations in the Qing Empire. Too often seen as a half-hearted adaptation in the face of external Western aggression, the reforms of the Tonghzi Restoration significantly overhauled Qing methods of rule, while paradoxically reinforcing many of the empire's more orthodox and traditional features. In the face of the millenarian Taiping challenge in the empire's Sinic core, the Manchus doubled down on their reliance on traditional elites – specifically the Confucian literati and their associated loyalist militia – to uphold Qing rule. At the same time, the Manchus

---

[40] See for example C. A. Bayly, 'Distorted development: The Ottoman Empire and British India, circa 1780–1916', *Comparative Studies of South Asia, Africa and the Middle East*, 27 (2) (2007), 340; K. Mantena, *Alibis of Empire: Henry Maine and the ends of liberal imperialism* (Princeton: Princeton University Press, 2010), chapter 5; and more generally T. R. Metcalf, *Ideologies of the Raj* (Cambridge: Cambridge University Press, 1997).

[41] J. Darwin, *Unfinished Empire: The global expansion of Britain* (New York: Bloomsbury Press, 2012), p. 212.

progressively redefined their relations with tributary polities, synthesizing elements from traditional tributary diplomacy with localized adaptations of Western diplomatic norms. Importantly, this renovation occurred within the context of Britain's Cooperative Policy towards the Qing Dynasty. This policy sought not to destroy the empire, but to support its resuscitation as the core of an East Asian order that would be centred on a strong Qing Empire, while remaining permeable to Western commercial penetration.[42]

My essential point is that even in the face of ostensibly powerful modernizing pressures, the path-dependent legacies of an earlier era of customized conquest constrained imperial elites in both the British Raj and the Qing Empire from the mid-nineteenth century. The British and Qing empires experienced symmetrical and structurally similar crises of imperial authority at this time.[43] These crises spurred conservative renovations of existing diversity regimes, rather than exemplifying a form of nineteenth-century 'rational state-building'.[44] Out of these crises, Western colonialism consolidated in South Asia and was extended informally into East Asia, effectively yoking maritime Asia under an integrated web of Western hegemony from the Bay of Bengal through to the East China Sea for the first time. In both South and East Asia, however, this consolidation and extension rested on a delicate fabric of local acquiescence and on the twin foundations of the British Raj and the Manchu Raj, which subsequently remained entwined in distrustful symbiosis down to the early twentieth century.

Plan of the Book

This book proceeds as follows.

Chapter 1 situates my inquiry by first critically reviewing accounts of empires' emergence that have tried to explain the Western ascendancy in Asia. I then make the case for reframing the puzzle of this ascendancy away from a traditional formulation of the Rise of the West, and towards an alternative puzzle of How the East was Won. This alternative formulation stresses the necessity of examining the Western ascendancy comparatively and interactively, in the context of its entanglements with its

---

[42] See generally Fairbank, 'Synarchy under the treaties'.
[43] On this crisis, see generally M. Geyer and C. Bright, 'World history in a global age', *American Historical Review*, 100(4) (1995), 1034–60; see also Maier, *Leviathan 2.0*, chapter 2.
[44] B. Buzan and G. Lawson, 'The global transformation: The nineteenth century and the making of modern international relations', *International Studies Quarterly*, 57(3) (2013), 621.

Asian precedents and counterparts. The chapter concludes with a presentation of the book's theoretical argument.

Chapter 2 situates my inquiry historically by sketching the Eurasian Transformation that made later Mughal, Manchu and Western empire-building projects possible. I argue that late-medieval Eurasia was transformed through an interlocking quartet of geopolitical, economic, administrative and ideological processes of 'hemispheric integration'.[45] These processes dramatically expanded Eurasia's interaction capacity. They also reconfigured the existing distribution of military, economic, administrative and cultural forms of capital, making new forms of militarized commercial state-building possible on Eurasia's steppe, forest and sea frontiers. This paved the way for the emergence of the commercially sophisticated, administratively durable and culturally polyglot empires that subsequently dominated Eurasia, and that form the subject of this book.

Having laid out the inquiry's theoretical foundations and historical context, the rest of the book proceeds in a chronological fashion.

Chapter 3 examines the rise of the Mughal and Manchu empires. These empires were Asia's two greatest terrestrial powers in terms of population, commercial wealth and military strength, and were the respective regional hegemons in South and East Asia when Westerners first insinuated themselves along Asia's maritime frontiers. Their parallel origins – congruent challenges of consolidation and legitimation, and divergent diversity regimes – form the primary axes of comparison.

Chapter 4 then considers Western incorporation into the Mughal and Manchu empires. Here I place particular stress on the differing degrees to which Western maritime powers were incorporated into the Mughal and Qing empires, and the long-term consequences of this differential integration for the subsequent fate of international orders in South and East Asia.

Chapter 5 explains the great Asian divergence after 1700, which saw the Mughal Empire rapidly decline at the same time that the Qing Empire doubled in size and peaked in its material and ideational power. The Manchus proved more effective than the Mughals in accommodating cultural diversity as they conquered new territory – a discrepancy that was key to explaining their empires' diverging fates. The Mughals' Persephone model of syncretic incorporation proved insufficiently elastic in integrating new intermediaries from the Deccan, a weakness that

---

[45] On hemispheric integration as a key driver of Eurasian political development in the millennium up to 1500 CE, see generally J. H. Bentley, 'Hemispheric integration, 500–1500 CE', *Journal of World History*, 9(2) (1998), 237–54.

Emperor Aurangzeb's sectarian inclinations aggravated. Conversely, the Manchus' model of segregated incorporation enabled them to encompass vast new territories in Tibet and Xinjiang in the eighteenth century, in the process also eradicating the threat of steppe conquest that had plagued all preceding rulers of China.

Chapter 6 explains the East India Company's rise to paramountcy in South Asia from 1740–1820, following the Mughal Empire's implosion. Consistent with the book's central claim, I argue that we can understand the rise of the Company Raj only by acknowledging the derivative character of company imperialism, which drew systematically on practices of conquest by customization first pioneered by earlier waves of Asian imperialists. At the same time, I acknowledge the unique regime of ecumenical incorporation the EIC mobilized to manage cultural diversity, and the distinctive vulnerabilities that it introduced into the company's system of rule.

Chapter 7 rounds out the narrative by examining the interlocking crises that engulfed the British Raj and the Qing Empire in the mid-nineteenth century, and compelled sweeping renovations in the orders they respectively dominated. From the early 1800s, the British in Asia embraced a transformational liberalism that sought not to accommodate cultural diversity, but to subsume it to a single anglicized civilizational standard. The Indian Mutiny that this transformation sparked almost destroyed British rule, and resulted in a reconstitution of imperial order again firmly anchored in the incorporation of cultural difference, rather than its forced assimilation. Synchronous crises that nearly toppled the Qing Empire meanwhile prompted a parallel downgrading of British liberal aspirations in East Asia, and cooperation with a revived Qing Dynasty now more firmly wedded than ever to a conservative model of rule through the segregated incorporation of its diverse imperial constituencies. These mid-century crises confirmed the resilience of the British Raj and the Qing Empire, while also straitjacketing them within systems of rule that would ultimately condemn them to oblivion in the first half of the following century.

The Conclusion recaps the book's central argument, and teases out its main lessons for both the dynamics of universal conquest within international systems, as well as the rise of the West in world history.

1   From the Rise of the West to How the East Was Won

For 200 years, a gargantuan power imbalance has defined world politics – the West's dominance over historically more powerful societies in South and East Asia. From the late 1700s, military and economic power slid from East to West as tectonically as if Eurasia had been tilted on its side. So unprecedented was this power shift, and so profound its impact on world politics, that the 'rise of the West' remains today one of the social sciences' defining questions.

In this chapter, I draw critically but appreciatively from this vast literature on the rise of the West as a point of departure. But my interest is not to critique this literature simply to produce a better explanation for the Western ascendancy per se. Rather, I argue that we must shake off the habit of studying the rise of the West in isolation, and instead consider it comparatively within the early modern Eurasian context that made it possible.

Accordingly, this chapter is organized in three sections. I begin with a critical review of existing accounts of the rise of the West. I focus especially on arguments that respectively stress Western exceptionalism, the logic of uneven and combined development, and 'pericentric' theories of empire,[1] that focus on the ideational or network-relational preconditions for colonial collaboration. This review reveals common limitations to these approaches that warrant a shift from the rise of the West, towards the alternative puzzle of 'How the East was won'. The second section makes the case for this shift in explanatory focus in greater detail. The final section lays out this book's conceptual framework and core argument.

Exceptionalism, Entanglements and Encounters: Explaining the Rise of the West

This section engages many of the most prominent accounts of the West's rise to global supremacy. To give order to the discussion, I have grouped

---

[1] On pericentric theories of empire, see generally M. W. Doyle, *Empires* (Ithaca: Cornell University Press, 1986), pp. 25–6.

22

these approaches under the themes of (a) Western exceptionalism; (b) global entanglements; and (c) frontier encounters. These frameworks respectively privilege modes of explanation cast at the scale of the (Western) civilizational, the global, and the colonial conquest frontier. Together they provide both inspiration and foil for my alternative framework, cast at the hemispheric/Eurasian scale, and outlined in the next two sections.

Western Exceptionalism

Some of the most influential efforts to explain the rise of the West attribute it to characteristics supposedly unique and endogenous to the West itself. Western exceptionalism can be found in fields as diverse as global history, historical sociology, military history, and institutional economics. Given this diversity, my engagement with this literature is necessarily selective. Here I focus on two of its most prominent expressions: the military superiority thesis, and the economic superiority thesis.

The Western military superiority thesis ascribes the East-West power flip primarily to the West's supposedly unique propensity for military innovation. The sparest of these accounts argue that a succession of 'military revolutions', beginning in the sixteenth century and accelerating with the nineteenth-century industrial revolution, equipped the West with supposedly world-beating military capabilities.[2] These capabilities – ranging from technological to organizational to cultural – developed in the crucible of continuous geopolitical competition in medieval and early modern Europe. Military superiority advocates contend that the winnowing effects of continuous warfare endowed Europeans with the war-fighting capabilities that eventually won them global supremacy by the nineteenth century.[3] Augmenting this line of argument, neoclassical realists further contend that non-European polities' administrative weakness and societal divisions generally prevented them from meeting the Western challenge, condemning them to colonial or semi-colonial status.[4]

---

[2] See for example W. H. McNeill, *The Rise of the West: A history of the human community* (Chicago: University of Chicago Press, 1963); and Parker, *The Military Revolution*. For an outstanding recent critique of the military revolution thesis as an explanation for the West's late rise to global dominance, see J. C. Sharman, *Empires of the Weak: The real story of European expansion and the creation of the new world order* (Princeton: Princeton University Press, 2019).

[3] See for example M. Mann, *The Sources of Social Power*, 4 vols., III: *Global Empires and Revolution, 1890–1945*, 2nd ed. (Cambridge: Cambridge University Press, 2012), pp. 23–6; and C. Tilly, *Coercion, Capital and European States, AD 990–1992* (New York: Wiley-Blackwell, 1992), p. 162.

[4] See for example S. Rosen, *Societies and Military Power: India and its armies* (Ithaca: Cornell University Press, 1996); and J. W. Taliaferro, 'State building for future wars: Neoclassical realism and the resource-extractive state', *Security Studies*, 15(3) (2006), 464–95.

The military superiority thesis can be faulted on three main grounds. First, at least with respect to the West's colonial expansion in Asia, there is the simple question of timing. Historians who have studied the formation of the West's territorial colonial empires in Asia explicitly discount Western military-technological supremacy as an explanation for the East-West power flip. 'Britain's empire [in Asia] was a Bonapartist, not a Wilhelminic achievement',[5] which crystallized in the late eighteenth and early nineteenth centuries. It thus substantially predated the late-nineteenth-century military innovations that later temporarily established unqualified Western military dominance over its Afro-Asian rivals. Writing of Britain's conquest of India, Douglas Peers admonishes:

We must not extrapolate backward, that is, assign timelessness to the kinds of technological differentials so obvious in the late nineteenth and twentieth centuries. By then, the discrepancies between highly industrialized societies and recently conquered peoples in Asia and Africa had become unmistakably clear. Quick-firing artillery, breech-loading rifles with smokeless powder, machine guns, tele-graphs, steam-powered vessels, and other innovations, which collectively comprise the kinds of weapons associated with modern industrial warfare, did not enter widespread service until the late nineteenth century.[6]

Military-industrial supremacy did undeniably consolidate the West's global dominance *after* 1870. Between 1870 and 1915, Western states distributed or redistributed approximately a quarter of the world's land surface between them as colonial possessions.[7] Industrial technologies such as steam-driven transportation systems facilitated these conquests, as did more purely military innovations such as the repeating rifle and the machine gun. But the lopsidedness of cross-cultural military encounters from the late nineteenth century was 'extraordinary as well as transitory',[8] and did not reflect the far more even military balance that prevailed between Europeans and Asians before this time.[9] Most notably, such a perspective also ignores the fact that – on land at least – Europeans

---

[5] D. H. A. Kolff, 'The end of the *Ancien Régime:* Colonial war in India, 1798–1818' in J. A. de Moor and H. L. Wesseling (eds.), *Imperialism and War: Essays on colonial wars in Asia and Africa* (Leiden: E. J. Brill, 1989), p. 22.

[6] D. M. Peers, 'Revolution, evolution, or devolution: The military and the making of colonial India' in W. E. Lee (ed.), *Empires and Indigenes: Intercultural alliance, imperial expansion, and warfare in the early modern world* (New York: New York University Press, 2011), p. 92.

[7] E. Hobsbawm, *The Age of Empire, 1875–1914* (London: Vintage, 1989), p. 59.

[8] W. H. McNeill, *The Age of Gunpowder Empires, 1450–1800* (Washington, DC: American Historical Association, 1989), p. 12.

[9] On this point, see generally P. A. Lorge, *The Asian Military Revolution: From gunpowder to the bomb* (Cambridge: Cambridge University Press, 2008); and Sharman, *Empires of the Weak.*

were more often supplicants than suzerains to Asian powers, at least prior to the mid-eighteenth century.

Besides the question of timing, the Western military superiority thesis also suffers when we consider the actual dynamics of large-scale colonial conquest, once Westerners did embark on territorial expansion in Asia from the 1750s. Certainly, the military innovation of the broadside-firing battleship had previously helped Westerners eke out a tenuous toehold on Asia's littoral frontiers from the sixteenth century. Blue water naval supremacy was critical in enabling Westerners to muscle in on Asian markets from the 1500s, and thus become meaningful participants in a larger Eurasian commercial and strategic order.[10] Consequently, it looms large in the narrative to follow. But other signature innovations stemming from the early modern Western 'military revolution' were either not exclusively Western (gunpowder artillery),[11] were easily and rapidly adopted by non-European powers (drilled infantry armies),[12] or were for other reasons unsuitable for purposes of colonial conquest (modern *trace italienne*-style fortresses).[13] Westerners were moreover able to undertake large-scale territorial conquest in Asia only through the massive mobilization of Asian resource portfolios and indigenous collaborators. The East India Company's (EIC) conquest of India, for example, was supported overwhelmingly through Indian-manned armies, while it raised 90 per cent of its war credit from Indian bankers.[14] Indian spies likewise sustained the 'empire of information'[15] on which the Company Raj was built, while Indian contractors supplied the logistical infrastructure that sustained the company's armies in the field.[16] In contrast to Westerners' experience in the New World, the path to conquest in Asia was not eased by pandemics that destroyed most vestiges of indigenous resistance in the early stages of expansion. Collaboration – rather than the overwhelming application of superior firepower against weaker opponents – consequently proved

---

[10] See for example T. Andrade, 'Was the European sailing ship a key technology for European expansion? Evidence from East Asia', *International Journal of Maritime History*, 23(2) (2011), 17–40.

[11] Lorge, *The Asian Military Revolution*, p. 86.

[12] T. Andrade, *The Lost Colony: The untold story of China's first great victory over the West* (Princeton: Princeton University Press, 2011), p. 131.

[13] Sharman, *Empires of the Weak*, pp. 77–8.

[14] T. Roy, 'Rethinking the origins of British India: State formation and military-fiscal undertakings in an eighteenth century world region', *Modern Asian Studies*, 47(4) (2013), 1139.

[15] C. A. Bayly, *Empire of Information: Intelligence gathering and social communication in India, 1780–1870* (Cambridge: Cambridge University Press, 1999).

[16] See generally K. Roy, 'Military synthesis in South Asia: Armies, warfare and Indian society, c. 1740–1849', *Journal of Global History*, 69(3) (2005), 651–90.

imperative in enabling large-scale territorial expansion, and must therefore be central to any inquiry into the origins of the East-West power flip.

Third and most importantly, the Western military superiority thesis falls short because it fails to situate Western colonial conquests in Asia within a larger Eurasian comparative context. The West's establishment of colonial dominance over commercially sophisticated, vastly more populous and culturally diverse populations in Asia was undoubtedly remarkable. *But it was far from unique in the context of early modern Eurasia.* By the late eighteenth century, similar power transitions had already enabled Muslim Timurid Mughals to dominate Hindustan, and had also catapulted 'barbarian' Manchus to power in Sinic East Asia. Cultural difference, geographic distance and indigenous resistance had each been overcome by Mughal and Manchu parvenu conquerors long before the English East India Company's rise to paramountcy in India. Crucially, these Asian precursors to Western colonial rule had moreover pioneered techniques of conquest that later provided decisive precedents for Western expansion. Mughal and Manchu conquerors mastered the challenges of mobilizing culturally diverse conquest coalitions, binding them to nascent structures of imperial rule, and then pre-emptively disrupting the emergence of countervailing coalitions that could threaten their power. These were imperatives that Western colonialists also later confronted, and to which they responded in strikingly similar ways. Whereas the Western military superiority thesis stresses the disruptive power of European *innovation*, comparative scrutiny alternatively illuminates the profoundly *imitative* roots of Western colonial conquest in Asia. Western colonialists succeeded in dominating first South and then East Asia as much because of their similarities with preceding Asian hegemons as for their differences – an observation that substantially undercuts military exceptionalist accounts of the Western ascendancy.

Besides the military superiority thesis, a popular alternative explanation credits the rise of the West not to its supposedly unique martial prowess, but to economic dynamism flowing from superior governance institutions. Specifically, this form of neo-Weberian institutionalism attributes the Western ascendancy to a constellation of institutions, ranging from strong bureaucratic states through to limited constitutional government, and including also property regimes that favoured private capital accumulation.[17] These institutions supposedly provided the matrix within which the industrial revolution could germinate, ensuring the

---

[17] See for example F. Fukuyama, *The Origins of Political Order: From prehuman times to the French Revolution* (New York: Farrar, Straus and Giroux, 2012); E. Jones, *The European Miracle: Environments, economies and geopolitics in the history of Europe and Asia* (Cambridge: Cambridge University Press, 2003); and D. C. North, *Institutions,*

revolutionary increase in productive and destructive capacities that won the West world hegemony.

Neo-Weberian institutionalism offers a more holistic and less anachron-istic explanation for the East-West power flip than the military superiority thesis. Again, however, it has sparked criticisms which have substantially qualified its persuasiveness. Drawing inspiration from Kenneth Pomeranz' pioneering study of the 'great divergence' between Western Europe and China after 1750,[18] the California school of historians has marshalled a vast body of evidence to contest institutionalist variants of Western exception-alism. These critiques have challenged the timing and length of the great divergence between Asia and the West, dating the divergence's onset from the late eighteenth century, rather than either the sixteenth century or even earlier.[19] Following Pomeranz' lead, California school historians have likewise questioned the causal sufficiency of Western governance institu-tions as the main reason for the West's ascendancy. Instead, Pomeranz and his supporters have stressed the importance of conquest and contingency in driving the rise of the West. Pomeranz thus contends that it was the West's earlier conquest of the Americas, together with the fortuitous location of coal reserves in Great Britain, that enabled North-western Europe alone to escape ecological bottlenecks that stopped all other early modern societies from moving beyond proto-industrialization.[20]

While the debate between Western exceptionalists and their California school critics remains far from settled, even champions of the former acknowledge that exclusively endogenous accounts of the Western ascendancy are now difficult to sustain.[21] The pull of early modern Asian prosperity was undeniably the crucial catalyst propelling Western maritime expansion from the early sixteenth century. Historians have moreover conclusively demonstrated the indispensability of New World precious metals and cash crops in enabling large-scale Western participa-tion in Asian trading networks.[22] And – as I argue below – the injection of

Institutional Change and Economic Performance (Cambridge: Cambridge University Press, 1990).

[18] Pomeranz, *The Great Divergence.*

[19] See for example generally A. G. Frank, *ReOrient: Global economy in the Asian age* (Berkeley: University of California Press, 1998); J. A. Goldstone, 'Efflorescences and economic growth in world history: Rethinking the "rise of the West" and the industrial revolution', *Journal of World History*, 13(2) (2002), 323–89; R. B. Wong, *China Transformed: Historical change and the limits of the European experience* (Ithaca: Cornell University Press, 1997).

[20] Pomeranz, *The Great Divergence.*

[21] M. Mann, 'Review article: The great divergence', *Millennium: Journal of International Studies*, 46(2) (2018), 241–8.

[22] See for example D. O. Flynn and A. Giráldez, 'Born with a "silver spoon": The origin of world trade in 1571', *Journal of World History*, 6(2) (1995), 201–21.

New World resources into Asia also had transformative geopolitical effects among Asian polities themselves, which are typically ignored in accounts that fixate exclusively on explaining the Western ascendancy.

Acknowledging the centrality of these inter-societal exchanges in reshaping early modern Eurasia by no means negates the importance of Western institutional innovation to this process. In particular, the institution of the chartered company-state played a critical role, alongside Western naval superiority, in enabling Westerners to project power across transcontinental distances, and so insinuate their way permanently into originally wealthier and more powerful Asian host polities. But the efficacy of even institutions such as the company-state depended on their ability to 'plug in' to indigenous Asian customs of commercial extraterritoriality as a prerequisite for their expansion. This again highlights the interactive and synergistic character of the West's initial forays into littoral Asia, again counselling against purely endogenous accounts of the Western ascendancy.

Global Entanglements

In contrast to exceptionalist accounts, global historical sociologists and scholars of uneven and combined development (UCD) have alternatively marshalled arguments cast at the global (as opposed to the civilizational) level of analysis, and privileged inter-societal relations of unequal exchange over innate Western advantages to explain the rise of the West.

Working within the tradition of global historical sociology, John Hobson's analysis of Western civilization's 'eastern origins' and Barry Buzan and George Lawson's account of the nineteenth-century 'global transformation' directly engage the puzzle of the East-West power flip.[23] Explaining the West's late and historically exceptional ascendancy over Asia, Hobson argues that the West rose to global dominance first by assimilating Asian (primarily Chinese) technologies, and then later by engaging in the large-scale racist imperial appropriation of Afro-Asian resource portfolios.[24] In contrast to liberal accounts of the rise of the West, Hobson foregrounds the centrality of an interventionist British state in consciously engineering British industrialization, and in coercively subordinating non-European polities to British imperatives.[25] He furthermore stresses the role that an expansionist ideology – centred around non-Europeans' forced cultural conversion and their economic

---

[23] Buzan and Lawson, 'The global transformation', 630–4; Buzan and Lawson, *The Global Transformation*; and Hobson, *The Eastern Origins of Western Civilization*.

[24] Hobson, *The Eastern Origins of Western Civilization*, p. 257.   [25] Ibid., pp. 245–7.

containment – played in simultaneously industrializing the West while de-industrializing Asia.[26]

Hobson's commitment to a multi-causal mode of explanation finds echoes in Buzan and Lawson's more recent account of the nineteenth-century global transformation. Addressing the East-West power flip, Buzan and Lawson observe that 'the shift in global power distribution from Asia to Europe took place because of a novel configuration that linked industrialization, the rational state and ideologies of progress'.[27] The European breakthrough towards industrial modernity was thus 'asynchronous and interactive', and depended critically on processes of unequal exchange and primitive accumulation linking North-western Europe to exploited peripheries.[28] The global transformation thesis nevertheless accords a more equal weighting to a modernizing triad of interlocking ideational, institutional, and economic transformations, which collectively propelled the societies of North-western Europe to global dominance.

Hobson and Buzan and Lawson's contributions illuminate critical dimensions of the East-West power flip, and their multi-causal mode of analysis cleaves closely to that which informs my own argument. They nevertheless share two main limitations. First, like the military superiority and institutionalist arguments already canvassed, historical sociological accounts of the East-West power flip are also confounded by the timing of Western imperialism in Asia. Hobson places the date of the Western ascent at around 1840, coincident with the First Opium War.[29] Likewise, Buzan and Lawson follow Hobson in nominating the First Opium War as an especially significant signpost in the West's military-industrial ascent over Asia.[30] This is problematic, given the earlier timing of Western territorial conquests in Asia previously noted. By the end of the Third Anglo-Maratha War (1817–19), the EIC had in India won control over approximately 15 per cent of the world's population, seeing off well-organized opponents that enjoyed equivalent technological advantages in the process.[31] The company's conquest of Java (another of pre-industrial Asia's main power centres) during the British interregnum there likewise occurred decades prior to the Second Industrial Revolution.[32] In both these and other instances, Asian military

---

[26] Ibid., pp. 259–60.   [27] Buzan and Lawson, 'The global transformation', p. 625.
[28] Ibid., p. 621.   [29] Hobson, *The Eastern Origins of Western Civilization*, p. 20.
[30] Buzan and Lawson, 'The global transformation', 632.
[31] On this period as the critical epoch in establishing the West's growing global military ascendancy, see generally C. A. Bayly, 'The first age of global imperialism, c. 1760–1830', *Journal of Imperial and Commonwealth History*, 26(2) (1998), 28–47.
[32] M. Ricklefs, *A History of Modern Indonesia since c. 1300* (Berkeley: Stanford University Press, 1993), p. 113.

manpower formed an indispensable asset in constructing and consolidating Western hegemony. A convincing account of the East-West power flip must explain how the EIC succeeded in mobilizing and harnessing indigenous military capabilities and turning them to imperial ends in this way.

Second, while these scholars rightly emphasize the immense violence of European imperialism, they neglect the essential role non-European intermediaries played in shoving and shaping the course of European expansion in Asia, and the resulting hybridity of the pan-regional order that consolidated in maritime Asia under Western suzerainty by the mid-nineteenth century. This neglect is for example evident in Hobson's characterization of the 'unequal treaty' system that governed the Sino-Western relationship from 1842 to 1943. Hobson portrays this system as 'dictated solely on Western terms to the detriment of Chinese sovereignty and self-determination'.[33] But recent scholarship qualifies this characterization.[34] For the unequal treaty system built on long-established Chinese customs of commercial extraterritoriality, and operated alongside China's traditional tributary relations with its Confucian satellites down to the late nineteenth century. Far from 'shatter[ing] the whole moral/normative structure on which the Chinese state and society had been founded',[35] Western intervention proved distinctly secondary to internal rebellion as the Qing Dynasty's pre-eminent threat. After the Sino-Japanese war (1894–5), foreign predation admittedly grew more threatening, and eventually helped destroy the Qing Empire. But for the preceding fifty years, Qing courtiers, Confucian Chinese scholar gentry and barbarian Western interlopers improvised and co-managed a 'synarchic' order in East Asia, which rested on a distinctly hybrid synthesis of European and Asian interests and practices.[36]

Privileging the master mechanism of Uneven and Combined Development (UCD), Alex Anievas and Kerem Nişancioğlu have offered an alternative account of the Western ascendancy, which given its prominence also warrants critical scrutiny.[37] Like Hobson and Buzan and Lawson, Anievas and Nişancioğlu array themselves against Western exceptionalism, in favour of a sustained examination of the interregional

---

[33] Hobson, *The Eastern Origins of Western Civilization*, p. 261.

[34] See for example generally T. Kayaoglu, *Legal Imperialism: Sovereignty and extraterritoriality in Japan, the Ottoman Empire, and China* (Cambridge: Cambridge University Press, 2010).

[35] Hobson, *The Eastern Origins of Western Civilization*, p. 262.

[36] Fairbank, 'Synarchy under the treaties', pp. 222–3.

[37] A. Anievas and K. Nişancioğlu, *How the West Came to Rule: The geopolitical origins of capitalism* (London: Pluto Press, 2015); and A. Anievas and K. Nişancioğlu, 'How did the West usurp the rest? Origins of the great divergence over the *longue durée*', *Comparative Studies in Society and History*, 59(1) (2017), 34–67.

and global forces that drove the rise of the West. More specifically, they stress the importance of the uneven development and configuration of different societies (e.g., the initial 'backwardness' of Western Europe relative to Asia), and the centrality of 'geopolitical combination' between these heterogeneous orders, to account for the East-West power flip.[38] Through this lens, a backward feudal-cum-capitalist West eventually developed a comparative advantage in certain means of violence – especially in the maritime domain – relative to the 'tributary East', where powers such as China remained largely preoccupied with fending off terrestrial and especially nomadic challengers.[39] Within the specific context of India, Mughal over-extension and a resulting fiscal-agrarian crisis from the late seventeenth century created an opening for the EIC to establish territorial rule.[40] The resulting capture of centrally located Asian territories and armies thereafter granted the British the coercive wherewithal needed to eventually subordinate much of the rest of the world to Western dominance.[41]

There is much to commend Anievas and Nişancioğlu's account. In particular, their recognition of the mutually conditioned and co-constitutive character of the 'decline of the East' and the 'rise of the West' resonates with my own stress on the synergistic and entwined character of Western and Asian early modern empire-building.[42] We likewise agree on the centrality of Indian military power in enabling the West's brief period of dominance over Asia. These convergences aside, three points of differentiation distinguish our approaches.

First, UCD accounts leave the collaborative dynamics of Western colonial conquest under-specified. Anievas and Nişancioğlu acknowledge in passing the importance of 'Eastern agency',[43] through the collaboration of Asian intermediaries, in enabling the East-West power flip. But they remain silent on the processes through which the EIC recruited, mobilized, organized, and eventually suborned the vast networks of local collaborators on which its empire was built. This is a critical lacuna, because it was precisely these processes that were key to transforming the EIC from a parasitic player on India's maritime margins, towards a full-fledged territorial power capable of conquest on a subcontinental scale. The 'decisive comparative advantage in the means of violence' that 'largely explains Europe's eventual ascendancy to global pre-eminence' was terrestrial as much as maritime.[44] And it was critically forged in India via complex processes of cross-cultural appropriation, customization and

---

[38] Anievas and Nişancioğlu, 'How did the West usurp the rest?', 65.
[39] Anievas and Nişancioğlu, *How the West Came to Rule*, p. 260.   [40] Ibid., p. 265.
[41] Ibid., p. 272.   [42] Ibid.   [43] Ibid., p. 271.   [44] Ibid., p. 260.

institutional conversion that yielded a distinctly hybrid – even *mestizo* – character to the Company Raj.

Second, following directly from this observation, UCD accounts echo the historical sociological arguments critiqued previously in underplaying the eclectic and distinctly Eurasian character of the international order that underwrote the West's brief period of hegemony in maritime Asia after 1800. Like the Mughals and Manchus that preceded them, the EIC did not embark on large-scale conquest with a 'clean slate', but succeeded only through repurposing indigenous institutions and reorganizing existing patterns of cultural affiliation to suit their ends. The collaborative dynamics of conquest and rule on the Indian subcontinent moreover powerfully constrained subsequent British attempts at territorial and commercial expansion, both in India and in East Asia, as well as blunting efforts at ideological proselytization and the forced anglicization of subject populations. Recognition of this reality is important for its own sake, in helping us to understand the processes through which imperial hierarchies emerge and endure. But it is also key to comprehending the constitution and operation of the Western-dominated international order in Asia – an order that was less 'Western', and more indebted to Asian precedents and practices, than existing accounts acknowledge.

Finally, the UCD account shares with other perspectives previously critiqued a blindness concerning the intimate interconnections and deep parallels linking Asian and Western empire-building in the early modern period. The EIC's pattern of expansion was undeniably distinctive, and the company brought with it advantages – from blue water naval supremacy through to the chartered company-state form – that distinguished it from its Asian siblings. But Europeans – like the Mughals and the Manchus – gained a foothold on Asia's frontier zones primarily through their ability to tap into trans-regional trading networks, and mobilize the resulting surpluses to finance large-scale conquest. The tasks of cobbling together multi-ethnic conquest coalitions, appropriating indigenous military techniques and technologies, and stabilizing their empires through the assembly of diversity regimes based on the principle of 'define and rule' were also common to these imperial orders. Recognition of these parallels is key to understanding Asia's historical evolution. It moreover demands a more fine-grained focus on the dynamics of identity formation and colonial collaboration than is possible through explanations cast at a global level of analysis.

Colonial Encounters on Conquest Frontiers

The final set of perspectives considered here addresses many of the aforementioned concerns, by directly examining the crucial question of how Western colonialists elicited the local collaboration necessary to build and sustain their empires. Network-relational accounts focus on the enabling configurations of social ties that made it possible for colonial empires to emerge in the first place. Postcolonial scholars have meanwhile insightfully analysed how Western colonialists curated indigenous identities to consolidate their dominance over conquered populations in the longer term. Together, these approaches provide inspiration for my own argument, with the caveat that their exclusive focus on Western colonialism obscures critical parallels between Western and Asian empire building, that I foreground for the remainder of this inquiry.

Paul MacDonald's work on the network-relational dynamics of nineteenth-century colonial conquest constitutes one of the most important recent attempts to explain the Western ascendancy.[45] Stripped to its essentials, MacDonald argues that colonial expansion depended on Westerners' ability to surmount the barriers of 'distance and resistance' to transcontinental conquest.[46] This in turn necessitated extensive indigenous collaboration. Where dense social ties existed between Western colonialists and local elites, and where elites themselves were fragmented, collaboration and successful colonial conquest was most likely.[47] Conversely, conquest was least likely where ties between colonialists and indigenous elites were weak, and intra-elite indigenous ties (and thus capacities for collective resistance to colonial incursion) were strong.[48]

MacDonald's argument provides crucial insight into the local societal foundations of the 'divide and conquer' strategies that characterize large-scale conquest. More generally, network-relational approaches to empires' emergence help explain precisely when and how vastly outnumbered outsiders have succeeded in assembling diverse conquest coalitions. Surmounting this challenge was equally crucial for the rise of the Mughal, Qing and British empires, and so is of pivotal relevance to this book. But an exclusive focus on divide and conquer strategies obscures the equally critical 'define and conquer' aspects of imperial statecraft that were also key to empires' emergence. Likewise, the 'divide and rule' methods of governance and legitimation that sustained Asian and Western empires alike in the long term also presupposed 'define and rule'[49] practices as their necessary precondition.

Postcolonial accounts of empire have gone furthest in teasing out the define and conquer and define and rule aspects of Western colonialism. Most famously, postcolonialists revealed Orientalist scholars' fundamental

---

[45] MacDonald, *Networks of Domination*.   [46] Ibid., p. 45.   [47] Ibid., p. 7.   [48] Ibid.
[49] Mamdani, *Define and Rule*.

role in constructing and entrenching the Hindu/Muslim binary as India's defining antagonism, with its containment and management emerging as a primary warrant for company rule from the early nineteenth century.[50] Beyond India, postcolonialists have elaborated in detail on the ways that Western colonialists relentlessly prosecuted strategies of 'rule through difference',[51] and fostered a mosaic of tribal, clan, religious and ethnic identities among conquered peoples in order to sustain white minority rule.[52]

Echoing my appreciation of network-relational accounts of empire, I agree with the substance of postcolonialist insights on the identity-constitutive strategies that underpinned Western colonial domination. My critique of both network-relational and postcolonial accounts of empire lies not in their substance, but in their exclusive application to Western cases. There is nothing inherent to either approach that precludes fruitful comparison between Western as well as non-Western empires. Indeed, as I hope to show, the network-configurative and identity-constitutive dimensions of imperial conquest and consolidation were markedly similar across the three empires – two Asian and one Western – that cumulatively did the most to mould modern Asia. But postcolonialists in particular often tacitly presume that colonial strategies of define and conquer and define and rule grew out of uniquely Western pathologies.[53] This presumption constricts our field of vision, blocking due recognition of both the critical parallels between Western and Asian colonial empire-building, as well as the Asian precedents on which later Western dominance rested.

The East-West power flip remains modernity's most momentous power transition. And there is no denying the distinctiveness of Western colonialism in Asia. The West *did* wield exceptional military and institutional advantages, notably blue water naval capabilities and chartered company-states. Without

---

[50] See for example B. S. Cohn, *Colonialism and its Forms of Knowledge: The British in India* (Princeton: Princeton University Press, 1996); E. Said, *Orientalism* (London: Routledge Kegan & Paul, 1978).

[51] On 'rule through difference' as a constitutive characteristic of empires as a distinct form of polity, see generally J. Burbank and F. Cooper, *Empires in World History: Power and the politics of difference* (Princeton: Princeton University Press, 2010).

[52] See for example M. Mamdani, *Citizen and Subject: Contemporary Africa and the legacy of late colonialism* (Princeton: Princeton University Press, 1996); Mamdani, *Define and Rule*; and Newbury, *Patrons, Clients, and Empire*.

[53] There are of course important studies that have foregrounded the politics of difference as key to the rise and functioning of empires beyond the Western maritime colonial context, though these perspectives do not generally locate themselves explicitly within the postcolonial tradition. See Barkey, *Empire of Difference*; Burbank and Cooper, *Empires in World History* and also V. A. Kivelson and R. G. Suny, *Russia's Empires* (Oxford, Oxford University Press, 2017).

them, it would have been impossible for Europeans either to first insinuate their way into Asia's thriving maritime commercial networks, or to then dramatically expand their presence after Asians had absorbed the initial impact of Western intrusion. Globally, primitive accumulation and relations of unequal exchange – especially surpluses wrenched from the New World and then sold on to Asian buyers – *were* likewise clearly essential to facilitate Western commercial and political penetration into Asia. And the emergence of a highly commercialized and militarized maritime frontier in southern India *did* nourish the networks of local intermediaries that Western colonialists later mobilized to conquer on a subcontinental scale, through strategies of define, divide and conquer.

Its distinctiveness aside, the broader point stands that Western colonialism in Asia is best understood when situated in its larger early modern Eurasian context. For Westerners were first pulled into an Asian-dominated global economy by a prosperity born in part from earlier waves of Asian imperial expansion. Contrasting Mughal and Qing diversity regimes then decisively shaped the divergent trajectories of Western expansion and incorporation into India and China. Later still, Western modes of empire-building and consolidation remained profoundly derivative, imitating Asian precedents more often than they innovated genuinely new methods of colonial conquest and rule. Finally, even at the apogee of Western supremacy from the mid-late nineteenth century, a crippling dependence on local clients largely doomed efforts to comprehensively modernize and Westernize political orders in South and East Asia. Understanding the intimately braided interrelationships between Western and Asian empire-building is key to properly comprehending the historical evolution of Asian international orders from the sixteenth century onwards. And doing so requires not a change in theoretical approach, so much as a reframing of the puzzle being addressed – from 'the rise of the West' to 'how the East was won'.

From the Rise of the West to How the East Was Won: Reframing the Transformation of International Order in Early Modern Eurasia

The rise of the West is rightly seen as one of modernity's pivotal transformations. But an exclusive preoccupation with the Western ascendancy – to the exclusion of its Asian precedents and counterparts – is problematic for the following reasons.

First, analyses of the Western ascendancy elongate and exaggerate the era of Western dominance, particularly in Asia. Invocations of a 'Vasco da Gama' epoch of Western hegemony, that is supposedly only now drawing to a close with the contemporary resurgence of Asian Great Powers, constitute an especially egregious expression of this tendency.[54] Notwithstanding their strength at sea, Westerners were either tolerable irritants or intermittently useful commercial and military partners for most Asian hosts down to the mid-eighteenth century.[55] Moreover, even following the consolidation of Western territorial power in South and Southeast Asia, Western paramountcy there remained patchy, tenuous and incomplete.[56] Further afield, Western intrusion into Qing-dominated Northeast Asia gained real momentum only after the First Opium War (1839–42), and was in any case contained in its reach and limited in its impact on the East Asian regional order down to the final collapse of the Sinocentric tributary system in the 1890s.[57]

Second, the 'rise of the West' paradigm misreads the character of Western hegemony when it did finally consolidate in Asia in the nineteenth century. To take one example, 'vanguardist' accounts of the expansion of a Western-dominated international society conceive it as one of straightforward top-down imposition.[58] Asian polities through this lens were either gobbled up by Western colonial empires, or press-ganged into conformity with Western diplomatic practice and its accompanying 'standard of civilization'.[59] There is of course much truth in this portrayal. But unqualified acceptance of the 'vanguardist' narrative obscures the critical dependence of Western expansion on indigenous collaboration, and the unavoidable normative and institutional hybridity of the regional orders that emerged out of this collaboration at the high tide of colonialism. Nineteenth-century Western 'expansion' continued to manifest many of the syncretic characteristics of the early modern era that had preceded it, albeit with Westerners rather than locals now dictating the terms of interaction. The Raj's sprawling network of indirectly ruled states in South Asia, the Persian Gulf and Southeast Asia, and the mishmash of Western and Sinic diplomatic practices that sustained

---

[54] This tendency was evident in earlier historical interpretations of early modern Asia, but has since been superseded in the specialist literature. For an influential example of this earlier Eurocentrism, see K. M. Panikkar, *Asia and Western Dominance: A survey of the Vasco da Gama Epoch of Asian history, 1498–1945* (London: George Allen & Unwin, 1953). The 'Vasco da Gama epoch' trope nevertheless still finds life in some more recent interpretations of contemporary Asian geopolitics. See for example C. Bell, *The End of the Vasco da Gama Era* (Sydney: The Lowy Institute, 2007).

[55] F. Fernandez-Armesto, *Pathfinders: A Global History of Exploration* (New York: W.W. Norton, 2017), p. 181.

[56] Bose, *A Hundred Horizons*, pp. 51–2.

[57] See generally Fairbank, 'Synarchy under the treaties'.

[58] I take the terminology of 'Vanguardism' from Barry Buzan, in Buzan, 'Culture and international society', 1–25.

[59] See for example G. W. Gong, *The Standard of 'Civilization' in International Society* (Oxford: Oxford University Press, 1984).

order in Northeast Asia following the Opium Wars, are but two instances of this syncretism. They attest to the reality that Western hegemony in Asia rested on hybrid foundations, with fleeting attempts to standardize Asian polities along Western lines being more the disastrous exception than the rule.

Western hegemony in Asia was both briefer, and less 'Western' in its institutional or normative character, than rise of the West narratives suppose. Beyond these specific concerns, an exclusive focus on the Western ascendancy also obscures crucial parallels between Asian and Western imperialism, and the dependence of the latter on the precedents set by prior waves of Asian empire-building. Mughal and Manchu imperialists pioneered a style of commercialized conquest-state formation on Eurasia's inner land frontier that Europeans later mimicked on Eurasia's maritime fringe. They also provided between them the institutional frameworks that mediated Western infiltration into most of maritime Asia. Finally, in expanding their empires to encompass unprecedentedly large swathes of South, East and Central Asia, the Mughals and Manchus permanently expanded the interaction capacity – and thus the level of integration – within these regions. This laid the basis for the regional orders that Westerners then later enfolded at the height of nineteenth-century colonialism.

Scholars of IR have customarily identified modernity's origins with the emergence of a Westphalian sovereign state system, and its subsequent globalization via succeeding waves of colonialism and decolonization.[60] This perspective has its merits. But from a Eurasian standpoint, Westphalia is a parochial exception to a hemispheric trend towards greater imperial integration after c. 1500.[61] In South and East Asia especially, the early modern era was marked by waves of conquest spearheaded by frontier warrior elites. The orders that arose from these conquests had few precedents in territorial scale, and exerted permanently transformative effects on both regions. Though outside the scope of this book, we can also see parallel processes of regional consolidation, in Ottoman conquests in Southwest Asia and Muscovy's expansion into Siberia, at this time.[62]

---

[60] See for example T. Dunne and C. Reus-Smit (eds.), *The Globalization of International Society* (Oxford: Oxford University Press, 2017).

[61] On early modern Europe as the historic exception to the rule that anarchic systems will tend towards hegemonic domination, see generally J. Moller, 'Why Europe avoided hegemony: A historical perspective on the balance of power', *International Studies Quarterly*, 58(4) (2014), 660–70.

[62] On the dynamics of Ottoman expansion and accompanying mobilization and management of cultural difference, see again Barkey, *Empire of Difference*. On Muscovy's expansion throughout much of Eurasia, see again generally Kivelson and Suny, *Russia's*

From a Eurasia-wide perspective, then, the Westphalian *Sonderweg* was a sideshow to the main event: the roughly synchronous consolidation of imperial international orders across the Old World, under the aegis of 'liminal actors' originating from Eurasia's militarized and commercialized frontiers.[63] In Mughal India and Qing-dominated East Asia, vastly outnumbered and culturally marginal frontier warriors tapped in to Eurasia-wide trading networks to hoard the resources necessary to begin conquest. Having carved out nuclei of power at the edges of existing regional systems, they then recruited multi-ethnic conquest coalitions to 'roll up' these systems.[64] This culminated in the consolidation of new imperial international orders, sustained by vast networks of indigenous collaborators bound to the new order through distinct diversity regimes anchored in the perpetuation of 'rule through difference'.

The East-West power flip from the late eighteenth century depended – and in important respects crucially mimicked – this earlier phase of Asian colonialism. Explaining 'how the East was won' is thus critical for understanding the later 'rise of the West', hence the shift in perspective that grounds this inquiry.

I am of course far from the first person to have identified parallels and precedents between Asian and European empire-building in early modern Asia. Herfried Munkler has for example acknowledged early commonalities in Inner Asian steppe and European seaborne empires, not least in their capacity to expand over vast geographic distances, and their tendency (at least in their early phase) towards relatively weak and decentralized forms of political integration.[65] Victor Lieberman has been even more explicit, going so far as to dub the Dutch in Southeast Asia as 'white Inner Asians', who became 'agents of early modern transformation in somewhat the same way that Inner Asians influenced China and South Asia, or the British ultimately altered Indian trajectories'.[66] John Darwin's pithy characterization of the Qing Empire as a 'Manchu Raj', and Michael Adas' more sustained treatment of the Manchus as masters

---

Empires. For Russian expansion into Siberia and its parallels with Western colonialism, see M. Aust, '*Rossia Siberica*: Russian-Siberian history compared to medieval conquest and modern colonialism', *Review (Fernand Braudel Center)*, 27(3) (2004), 181–205.

[63] On 'liminal actors' and the phenomenon of outsider conquest and system domination, see generally M. A. Glosny and D. Nexon, 'The Outsider Advantage: Why Liminal Actors Rise to System-Wide Domination', unpublished manuscript presented at the Weatherhead Center for International Affairs, Harvard University, 2018.

[64] Nedal and Nexon, 'Anarchy and authority', 170.

[65] Herfreid Munkler, *Empires: The Logic of World Domination from Ancient Rome to the United States* (London: Polity Press, 2007), pp. 57–8.

[66] V. Lieberman, *Strange Parallels: Southeast Asia in global context*, 2 vols., II: *Mainland Mirrors, Europe, Japan, China South Asia, and the Islands* (Cambridge: Cambridge University Press, 2009), p. 770.

of a colonial empire, further underscore important family resemblances between Western and Asian imperial projects.[67]

Notwithstanding the increasing frequency of these allusions, students of empire have yet to systematically theorize the parallels and inter-actions between Western and Asian empires throughout the early mod-ern period. In particular, the possibility that the two might be united through common – or at least congruent – processes of imperial hier-archy formation has not been comprehensively developed. Within IR, theorists of comparative international systems *have* made progress developing frameworks for understanding how balance-of-power mech-anisms might be subverted and regional state systems displaced by empire builders. But this literature has drawn most fruitfully from cases in antiquity (notably Warring States China), rather than identify-ing more temporally proximate cases where the logic of domination prevailed over the logic of balancing. Most fundamentally for this inquiry, existing treatments of the logic of domination juxtapose Western anarchy with Asian hierarchy. This leads them to ignore key commonalities in Western and Asian processes of empire formation that not only occurred far more recently, but also eventually became inex-tricably entwined.

It is to an articulation of the theoretical framework explaining the com-mon 'logic of domination' that underpinned Mughal, Manchu and later British imperialism in Asia that I now turn.[68]

Conquest by Customization: The Logic of Domination and the Rise of Imperial Orders Along Early Modern Eurasia's Land and Sea Frontiers

The Mughal, Qing and British empires in Asia respectively constituted the world's largest and most powerful Islamic, East Asian and Western maritime empires. Notwithstanding their great differences, each evolved through roughly comparable stages of emergence, expansion and consolidation. Accordingly, the following presentation of my the-oretical argument maps on to these successive phases of imperial evolution.

---

[67] M. Adas, 'Imperialism and colonialism in comparative perspective', *International History Review*, 20(2) (1998), 371–88; J. Darwin, *After Tamerlane: The rise and fall of global empires, 1400–2000* (London: Bloomsbury Press, 2008), p. 132.

[68] On the 'logic of domination' as an alternative to the 'balance of power' logic in driving international systems' evolution, see generally V. T.-B. Hui, 'Toward a dynamic theory of international politics: Insights from comparing ancient China and early modern Europe', *International Organization*, 58(1) (2004), 175–205.

Imperial Emergence on the Early Modern Eurasian Frontier

Historically, the irruption of vast territorial empires was far from uncommon across the Eurasian steppe. But what distinguished the empires that emerged after 1500 was their unprecedented diversity, wealth, administrative complexity and durability. Previous steppe conquerors, most notoriously Genghis Khan and Tamerlane, had of course harnessed their mastery of cavalry warfare to carve out vast territorial empires.[69] But these empires generally proved short-lived, rapidly fragmenting following the death of charismatic founders. Early modern conquerors were hardly better at fighting or ruling than their medieval predecessors. But they *were* more successful in appropriating the material, institutional and ideational resources of conquered societies, and converting them to sustain new projects of empire. I attribute this success in the first instance to a reconfiguration of Eurasia's social ecology, which I dub the Eurasian Transformation. This reconfiguration made new forms of polity formation possible, nourishing the rise of 'liminal actors' at the margins of South and East Asian sedentary power centres that eventually formed the nuclei of new imperial orders in both regions.

A sustained discussion of the Eurasian Transformation follows in Chapter 2. For now, it is enough to note that the Eurasian Transformation comprised a quartet of interlocking transformations – economic, military, administrative and cultural – that together made new forms of empire-building possible in the early modern world.

Economically, the growth of long-distance trade across Eurasia's land and maritime frontiers provided new possibilities for entrepreneurial warlords to muscle in on these commercial networks, and siphon off some of the wealth to build the war chests needed to finance wars of conquest.[70] The rising trade in low-volume/high-value luxury commodities provided especially lucrative arbitrage opportunities from the early sixteenth century onwards. European appetites for Asian fine spices famously provided first the Portuguese and then later the European company-states with the impetus to found the 'militarized trade diasporas' that formed the nuclei of their maritime empires in Asia.[71] Less well known but just as important, Ming Chinese hunger for hinterland

---

[69] For a good overview of steppe imperialism and its varied impact on sedentary societies, see T. J. Barfield, 'Steppe empires, China, and the silk route: Nomads as a force in international trade and politics' in A. M. Khazanov and A. Wink (eds.), *Nomads in the Sedentary World* (London: Routledge, 2001), pp. 234–49.

[70] See generally J. Abu-Lughod, *Before European Hegemony: The world-system AD 1250–1350* (Oxford: Oxford University Press, 1991).

[71] On 'militarized trade diasporas' as drivers of European expansion, see P. D. Curtin, *Cross-Cultural Trade in World History* (Cambridge: Cambridge University Press, 1984), p.

luxuries like ginseng and sable provided an equivalent spur for the genesis of the militarized trading monopoly that ultimately became the Qing Empire.[72]

By itself, the growth of long-distance trade was insufficient to enable new nuclei of power to emerge on Eurasia's frontiers. But alongside this commercial expansion, far-reaching increases in Eurasia's violence inter-action capacity meanwhile provided a further impetus for change.[73] Nomadic steppe pastoralists had long enjoyed a comparative advantage in violence over their sedentary neighbours, in their mastery of cavalry warfare. This persisted into the early modern period, and indeed remained the primary military foundation of empires in South Asia especially down to the mid-eighteenth century.[74] Added to this initial advantage, however, pastoralists' adoption of gunpowder weaponry (notably field and siege artillery) in the early modern period enabled them to conquer, pacify and absorb sedentary power centres more effectively than before.[75] On Eurasia's maritime frontier, meanwhile, Europeans' introduction of broadside-firing battleships soon won them mastery on the high seas.[76] This mastery not only underwrote their protection racket in the Indian Ocean, but also helped them to eke out networks of fortified trading settlements across the Eurasian littoral.[77]

The combination of expanding trade and mastery of niche military advantages together nourished liminal actors on Eurasia's frontiers that later mutated into territorial empires. But concurrent administrative and

---

[57.] See also D. Ringrose, *Europeans Abroad, 1450–1750* (London: Rowman & Littlefield, 2018), pp. 152–4.

[72] L. Narangoa and R. Cribb, *Historical Atlas of Northeast Asia 1590–2010: Korea, Manchuria, Mongolia, Eastern Siberia* (New York: Columbia University Press, 2014), p. 27.

[73] I take the concept of violence interaction capacity from D. H. Deudney, 'Regrounding realism: Anarchy, security, and changing material contexts', *Security Studies*, 10(1) (2000), 2–3.

[74] J. Gommans and D. H. A. Kolff, 'Introduction' in J. Gommans and Dirk H. A. Kolff (eds.), *Warfare and Weaponry in South Asia 1000–1800* (Oxford: Oxford University Press, 2001), p. 42.

[75] On Muslim-majority steppe empires that evolved from the synthesis of steppe cavalry warfare and gunpowder weaponry, see for example generally D. E. Streusand, *Islamic Gunpowder Empires: Ottomans, Safavids, and Mughals* (London: Routledge, 2010). On the significance of gunpowder weaponry in empowering the Manchu conquest of China and large parts of East and Central Asia, see N. di Cosmo, 'Did guns matter? Firearms and the Qing formation' in L. A. Struve (ed.), *The Qing Formation in World-Historical Time* (Cambridge, MA: Harvard University Press, 2004), pp. 121–66.

[76] C. M. Cipolla, *Guns, Sails and Empires: Technological innovation and the early phases of European expansion* (New York: Minerva Press, 1965). See also A. Clulow, 'European maritime violence and territorial states in early modern Asia, 1600–1650', *Itinerario*, 33 (3) (2009), 72–94.

[77] Clulow, 'European maritime violence', 78.

cultural transformations within Eurasia's sedentary cores indirectly abetted this process.

From the late medieval period onwards, Eurasia's sedentary power centres had witnessed a series of cumulating cycles of administrative centralization and territorial consolidation. Rulers' 'infrastructural power' – in particular their capacity to tax agriculture and commerce while expanding their territorial reach – increased during this time.[78] This process was geographically uneven to be sure, with China hugely surpassing other power centres in bureaucratic sophistication and capacities for direct rule.[79] It was also far from linear in its progression, with cycles of administrative self-strengthening regularly interspersed with periods of entropy and collapse. Nevertheless, the secular trend was towards bigger and more administratively capable polities.[80] These increased capacities for territorial administration – and in particular capacities to tax South and East Asia's vast reserves of commercial and agricultural wealth – provided potent temptations for frontier warlords. For they generated a more sophisticated machinery of government that conquerors might potentially appropriate. This would in turn offer them far more sustained access to wealth than earlier models of plunder and tribute-taking had offered.

In Persephone Southwest Asia and Sinic East Asia, cultural transformations in sedentary power centres provided a final condition of possibility for early modern empire formation. In both regions, late medieval waves of conquest had spurred the development of ambitious programmes of normative pacification, as administrative and clerical elites sought to acculturate warrior elites to emerging conceptions of courtly and urban civility. Within the Persephone world, rulers' legitimacy increasingly became tied to their conformity to norms and standards of 'gentlemanly conduct' (*adab*).[81] Persephone cultural elites likewise sought to tame the violence of rule by conceiving it as a form of discipline (*siyasat*) acceptable only to the extent that it curbed humanity's animal instincts and allowed civilization to flourish.[82] A comparable 'civilizing project' in China concurrently sought to codify the civilized/barbarian distinction. This

---

[78] I take the idea of infrastructural power from M. Mann, *The Sources of Social Power*, 4 vols., I: *A History of Power from the Beginning to AD 1760*, 2nd ed. (Cambridge, Cambridge University Press, 2012), p. 170.

[79] Lieberman, *Strange Parallels*, p. 504.   [80] Ibid., pp. 9–10.

[81] On *adab*, see Ira M. Lapidus, 'Knowledge, virtue, and action: The classical Muslim conception of *adab* and the nature of religious fulfilment in Islam' in B. D. Medcalf (ed.), *Moral Conduct and Authority: The place of adab in South Asian Islam* (Los Angeles: University of California Press, 1984), pp. 38–61.

[82] S. A. Arjomand, 'The salience of political ethic in the spread of Persianate Islam', *Journal of Persianate Studies*, 1(1) (2008), 11–2.

entailed both prescribing a strict behavioural code for the Confucian scholar-gentry, as well as tying governmental legitimacy to the idea of a Heavenly Mandate, where the ruler's legitimacy remained conditional on their ability to perform the rites necessary to maintain a state of cosmic and temporal harmony.[83]

Persephone and Sinic sedentary elites each aimed to articulate a coherent ideology of rule, and to prescribe rituals and norms that could pacify and acculturate warrior elites to these new civilizational standards. Both sought in part to tame the violence of Eurasia's steppe frontier by demarcating a civilized/barbarian distinction, pre-emptively delegitimizing the prospect of rule by barbarians'.[84] Ironically, however, these new 'civilizing projects' also provided a potentially potent source of legitimation for frontier conquerors. For both Persephone and Sinic 'civilizing projects' were predicated on the possibility that 'barbarians' could be acculturated to 'civilization'. In this respect, they offered strikingly cosmopolitan conceptions of rightful rule that were divorced from conceptions of exclusive ethnic proprietorship. This left the door open for liminal actors to appropriate these civilizing projects and repurpose them to legitimize new projects of empire – a prospect that they spectacularly and repeatedly realised in the early modern period.

The Eurasian Transformation thus both nourished new polities on Eurasia's frontiers, while simultaneously making South and East Asia's main power centres even more tempting as targets for conquest. Increased trade in long-distance luxuries provided frontier warlords with lucrative new profit-making opportunities. This gave them the liquid wealth necessary to finance more durable polities, and to entice and sustain broader coalitions of allies beyond their immediate retinues. The integration of gunpowder weaponry into the existing military repertoires of steppe cavalrymen and European mariners meanwhile granted them niche military advantages, which they could leverage to more effectively extort tribute from Asia's core centres of wealth and power.

Simultaneously, the growing administrative sophistication of South and East Asian sedentary polities paradoxically increased their susceptibility to conquest during periodic cycles of internal weakness. The consolidation of a literate bureaucracy with more sophisticated capacities for revenue extraction, and the increased wealth generated under the protection of these more advanced sedentary states, both proved powerful

---

[83] See generally W. Gungwu, 'The Chinese urge to civilize: Reflections on change', *Journal of Asian History*, 18(1) (1984), 1–34.

[84] I discuss these parallel 'civilizing missions' in greater detail in A. Phillips, 'Civilizing missions and the rise of international hierarchies in early modern Asia', *Millennium: Journal of International Studies*, 42(3) (2014), 697–717.

magnets for frontier predators. Finally, the maturation of Persephone and Sinic civilizing projects provided an additional key enabler of early modern conquest. In particular, these projects' susceptibility to barbarian appropriation rendered them a potent legitimation resource for parvenu rulers looking to win the acquiescence of indigenous elites.

Protracted in its course and uneven in its impact, the Eurasian Transformation nevertheless radically reshaped the distribution of different forms of capital – economic and military, but also administrative and cultural – across the Old World. It therefore provided crucial conditions of possibility for the forms of frontier empire-building that took hold after 1500. Beyond this enabling context, however, we must also acknowledge the distinct mode of aggrandizement that characterized frontier empire-building in its emergent and most protean phase. Borrowing from Karen Barkey's characterization of the early Ottoman Empire as a 'brokered frontier state',[85] I argue that it was far from random that the Mughal, Qing and European maritime empires in Asia first took shape along Eurasia's land and maritime frontier zones, adjacent to but beyond the firm reach of established centres of sedentary power. For these contested and typically under-governed 'middle ground' contact zones were 'places of fluid cultural and economic exchange', where multiple power networks contended for supremacy.[86] Within such environments, favourably positioned actors could potentially insinuate themselves at the intersection of diverse social networks, splicing together resources drawn from each and recombining them into qualitatively new nuclei of power.

In their emergent phase, entrepreneurial warlords assembled new conquest proto-states through a particular form of brokerage – arbitrage – that is most prevalent in frontier zones.[87] Arbitrageurs accumulate power by exploiting price differentials between economic, cultural and political goods across different geographic and social contexts.[88] In the context of this inquiry, economic arbitrage looms as the most obvious example of this phenomenon at work. The business model of the European maritime empires was entirely dependent on the arbitrage possibilities that Western appetites for Asian fine spices opened up. Nurhaci, the Qing Dynasty's founder, likewise consolidated power first by illegally buying up Chinese trading patents regulating the trade in luxury goods from Northeast Asian resource enclaves to the Ming court.

---

[85] Barkey, *Empire of Difference*, p. 1.
[86] C. P. Giersch, *Asian Borderlands: The transformation of Qing China's Yunnan frontier* (Cambridge, MA: Harvard University Press, 2006), pp. 3–4.
[87] A. I. Ahram and C. King, 'The warlord as arbitrageur', *Theory and Society*, 41(2) (2012), 174.
[88] Ibid., p. 169.

Beyond economic arbitrage, the empire builders that dominate this inquiry also engaged in extensive cultural arbitrage as well. Thus, in the early sixteenth century, Babur followed steppe precedent in exploiting the cultural capital inherent in his genealogical links to Genghis Khan and Tamerlane to mobilize clan allies for conquest.[89] Simultaneously, however, his familiarity with Persephone courtly culture also enabled Babur to reach out to the commercial and administrative elites in Hindustan essential to more permanently secure his nascent empire.[90] Babur's liminal position at the interstices of the Timurid and Persephone cultural worlds therefore empowered him to exploit the alliance-building possibilities inherent in both traditions. Nearly a century later, Nurhaci similarly drew freely from Mongol, Sinic, Jurchen and Korean cultural resources to construct a new hybrid identity for the emergent 'Manchu' constituency that would form the core of the embryonic Qing Empire.[91]

The Eurasian Transformation reconfigured the existing distribution of economic, military, administrative and cultural capital in ways that made it *possible* for new empires to form after 1500. Within this larger hemispheric context, the emergence of new brokerage opportunities concentrated on Eurasia's land and maritime frontier zones further increased the likelihood of liminal empires emerging at the edges of established sedentary power centres. Ultimately, however, it was the agency of entrepreneurial warlords – and in particular their pursuit of strategies of aggrandizement grounded in diverse forms of arbitrage – that yielded the nuclei of new empires from this time. How these protean polities then mutated and expanded, from peripheral parasites to system-dominating empires, is a question I will now address.

Define and Conquer: Cultural Diversity and the Expansion of Eurasian Early Modern Empires

Eurasia's growing interaction capacity helped spawn diverse polity forms during the early modern period. In particular, the arbitrage opportunities that arose during this period fostered the rise of new imperial nuclei on Eurasia's land and sea frontiers. But the demographic insignificance of

---

[89] L. Balabanlilar, *Imperial Identity in the Mughal Empire: Memory and dynastic politics in early modern South and Central Asia* (London: I. B. Tauris, 2012), p. 19.
[90] See generally S. P. Blake, 'Courtly culture under Babur and the early Mughals', *Journal of Asian History*, 20(2) (1986), 193–214.
[91] On the formation of a distinct Manchu identity from multiple cultural resources, see for example Crossley, *A Translucent Mirror*, p. 3; and E. S. Rawski, 'The Qing Empire during the Qianlong reign' in R. W. Dunnell, M. C. Elliott, P. Foret and J. A. Millward (eds.), *New Qing Imperial History: The making of inner Asian empire at Qing Chengde* (London: Routledge, 2004), p. 17.

these frontier proto-polities at first posed formidable obstacles to their expansion. To transition from fringe predators to system-dominating empires, these actors needed to build conquest coalitions big enough to overwhelm neighbouring sedentary power centres. Given their cultural liminality as stigmatized barbarians lurking on the fringes of existing regions, this alliance-building also required overcoming barriers of cultural difference that separated would-be empire builders from potential allies. Bribes and bullying could secure followers in the short term. But to build more enduring relationships, aspiring imperialists needed to harness allies' active allegiance, and yoke them firmly to emerging structures of imperial rule.[92] Finally, even as they organized their own coalitions for conquest, empire builders simultaneously needed to undermine, disrupt or pre-empt the formation of counter-coalitions that could prevent their rise. These three imperatives – *building* diverse conquest coalitions, *binding* these coalitions to nascent imperial nuclei and *breaking* existing or potential counter-coalitions – formed the essence of early modern statecraft on Eurasia's frontiers. Below I consider each in turn to establish how these imperatives informed the strategies of liminal warlords, and how they then shaped the empires that arose in the wake of their triumphs.

Building a viable conquest coalition beyond their immediate retinue constituted the most basic imperative facing early modern Eurasian empire builders. The reason for this was simple. Niche capabilities in cavalry and naval warfare undeniably offered frontier warlords great scope for opportunistic predation. But to generate the hard power resources necessary to both seize *and* hold large-scale empires for the longer term, it was essential that empire builders tap into the vast reservoirs of indigenous military labour resident in Asia's sedentary power centres. The trajectories of the Mughal, Qing and British empires consistently bear out this observation. Both the Mughals and the British won paramountcy in India only by tapping into (and in Britain's case, eventually monopolizing) the subcontinent's incomparably large market for mercenaries.[93] The Manchus likewise conquered the Ming Empire with highly diverse armies, in which Han Chinese were nevertheless overwhelmingly numerically preponderant.[94]

Moving from predation to paramountcy thus necessitated a scale shift in the size and complexity of warlords' military capabilities. Given their small numbers and liminal status as stigmatized outsiders, would-be conquerors had to find a way to overcome the barriers of cultural difference that estranged them from potential allies. *Put more positively, the mobilization of*

---

[92] On 'yoking' as a key process driving the formation of complex entities, including polities, see P. T. Jackson and D. H. Nexon, 'Relations before states: Substance, process and the study of world politics', *European Journal of International Relations*, 5(3) (1999), 313–17.
[93] Gommans and Kolff, 'Introduction', p. 16.   [94] Crossley, *A Translucent Mirror*, p. 30.

military power demanded a corresponding management of cultural difference in ways that supported imperial expansion. The generation of material capabilities and the organization of cultural diversity were two sides of the same coin. Constructing armies big enough to support large-scale conquest and rule presupposed the successful management and manipulation of cultural diversity. Across my cases, empire builders pursued this goal by self-consciously curating the identities of the various constituencies that made up their conquest coalition – a process I refer to as define and conquer.

Define-and-conquer strategies constitute a particular form of cultural statecraft, where aspiring hegemons seek to split allies from rivals, while yoking their allegiances to emerging imperial hierarchies. These strategies presuppose that potential collaborators' identities are sufficiently malleable that they can potentially be re-sculpted to support imperial expansion. At the same time, however, even the most ambitious empire builders do not undertake expansion with the benefit of a cultural clean slate. Instead, the curatorship of constituencies involves the extensive appropriation and conversion of existing indigenous forms of symbolic and cultural capital, and their remixing into new forms of collective identity amenable to incorporation within emerging imperial hierarchies.[95] Empire builders are therefore innovators, to the extent that they seek to reorder forms of cultural difference to enhance their own capacities for military mobilization, while at the same time chipping away at the allegiances and alliances underpinning the hard power military capabilities of rivals. At the same time, however, their scope for cultural innovation is necessarily constrained by the prevailing identity topography within regions targeted for conquest – and in particular the degree of 'stickiness' tying locally resonant legitimation resources to existing power structures.

A brief contrast between the Mughals and the Manchus suffices to illustrate the impact of existing identity topographies on patterns of imperial expansion. As the Mughals expanded into northern India, they were forced to reckon with the Rajputs. Predominantly Hindu landed nobles, the Rajputs were fragmented into patrilineal brotherhoods, and jockeyed for power through participation in intricate webs of dynastic diplomacy, through which lower-ranked nobles sought to marry into wealthier and more powerful families.[96] Fiercely independent outside of

---

[95] On the centrality of mobilizing diverse forms of capital in constructing and sustaining international hierarchies, see generally D. H. Nexon and I. B. Neumann, 'Hegemonic-order theory: A field-theoretic account', *European Journal of International Relations*, 24(3) (2018), 662–86. The language of imperial constituencies I deploy throughout this book is drawn from Crossley, *A Translucent Mirror*, pp. 5–6.

[96] J. F. Richards, *The New Cambridge History of India*, V: *The Mughal Empire*, Pt I (Cambridge: Cambridge University Press, 1993), p. 22.

these familial patron-client ties, the Rajputs furthermore understood their identity by reference to their *dharma*, a divinely ordained code of conduct that tethered their sense of selfhood and ontological security firmly to the enactment of martial valour.[97]

Historically, the Rajputs had fiercely resisted previous Islamic invaders, and so presented a potentially formidable obstacle to Mughal rule. However, thanks to the Emperor Akbar's skilled deployment of define and conquer techniques, most Rajput nobles eventually enlisted to the Mughal cause, becoming pillars of the imperial establishment. Akbar and his successors managed to exploit Rajput traditions of dynastic diplomacy to position the Mughal emperor as the pre-eminent patron within Rajput marital networks.[98] But they were only able to do so because Rajput notions of identity were neither ethnically exclusive, nor were they especially fixated on a Hindu/Muslim binary – a fateful fault-line in South Asia that had yet to solidify in the sixteenth century. Instead, dharmic conceptions of Rajput identity proved both malleable and adaptable to Mughal purposes. For the Rajputs, war in the loyal service of any truly powerful patron constituted a potent source of dharmic fulfilment, regardless of ostensible ethnic or religious differences that might otherwise differentiate patron from client. This made it relatively easy for both Mughal patrons and Rajput clients to mobilize indigenous forms of cultural capital (mainly Hindu mythology and Rajput bardic literature) to legitimize the Mughal-Rajput alliance, and thus incorporate a potent source of Indian military power permanently into the Mughal war machine.[99]

By contrast, the Manchus at first had a far tougher time enlisting the Han Chinese warriors and administrators they needed to challenge the Ming Dynasty for hegemony in East Asia. In particular, the stigma of Manchu barbarism initially proved a major barrier to the expansion of the Manchu conquest coalition.[100] This was especially so during the early years of the Manchu challenge, when the Ming emperor appeared to retain the Heavenly Mandate. Sinic conceptions of sacerdotal kingship, centred on a Confucian civilizing project, proved 'sticky' and not easily transferrable to barbarian would-be usurpers. This was so even as the Ming Dynasty slowly succumbed to internal decay, and its material capacity to resist external challengers started to ebb. The Manchus

---

[97] Ibid., p. 24.   [98] Ibid.

[99] D. E. Streusand, *The Formation of the Mughal Empire* (Delhi: Oxford University Press, 1991), pp. 94–102. See also M. H. Fisher, *A Short History of the Mughal Empire* (London: I. B. Tauris, 2016), p. 88.

[100] Evelyn Rawski notes that this perception of Manchu 'barbarism' was not merely confined to China, but extended also to other Confucian kingdoms such as Korea as well. See E. S. Rawski, *Early Modern China and Northeast Asia: Cross-border perspectives* (Cambridge: Cambridge University Press, 2015), p. 216.

responded by trying to either ignore or side-step this obstacle, relying on a combination of bribes and intimidation to coax Han Chinese soldiers to defect to the Manchu cause.[101] Ultimately, however, it was only once the Manchus seriously dedicated themselves to claiming the Heavenly Mandate – that is, by embracing the Confucian civilizing mission as their own – that they were able to induce bandwagoning on a sufficient scale to topple their Ming rivals.[102] Though they never abandoned their separate identity as Manchus, Northeast Asia's identity topography proved sufficiently restricting to force them to also cast themselves as 'civilized' inheritors of the Heavenly Mandate as a prerequisite for building a successful conquest coalition.[103] The resulting tension between Confucian universalism and ethnic particularism would prove an enduring source of instability within the Qing Dynasty, which they struggled to reconcile for the remainder of their rule.[104]

Notwithstanding their differences across my cases, define-and-conquer strategies remained equally pivotal to Mughal, Manchu and British empire builders' efforts to cobble together the conquest coalitions necessary to undertake large-scale expansion. Having built a conquest coalition through the curation of diverse imperial constituencies, *binding* these constituencies to emerging structures of imperial rule, and *breaking up* the possibility of rival coalitions emerging, then proved empire builders' next key governance challenges.

Rapid territorial conquest by itself offered no guarantees as to the longevity of nascent empires. Indeed, historically, coalitions bound exclusively by the promise of plunder most often disintegrated following the first flush of victory, as their component factions clashed over the division of spoils.[105] Likewise, especially in their early and inchoate phase, infant empires remained acutely vulnerable to the threats of secession and subversive collaboration between nominally subordinate allies. Consequently, to preserve unity, empire builders had to contrive legitimation strategies that bound their constituencies to the imperial centre, while preventing them from collaborating either with one another, or with rival power centres external to the coalition.

Customization – referring to the articulation of discrete legitimating codes for diverse constituencies – is the term I use to denote the approach

---

[101] G. R. Li, 'State building before 1644' in W. J. Peterson (ed.), *The Cambridge History of China*, 15 vols., IX: *The Ch'ing Empire to 1800*, Pt I (Cambridge: Cambridge University Press, 2002), pp. 57–8.
[102] Lieberman, *Strange Parallels*, pp. 594–5.   [103] Ibid.   [104] Ibid., p. 595.
[105] One of the most historically significant manifestations of this phenomenon was the near disintegration of Babur's embryonic Mughal Empire following his death in 1530. See S. F. Dale, *The Muslim Empires of the Ottomans, Safavids, and Mughals* (Cambridge: Cambridge University Press, 2010), p. 97.

early modern empire builders took to preserve the unity of their conquest coalitions. Where define-and-conquer refers to the early curation of constituents' collective identities, customization alternatively captures the define and rule techniques empire builders employed to stabilize these identities and secure allies' continued loyalty and subordination to the imperial centre. Strictly speaking, customization techniques feature in both the expansion and consolidation phases of empires' development. Here I confine myself to a preliminary discussion of the logic of customization in the expansion phase, deferring a discussion of its more comprehensive institutionalization to the following section.

Customization follows and further fleshes out the basic logic of heterogeneous contracting that Daniel Nexon has developed elsewhere to characterize the network-relational composition of early modern empires.[106] Nexon argues that empire builders situate themselves at the centre of a hub-and-spoke governance structure that maximizes their power over dependent allies and intermediaries, while minimizing possibilities for collaboration between these dependent nodes.[107] Empire builders seek to legitimate these hub-and-spoke arrangements through resort to 'polyvalent signalling',[108] that is, legitimation techniques designed to resonate separately with local intermediaries, without either alienating them, or providing an affective or ideological basis for cross-node mobilization against the centre.

The concept of customization thus more tightly specifies 'polyvalent signalling', teasing out its strategic logic and elaborating on its core techniques. Following Nexon, I argue that empires rest on the centre's ability to bind dependent allies to itself, while either disrupting or preempting the formation of rival coalitions. These imperatives are generally present in all imperial formations. But they obtained with particular force for the empires considered here, given empire builders' extreme dependence on culturally diverse conquest coalitions to enable large-scale expansion. Customization refers specifically to the imperial centre's tailoring of idioms of legitimation specific to its constituent allies, and the construction, reification and naturalization of cultural boundaries between them to prevent subsequent efforts at cross-constituent mobilization.[109] In empires' mature phase, customization strategies become institutionalized in the form of diversity regimes, described in the next section. These

---

[106] Nexon, *The Struggle for Power in Early Modern Europe*; and D. H. Nexon and T. Wright, 'What's at stake in the American empire debate', *American Political Science Review*, 101 (2) (2007), 253–71.

[107] Nexon, *The Struggle for Power in Early Modern Europe*, pp. 105–8.   [108] Ibid., p. 114.

[109] For an early attempt to elaborate on the logic of customization, see Phillips, 'Making empires', pp. 43–65.

regimes nevertheless evolve from far more fluid and improvised practices of define and conquer that empire builders continuously adapt over the initial course of imperial expansion.

Once again, two empirical examples must suffice to illustrate what customization looks like in practice. During the Manchus' initial wave of expansion, as they recruited Mongols and Han Chinese to their ranks, the Manchu leadership innovated a system of military *qua* ethnic organization known as the banner system.[110] The banner system – which became one of the Qing Empire's signature institutions – explicitly institutionalized ethnic difference as a core organizing principle of the Qing military establishment. Mongol, Manchu and Han Chinese warriors were thus funnelled into ethnically and linguistically exclusive banners.[111] These banners were not merely fighting formations fashioned as temporary expedients for conquest. Rather, they became all-encompassing institutions for the multi-ethnic Qing conquest elite, becoming a site for the allocation of core privileges such as pensions and land entitlements.[112] More fundamentally, they also provided an institutional framework through which the Qing emperor could target customized legitimation narratives to discrete segments of the imperial elite after conquest.[113] The banner system was far from the only consequential governance institution in the Qing Empire, co-existing for example with other practices that confirmed the Manchus as pre-eminent within the Qing conquest coalition.[114] But it did nevertheless provide an early template for organizing difference – and customizing legitimating narratives – that privileged ethnic and linguistic diversity as the basis for the 'define and rule' strategies that would sustain the Qing Empire for the duration of its existence.

The British were even more explicit in employing define and rule strategies of customization to first expand and then later consolidate their empire in India. Lord Elphinstone, one-time governor of EIC's Madras and Bombay Presidencies, captured this imperative thus: 'The safety of our great iron steamers ... is greatly increased by building them in compartments. I would ensure the security of our Indian empire by

---

[110] For an excellent overview of the banner system, see M. C. Elliott, 'Ethnicity in the Qing Eight Banners' in P. K. Crossley, H. F. Sui and D. S. Sutton (eds.), *Empire at the Margins: Culture, ethnicity and frontier in early modern China* (Berkeley: University of California Press, 2006), pp. 27–57.

[111] See generally M. C. Elliott, *The Manchu Way: The Eight Banners and ethnic identity in late Imperial China* (Stanford: Stanford University Press, 2001).

[112] M. G. Chang, *A Court on Horseback: Imperial touring and the construction of Qing rule, 1680–1785* (Cambridge, MA: Harvard University Press, 2007), p. 21.

[113] Elliott, 'Ethnicity in the Qing Eight Banners', p. 29.

[114] On ethnic particularism as a key and enduring feature of Qing ideology and practice, see J. Leibold, *Reconfiguring Chinese Nationalism: How the Qing frontier and its indigenes became Chinese* (New York: Palgrave Macmillan, 2007), p. 27.

constructing our native army on the same principle.'[115] In the company's early territorial expansion, the EIC consciously institutionalized religious difference as a key basis for its customization strategies. Thus, in Bengal, the EIC deliberately cultivated a high caste identity among its native infantry. By sponsoring a form of militarized Brahmin identity that elevated peasant recruits' status within their communities, but tied this status elevation to military service for the company, the EIC was able to significantly strengthen its ideological outreach to a key constituency.[116] In the Ceded and Conquered territories around Delhi, by contrast, the company systematically appropriated Mughal idioms of legitimacy to attract Muslim cavalrymen into its service and bind them to the emerging Raj.[117] In both instances, the EIC appropriated and adapted existing indigenous cultural capital to its own ends, solidifying communal divisions in the process. These customization strategies both bound militarily vital constituencies to the company, while dividing them from each other. In so doing, they reflected the define and rule logic on which the divide and rule principle of British rule in Asia rested.

Governing Diversity Through Define and Rule: The Consolidation and Legitimation of Empires

The processes of identity curation (define and conquer) and the customization of legitimating narratives (define and rule) are separated here for analytical convenience. But in practice, they are both hard to disentangle, and are also continuously operative throughout the early stages of the imperial life cycle, from emergence and expansion through to consolidation. The imperatives of building and binding conquest coalitions while blocking or breaking up potential counter-coalitions never vanish, even once conquest ends and empire builders turn their attention to consolidation. This caveat aside, the consolidation phase possesses distinctive features, which I briefly canvass to round out the book's theoretical framework.

The initial processes of imperial emergence and expansion are often opportunistic – even chaotic – and are characterized more by haphazard improvisation than by the calculated pursuit of a grand strategy. But as empires transition from expansion to consolidation, the need to stabilize them through the imposition of greater ideological and institutional

---

[115] Lord Elphinstone, cited in D. Omissi, "'Martial races': Ethnicity and security in colonial India, 1858–1939', *War and Society*, 9(1) (1991), 9.

[116] S. Alavi, *The Sepoys and the Company: Tradition and transition in Northern India, 1770–1830* (Delhi: Oxford University Press, 1995), p. 45.

[117] See generally S. Alavi, 'The makings of company power: James Skinner in the ceded and conquered provinces, 1802–1840', *Indian Economic and Social Review*, 30(4) (1993), 437–66.

coherence intensifies. This need is particularly pronounced for the service elites that constitute the empire's upper echelons. Once empire builders have completed the process of 'systemic roll-up'[118] and won regional paramountcy, they must contrive an overarching purpose for imperial rule that can provide a focal point of unity and sense of shared mission for service elites.[119] To be sure, ideological coherence does not imply uniformity. The heterogeneity of initial conquest coalitions, and the continuing necessity of define and divide and rule imperatives, both counselled against ambitious projects of system-wide cultural standardization in the empires under consideration here. Nevertheless, even as they exploited cultural diversity to sustain their power, Mughal, Qing and British empire builders also needed to reflect this diversity in an incorporative ideology that legitimized their domination and gave a unifying purpose to imperial rule.

In each of the empires under consideration, empire builders eventually settled on Janus-faced ideologies of rule to fulfil this purpose. These legitimizing ideologies both differentiated the inner circle of ruling elites from subject populations, while also providing a coherent basis for collaboration with indigenous intermediaries. The first, inward-looking 'face' of imperial ideology was meant for inner elites' private consumption, and justified their domination on particularistic grounds. Thus, the Mughals claimed a semi-divine right to rule on the basis of their genealogical ties to Genghis Khan and Tamerlane.[120] Though protégés could be adopted into the Timurid household, this practice paradoxically confirmed the presumption that the right to rule remained anchored in charismatic authority transmitted through genealogical ties.[121] The Manchus similarly contrived a mythic foundation for Manchu 'specialness' that differentiated them as a separate conquest elite from their subjects. Anchored heavily in animism and in shamanistic rituals and symbolism, Manchu self-conceptions stressed their innate martial valour as core to their collective identity, and a sufficient warrant by itself for Manchu domination.[122] The British lastly also laid claim to a special right to rule, though one that mutated from one grounded in Britons' supposedly more 'civilized' status, towards a justification for domination

---

[118] Nedal and Nexon, 'Anarchy and authority', 170.
[119] On the importance of cultivating a 'cultural-religious allure' to bind intermediaries to the imperial center in early modern Eurasian empires, see J. Duindam, 'Rulers and elites in global history: Introductory observations' in M. van Berkel and J. Duindam (eds.), *Prince, Pen, and Sword: Eurasian perspectives* (Leiden: Brill, 2018), p. 5.
[120] See generally Balabanlilar, *Imperial Identity in the Mughal Empire.*   [121] Ibid.
[122] See for example Elliott, 'Ethnicity in the Qing Eight Banners', p. 38.

increasingly grounded in scientific racism by the mid-late nineteenth century.[123]

The inward-looking 'private' face of imperial ideology generated a strong sense of *esprit de corps* among imperial elites, and a coherent justification for systems of domination grounded in minority rule. But by itself it could never have legitimized rule to the diverse constituencies that composed the empires considered here. To win and keep indigenous intermediaries' allegiance, empire builders needed to contrive a more inclusive, more cosmopolitan and above all more 'outward-facing' imperial mission. Accordingly, Mughals, Manchus and Britons each articulated explicitly incorporative ideologies of rule to engage the collaborators necessary to hold their empires together.

These imperial ideologies explicitly foregrounded empires' heterogeneity, and provided coherent systemic justifications for authoritarian imperial rule based on the effective management of this diversity. They were incorporative in that they acknowledged empires' cultural diversity rather than seeking to either erase or transcend it. But beyond merely passively accepting cultural diversity, empire builders in early modern Eurasia explicitly integrated a positive message of 'unity in diversity' into their legitimating ideologies.

The Mughals thus conceptualized the emperor as *padshah*, a universal monarch who reconciled his imperial constituencies through the centripetal charisma of his semi-divine character.[124] This vision of 'peace for all' envisioned a partial synthesis of the Empire's religious traditions, exemplified in a cosmopolitan and self-consciously hybrid court culture.[125] The Manchus likewise mobilized incorporative themes in their legitimating ideology to sustain their rule. But whereas the Mughals opted for the reconciliation of difference through syncretism, the Manchus conversely conceived the emperor as separately and simultaneously embodying the cosmological orders of his chief constituencies.[126] The management of diversity through segregation rather than syncretism would remain the foundation for Manchu power for the Qing Dynasty's duration.[127]

The British differed once again in their legitimating ideology. They did not seek to reconcile their constituents' diversity through Mughal-style syncretism. Nor did they seek to separately incarnate their constituencies' identities, after the segregated model of the Manchus. Instead, the British

---

[123] On the evolution of British justifications for rule in India, see generally Metcalf, *Ideologies of the Raj*.

[124] I. A. Khan, 'Tracing sources of principles of Mughal governance: A critique of recent historiography', *Social Scientist*, 37(5–6) (2009), 50.

[125] Ibid., p. 51.   [126] See generally Crossley, *A Translucent Mirror*.   [127] Ibid.

harnessed an incorporative ideology centred around the theme of *ecumenicism*. Like their Asian counterparts, the British pursued define and rule strategies designed to prevent wholesale collaboration between their constituencies. But they justified their rule through reference to an imperial mission that foregrounded religious difference as the defining fault-line within their Indian empire. More specifically, company propagandists conceived Indian 'civilization' as Hindu in its essential character.[128] Supposedly brought low by the despotism of earlier barbaric Muslim conquerors, India could be redeemed only through the intercession of the civilized British. This intercession would entail the separate governance of India's constituencies, and their rule through separate legal codes that purportedly honoured and reflected these constituencies' distinct religious traditions.[129]

Incorporative legitimation strategies informed the overarching purpose of the empires considered here. They provided a semblance of ideological coherence, and a focal point for mutual identification, between empires' inner elites and indigenous intermediaries. But these legitimating ideologies did not float freely. Rather, they deeply infused practices of imperial administration, leaving a fundamental imprint on how empire builders organized political authority, managed their empires, and preserved minority rule. Accordingly, besides consideration of empires' legitimating ideologies, this book finally foregrounds what Chris Reus-Smit has dubbed 'diversity regimes' as a core feature of the imperial systems considered here.[130]

Reus-Smit defines diversity regimes as 'systems of norms and practices that simultaneously configure authority and construct [cultural] diversity'.[131] He furthermore argues that diversity regimes perform the following functions: (a) They legitimize certain forms of political authority and define the scope of legitimate political action; (b) they define categories of cultural difference and organize them normatively and (c) they relate legitimate units of political authority to authorized categories of cultural difference.[132] Within the context of this study, diversity

---

[128] E. M. Collingham, *Imperial Bodies: The physical experience of the Raj, c. 1800–1947* (London: Polity, 2001), p. 15.

[129] Cohn, *Colonialism and its Forms of Knowledge*, p. 146. See also L. Benton, 'Colonial law and cultural difference: Jurisdictional politics and the formation of the colonial state', *Comparative Studies in Society and History*, 41(3) (1999), 570.

[130] Reus-Smit, 'Cultural diversity and international order', 876. For a roughly cognate concept from the historiography of the Russian Empire, see generally Burbank's discussion of the Tsarist 'imperial rights regime' in J. Burbank, 'An imperial rights regime: Law and citizenship in the Russian empire', *Kritika: Explorations in Russian and Eurasian History*, 7(3) (2006), 397–431.

[131] Ibid.   [132] Ibid.

regimes represent the culmination of practices of identity curation and customization empire builders first pioneered in the course of multicultural conquest coalitions.

Hammering home an earlier point, conquering on a subcontinental scale in the early modern period required large-scale resource mobilization, beyond the means ordinarily available to liminal actors. To tap into the indigenous manpower reserves and specialist military skills of Asia's sedentary power centres, empire builders in turn had to both assemble and control culturally diverse conquest coalitions, before then binding them to emerging imperial hierarchies, and preventing subaltern attempts at subversive collaboration or secession. Define and conquer (identity curation) and define and rule (customization) provided the bases for the divide and conquer/divide and rule strategies that composed composite behemoths such as the Mughal, Manchu and British empires. Incorporative legitimating ideologies and their accompanying diversity regimes marked the endpoint of these processes, as more improvised efforts at define and conquer/rule became codified into legitimating ideologies and modes of imperial administration.

In this key respect, then, empires' diversity regimes had similar origins, and performed equivalent functions, across my Western and non-Western cases. Notwithstanding these commonalities, the Mughal, Manchu and British diversity regimes naturally varied, in accordance with the diversity narratives that infused them.

The Mughal model of syncretic incorporation thus sustained an order where the peripatetic Mughal court remained the focal point of political power and elite acculturation. Especially under Akbar, the Mughal ideology of universal reconciliation carefully sponsored cross-pollination between the empires' religious and political elites.[133] This syncretism – centred on the semi-mobile Mughal court – sought to loosen intermediaries' commitments to more parochial forms of identity, thus weakening their ability to mobilize local power bases against the imperial household.[134] At the same time, however, the Mughals preserved their power by adopting an extremely loose model of suzerain overrule. Rather than crushing and absorbing rival power centres *in toto*, the Mughals preferred to incorporate them within a territorially non-exclusive system of rule, in which sovereign prerogatives were 'co-shared' with subordinate rulers.[135] In cultivating a distinctive form

---

[133] Khan, 'Tracing sources of principles of Mughal governance', 51.

[134] On the importance of the semi-mobile court as an early part of the Mughals' imperial repertoire, see generally J. Gommans, 'Warhorse and post-nomadic empire in Asia, c. 1000–1800', *Journal of Global History*, 2(1) (2007), 13–17.

[135] On this conception of shared sovereignty, see F. Hasan, *State and Locality in Mughal India: Power relations in Western India, c. 1572–1730* (Cambridge: Cambridge University Press, 2004), p. 43. On the tensions between this model of sovereignty and a later Western absolutist conception of sovereignty, see Bose, *A Hundred Horizons*, pp. 70–1.

of emperor-centric Persephone cosmopolitanism, the Mughals thus sought to organize diversity in such a way as to simultaneously elevate and separate indigenous intermediaries culturally from their parochial power bases. The extremely loose system of suzerain overrule meanwhile facilitated continuous territorial expansion, with the Mughal empire incorporating and interweaving with existing power structures, rather than seeking to obliterate them.

The diversity regime of *segregated incorporation* underpinning the Qing Empire differed profoundly from the Mughal model. For the Manchus, the banner system of military organization provided the initial and enduring template for organizing diversity throughout the empire. Rather than seeking to win intermediaries through syncretic socialization and strategic cross-pollination, the Manchus systematically siloed their interactions with indigenous elites. The emperor discretely embodied the different cosmologies of his separate peoples, code-switching as necessary to secure their continued fealty.[136] This segregated model of rule was replicated in Manchu administration and diplomacy. In the empire's wealthy Sinic core and in its diplomacy with Confucian neighbours, the Manchus adopted a fractal model of suzerainty, whereby the political order reflected the paternal hierarchy of the classic patriarchal Confucian household. Direct territorial administration prevailed domestically, while the Manchus appropriated and replicated Ming-era models of tributary diplomacy to deal with Confucian kingdoms.[137] In dealing with the steppe, by contrast, the Manchus created a new institutional framework – the court for the administration of the outer provinces (the Lifan Yuan).[138] Essentially a system of colonial indirect rule, the Lifan Yuan linked the emperor-as-*khan* to local vassals, granting these subordinates extensive (but revocable) privileges of self-rule.[139] In configuring imperial authority claims to indigenous norms and power structures, the Lifan Yuan thereby reproduced a system of segregated incorporation that preserved Qing hegemony throughout eastern Eurasia down to the mid-nineteenth century.

British India's diversity narrative of *ecumenical incorporation* lastly found institutional expression in a complementary diversity regime. The empire was from the start grounded in the conviction that India – 'a mere

---

See also S. J. Tambiah, 'What did Bernier actually say? Profiling the Mughal Empire', *Contributions to Indian Sociology*, 32(2) (1998), 380.

[136] Leibold, *Reconfiguring Chinese Nationalism*, p. 27.

[137] See for example generally S.-H. Yoon, 'Repertoires of power: Early Qing–Chosŏn relations (1626–1644)', *Chinese Historical Review*, 21(2) (2014), 97–120.

[138] See generally N. di Cosmo, 'Qing colonial administration in inner Asia', *International History Review*, 20(2) (1998), 287–309.

[139] Ibid.

geographic expression'[140] – encompassed diverse communities that could only be governed with a firm hand. As noted, the proverbial (and largely contrived) binary antagonism between Hindus and Muslims provided a primary warrant for foreign rule. Foregrounding religious fault-lines as key to India's constitution, British authority rested on Britons' ability to institutionally mediate and manage these tensions in ways that might potentially facilitate Indian civilization's eventual renewal.[141] Within those portions of India directly under British rule, British sponsorship of a religiously defined form of legal pluralism provided the keystone component of its diversity regime.[142] British scholars and administrators sponsored distinct bodies of 'Anglo-Hindu' and 'Anglo-Muhammaden' law as the primary means of realizing this vision.[143] Elsewhere, in that portion of India under indirect rule, the British meanwhile scrupulously sponsored local dynasties to accent both their parochial distinctiveness, as well as the authenticity of their right to rule.[144] British India's appropriation of the Mughal ritual of the *durbar*, and the later elevation of the British monarch as emperor/empress of India, finally provided a focal point for elite integration into the empire.[145] In stark contrast to the Mughals, though, British imperial *durbars* did not seek to acculturate their top intermediaries into a syncretic court culture. Instead, they offered an opportunity to publicly display the empire's diversity to itself – underscoring in the process India's innate and irrepressible heterogeneity, and with it the absolute necessity of British rule.[146]

Conclusion

This chapter has situated this book with the longstanding debate on the Western ascendancy as its point of departure and argued for a shift in focus to foreground the Eurasia-wide wave of empire-building that defined early modernity. I have also advanced the theoretical framework that will drive my explanation for 'how the East was won' for the remainder of the book.

---

[140] Darwin, *Unfinished Empire*, p. 212.   [141] Collingham, *Imperial Bodies*, pp. 14–17.

[142] See generally M. R. Anderson, 'Islamic law and the colonial encounter in British India' in D. Arnold and P. Robb (eds.), *Institutions and Ideologies: A SOAS South Asia reader* (London: Routledge Curzon, 1993), pp. 165–85.

[143] Ibid.

[144] See for example D. Cannadine, *Ornamentalism: How the British saw their empire* (Oxford: Oxford University Press, 2002), pp. 42–5. See also generally B. S. Cohn, 'Representing authority in Victorian India' in E. Hobsbawm and T. Ranger (eds.), *The Invention of Tradition* (Cambridge: Cambridge University Press, 1983), pp. 165–210.

[145] See for example Alavi; 'The makings of company power', 440.

[146] Cohn, 'Representing authority in Victorian India', p. 184.

Revisiting the chapter's main points, I began with a consideration of explanations for the Western ascendancy, which respectively fore-grounded the themes of Western exceptionalism, global entanglements and frontier colonial encounters. Conceding the West's niche strength in naval warfare and the role of chartered companies in facilitating Western insinuation into maritime Asia, I nevertheless sided with critics who have rejected the larger narrative of civilizational exceptionalism as an accurate explanation for the Western ascendancy. Siding with global historical sociologists and UCD scholars, I conceded the importance of primitive accumulation (especially the West's exploitation of New World resources) in facilitating Western incorporation into Asia's courts and ports. But I also noted key limitations of these perspectives, most notably their tendency to downplay important parallels between Western and Asian forms of empire-building, and their under-specification of the mechanisms of local collaboration that made this empire-building pos-sible. Network-relational and postcolonial accounts offer an important remedy to this latter defect. But their exclusive focus on Western coloni-alism obscures its fundamentally mimetic character, and its extreme dependence on Asian precedents and practices to succeed.

The second section of this chapter then expanded on this critique, making the case for reorienting the study of Western colonialism in Asia to consider it *comparatively* within its broader Eurasian context. Building on existing studies of non-Western empire-building, my main point was to stress the mimetic character of Western colonialism once the EIC embarked on large-scale conquest from the mid-eighteenth century. At every step, Western colonialism built upon Asian precedents, depended on Asian collaborators, legitimized itself through the remixing of Asian cultural resources and operated within densely integrated regional orders in South and East Asia that earlier Asian empire builders had built. The question of 'how the West came to rule' from the late 1700s is therefore inseparable from the era of early modern Asian colonialism (1500–1750) that immediately preceded it.

At an even more basic level, situating the Western ascendancy within its broader Eurasian context is vital to gaining a more representative impres-sion of international systems' comparative development in Eurasia after 1500. Analyses of international systems' historical evolution remain marred by Eurocentrism, whether in its parochial or exceptionalist incar-nations. Eurocentric parochialism has conceptualized international sys-tems' development exclusively through the (north-western) European experience, for instance foregrounding the evolution of norms of sover-eign statehood and the balance of power as being the defining develop-ments constitutive of political modernity. Eurocentric exceptionalists have conversely paid more attention to Western colonialism, but have cast it as a *sui generis* phenomenon.

By contrast, this book recognizes that Europe's shift from medieval heteronomy to sovereign anarchy was an exception to the Eurasian rule of regional imperial consolidation. Elsewhere, from Ottoman-ruled southwest Asia and the Russian steppe, to Mughal India and Qing-centric East Asia, an imperial logic of domination prevailed over a European-style balance of power. In each of these other world regions, liminal frontier warlords 'rolled up' existing orders, eventually subsuming them within new imperial international systems. It is this story – of the roughly synchronous consolidation of imperial international systems across Eurasia – that rightly belongs at the centre of our accounts of early modern world politics, rather than either the Westphalian moment or the European conquest of the New World. Consequently, it is this Eurasian focus that frames this inquiry.

Having critiqued various explanations for the Western ascendancy and then offered my defence of a shift towards a comparative analysis of Western and Asian empire-building, I finally advanced this book's theoretical argument. Recapping briefly, I have argued that the Eurasian Transformation transformed the distribution of forms of economic, military, political and cultural capital throughout the Old World, in ways that made new forms of hybrid empire-building possible. In particular, one of the Eurasian Transformation's key impacts was that it enabled liminal warlords on Eurasia's land and maritime frontiers to pursue commercialized state-building strategies via practices of economic and cultural arbitrage. In combination with warlords' possession of niche military advantages (either in cavalry or naval warfare), these arbitrage opportunities nourished the formation of new nuclei of power, around which system-dominating empires would eventually form.

While practices of arbitrage birthed imperial proto-states, I have argued that the shift from parasite to paramount power necessitated that would-be empire builders overcome their small numbers and the barbarian stigma that estranged them from potential allies. More directly, I have maintained that transitions to large-scale territorial expansion demanded that empire builders build culturally diverse conquest coalitions, before binding them to imperial hierarchies and then pre-empting or breaking up rival counter-coalitions. Define and conquer strategies of curating imperial constituents' identities and define and rule strategies of customization were both central to successful empire-building. The first enabled empire builders to organize heterogeneous allies into coherent and cohesive conquest coalitions. The second meanwhile maximized empire builders' chances of maintaining dominance over subordinate allies, while impeding chances of imperial constituencies either seceding or otherwise subversively cooperating against the imperial centre.

Finally, drawing on Chris Reus-Smit's notion of diversity regimes, I argue that empires consolidate in their mature post-conquest phase around particular projects for organizing cultural diversity, which are institutionalized in distinctive models of imperial rule. In the cases considered, the Mughals, the Qing Dynasty and the British Empire all generally favoured diversity regimes centred on notions of incorporation, rather than coercive assimilation to a unitary civilizational standard. As we will see, this is a generalization rather than an absolute truth, with rare deviations from incorporative models occasioning disaster for each of the empires under review. However, while incorporative diversity regimes predominated for both Western and Asian empires, their specific forms (syncretic, segregated and ecumenical) varied dramatically. This variation reflected these empires' distinct historical trajectories, as well as the specific visions of the good that informed imperial rule.

With the book's conceptual apparatus laid out, I now turn to the historical narrative – beginning with an account of the Eurasian Transformation.

2   The Eurasian Transformation

This chapter aims to understand how the Eurasian Transformation made it possible for 'barbarians' to establish primacy over pre-existing international systems in South and East Asia, despite their limited numbers and stigmatized status. To make sense of this liminal imperialism, we must appreciate: (a) the systemic context out of which it emerged; (b) the changed structural conditions of possibility that made it possible and (c) the agent-centred strategies of arbitrage through which it ultimately took form. My analysis is structured accordingly, respectively anatomizing Eurasia's systemic context at 1500, the new conditions of possibility embodied in the Eurasian transformation and the strategies of proto-empire formation that land and sea 'barbarians' fashioned in response to these changed conditions.

Eurasia at 1500

Before considering Eurasia's systemic context in 1500, I must first define my use of the term *international systems*, which I employ here in two distinct senses. Following Buzan and Little, I distinguish 'full international systems' from 'economic international systems'.[1] The former refers to polities enmeshed in dense and overlapping webs of military, political, economic and sociocultural interaction, and which are bound together by shared fundamental institutions of cooperation and conflict management.[2] The latter refers to 'thinner' social systems, where polities are loosely connected through commercial interaction, but otherwise lack the dense political and sociocultural patterns of interaction or shared institutions that mark out full international systems.[3] By way of illustration, both Latin Christendom and the sovereign state system that succeeded it constitute classic examples of full international systems. Conversely, the Silk Road trading circuits that integrated late medieval

[1] B. Buzan and R. Little, *International Systems in World History: Remaking the study of international relations* (Oxford: Oxford University Press, 2000), p. 96.
[2] Ibid.   [3] Ibid.

and early modern Eurasia more closely approximate economic international systems. The distinction is imperfect, for as we will see,
Eurasia's two main economic international systems were also importantly
constituted by non-economic patterns of exchange. But for now it is
a necessary demarcation, marking a key contrast between Eurasia's principal sedentary power centres, and their steppe and sea frontiers.

Eurasia's full international systems in 1500 naturally cohered around
its main centres of population and agricultural productivity. Both then as
now, populations clustered around Eurasia's most fertile deltaic and
coastal regions. The Rhine-Danube basin, the Indo-Gangetic plain and
the Yangtze River delta watered flourishing agricultural economies, providing a ready tax base for aspiring rulers.[4] Proximity to riverine and
coastal waters and inland seas (most famously in the West, the
Mediterranean) meanwhile provided merchants with cheap means of
transportation.[5] This encouraged trade, again promoting concentrations
of wealth that rulers could harness to consolidate power and expand their
politico-military reach. Proximity to the sea was a mixed blessing for
rulers to be sure, with the Indian Ocean in particular eventually emerging
as an increasingly militarized commercial frontier from the sixteenth
century. But for most of history until that point, reliable access to riverine
and coastal territories had been far more of a blessing than a curse, the
connecting power of water significantly aiding both commerce and state
formation.

Early modern Eurasia was dominated by a diverse range of different
sedentary power centres. Here I confine my focus to those located in what
we now refer to as India and China.

India at 1500 lacked an overarching political unity. *No single full international system spanned the subcontinent.* India's polities of course collectively exerted immense cultural influence and economic dynamism, within
and beyond Asia. The spread of Sanskrit and Buddhism, and later the
'Indianization' of societies in the Malay Archipelago, attest to the
former.[6] India's status as the fulcrum of Indian Ocean-wide trading
networks, and its long history of economic innovations (for example in
revolutionizing the cultivation of sugar and cotton) evidence the latter.[7]
Notwithstanding the immensity of these achievements, it makes no

---

[4] S. Solomon, *Water: The epic struggle for wealth, power, and civilization* (New York: Harper
Perennial, 2011), p. 24.
[5] Ibid., p. 59.
[6] See for example generally L. Shaffer, *Maritime Southeast Asia to 1500* (New York:
M. E. Sharpe, 1996), p. 24.
[7] See generally L. Shaffer, 'Southernization', *Journal of World History*, 5(1) (1994), 1–21.

historical sense to credit them to a unitary 'India', which did not exist either as a single empire or as a consolidated states system at this time.

Instead, India at 1500 remained irrepressibly plural, and split between very different international systems in the north and south. Thus, in northern India, a highly protean state system predominated, marked by dense political, cultural, economic and above all military interaction between indigenous and foreign warlords. Successive Muslim invasions from the twelfth century had drawn northern India into more sustained contact with Afghan, Turkic, Persian and Central Asian peoples.[8] This had accelerated processes of cultural borrowing and military innovation, fuelling the consolidation of more powerful local kingdoms. Before Tamerlane's sacking of the capital in 1398, the Delhi Sultanate had stood as north India's most potent power.[9] A self-consciously Muslim conquest state, the Delhi Sultanate had succeeded in spreading Islam as far east as Bengal.[10] Following its decline, however, smaller independent sultanates and Rajput kingdoms emerged in its place.[11] By the late fifteenth century, these polities acknowledged no common superior. Nor had they progressed towards the 'mature anarchy' of a consolidated sovereign state system, marked by shared subscription to deeply institutionalized mechanisms of co-operation and conflict management.[12] However, and though history would later confound this judgement, the apparent trend in the north was towards greater political fragmentation, pointing to the eventual coalescence of something resembling a regional state system.

By contrast, the situation in India south of the Narmada river in 1500 was very different. Here, the empire of Vijayanagar enjoyed regional dominance, claiming suzerainty over a weakly integrated assortment of tributaries and satrapies.[13] The most militarily powerful and expansive of south India's polities, Vijayanagar has often been miscast as a muscular Hindu counterpoint to Muslim expansion from the north.[14] On the contrary, successive Vijayanagar rulers drew eclectically from their

---

[8] C. B. Asher and C. Talbot, *India Before Europe* (Cambridge: Cambridge University Press, 2008), p. 25.

[9] Ibid., p. 45.

[10] R. M. Eaton, *The Rise of Islam and the Bengal Frontier, 1204–1760* (Berkeley: University of California Press, 1993), p. 32.

[11] Asher and Talbot, *India Before Europe*, p. 99.

[12] On the distinction between mature and immature anarchy as it relates to state systems, see B. Buzan, *People, States and Fear: The national security problem in international relations* (London: Harvester Wheatsheaf, 1983), pp. 96–101.

[13] Asher and Talbot, *India Before Europe*, p. 54.

[14] For a background to and critique of this portrayal, see P. B. Wagoner, '"Sultan among Hindu kings": Dress, titles, and the Islamicization of Hindu culture at Vijayanagara', *Journal of Asian Studies*, 55(4) (1996), 851–2.

subjects' diverse cultural traditions, as they wove local intermediaries into loose networks of imperial protection and obedience.[15] In adopting syncretic legitimation strategies, Vijayanagar both mimicked the more compact Islamicate and Rajput polities to the north, as well as anticipating the policies of the Mughal Empire that eventually succeeded it.

Even more than its Mughal successors, Vijayanagar also exerted only very indirect control over its vassals. Throughout coastal south India especially, Vijayanagar largely left indigenous lords (*nayakas*) to their own devices.[16] The emperor expected these vassals to render tribute and provide warriors to the empire when needed.[17] And Vijayanagar was hardly indifferent to the economic and strategic value of Indian Ocean commerce, which it tried to channel towards its vassals and away from potential rivals.[18] But the empire's loose rein over its coastal feudatories, combined with its indifference to naval affairs, allowed a string of prosperous entrepots to thrive across the length and breadth of India's southern coast.[19] These cosmopolitan nodes plugged the subcontinent into vast Afro-Eurasian circuits of commercial exchange – and would later prove vital toeholds for European imperialists.

As one of the world's two greatest sedentary population centres, India at 1500 remained deeply split regionally between north and south. Its most powerful polities in both regions moreover already possessed many of the key features (a preference for cultural syncretism and decentralized rule, an indifference to naval affairs) that would later also define the Mughal Empire.

China by contrast was ruled by the Ming Dynasty, which at 1500 still enjoyed unrivalled paramountcy as the hub of a full international system encompassing most of sedentary East Asia. China's last Sinic dynasty, the Ming Empire was more tightly integrated than any of its Eurasian contemporaries. The prodigiously fertile Yangtze River delta supported a huge agricultural population, which provided the tax base necessary to support a central state that was precociously modern in its bureaucratic sophistication and capacity for direct rule.[20] The accelerating tempo of steppe invasions and experiences of 'barbarian' rule immediately before the Ming Dynasty had moreover consolidated a powerful sense of *esprit de corps* and solidarity among China's Confucian lettered elites. In particular, the Confucian literati harboured a strong conception of themselves as the chief custodians of 'civilization', and worked as junior partners to the emperor to defend against the 'barbarian' threat posed by potential enemies from the steppe.[21]

---

[15] Ibid., p. 853.   [16] Asher and Talbot, *India Before Europe*, pp. 57–8.   [17] Ibid.
[18] Ibid., p. 77.   [19] Ibid., p. 78.   [20] Lieberman, *Strange Parallels*, p. 604.
[21] Ibid., pp. 591–3.

Ming China was far smaller in both population and territory than either the Qing Dynasty that succeeded it, or the contemporary People's Republic of China. But in 1500, it was already undeniably East Asia's dominant military, cultural and economic power. In contrast to South Asia, East Asia much more closely approximated a full international system, organized under the suzerainty of the Middle Kingdom. Within this system, hierarchical international relations were most clearly defined and institutionalized between Ming China and neighbouring Confucian kingdoms, namely Korea and Vietnam. These polities acknowledged the emperor's supreme authority, and routinely participated in the Sinocentric system of tributary diplomacy.[22] Korean and Vietnamese kings also directly claimed their domestic authority from the emperor's imprimatur, with investiture missions constituting a key ritual reaffirming the ties of benevolence and obedience binding the emperor to his 'civilized' Confucian neighbours.[23]

For all of its immense power, however, Ming China's regional dominance was far from total. While Japan had briefly participated in the Ming system of tributary diplomacy, by 1500 it had already foresworn this allegiance. From then on, it lurched between simply asserting its independence from Ming China (while maintaining its own rival mini-tributary system), to at one point directly challenging the Ming Dynasty for Northeast Asian dominance.[24] Non-Sinic Southeast Asian polities meanwhile participated only partially and fitfully in the tributary system, their ties to the Ming Dynasty being mediated more by unofficial trade than by ritual diplomacy.[25] Besides its state-like neighbours, the Ming Dynasty also had to manage a host of non-state challengers on its terrestrial and maritime frontiers. From the empire's northern steppe and forest frontiers, the empire constantly faced off against 'barbarian' polities, which ranged in the perils they presented from mere nuisance to existential challenge.[26] By contrast, the pirates (*wakou*) that plagued East Asian waters never posed the same kind of threat to the Ming Dynasty. But their wilful undermining of China's system of managed tributary trade

---

[22] See generally Kang, 'Hierarchy and legitimacy in international systems'.

[23] See for example J.-Y. Lee, 'Diplomatic ritual as a power resource: The politics of asymmetry in early modern Chinese-Korean relations', *Journal of East Asian Studies*, 13 (2) (2013), 309–36. Lee nevertheless notes the crucial power-political dimensions of ritual diplomacy, even when the cultural concordance between China and its tributaries appeared most robust.

[24] On this latter direct challenge to Chinese hegemony, see K. M. Swope, 'Deceit, disguise, and dependence: China, Japan, and the future of the tributary system, 1592–1596', *International History Review*, 24(4) (2002), pp. 757–82.

[25] G. Wade, 'Engaging the south: Ming China and Southeast Asia in the fifteenth century', *Journal of the Economic and Social History of the Orient*, 51(4) (2008), 615–16.

[26] Lieberman, *Strange Parallels*, p. 581.

precluded the Ming Dynasty from ever emulating Indian rulers' *laissez faire* attitude to maritime affairs. Instead, Ming China maintained far closer control over resident trading communities in its coastal enclaves, and asserted far more robust claims over its maritime periphery, than was evident in India.[27]

The main point from this survey is the great diversity of the international systems that predominated in key Eurasian power centres at the start of the sixteenth century. Focusing on India and China, we see a range of regional orders, from nascent state systems (north India), through loose empires (south Asia) towards consolidated and strongly institutionalized imperial international orders (Ming-centric East Asia). But besides these full international systems, the entire Eurasian landmass was also traversed by two further (primarily economic) international systems: the Eurasian steppe (Saharasia) and maritime Afro-Asia (the Indosphere).[28] These were just as decisive for Eurasia's post-1500 evolution as their more conventional sedentary counterparts, and so are introduced here.

'Saharasia' refers to the Eurasian steppe – a huge arc of territory, stretching from just east of Vienna to just north of Beijing that formed the principal land frontier for Eurasia's sedentary population centres.[29] Saharasia is significant for this inquiry as a site of Eurasian 'hemispheric integration',[30] functioning as 'a huge continental *mediterranée*, a vibrant interstitial region that widened the horizon of all its adjoining societies and opened new channels for pastoralists, warriors, merchants, pilgrims and other restless wanderers'.[31] In the lead-up to 1500, Saharasia was most famous as home to the Silk Road trading routes. From X'ian to Constantinople, caravanserai networks formed the nuclei of a string of cosmopolitan oasis towns and cities. These towns and cities served as the commercial connective tissue uniting Eurasia's sedentary power centres, providing the main medium through which Eurasia's long-distance trade was conducted.[32] Beyond their importance as trading centres, Silk Road

---

[27] J. E. Wills Jr, 'Introduction' in J. E. Wills Jr (ed.), *China and Maritime Europe, 1500–1800: Trade, settlement, diplomacy, and missions* (Cambridge: Cambridge University Press, 2010), p. 4.

[28] I advance more developed overviews of these early modern international systems in Andrew Phillips, 'International Systems' in Tim Dunne and Christian Reus-Smit (eds.), *The Globalization of International Society* (Oxford: Oxford University Press, 2017), pp. 43–62.

[29] I take the term Saharasia from Gommans, 'Warhorse and post-nomadic empire in Asia', 11.

[30] Bentley, 'Hemispheric integration'.

[31] J. Gommans, 'The Eurasian frontier after the first millennium AD: Reflections along the fringe of time and space', *Medieval History Journal*, 1(1) (1998), 130.

[32] R. Foltz, *Religions of the Silk Road: Premodern patterns of globalization* (New York: Palgrave Macmillan, 2010), p. 10.

caravanserai networks that helped constitute Saharasia moreover served as primary vectors for the transmission of ideas, culture and even diseases across the Old World.[33]

Moving on from its generic significance as a zone of inter-regional exchange, Saharasia's ecology and strategic geography also made it uniquely important as a source of military threat to sedentary Eurasia. Beginning with its ecology, Saharasia is significant principally for its aridity and vast grasslands. Saharasia's low rainfall, combined with its isolation from the coast and from major river systems, inhibited the emergence in the Eurasian interior of highly urbanized sedentary societies.[34] At the same time, Saharasia's grasslands and insulation from the tropical diseases of monsoon Asia made it ideal for horse-breeding.[35] This distinct ecological combination had several key consequences. Unable to sustain large human populations, Saharasia instead supported nomadic and semi-nomadic pastoralists. Though historically resistant to centralized state-building, these peoples were intimately familiar with cavalry warfare techniques, especially following the incorporation of the stirrup into steppe societies from the eleventh century.[36] Saharasia's unmatched suitability for horse-breeding meanwhile led to its emergence as Eurasia's primary warhorse production centre, especially as demand from India and China provided further market inducements to pastoral horse breeders.[37]

The combination of fiercely independent pastoralist communities, possessing intimate knowledge of cavalry warfare and having ready access to a near-unlimited supply of warhorses, was of momentous import. For it guaranteed that steppe pastoralists from Eurasia would pose *the* primary military threat to Eurasia's sedentary power centres down to the mid-eighteenth century. Throughout South and East Asia especially, cavalry remained the decisive instrument of war throughout the medieval and early modern periods. Nomadic pastoralists' mastery of cavalry warfare and unrivalled access to mounts enabled them to continuously prey on wealthier and far more populous sedentary societies.[38] When sedentary societies were weak, pastoralists could and did pose an existential military threat to incumbent dynasties. Conversely, even when sedentary societies were strong, their steppe neighbours could still threaten them by resorting

---

[33] Ibid., p. 98.

[34] R. A. Palat, 'Power pursuits: Interstate systems in Asia', *Asian Review of World Histories*, 1 (2) (2013), 235–6. See also P. C. Perdue, *China Marches West: The Qing conquest of Central Asia* (Cambridge, MA: Harvard University Press, 2005), p. 23.

[35] Gommans, 'Warhorse and post-nomadic empire in Asia', 5.

[36] J. Gommans, 'Warhorse and gunpowder in India c. 1000–1850' in J. Black (ed.), *War in the Early Modern World* (London: Routledge, 2004), p. 110.

[37] Gommans, 'Warhorse and post-nomadic empire in Asia', 9.   [38] Ibid., p. 5.

to raiding and intermittent extortion to siphon off a portion of the former's wealth.[39] Saharasia's strategic geography moreover made these pastoralists relatively invulnerable to retaliation. This is because the vastness
of the steppe meant that they could when necessary retreat beyond the
range of punitive expeditions that sedentary societies periodically sent out
to destroy them.[40]

Saharasia's ecological conditions and resulting strategic geography thus
made for permanent insecurity along Eurasia's land frontiers. *In particular,
the threat pastoralist predators posed to sedentary power centres vastly exceeded
the former's demographic strength.* The Eurasian 'horse-warrior revolution'[41]
gave them the asymmetric military advantage necessary to perpetually
threaten and occasionally invade and overwhelm far more populous and
wealthy neighbours. The formidable loss of strength gradient sedentary
societies confronted, as they tried to project punitive power into the steppe,
meanwhile granted pastoralist predators a strong measure of impunity,
preventing their speedy destruction.[42] Offsetting these advantages, steppe
pastoralists lacked the internal coherence and the administrative sophistication necessary to govern the vast new empires they occasionally managed
to conquer, at least for any length of time. Empires such as that of Genghis
Khan and Tamerlane were as ephemeral as they were enormous, felled by
faction and by pastoralist elites' ambivalence – if not outright hostility – to
central rule.[43] Accordingly, at least down to c. 1500, a fractious stalemate
mediated relations between the steppe and Eurasian sedentary societies.
Steppe pastoralists could occasionally conquer their sedentary neighbours,
but found it difficult to govern and preserve what they had conquered.
Sedentary societies, meanwhile, could typically either buy off or blockade
pastoralists, but could rarely either destroy them outright, or else contrive
some other military response to permanently neutralize the threat they
represented.

As a Eurasia-wide inter-regional system, the Saharasian frontier was thus
doubly important for the Old World's development, as a commercial super-
circuit but also as a source of military insecurity. The Indosphere – the vast
stretch of littoral territory extending across the Indian Ocean, and up into

[39] See generally T. J. Barfield, 'The shadow empires: Imperial state formation along the
Chinese-nomad frontier' in S. E. Alcock, T. N. D'Altroy, K. D. Morrison and Carla
M. Sinopoli (eds.), *Empires: Perspectives from archaeology and history* (Cambridge:
Cambridge University Press, 2001), pp. 10–41.
[40] See for example Perdue, *China Marches West*, p. 522.
[41] J. Gommans, 'The silent frontier of South Asia, c. AD 1000–1800', *Journal of World
History*, 9(1) (1998), 11.
[42] Perdue, *China Marches West*, p. 522.
[43] See for example D. Morgan, 'The decline and fall of the Mongol Empire', *Journal of the
Royal Asiatic Society*, 19(4) (2009), 427–37.

Southeast Asia and beyond – conversely constituted a more exclusively economic international system before 1500. Ecological and climatic conditions had long favoured the Indosphere as an inter-regional zone of exchange. The near-continuous stretch of littoral territory around the Indian Ocean encouraged trade, for it enabled 'short-legged' ships to hop between coastal settlements, without having to navigate treacherous expanses on the scale of the Atlantic or Pacific Oceans.[44] Likewise, the regularity of the monsoonal winds further aided sail-based maritime trade and exploration.[45] Seasonal variations moreover meant that merchants were compelled to remain resident in coastal towns and cities until the direction of the monsoon winds changed.[46] As a result, these entrepots quickly became home to a cosmopolitan melange of resident trading diasporas.[47] Granted rights of residence and self-government by rulers anxious to skim the customs revenues that came with trade, these diasporas helped sustain vast inter-regional webs of commerce, forming a robust maritime complement to the Saharasian Silk Road.[48]

Already an important trading circuit, the Indosphere's importance only increased in the fourteenth century following the collapse of Genghis Khan's empire, and the ensuing insecurity along the Silk Road as feuding Turco-Mongol warlords fought to revive a universal imperium.[49] Notwithstanding its commercial centrality, Eurasia's maritime frontier lacked the military dynamism of its terrestrial counterpart before 1500. In contrast to Western precedents dating from antiquity, no incumbent power in littoral Asia asserted proprietary control or even claims to exclusive custodianship over the high seas. In the Indian Ocean in particular, the high seas were perceived as an 'asocial medium', over which it would be absurd for rulers to assert any claims of monopolistic control.[50] With the fleeting exception of Ming China's fifteenth-century expeditions into the Indian Ocean, rulers in India and China in particular evinced little interest in developing capacities for long-distance maritime power projection, of the kind that would later spearhead the West's commercial infiltration into Asia.[51] This is noteworthy because maritime Eurasia's

---

[44] J. H. Bentley, 'Sea and ocean basins as frameworks of historical analysis', *Geographical Review*, 89(2) (1999), 218–19.

[45] S. R. Prange, 'Scholars and the sea: A historiography of the Indian Ocean', *History Compass*, 6(5) (2008), 1382.

[46] T. Roy, *India in the World Economy: From antiquity to the present* (Cambridge: Cambridge University Press, 2012), p. 9.

[47] Ibid.   [48] Ibid.   [49] Abu-Lughod, *Before European Hegemony*, p. 183.

[50] P. E. Steinberg, *The Social Construction of the Ocean* (Cambridge: Cambridge University Press, 2001), p. 46.

[51] This is not to say that resident Indian Ocean powers never pursued strategies of predation, but rather that when they did so, these tended to be localized exceptions rather than common regional practice. For details of these exceptions, see for example S. R. Prange,

strategic geography potentially favoured a style of frontier raiding and harassment similar to that found on the steppe. The Indian Ocean in particular offered opportunities for maritime warlords to harass port cities and interdict the region's heavily trafficked trading routes.[52] The existence of a huge network of loosely governed port cities and enclaves near to one another – and the absence of indigenous blue-water naval capabilities – moreover made it possible for outsiders to strike coastal settlements without warning, before withdrawing beyond the reach of retaliation from primarily land-oriented indigenous states and empires. Before 1500, these possibilities were hypothetical. But their very existence suggests parallel pathways to empire, which both steppe- and sea-based empire builders pursued with vigour with the onset of the Eurasian Transformation – a tectonic power shift I will now explore in detail.

The Eurasian Transformation

The Eurasian Transformation and the Changing Systemic Context of Empire-Building in the Old World

The Eurasian Transformation refers to a conjunction of military, administrative, cultural and economic macro-processes that provided critical preconditions for the rise of liminal imperialism (both its Asian and European variants) from the sixteenth century onwards.[53] It is difficult to precisely bound the Eurasian Transformation temporally, for while its full effects were felt only during the early modern period, the macro-processes that composed it were cumulatively building for hundreds of years beforehand. With this caveat in mind, I articulate below the Eurasian Transformation's constituent features, before spelling out how the changed conditions they generated produced new opportunities for conquest that Asians and later Europeans both exploited to the full after 1500.

The Eurasian Transformation was defined first by a dramatic growth in violence interdependence throughout the Old World.[54] Though they are

---

'A trade of no dishonor: Piracy, commerce, and community in the western Indian Ocean, twelfth to sixteenth century', *American Historical Review*, 116(5) (2011), 1269–93.

[52] Ibid.

[53] For an early sketch of the Eurasian Transformation and its impact on Eurasian political development and world history, see A. Phillips, 'The global transformation, multiple early modernities, and international systems change', *International Theory*, 8(3) (2016), 481–91.

[54] I take the concept of violence interdependence from D. H. Deudney, *Bounding Power: Republican security theory from the polis to the global village* (Princeton: Princeton University Press, 2008), pp. 29–30.

rarely (if ever) considered together, Genghis Khan and Tamerlane's late-medieval conquests and Western Europeans' later infiltration into maritime Asia together marked profound increases in the military interconnectedness of Old World societies. As noted previously, the spread of the stirrup throughout Saharasia had helped spur a 'horse-warrior revolution' as early as the eleventh century, and with accelerating speed and impact from the twelfth century.[55] Added to pastoralists' existing horsemanship skills and unrivalled access to mounts, this innovation enabled them to pose a more sustained and intense threat to Eurasia's sedentary power centres than before.[56] Likewise, European innovations in sail and shipbuilding technologies had long helped them to range well beyond their north Atlantic confines. Though on land militarily inferior to Afro-Asian societies in most respects, Western Europeans honed their (initially marginal) advantages in seafaring throughout the late medieval period.[57] These advantages would eventually give them the capacity to project power along the Old World's sea frontiers, eking out the tiny toeholds from which full-blown empires would much later emerge.

Alongside their respective strengths in horsemanship and seafaring, both Asian pastoralists and European mariners also benefited from the spread of gunpowder weapons throughout Eurasia during the late medieval period. Initially a Chinese invention, gunpowder and gunpowder-driven projectile weapons rapidly diffused throughout the Old World, being assimilated and adapted to a range of existing military traditions.[58] For steppe pastoralists, gunpowder weapons initially offered little advantage on the battlefield. Mounted archers could already fire arrows with great speed and accuracy, nullifying the value of early matchlock rifles and muskets.[59] On the other hand, pastoralists' eventual adoption of siege artillery (most often with the aid of foreign mercenaries or captives) dramatically increased their ability to besiege and conquer fortified cities, further amplifying their threat to sedentary societies.[60] Gunpowder weaponry proved even more important for Europeans. For it was Europeans' incorporation of cannons into naval warfare that eventually gave them

---

[55] Gommans, 'The silent frontier of South Asia', 11.   [56] Ibid., pp. 16–17.

[57] T. Andrade, 'Beyond guns, germs, and steel: European expansion and maritime Asia, 1400–1750', *Journal of Early Modern History*, 14(1–2) (2010), 177. Andrade nevertheless notes that Europeans did not long monopolize their naval technological advantages, which polities such as the Yarubi Dynasty in Oman and the Zheng confederacy in Taiwan did manage to emulate.

[58] See generally T. Andrade, *The Gunpowder Age: China, military innovation and the rise of the West in world history* (Princeton: Princeton University Press, 2017); Lorge, *The Asian Military Revolution*; Streusand, *Islamic Gunpowder Empires*.

[59] Gommans, 'Warhorse and gunpowder in India', p. 116.

[60] See for example Streusand, *Islamic Gunpowder Empires*, p. 207.

a marked comparative advantage in violence on the high seas. This enabled first the Portuguese, and then later the Dutch and the British to militarize Eurasia's maritime frontier, and employ the threat of bombardment and naval predation to extort commercial privileges from Asia's main terrestrial powers.[61]

The spread of key military technologies (the stirrup and gunpowder weaponry) from their sedentary Asian origins to Eurasia's frontiers thus significantly enhanced the respective threats pastoralist horsemen and European mariners posed to key power centres in South and East Asia. These threats were of course originally by no means comparable in magnitude. Steppe conquerors could and did occasionally threaten the very existence of kingdoms and empires across the Old World.[62] Conversely, Europeans down to the mid-eighteenth century remained in most cases no more than irritants to the societies on which they preyed.[63] But the fact remains that late medieval and early modern Eurasia saw sustained increases in violence interdependence across the board. The perennially perilous Eurasian land frontier became even more dangerous. And for the first time, Asian waters were becoming comprehensively militarized, as Europeans violently asserted custodianship over long-distance maritime trading routes in ways that lacked any indigenous precedent.[64]

Military innovations on Eurasia's land and sea frontiers, and the corresponding increase in violence interdependence they yielded, thus proved critical in defining the Eurasian Transformation. Paralleling these innovations on the frontiers, however, from the late medieval period onwards Eurasia's power centres experienced their own dramatic changes. Administratively, the era witnessed the continued growth of a clerical administrative class, and the growth of more centralized forms of rule. As ever, China was the most precocious in its development, with the Chinese model of bureaucracy and elite recruitment through examination dating from as early as the T'ang Dynasty.[65] However, this trend – though cyclical and uneven – was general throughout Eurasia's sedentary power centres.[66] Most critically, Eurasia's administrative rationalization was inextricably tied up with the consolidation of new identities among its lettered and warrior elites. Specifically, and in part in response to intensifying predation from steppe pastoralists, Eurasia's sedentary societies saw

---

[61] Clulow, 'European maritime violence', 73.   [62] Lieberman, *Strange Parallels*, p. 581.
[63] Fernandez-Armesto, *Pathfinders*, p. 181.
[64] For limited and localized exceptions to this rule, see for example S. R. Prange, 'The contested sea: Regimes of maritime violence in the pre-modern Indian Ocean', *Journal of Early Modern History*, 17(1) (2013), 9–33.
[65] Lieberman, *Strange Parallels*, pp. 507–8.   [66] Ibid., pp. 52–3.

the growth of 'civilizing projects', aimed at normatively pacifying warrior elites and integrating them into more ambitious and expansive systems of centralized rule.[67]

Historical sociologists have extensively explored the evolution of 'civilizing processes' and more general projects of normative pacification in the context of medieval and early modern Europe.[68] But these processes were common throughout Eurasia. In South and East Asia especially, the growing violence interdependence spawned by the horse warrior revolution was particularly critical in catalysing this process.

Thus, in China, repeated steppe invasions radically sharpened existing civilized/barbarian dichotomies at this time, and crystallized the emergence of a more programmatic Confucian civilizing project. Reaching its apogee under the Ming Dynasty, the Confucian civilizing project stressed Confucianism's universality as a cosmology, a philosophy of rule, and a way of life. The Confucian scholar-literati conceived the world as divided into a polar opposition between civilized (i.e. Confucian) and barbarian peoples, and blamed the violence of steppe pastoralists on their barbarous nature.[69] At the same time, however, many also believed that Confucianism's universality held out the possibility that barbarians could be pacified through exposure to Confucian norms and Chinese language and culture.[70] Repeated barbarian invasions served if anything to fortify this conviction. They also strengthened Chinese elites' corollary belief that peace could be permanently secured with barbarians only through their conformity to Confucian norms and practices – an idea that would have longstanding implications for China's management of both steppe and sea-based threats to its hegemony in Northeast Asia.

In south and southwest Asia, steppe invasions sparked similar projects of normative pacification. Throughout a broad swathe of the Middle East, Central and northern India, Persianate high cultures predominated in royal courts, and among urban lettered elites.[71] Just as mastery of Confucianism and Chinese classical education formed a defining marker of civilized identity in Northeast Asia, so too did equivalent conceptions

---

[67] I first explored this development in A. Phillips, 'Civilizing missions and the rise of international hierarchies in early modern Asia'.

[68] The classic work remains N. Elias, *The Civilizing Process: Sociogenetic and psychogenetic explanations* (London: Blackwell Publishing, 2000). For a more recent exploration, see M. van Berkel and J. Duindam (eds.), *Prince, Pen, and Sword: Eurasian perspectives* (Leiden: Brill, 2018).

[69] Lieberman, *Strange Parallels*, p. 592.   [70] Ibid., p. 591.

[71] See generally S. A. Arjomand, 'Unity of the Persianate world under Turko-Mongolian domination and divergent development of imperial autocracies in the sixteenth century', *Journal of Persianate Studies*, 9(1) (2016), 1–18; and R. L. Canfield (ed.), *Turko-Persia in Historical Perspective* (Cambridge: Cambridge University Press, 2002).

of civility gain greater purchase and prominence among Persephone elites from the late medieval period.[72] Certainly, Persianate ideas and conceptions of collective identity were not as all-encompassing for Central Asians and north Indians, relative to the dominance of Confucianism among Northeast Asian sedentary elites. Instead, Persianate high culture and norms of civility layered on top of existing indigenous identities, without effacing them.[73] This qualifier aside, Persianate conceptions of civility shared key similarities with Confucianism, in their content, purpose and practices.

The familiar polarity between civilized urbanites and barbarous nomads was central to Persianate conceptions of civility. For Persianate lettered elites (the *ashraf* class), civility was virtually synonymous with urbanity, and contrasted with the rudeness, ignorance and savagery of the nomad.[74] Like the Confucian scholar-literati, Persianate elites conceived their relationship with Saharasian warrior elites in terms of existential antagonism.[75] Importantly, however, they also shared with Confucianism a faith in human nature's essential malleability, and in barbarians' potential to be redeemed (or at least constrained) through exposure to civilization. In particular, the idea of *akhlaq* (lit. 'disposition of the soul') occupied a key role in Persianate civilizing projects.[76] Specifically, Persianate ideas of civility rested on the idea that moral virtues could be cultivated through education. The ruler was obliged to encourage virtue among his subjects through a combination of ritual, moral example and the provision of justice.[77] Subjects likewise had a duty to cultivate moral virtues within themselves through immersion in Persianate literature (especially poetry) and culture, and also through the self-conscious adoption of rightful conduct and manners (*adab*) befitting a civilized 'gentleman.'[78]

Despite their natural differences, Confucian and Persianate civilizing projects were manifestations of a Eurasia-wide process of normative pacification, spurred in response to the Old World's rising violence interdependence from the late medieval period. Both projects also aided administrative centralization in Eurasia's sedentary power centres in

---

[72] See generally Arjomand, 'The salience of political ethic in the spread of Persianate Islam', 5–29.
[73] See generally S. A. Arjomand, 'Persianate Islam and its regional spread' in P. Michel, A. Possamai and B. S. Turner (eds.), *Religions, Nations, and Transnationalism in Multiple Modernities* (London: Palgrave Macmillan, 2017), pp. 67–84.
[74] M. Kia, 'Moral refinement and manhood in Persian' in M. Pernau et al. (eds.), *Civilizing Emotions: Concepts in nineteenth century Asia and Europe* (Oxford: Oxford University Press, 2015), p. 148.
[75] Ibid.
[76] J. E. Wilson, 'Early colonial India beyond empire', *Historical Journal*, 50(4) (2007), 956.
[77] Kia, 'Moral refinement and manhood in Persian', p. 148.   [78] Ibid.

various ways. Confucian and Persianate conceptions of political authority were rigidly hierarchical and emperor-centric, and so were well-suited to propping up dynastic forms of rule. In their emphasis on human malleability and the civilizing power of education and good manners, these projects were also cosmopolitan in that they were separable from ideas of ethnic proprietorship.[79] This made them well-suited as a means of ideologically integrating military and lettered elites from diverse cultural backgrounds, aiding immeasurably in the acculturation and consolidation of service elites subordinate to central rule. Crucially, the cosmopolitan character of Confucian and Persianate civilizing projects also left them susceptible to later appropriation and repurposing by barbarian conquerors, though this is jumping ahead in my analysis.

A final key point of symmetry between Confucian and Persianate civilizing projects is that normative pacification in both instances was not simply a matter of ideological indoctrination. To be considered truly civilized, one also had to master certain bodily practices and forms of consumption as essential exterior markers of civilized identity. For Confucian and Persianate elites (as also for their counterparts in Western Europe), civilization extended to the refinement of manners in areas ranging from polite conversation, through to bodily comportment, culinary practices and sexual conduct.[80] Moreover, though Confucian and Persianate moralists condemned excess and celebrated the virtue of moderation, in practice the cultivation of civilized identities fuelled hugely increased demand for the consumption of exotic luxury commodities as a tangible status of elite refinement. Exotic clothing, food and stimulants in particular emerged as signifiers of elite civilized status – contributing directly to the Eurasian Transformation's final defining macro-process of hemispheric economic integration.[81]

Scholars have long recognized trade's importance as a force of Eurasian integration from the late medieval period.[82] Here I build on these insights, but with an emphasis on the normative and cultural drivers of

---

[79] See for example Lieberman, *Strange Parallels*, p. 592. On Turko-Mongol successes in appropriating Persianate conceptions of civility and monarchical authority for their own imperial purposes, see generally J. Brack, 'Theologies of auspicious kingship: The Islamization of Chinggisid sacral kingship in the Islamic world', *Comparative Studies in Society and History*, 60(4) (2018), 1143–71.

[80] Lieberman, *Strange Parallels*, pp. 591–2. On *adab*, the code of ethics, etiquette and personal comportment that shaped elite behaviours in much of the Persianate world and eventually helped sustain the Mughal Empire, see generally Lapidus, 'Knowledge, virtue, and action', pp. 38–61.

[81] C. A. Bayly, '"Archaic" and "modern" globalization in the Eurasian and African arena, c. 1750–1850' in A. G. Hopkins (ed.), *Globalization in World History* (New York: W. W. Norton, 2001), p. 51.

[82] See for example generally Abu-Lughod, *Before European Hegemony*.

this trend. For just as increased violence interdependence spurred administrative rationalization and normative pacification, so too did sedentary 'civilizing projects' help drive demand for the long-distance trade in luxury commodities, further integrating Eurasia as a result. As noted, the consumption of exotic clothing, food and stimulants emerged as an important signifier of civilized status in Eurasia's sedentary power centres. Critically, however, diverse religious and medicinal beliefs and canons of taste generated with them regionally distinctive 'patterns of exotic consumption and comportment'.[83] The Confucian scholar-gentry's appetite for luxuries such as sea slugs, edible birds' nests and ginseng provided a strong impetus for increased Chinese trade with both Southeast Asia and in remote hinterlands in northeast Asia, though these commodities had limited appeal elsewhere.[84] Likewise, Middle Eastern and South Asian (and later, European) aristocratic and merchant elites prized Southeast Asian fine spices (e.g., cloves, nutmeg, and mace), which held little value for Northeast Asians.[85] This regional diversity – alongside the more universal fetishization of goods acquired from distant lands – provided a massive impetus to trade in low volume/high value luxury commodities.

Civilizing projects and accompanying processes of elite acculturation and stratification provided a key cultural driver of Eurasian economic integration before 1500. This trend only accelerated during the early modern period, especially following Europeans' forced entry into the Indosphere. European demand for fine spices and Asian textiles, and the arbitrage opportunities this demand created, provided the foundation for the 'militarized trade diasporas' that spearheaded Western infiltration into South and Southeast Asia.[86] New World commodities – such as chillies and tobacco – meanwhile provided an additional signifier of exoticism and status for Eurasian elites, and an important alternative to New World bullion reserves for Westerners anxious to buy their way into Asian markets.[87] The spectacular growth in the luxury commodity trade during the early modern period would prove especially critical in helping to finance the rise of both the Manchus and also the Western maritime empires in Asia.[88] The Mughals, meanwhile, began their rise to power at least in part through their ability to siphon wealth from the Silk Road

[83] Bayly, '"Archaic" and "modern" globalization', p. 51.   [84] Ibid., p. 70.
[85] K. N. Chaudhuri, *Trade and Civilization in the Indian Ocean: An economic history from the rise of Islam to 1750* (Cambridge: Cambridge University Press, 1985), p. 21.
[86] P. D. Curtin, *The World and the West: The European challenge and the overseas response in the age of empire* (Cambridge: Cambridge University Press, 2012), p. 4.
[87] Bayly, '"Archaic" and "modern" globalization', p. 70.
[88] On trade in luxuries as a key fillip for Manchu empire-building, see generally L. Sun, 'The Economy of Empire Building: Wild ginseng, sable fur, and the multiple trade

trading routes freshly energized by rising demand for luxury commodities.[89] Below I will consider exactly how these barbarians were able to parlay these economic opportunities into large-scale and long-term conquest. For now, it is necessary to note that the early modern globalization that helped make these conquests possible drew on deep medieval roots. And that the trade that helped spawn these empires was paradoxically stimulated in part by civilizing projects conceived in part to neutralize the threat of barbarian invasion.

The Eurasian Transformation and Changing Opportunity Structures along Eurasia's Land and Sea Frontiers

The Eurasian Transformation exerted far-reaching and diverse impacts on political orders throughout the Old World. But the enhanced opportunities it provided for empire-building from liminal actors on Eurasia's sea and land frontiers were easily the most consequential.[90] In reviewing these enhanced empire-building opportunities, we must first recall the obstacles that had formerly mediated relations between sedentary Eurasia and the barbarians on its land and sea frontiers. Down to the sixteenth century, a tense but seemingly durable stalemate governed relations between steppe and sedentary peoples. Nomadic pastoralists possessed the military means to harass, extort and even temporarily conquer their sedentary neighbours.[91] But the small numbers and culturally marginal cultural status of barbarians nevertheless thwarted many bids for conquest. And even where barbarians were successful in temporarily conquering sedentary societies, these same obstacles of demographic inferiority and cultural marginality significantly complicated efforts to translate military victories into durable long-term rule.[92] The geographic vastness of the steppe, and the inhibiting effects of loss of strength gradients, meanwhile meant that sedentary societies could at best contain steppe pastoralists, rather than vanquishing them entirely.[93]

networks of the early Qing Dynasty, 1583–1644' (DPhil diss., University of Oxford, 2018). On arbitrage in the Europe-Asia spice trade as a catalyst for the rise of European maritime empires, see generally D. A. Irwin, 'Mercantilism as strategic trade policy: The Anglo-Dutch rivalry for the East India trade', *Journal of Political Economy*, 99(6) (1991), 1296–314.

[89] J. Gommans, *Mughal Warfare: Indian frontiers and highroads to empire, 1500–1700* (London: Routledge, 2002), pp. 24–5.

[90] The concept of liminal actors as agents of conquest in international systems is drawn from Glosny and Nexon, 'The outsider advantage'.

[91] Gommans, 'Warhorse and post-nomadic empire', 5.

[92] Lieberman, *Strange Parallels*, pp. 586–7.   [93] Perdue, *China Marches West*, p. 522.

The Eurasian Transformation reordered the distribution of military, administrative, cultural and economic capabilities across the Old World, in ways that cumulatively allowed barbarians on Eurasia's steppe and sea frontiers to overcome earlier obstacles to long-term empire-building. This shift occurred earlier and in a much more pronounced way along Eurasia's land frontier, to be sure. But it was ultimately evident on both land and sea, and was critically important for the Asian and European empire-building projects that transformed South and East Asia.

The first and most noteworthy change the Eurasian Transformation brought with it was in the enhanced opportunities for barbarian actors to construct hybrid military forces, better suited to both conquering *and* permanently occupying Asia's commercially sophisticated and densely populated sedentary power centres. As noted, one of the defining features of Eurasia's barbarian fringe-dwellers was their possession of asymmetric strengths in cavalry and maritime warfare respectively. These capabilities were key in enabling them to extort trading privileges from Indian and Sinic polities, and so to create 'shadow empires' that parasitically fed off Asian prosperity.[94] From the late medieval period onwards, the incorporation of Asian military innovations (notably the stirrup and gunpowder weaponry) had further strengthened these actors' niche military skills.

These improvements notwithstanding, barbarian conquerors remained hamstrung by a lack of access to armed forces of sufficient quantity and loyalty to properly enforce their domination over sedentary rivals. The challenges of both conquest and indefinite occupation necessitated hybrid military establishments that retained liminal actors' niche military advantages, while combining them with huge reserves of military manpower largely drawn from sedentary power centres. To scale up from being marginal predators to viable long-term rulers, barbarian would-be conquerors needed to combine their established advantages in speed and shock, with the advantages of mass that access to sedentary Eurasia's vast military manpower resources permitted. And in order to secure reliable access to these resources, barbarians had to find a means to win the sustained collaboration and allegiance of the indigenous allies needed to recruit, man and administer their armies.

Collaboration was therefore key to liminal imperialists' abilities to make the transition from fringe-dwelling parasites to paramount conquerors. The Eurasian Transformation inadvertently made this easier in

---

[94] See generally Barfield, 'The shadow empires'; and V. Lieberman, 'Protected rimlands and exposed zones: Reconfiguring premodern Eurasia', *Comparative Studies in Society and History*, 50(3) (2008), 721–2.

three key ways. First, administrative centralization – and the growing strength of state-based forms of rule – paradoxically made it easier for outsiders to capture sedentary governance institutions and elites, and reroute them to serve conquerors' own objectives. In particular, the consolidation of increasingly coherent identities among South Asia's *ashraf* class and the Confucian scholar-literati proved a long-term boon for liminal imperialists. This is because barbarians could only conquer and rule subcontinental empires over the longer term if they could collect the taxes needed to finance the military establishments on which their dominance ultimately depended.[95] The rise of increasingly coherent identities among Persianate and Confucian lettered service elites, in South and East Asia respectively, created region-wide constituencies that could potentially be co-opted for precisely this purpose.[96]

Second, and relatedly, the elaboration of Persianate and Confucian civilizing projects from the late medieval period provided barbarians with a potent ideological point of entry into sedentary power centres. This is ironic, because as we have seen, Persianate and Confucian civilizing projects originally arose as an ideological defence to barbarian aggression. Persianate and Confucian civilizing projects aimed to normatively pacify steppe and sea aggressors through assimilation, obliterating their cultural distinctiveness and erasing the habits of untamed violence that had originally made them such a threat to sedentary societies. But beliefs in barbarians' essential malleability paradoxically left open the possibility that these outsiders could themselves appropriate and repurpose civilized forms of cultural capital for their own ends. As we will see, exposure to Persianate and Confucian civilizing influences did not expunge the separate identities of Mughal, Manchu or British conquest elites. But increased familiarity with these influences did give them valuable ideological resources, which they could eventually leverage to win over the collaborators they needed to conquer and control their more civilized neighbours. This normative ju-jitsu would prove crucial in propelling barbarian imperialism from the sixteenth century – and would not have been possible without the new forms of cultural capital the Eurasian Transformation had wrought.

Finally, the surge in demand for exotic luxuries – itself partially derivative of the rise of Eurasia-wide civilizing projects – provided a potent potential source of financial aggrandizement for barbarian polity-builders. Hinterland luxury commodities – from fine spices to sea slugs

---

[95] M. van Berkel, 'The people of the pen: Self-perceptions of status and role in the administration of empires and polities' in M. van Berkel and J. Duindam (eds.), *Prince, Pen, and Sword: Eurasian perspectives* (Leiden: Brill, 2018), pp. 385–6.
[96] Ibid.

to furs (the 'soft gold' that drove Tsarist Russia's expansion into Siberia and North America) – had always commanded premium prices across the Old World.[97] But the Eurasian Transformation dramatically boosted this demand further, in part as a by-product of secular commercial expansion, but also because of the new association between luxury consumption and conformity to recently established ideals of urban civility. Though the beneficiaries of this increased luxury trade were legion, it disproportionately favoured those who could dominate Eurasia's principal land and sea trading routes, or at least tap into and siphon off wealth from critical nodes along them.

As the Eurasian Transformation unfolded, sedentary elites' growing demand for luxuries thus had important strategic as well as distributional consequences. Hunger for exotic luxuries drove a rise in long-distance trade that irrigated Eurasia's land and sea frontiers with huge new reserves of liquid wealth. This opened up opportunities for entrepreneurial warlords to pursue forms of frontier mercantilism, through which they sought to monopolize trade in high value/low volume luxuries, and then husband the resulting profits to finance further economic – and ultimately also territorial – expansion. The war chests won through frontier mercantilism could then in turn be used to recruit armies of the scale and sophistication necessary to conquer on a subcontinental scale.

To summarize: demographic inferiority and cultural marginality had long frustrated barbarian efforts to carve out enduring empires in sedentary Eurasia. But the Eurasian Transformation redistributed forms of military, administrative, cultural and economic capital in ways that significantly lowered these barriers, making possible the wave of Asian and European barbarian empire-building that transformed South and East Asia after 1500. In its earliest stages, the Eurasian Transformation allowed steppe and sea barbarians to incorporate Chinese military innovations with their own existing strengths in horsemanship and seamanship. These niche capabilities for coercion enabled them to harass – and in steppe warriors' instance, temporarily conquer – sedentary power centres.

But durable conquest required large-scale collaboration, and in particular the recruitment of the indigenous warriors and administrators necessary for this endeavour. The administrative centralization and consolidation of more coherent service elite identities in South and East Asia,

---

[97] Bayly, '"Archaic" and "modern' globalization", p. 70. On the sable trade as a key engine for Russian expansion into Siberia, see R. Willerslev and O. Ulturgasheva, 'The sable frontier: The Siberian fur trade as montage', *Cambridge Journal of Anthropology*, 26(2) (2006–2007), 79–100.

an integral part of the Eurasian Transformation, paradoxically made this task a lot easier. Likewise, the maturation of Persianate and Confucian civilizing projects proved double-edged. For rather than pacifying barbarians through cultural assimilation, it instead provided them with a potent means of ideological outreach to indigenous allies. The growth in the long-distance trade in exotic cultural commodities finally nourished new forms of frontier mercantilism at the edges of Eurasia's sedentary power centres. This endowed entrepreneurial barbarian warlords with the war chests necessary to entice large-scale recruitment of warriors and administrators from the societies they sought to conquer. This further destabilized the stalemate that had traditionally limited barbarian expansion, opening up new possibilities for conquest and imperial consolidation thereafter.

Translating Opportunities into Outcomes: Barbarian Agency and the Eurasian Transformation

Having considered the changed structural context of the Eurasian Transformation, and the expanded empire-building opportunities it brought with it, I now lastly sketch the main processes through which barbarians translated these opportunities into reality.

Economic arbitrage constituted the first process that nourished Asian and European empire-building on Eurasia's land and sea frontiers. Before they could assemble diverse conquest coalitions, barbarian empire builders first had to consolidate enough liquid wealth to make these ambitions possible. The arbitrage possibilities that came with the growth in Eurasian long-distance trade in luxuries enabled this process. This commonality aside, economic arbitrage functioned differently, and with varying levels of importance, across the cases considered. For the Mughals, direct involvement in economic arbitrage played an at best minimal role in their initial phase of imperial emergence. Instead, the positional advantages accruing from their possession of Kabul enabled Babur and his followers to passively skim profits from the long-distance trade, without directly becoming armed traders themselves.[98] Arbitrage was conversely far more important in fuelling the rise of the coalition that would eventually metastasize into the Qing Empire. The Manchus thus first emerged as a proto-imperial entity following Nurhaci's deliberate accumulation of Chinese trading patents, and his followers' creeping consolidation of control over the trade in ginseng and sable.[99] The European company-states were finally the most self-conscious and

---

[98] Gommans, *Mughal Warfare*, pp. 24–5.   [99] Li, 'State building before 1644", pp. 22–4.

systematic in pursuing armed arbitrage – originally in trade in the fine spices, and later in tea and opium – as the central focus of their activities.[100] Indeed, for the Europeans, territorial empire first emerged as a residual by-product – and not always a desirable one – of their militarized efforts to wrest exclusive control over the Europe-Asia luxuries trade.

In both direct and indirect ways, then, the expansion of Eurasia's trade in exotic luxuries and its accompanying arbitrage opportunities proved critical to empires' emergence along early modern Eurasia's land and sea frontiers. But as Asian and European imperial enterprises congealed and gained momentum, liminal imperialists had to recruit and mobilize a diverse conquest coalition to embark on large-scale territorial conquest. Doing so entailed articulating a vision of legitimate rule – a project of empire – that could attract and bind diverse constituencies to an emerging imperial hierarchy.[101]

Noting the centrality of 'projects' in helping to constitute complex networks of domination, sociologist Isaac Ariail Reed observes:

As social ties, chains of power are constructed, in part, out of signs that construe and comprehend those ties; they are simultaneously social and symbolic. In particular, when one person or group send and binds another person or group to pursue a project, the first embeds this sending-and-binding in a picture of the world that contains an idea of who is acting for whom, and under what authorization. The representation of *in whose name* action is authorized thus becomes important for the communication, coordination and justification of action.[102]

Recruiting and binding diverse conquest coalitions demanded empire builders conjure a 'picture of the world' compelling enough to local collaborators that it could overcome (or at least neutralize) the barbarian stigma that otherwise clung to Eurasia's liminal imperialists. Customization – the production of discrete appeals to different constituencies through define and conquer and define and rule strategies – proved central to this enterprise. Paradoxically, the civilizing projects that had already taken hold in sedentary power centres during the Eurasian Transformation provided potent cultural resources for such purposes.

---

[100] See generally Irwin, 'Mercantilism as strategic trade policy'. See also E. Rappaport, *A Thirst for Empire: How tea shaped the modern world* (Princeton: Princeton University Press, 2017); and C. Trocki, *Opium, Empire and the Global Political Economy: A study of the Asian opium trade, 1750–1950* (London: Routledge, 1999).

[101] On the importance of projects in cementing ties between super- and subordinate actors in emerging networks of power, see generally I. A. Reed, 'Chains of power and their representation', *Sociological Theory*, 35(2) (2017), 87–117.

[102] Ibid., p. 88.

Writing of the dynamics of hegemonic transition within the modern international system, Nexon and Neumann have observed: 'Hegemons cannot completely structure international order; they emerge in pre-existing social fields, and rarely, if ever enjoy a sufficient preponderance of meta-capital to rewrite those fields entirely.'[103] While Nexon and Neumann stress the constraining effects of extant forms of cultural capital on rising powers, in this inquiry, the emphasis is flipped on its head. Existing forms of cultural capital – specifically Persianate and Confucian civilizing projects – proved a source of empowerment as much as constraint, being malleable enough for barbarians to appropriate and repurpose to engage critical local constituencies. Mughals, Manchus and eventually also Britons all benefited from the cultural permeability and nominal universality of indigenous civilizing projects. At the same time, as parvenu conquerors entrenched along Eurasia's cosmopolitan land and sea frontiers, they were also able to leverage the advantages that came with being cross-cultural brokers. Situated along sedentary power centres' multicultural 'contact zones' and commercial frontiers, liminal imperialists had access to an unusually large range of cultural resources from which to weave their visions of empire.[104] This positioning primed them perfectly to craft discrete legitimation strategies for diverse imperial constituencies spread across the loosely governed land and sea frontiers of sedentary power centres, while simultaneously mobilizing the ideational power resources from these same sedentary cores to draw local collaborators into expanding barbarian-dominated imperial networks.

Beyond economic arbitrage and cultural customization, Asian and European barbarian empire builders finally consolidated their empires through the construction of imperial diversity regimes.[105] These diversity regimes both bound imperial constituencies to the centre, while pre-emptively breaking up the possibility of counter-coalitions forming either between imperial segments, or between imperial segments and rivals outside the imperial space. I have already sketched the syncretic, segregated and ecumenical regimes of incorporation that respectively underpinned Mughal, Manchu and British empire-building. For now, it is simply necessary to note that this process of institutional construction drew heavily on existing administrative and cultural resources already

---

[103] Nexon and Neumann, 'Hegemonic-order theory', 663.

[104] On contact zones, see M. L. Pratt, *Imperial Eyes: Travel writing and transculturation* (London: Routledge, 2006), p. 8.

[105] The concept of diversity regimes as a set of practices tethering authorized expressions of cultural difference to structures of political authority is introduced in Reus-Smit, *On Cultural Diversity*, and has since been further refined in Phillips and Reus-Smit (eds.), *Culture and Order in World Politics*.

present within sedentary power centres, even as it rearranged them to new imperial ends. The Mughal *mansabdari* system, the Manchus' Lifan Yuan, and the British system of 'indirect rule' over the Princely States all reflected distinctive visions of empire that understood and organized cultural diversity in unique ways that instantiated the particular predilections and strategic interests of their sponsors. But they also built systematically on local precedents, redeployed existing administrative and institutional arrangements, and converted existing administrative and cultural practices to build new diversity regimes. Empire-building thus entailed more remixing than wholesale reinvention. As we will see, this style of empire-building through remixing was for a time extremely effective. But it would also importantly constrain barbarian attempts to transcend the limits of initially successful models of rule, once the process of consolidation had stabilized and empire builders sought to further radically expand into new domains.

Conclusion

This chapter has situated the inquiry in both space and time. It has done so by providing a synoptic overview of Eurasia in 1500, as well as anatomizing the Eurasian Transformation that cumulatively transformed Eurasia's geopolitics, and paved the way for the barbarian Asian and European empires that dominated South and East Asia from the sixteenth century onwards. While Latin Christendom was making its protracted transition from medieval heteronomy to an absolutist system of sovereign states, South and East Asia meanwhile saw existing international systems rolled up and replaced by new imperial orders of gargantuan size and diversity. *The logic of domination, rather than the logic of balancing, defined South and East Asia's international politics throughout the early modern period.* Most incongruously, the masters of these new imperial orders were outnumbered and culturally marginal barbarians, whose success depended on their ability to overcome indigenous prejudices, consolidate and maintain culturally diverse conquest coalitions, and pre-empt the rise of competing counter-coalitions.

My central argument here has been that a concatenating series of macro-processes – military, administrative, cultural and economic – were critical in making these regional order transitions possible. The Eurasian Transformation saw a growth in violence interdependence throughout the Old World, as steppe and sea barbarians incorporated Asian military innovations into societies that already respectively possessed niche strengths in cavalry warfare and long-distance seafaring. This increased these actors' capacities to craft 'shadow empires' that parasitically diverted some of the wealth from sedentary neighbours through a combination of harassment, extortion and 'managed trade' in the form of selective trading privileges sedentary rulers doled out to pacify their frontiers.

Concurrent with the accelerating militarization of Eurasia's steppe and sea frontiers, Old World sedentary power centres meanwhile experienced growing administrative rationalization and centralization, and the consolidation of more coherent supra-local elite identities. Partially as a response to the growing threat of steppe barbarians in particular, the maturation of Persianate and Confucian civilizing projects respectively reshaped the ideational landscape of Southwest and Northeast Asia. These projects more sharply codified civilized/barbarian hierarchies than before, and aimed to pacify frontier zones and tame warrior elites through cultural assimilation. Nominally cosmopolitan, and divorced from notions of ethnic proprietorship, these civilizing projects aided the consolidation of state and empire formation in Eurasia's sedentary power centres in the short term. But they also represented a highly malleable form of cultural capital that could potentially be appropriated by outsiders to ensnare indigenous collaborators, and so enable liminal empire-building from Eurasia's steppe and sea margins.

The growth in Eurasia's long-distance trade in exotic luxury commodities, beginning in the late medieval period and accelerating rapidly after 1500, constituted the Eurasian Transformation's final macro-process. In part an artefact of the canons of taste associated with the rise of civilized identities in sedentary power centres, the surge in demand for exotic luxuries proved especially critical in aiding barbarian empire formation after 1500 because it expanded possibilities to capture and divert wealth from Eurasia's principal land and sea trading routes – possibilities that disproportionately favoured steppe and sea barbarians capable of projecting power along these routes. But it also stemmed more specifically from the expanded opportunities for arbitrage, and the associated ability to accumulate war chests to fund large-scale empire-building that arose from expanding long-distance trade. Sedentary elites' appetite for exotic luxuries thus directly nourished the nuclei of new empires on their steppe and sea frontiers, perversely making future barbarian conquests possible.

By the early sixteenth century, then, the Eurasian Transformation had begun to significantly transform both Asia's sedentary power centres, as well as its land and sea frontiers, in ways that radically expanded the scope for the durable liminal imperialism that reshaped East and South Asia the early modern era. After 1500, barbarians could far more easily build and bind the diverse coalitions they needed to conquer and govern sedentary power centres than was previously the case. Enhanced opportunities for arbitrage in the economic domain provided warlords with the necessary resources to entice the allies they needed to embark on large-scale conquest. And opportunities for cultural arbitrage meanwhile provided them with the means to later legitimize their rule over these allies, through customization strategies that culminated in the diversity regimes underpinning barbarian empires in their mature phase.

The trajectories of Mughal, Qing and British empire formation in early modern Asia were of course far from identical. The Mughals, for example, relied far less on direct involvement in trade and arbitrage in their initial phase of polity genesis, and confronted less consolidated cultural obstacles to their rise in northern India, than either the Manchus or the British. Likewise, in contrast to the Mughals and the Manchus, the EIC was at first a reluctant conqueror, hostage to commercial imperatives that powerfully constrained (but ultimately failed to stop) costly and unprofitable territorial acquisitions. Finally, though this book deliberately foregrounds the parallels between Asian terrestrial conquerors and European maritime imperialists, these parallels should not obscure their vital differences, the significance of which I will return to in the book's conclusion.

These caveats aside, this chapter has established that the great conquests that rolled up pre-existing international systems in South and East Asia after 1500 owed their origins to a conjunction of deep historical macroprocesses that began in the early centuries of the second millennium, and further intensified with the coming of early modernity. The Eurasian Transformation radically increased interaction capacity between Old World societies, steadily drawing together Eurasia as an increasingly integrated strategic environment well before the advent of European encroachment into maritime Afro-Asia. It also profoundly reshaped the distribution and composition of existing forms of military, administrative, cultural and economic capital, both within Eurasian sedentary power centres, but also along the Old World's terrestrial and maritime frontiers. Though its impacts were complex and diverse, the Eurasian Transformation's most noteworthy effect finally was to lower the barriers to liminal imperialism, enabling barbarians to build and bind diverse conquest coalitions, and so overcome the demographic and cultural barriers that had formerly frustrated most efforts at frontier empire-building. The resulting enterprises permanently transformed Asia's strategic geography, eventually bequeathing today's contemporary mega-states of India and China. In Chapters 1 and 2 I have intellectually located my inquiry, outlined this book's conceptual apparatus, and sketched the deeper macro-processes that made early modern liminal empire-building possible. With these preliminaries dispensed with, I can begin my empirical narrative by examining the rise of the Mughal and Manchu empires. It is to this comparison that Chapter 3 now turns.

3 The Rise of Asia's Terrestrial Empires

Introduction

In Chapter 2 I outlined in broad terms the revolutionary significance of the Eurasian Transformation for international relations in late medieval and early modern Eurasia. Having set the scene at a pan-regional level, in this chapter I examine the Eurasian Transformation's direct impact on international systems in South and East Asia. Specifically, I consider the rise of the Mughal and Qing empires, which together forged a template for rule that would define Asian and Western approaches to empire in the Old World down to the twentieth century. Notwithstanding their obvious differences, Mughal and Manchu conquest elites succeeded in establishing and maintaining rule over vastly more prosperous, populous and culturally sophisticated subject populations during the early modern era. They did so mainly through strategies of define and conquer and define and rule, entailing the extensive customization and repurposing of indigenous normative and institutional resources for imperial ends. Imperial elites creatively remixed these resources, both to create local constituencies in favour of barbarian rule, and also to generate the coercive reserves of hard power needed to defend their empires from internal and external hard challenges. Finally, rulers in both empires then stabilized their power through the establishment of distinct diversity regimes, which institutionalized existing practices of define and rule, while blocking the potential rise of anti-imperial coalitions.

This chapter proceeds in three parts. The first and second sections proceed in broadly chronological fashion, respectively examining the Mughal and Qing empires' emergence, expansion and consolidation. The third section then surveys the variations in forms of imperial hierarchy and diversity management that arose from these processes of imperial emergence, and foreshadows their significance for the later insinuation of European interlopers at these empires' maritime margins.

The Rise of the Mughal Empire in South Asia, 1500–1605

The Mughal Empire originated from the Fergana Valley in the late fifteenth century, when a warlord named Babur recruited a retinue of armed adventurers to wage opportunistic campaigns of plunder across Central Asia and northern India. Claiming direct descent from Genghis Khan and Tamerlane, Babur would go on to found in the Mughal Empire a superpower second only to China in its size, wealth and population. At its peak in the late 1600s, the Mughal Empire encompassed an area of 3.2 million square kilometres, extending from Afghanistan to the Bay of Bengal.[1] The Mughal emperor ruled a population of up to 150 million (twice that of Europe), and siphoned wealth from an imperial economy comprising approximately a quarter of the world's economic output.[2]

As a political entity, the Mughals eclipsed not only other contemporary Islamic empires (notably the Ottomans and the Safavids), but also the comparatively puny kingdoms of Latin Christendom. By way of comparison, by the early 1600s the Mughals ruled a population five to six times larger than either of Europe's two most powerful polities (France and Habsburg Spain), and collected twenty-five times more annual revenue than England's King James I.[3] If the scale of the Mughals' achievement was impressive, so too was the Mughals' capacity to assert and maintain their hegemony over vastly diverse subject populations. Sunni Muslims themselves, the Mughals established suzerainty over a polyglot population encompassing a bewildering array of sects and cultures, and centred political life around a profoundly cosmopolitan Persephone court culture that synthesized an array of traditions from the Indian subcontinent, Central Asia and the broader Turko-Persian world. Reflecting their empire's enormous heterogeneity, the Mughal ruling elite was primarily comprised of recent immigrants or descendants of recent immigrants (mainly from Central Asia, Iran and Afghanistan) but also included large numbers of local (especially Hindu Rajput) rulers as well.[4]

The Mughal Empire's foreign origins, its immense size and its enormous cultural diversity together warrant its prominence in this inquiry. For the Mughals powerfully embodied the radically new possibilities of political innovation the Eurasian Transformation wrought. A consideration of the Mughal Empire's initial emergence provides key insights into the dynamics of warlord polity formation along the steppe

---

[1] Richards, *The Mughal Empire*, p. 1.
[2] Fisher, *A Short History of the Mughal Empire*, p. 1.
[3] M. N. Pearson, 'Merchants and states' in J. D. Tracy (ed.), *The Political Economy of Merchant Empires: State power and world trade, 1350–1750* (Cambridge: Cambridge University Press, 1991), p. 52.
[4] Fisher, *A Short History of the Mughal Empire*, p. 4.

frontier, which the Eurasian Transformation's commercial dynamism made possible. The Mughals' harnessing of India's incomparably large military labour market likewise illustrates the importance of processes of institutional conversion in enabling foreign dynasties to gather the military resources necessary for expansion on a subcontinental scale. Lastly, the Mughals' syncretic ruling ideology and accompanying diversity regime, which legitimized Mughal rule by celebrating cultural diversity rather than trying to transcend it, provides an equally arresting illustration of the techniques of customization that consolidated the empires that emerged from the Eurasian Transformation. Accordingly, my analysis is structured around these themes of emergence, expansion and consolidation.

The Emergence of the Mughal Frontier Polity

To understand the Mughal Empire's emergence, we must first consider the physical and social ecology from which it emerged. Like its most important precursors, the empires of Genghis Khan and Tamerlane, the Mughal Empire originated from the Saharasian steppe, a vast territory that included 'all the arid and semi-arid zones of Eurasia, in the north skirting from the eastern outskirts of Vienna to the Chinese Wall, in the south stretching from the Atlantic coast of the Maghreb to the south-eastern extremes of the Indian sub-continent.'[5] Inhabited primarily by nomadic pastoralists, Saharasia – with its vast grasslands – historically served as Eurasia's primary breeding ground for warhorses.[6] From the eleventh century, as Saharasia's pastoralists integrated earlier technological developments such as stirrups and deeper saddles into their cavalry warfare, they took advantage of their unrivalled horsemanship and easy access to warhorses to establish dynamic new conquest dynasties, which preyed on the great wealth of neighbouring sedentary societies.[7] Transient though they were, these dynasties vastly accelerated Eurasia's cultural and commercial integration.[8] The historical memories of gargantuan conquest that these dynasties bequeathed to their descendants moreover stoked the latter's pretensions towards universal rule, profoundly shaping the ambitions of warlords such as the Mughal founder, Babur.[9]

---

[5] Gommans, 'The Eurasian frontier after the first millennium AD', 128.
[6] Gommans, 'Warhorse and post-nomadic empire in Asia', 6.   [7] Ibid., p. 4.
[8] See generally Abu-Lughod, *Beyond European Hegemony*; and J. Nichols, 'Forerunners to globalization: The Eurasian steppe and its periphery', *Studies in Slavic and General Linguistics*, 38 (2011), 177–95.
[9] L. Balabanlilar, 'Lords of the auspicious conjunction: Turco-Mongol imperial identity on the sub-continent', *Journal of World History*, 18(1) (2007), 6.

Traversed by the Silk Road, fifteenth-century Central Asia formed a focal point for commerce and war, and a fulcrum for cultural exchange between the Persian and Turkic worlds, as well as the Indian subcontinent. Commercially dynamic and culturally cosmopolitan, it remained politically divided, hosting an array of fractious warlords competing for supremacy. Babur, half-Mongol and half Turk and claiming direct descent from both Genghis Khan and Timur (Tamerlane), was one of these warlords. His august lineage granted Babur significant cultural and political capital among Central Asia's warrior elites, potentially providing an important source of legitimacy for his aspirations for rule and conquest.[10] Indispensable though it was as a legitimating resource, Babur's genealogy was nevertheless insufficient to prevent Uzbek rivals from ousting him from the Mughals' homeland in the Fergana Valley, forcing his relocation to Kabul in 1504.[11]

Strange though it might seem from a twenty-first century vantage point, Kabul in the early 1500s was an extremely promising cradle in which to nurse imperial ambitions. A booming entrepot, Kabul served as the hub for India's trade with Central Asia and (to a lesser extent) Iran.[12] Situated at the climatic as well as commercial interface of India and Central Asia, Kabul possessed both fertile agricultural lands (and thus taxable peasantry), as well as the extensive pasturage necessary to breed warhorses in large numbers.[13] Its status as a commercial hub for mediating inter-regional trade also made Kabul an important financial centre, where Indian bills of exchange could be cashed, and credit therefore raised to finance military expansion.[14] Novel military innovations, such as the Ottoman artillery and matchlock rifles Babur would use to defeat his enemies in northern India, were also readily available via the extensive trading networks converging on Kabul. Finally, Kabul was within striking distance of Hindustan – the immensely fertile (and thus immensely wealthy) Indo-Gangetic plain, further commending it as a springboard for conquest.[15]

Babur's genealogy invested him with a powerful claim to legitimacy that could potentially resonate with at least some of Central Asia's Turkic and Mongol warrior elite.[16] His strategic position in Kabul meanwhile gave Babur ready access to the material capital – taxable peasantry,

---

[10] M. K. Jha, 'South Asia, 1400–1800: The Mughal Empire and the Turco-Persianate tradition in the Indian Subcontinent' in J. Fairey and B. P. Farrell (eds.), *Empire in Asia: A new global history*, 2 vols., I: *From Chinggisid to Qing* (London: Bloomsbury Academic, 2018), p. 142.

[11] Fisher, *A Short History of the Mughal Empire*, p. 24.

[12] Gommans, *Mughal Warfare*, p. 25.   [13] Ibid., p. 24.   [14] Ibid., p. 25.   [15] Ibid.

[16] C. Lefèvre, 'In the name of the fathers: Mughal genealogical strategies from Babur to Shah Jahan', *Religions of South Asia* 5(1–2) (2011), 415.

abundant warhorses, credit and exotic weapons – necessary to support military conquest. And Kabul's proximity to Hindustan, then loosely ruled by decaying and vulnerable polities, offered wealthy and weak nearby targets for expansion.

This combination of authority, capacity and opportunity provided the preconditions for the Mughal Empire's later rise. But the empire's emergence was by no means foreordained. Babur was but one of a number of competing aspirants for power clustered throughout Central Asia and northern India. Moreover, though the Mughals eventually unified almost all of South Asia, India remained a consolation prize for both Babur and his immediate successor, Humayun, who both yearned fruitlessly to recapture their ancestral homelands in Central Asia.[17] Most critically for this inquiry, while Babur claimed the mantle of *Padshah* (universal ruler) as early as 1507,[18] the Mughals' expansion was initially opportunistic, even chaotic, in character. From the early 1500s, Babur assembled a ragtag confederacy of military adventurers to launch smash and grab raids against treasuries in northern India.[19] The promise of loot – as much as the charisma of his Timurid heritage – held Babur's coalition together, even following the conquest of Delhi in 1526. At the time of his death in 1530, Babur's embryonic empire consequently remained very weakly institutionalized, the Mughal state representing 'little more than a military occupation of north-western and northern Indian cities and fortresses rather than a broadly acknowledged sovereignty'.[20] Indeed, so tenuous was the Mughal grip on power that Babur's son and successor Humayun was for fifteen years evicted from India by the rival Indo-Afghan warlord Sher Shah, and forced into exile in Safavid Iran.[21]

Notwithstanding its improvised and ramshackle character, the Mughal Empire even in its earliest phase dramatized the new possibilities for political innovation that characterized the Eurasian Transformation. As 'bicultural frontiersmen'[22] originating from a commercially buoyant but politically fragmented frontier, the Mughals straddled multiple worlds, politically, culturally and economically. Their Turkic-Mongol heritage infused the Mughals with dreams of universal conquest, while enabling them to draw from the distinct martial traditions and resources of the Eurasian steppe.[23] Simultaneously, imperatives of commercialized military expansion drew the Mughals into intimate contact with a Persephone

---

[17] Jha, 'South Asia, 1400–1800', p. 142.   [18] Ibid.
[19] Fisher, *A Short History of the Mughal Empire*, p. 21.
[20] Dale, *The Muslim Empires of the Ottomans, Safavids, and Mughals*, p. 97.
[21] Richards, *The Mughal Empire*, p. 11.
[22] Gommans, 'Warhorse and post-nomadic empire in Asia', 12.
[23] Jha, 'South Asia, 1400–1800', p. 153.

universe, which provided a model of centralized bureaucratic administration, as well as a rich repertoire of ideological techniques for legitimating imperial rule over diverse populations.[24] If combined effectively with Hindustan's vast commercial and agricultural wealth (the Indian subcontinent possesses one of the world's largest acreages of arable land)[25], these resources could be harnessed to construct an empire of truly prodigious proportions. This was the task to which Akbar – Babur's grandson and the greatest of the Mughal Emperors – would dedicate himself for the entirety of his near fifty-year reign (1556–1605).

The Mughal Empire: Expansion

In January 1556, the Mughal emperor Humayun died suddenly, reportedly having slipped and fallen down a flight of stairs as he rushed to answer the call to prayer.[26] The empire that Akbar, his fourteen-year-old son, inherited remained a fragile enterprise. Mughal dominance in northern India was fiercely contested, primarily (though not exclusively) by rival Indo-Afghan warlords.[27] The Rajputs ('sons of kings'), a Hindu warrior aristocracy that had historically strongly resisted Muslim rule, also chafed at the Mughals' hegemonic pretensions.[28] Even the Mughal court remained divided, with many either jealous of Akbar's power, or obsessed with resuming campaigns to retake their Central Asian homelands.[29]

That Humayun had died less than a year after reconquering Delhi moreover meant that he had had little opportunity to firmly re-establish the Mughals' grip on India. Even besides the intrinsic perils of life under a regency government, then, Akbar faced formidable challenges securing his realm. Indeed, these obstacles were so gargantuan that at least one historian has characterized Akbar's reign as amounting to nothing less than a second Mughal conquest of India – one that would prove far more durable and consequential than that of his predecessors.[30] Given that

---

[24] On the importance of a Persianate high culture for helping to integrate late medieval and early modern multicultural polities in Central and South Asia, see for example R. M. Eaton, 'The Persianate cosmopolis (900–1900) and the Sanskrit cosmopolis (400–1400)' in A. Amanat and A. Ashraf (eds.), *The Persianate World: Rethinking a shared sphere* (Leiden: Brill, 2018), p. 73. More generally, on the hybridity characteristic of polities that drew their ideological inheritance from Turco-Mongol and Persianate sources, see generally Brack, 'Theologies of auspicious kingship'.

[25] Dale, *The Muslim Empires of the Ottomans, Safavids, and Mughals*, p. 127.

[26] Fisher, *A Short History of the Mughal Empire*, pp. 68–9.

[27] Richards, *The Mughal Empire*, p. 16.

[28] Streusand, *The Formation of the Mughal Empire*, p. 47.

[29] Richards, *The Mughal Empire*, p. 19.

[30] P. Nath, *Climate of Conquest: War, environment, and empire in Mughal north India* (Oxford: Oxford University Press, 2019), p. 3.

Akbar's reign saw both the empire's rapid expansion as well as its mature institutional consolidation, it forms the focus of our inquiry here.

If the Mughal Empire was to avoid the rapid disintegration that had historically befallen most steppe dynasties, it was essential that Akbar institutionalize more reliable and permanent military and administrative systems. Given the empire's great size and heterogeneity – which dramatically expanded further during Akbar's reign – it was also essential that he consolidate the empire by developing a suitably flexible and encompassing ruling ideology. To safeguard the empire from disintegration, it was likewise imperative that Akbar fashion a diversity regime sufficiently capacious and flexible to bind the empire's diverse constituencies permanently to the imperial centre. Here I first consider how Akbar overcame the challenges of occupation and expansion, before proceeding in the next section to questions of military mobilization, administration, legitimation and integration.

To appreciate the magnitude of the task Akbar faced in constructing a more permanent military machine, we must first acknowledge distinctive features of north India's social ecology that made this project an especially daunting enterprise. If we take as our benchmark Max Weber's definition of the state as an institution that claims a monopoly of legitimate violence,[31] then sixteenth-century north India appears as nothing less than a Weberian nightmare for would-be rulers. This is because at the time of the Mughals' consolidation (and for centuries afterwards), it hosted the world's largest market for military labour. This market generally comprised two overlapping elements: itinerant cavalry-based war-bands from Central Asia, Iran and Afghanistan, and local Indian grandees and their retainers, which included vast reserves of part-time peasant infantrymen.[32]

Contemporary estimates of the Indian military labour market during Akbar's reign indicate over 4.4 million imperial subjects with military qualifications, a figure far greater than the Mughals could possibly directly employ.[33] Historian Andrew de la Garza goes even further, observing that: 'South Asia was an environment militarized to the point of saturation. By some estimates, more than 10 percent of the adult male population was under arms in some capacity.'[34] India's superabundance of soldiers precluded the possibility of the Mughals imposing a monopoly on violence – an aspiration that in any case they never entertained. The

---

[31] M. Weber, *Political Writings* (Cambridge: Cambridge University Press, 1994), pp. 310–11.
[32] Gommans, *Mughal Warfare*, p. 68.   [33] Ibid., p. 74.
[34] A. de la Garza, *The Mughal Empire at War: Babur, Akbar and the Indian military revolution, 1500–1605* (London: Routledge, 2016), p. 136.

diverse economic opportunities military entrepreneurship offered, to actors ranging from Central Asian adventurers through to Indian peasants looking to augment their incomes outside of harvest season, were too powerful to suppress. The existence of entire social groupings (*jati*), whose sense of clan and religious identity was inextricably tied to the warrior vocation, further precluded any attempts to monopolize violence.[35] Accordingly, Akbar's immediate challenge was to introduce India's warrior elites to the special benefits – in terms of honour as well as profit – that they could accrue through imperial service, and then to develop a more systematic and comprehensive means 'to link the Indian military labour market to the Mughal apparatus of empire'.[36]

As with all of the empires considered here, the Mughal imperial enterprise then fundamentally depended on co-opting indigenous military labour, and constructing a broad conquest coalition from diverse local communities. In the Indian context, this imperative was especially pronounced, given the subcontinent's vast ecological as well as cultural heterogeneity. Historian Pratay Nath notes that from the early decades of conquest, the Mughals encountered radically distinct ecological conditions in different parts of their expanding empire. These ranged from the open plains of the Punjab and the Gangetic basin, which favoured cavalry-based warfare, to the densely forested highlands of central India, which instead necessitated protracted siege warfare to dislodge recalcitrant rulers from their hilltop fortresses.[37] India's ecological diversity meant that no single military technique or way of warfare was sufficient to spearhead universal conquest.[38] Additionally, it also reinforced the necessity of engaging indigenous allies, who often possessed the specialist military skills best adapted to meet the challenges of local conditions.

Within this broader context Akbar's co-optation of the Rajput nobility serves as an especially important and arresting example of how the Mughals were able to creatively harness indigenous military institutions, and co-opt and selectively curate the martial collective identities of local elites, to serve imperial ends. The Rajputs constituted a potentially formidable obstacle to Akbar's ambitions. In 1527, Babur had confirmed Mughal supremacy in northern India by defeating a confederacy of Rajput kings.[39] Thereafter, the Rajputs had nevertheless remained hostile to subjugation to an Islamic suzerain, and Akbar was compelled to wage several major campaigns in Rajasthan to bring them to heel.

[35] Richards, *The Mughal Empire*, pp. 22–3.   [36] Gommans, *Mughal Warfare*, p. 67.
[37] Nath, *Climate of Conquest*, p. 5.   [38] Ibid., p. xxxiv.
[39] Richards, *The Mughal Empire*, p. 8.

Notwithstanding this initial need for military subjugation, Akbar was eventually successful in co-opting the Rajputs as indispensable allies, and slotting them into a syncretic diversity regime as an integral part of a polyglot Mughal ruling elite. Paradoxically, a key prerequisite for this co-optation lay in the profoundly martial character of Rajput collective identity. The Rajputs formed part of the Kshatriya varna, the Hindu caste of kings and warriors. While the Kshatriya warrior ethos has ancient roots, Gommans notes that it experienced a revival from the eleventh and twelfth centuries, with the emergence throughout India of 'an assertive new aristocracy based on landed lordship'.[40] Comparable in many respects to the feudal nobility then also consolidating its power throughout Latin Christendom, the Rajput nobility subscribed to a deeply hierarchical world view, in which status and honour derived from a combination of landed wealth and martial prowess.[41]

Intuitively, the Rajputs' aristocratic independence, as well as their warrior ethos and religious devotion (the two were inextricably tied together), might seem to pose a forbidding impediment to their incorporation within the Mughal Empire. On the contrary, however, Akbar succeeded in drawing the most powerful Rajput nobles into the Mughal orbit, through a skilful combination of marital alliances and political patronage. While earlier Islamic rulers in northern India had occasionally taken Hindu wives, Akbar was the first to allow his Hindu wives to retain their faith, rather than convert to Islam.[42] He also recognized his sons born to Hindu wives as legitimate potential heirs, rather than excluding them from potential succession to the throne.[43] This apparent magnanimity not only reflected Akbar's legendary open-mindedness on religious matters. It was also diplomatically astute, for it enabled Akbar to more easily entice Rajput partners into quasi-permanent alliances, cemented through their daughters' marriage to the emperor.

Marital alliances bound the Rajputs by blood to the Mughal house, and as a result of Akbar's alliances, all subsequent Mughal emperors had Hindu ancestors. For Akbar's Rajput clients, marriage into the Mughal household also carried distinct advantages, not least being Akbar's willingness to back his in-laws in their disputes with rivals, both within their clans, and also with other Rajput clans.[44] Additionally, marriage into the Mughal court carried the promise of lucrative service – as both warriors and administrators – within the imperial government. Especially in light of Rajasthan's lack of natural agricultural wealth, imperial service offered the emperor's Rajput clients significant opportunities to enhance their

[40] Gommans, *Mughal Warfare*, p. 53.   [41] Ibid., pp. 53–4.
[42] Fisher, *A Short History of the Mughal Empire*, p. 85.   [43] Ibid.   [44] Ibid.

wealth, status and political influence, which were unavailable to more recalcitrant peers that refused the Mughals' overtures.[45] Over time, the additional resources derived from Mughal patronage tipped the local balance of power in Rajasthan in favour of the emperor's Rajput clients. This in turn further strengthened the Mughals' grip on Rajasthan, enabling them to largely conciliate a constituency that had previously proven highly resistant to outside rule.

Akbar's strategy towards the Rajputs yielded multiple dividends. Within Rajasthan itself, Akbar's sponsorship of Rajput clients created a new class of local intermediaries.[46] These clients could be counted on to facilitate the extension of Mughal influence, precisely because their own power depended on their access to imperial patronage. Selective engagement with favoured Rajput intermediaries moreover foreclosed the possibility that the Rajputs could again unite as they had previously done to resist Mughal suzerainty. Perhaps most importantly, in addition to bringing with them valuable military skills, the Rajputs' incorporation into the Mughal polity also strengthened the emperor, as it diluted the relative influence of Central Asian and Iranian court factions. This proved particularly important, given that imperial pretenders and in particular a powerful dissident Uzbek faction at one point posed the greatest threat to Akbar's hold on power.[47]

Without diminishing Akbar's strategic acumen in incorporating the Rajputs as dependent allies, it is crucial to note the features of Rajput social organization and identity that made this strategy possible in the first instance. At the time of the Mughals' ascent, patrilineal 'brotherhoods' formed the primary unit of social and political organization.[48] Within this social order, Rajput nobles (Thakurs) sought to enhance their power through marital alliances with other brotherhoods, with lower ranked nobles typically marrying their daughters off as a means of establishing or consolidating alliances with more wealthy and powerful Thakurs.[49] The fact that existing Rajput polities took the form of genealogically defined brotherhoods, which sought aggrandizement and upward mobility through vertical marriage alliances, provided a crucial point of entry for the expanding Mughal Empire. Specifically, Rajput traditions of marital diplomacy provided a ready-made institutional practice through

---

[45] Ibid., p. 89.
[46] P. Nath, 'Through the lens of war: Akbar's sieges (1567–69) and Mughal empire-building in early modern north India', *South Asia: Journal of South Asian Studies*, 41(2) (2018), 251–2.
[47] Streusand, *The Formation of the Mughal Empire*, pp. 94–102.
[48] Richards, *The Mughal Empire*, p. 22.   [49] Ibid., p. 24.

which the Mughals could plug in to existing power networks, and graft them onto their expanding imperial conglomerate.

The Rajputs' martial sense of collective identity, and their tradition of pursuing glory through devoted service to glorious master, further smoothed the way for Mughal expansion. Submission to the Mughals did not violate the Rajputs' *dharma*, their divinely ordained code of conduct that reflected sense of their place in the universe. Rather, the immense power of the Mughal emperor and his purported proximity to the divine enhanced the status of Rajput clients, by enabling them to bask in his reflected glory. On the indispensable harmony between the Rajputs' self-conception as a warrior-elite and their submission and service to the Mughals, historian John Richards observes:

Mughal service was compatible with the ethos of the warrior in service of a great master. Rajputs were enjoined to fight and die in the service of a master. A warrior's service was expressed in acts of complete self-sacrifice and devotion for the earthly master and for god ... In accepting Akbar's service, Rajput Thakurs thereby accepted him as a Muslim Rajput who possessed a far greater sovereignty than even the greatest of the Rajput masters.[50]

More than merely a munificent patron, Akbar and his successors were venerated as being semi-divine in character in Rajput bardic literature, further legitimizing Rajput submission to the empire. A Rajput poem extolling the emperor thus notes: 'The emperor upholds dharma. His rule stabilizes the earth ... The goddess Lakshmi shares her time between Vishnu's embrace and nestling at Akbar's breast.'[51] In this regard, then, Rajput incorporation into the Mughal Empire was not merely an act of expedience. Rather, existing Rajput identities proved sufficiently pliable to provide the basis for powerful legitimizing narratives, which were in turn indispensable for stabilizing the expanded ties of kinship and patronage that incorporated the Rajputs into the Mughal order.

The incorporation of Rajput nobility into the Mughal elite powerfully demonstrates the dexterity with which the Mughals harnessed existing social practices and collective identities to expand their empire. Consistent with my emphasis on define and conquer strategies, Rajput identities were not merely slotted unchanged into an expanding Mughal order. Rather, their identities were actively reshaped through processes of imperial incorporation. By way of illustration, the Rajputs had traditionally balanced their emphasis on aristocratic hierarchy with a countervailing stress on the egalitarianism of the clan brotherhood.[52]

---

[50] Ibid.   [51] Cited in Fisher, *A Short History of the Mughal Empire*, p. 88.
[52] J. Vivekanandran, *Interrogating International Relations: India's strategic practice and the return of history* (London: Routledge, 2011), p. 164.

Conversely, as prominent Rajput nobles became entangled in the Mughals' expanding web of patronage, they increasingly favoured aristocratic hierarchy over the collegiality of the clan, and sought to reduce the autonomy of junior relatives and allies accordingly.[53]

In particular, the Mughals' obsessive emphasis on genealogy encouraged mimicry among senior Rajputs, who emulated it in their own legitimation strategies.[54]

Bards had always encouraged their Rajput employers to assume aristocratic self-images closely linked with myths of origin that established their status as *ksatriyas* and traced their genealogies to, for instance, the great dynasties of ancient Indian history. *But now the political power and social status of the more successful lineages tended to be legitimised exclusively in the language of descent and kinship.*[55]

Likewise, Rajput kings also imitated their Mughal patrons in the administration of their own patrimonies, increasingly favouring more bureaucratic forms of local state-building and land administration than before.[56] As a result of these processes, Rajput clans became increasingly vertically stratified as local kingdoms coalesced under the canopy of Mughal suzerainty. This rendered the Rajputs more legible to the Mughals as imperial constituencies, and correspondingly more digestible as constituent components of the Mughals' expanding empire.

Important as expedients like the Mughal-Rajput alliances were for the empire's expansion, they were by themselves insufficient to institutionalize, legitimize and consolidate the empire as a whole. Instead, these improvisations laid the groundwork for more thoroughgoing efforts to entrench a system of rule that made a virtue of India's combination of dispersed military power and extreme cultural heterogeneity, by accommodating both as key features of the Mughal Empire.

As noted above, India's reserves of military power were too vast and too spread out to favour an imperial monopoly on coercion. Hence, rather than seeking to eliminate these nodes of power, Akbar enlisted them to the empire's service through a centralized system of patronage. The *mansabdari* ('rank-holder') system, which Akbar first introduced in 1572–3, quickly became the central institution of the Mughal polity.[57] *Mansabs* (rank-holders) were drawn from throughout the empire, and were obliged to serve as both imperial soldiers and administrators.

---

[53] Ibid.
[54] D. H. A. Kolff, *Naukar, Rajput, and Sepoy: The ethnohistory of the military labour market on Hindustan, 1450–1850* (Cambridge: Cambridge University Press, 1990), p. 72.
[55] Ibid., emphasis added.
[56] Vivekanandran, *Interrogating International Relations*, p. 165.
[57] Streusand, *Formation of the Mughal Empire*, p. 108.

Though the system varied across the empire's expanse, in essence it worked on the basis that a noble's rank was calibrated in proportion to the size of the military contingent he was expected to muster at the emperor's request.[58] While the emperor provided some cash subsidies to support his *mansabs*, the bulk of the burden for recruiting, paying and commanding soldiers lay with the *mansabs*, rather than the imperial household.[59]

The principal advantage of the *mansabdari* system was that the emperor 'secured the benefits of a large central army without the crushing financial and administrative burden such an entity usually carried with it'.[60] In this way, Akbar and his successors were able to make the empire's decentralized distribution of coercion work to their advantage. Beyond merely shifting the burdens of empire onto dependent allies, however, the *mansabdari* system also worked as the empire's primary mechanism of elite socialization and control. The ranking of each *mansab* was determined (at least theoretically) by the emperor himself, based on his assessment of the candidate's merits, and also on the basis of recommendations from high officials with more detailed knowledge of the candidate.[61] Rather than being fixed, a nobleman's position within the *mansab* hierarchy was moreover periodically reviewed. The power to promote or demote *mansabs* thus provided the emperor with an extremely powerful means of assuring the continued loyalty of his most powerful (and therefore potentially threatening) servants.[62]

Not merely a functional contract, the *mansabdari* system rested on the *mansabs'* ritual incorporation into the Mughal court. On important occasions, such as imperial birthdays or coronations, nobles were expected to present *peshkash* ('presentation gifts') as a form of tribute to the emperor.[63] In return, the emperor provided favoured supplicants with 'robes of honour' (*khilat*). Initially worn by the emperor himself, receipt of these items symbolized tributaries' incorporation into the Mughal household.[64] Alongside these forms of ritual gift exchange, the emperor moreover leveraged the intimacy of the *mansabdari* system to consolidate his power over his subordinates in other ways. To take one example, the court provided the venue in which the emperor legitimized his allies' authority, through ritual acts such as placing a vermillion mark (a *tika*) on a Hindu raja's forehead to ratify his status within the Mughal hierarchy.[65]

The final feature of the *mansabdari* system worth noting is that at least in its early incarnation under Akbar, it worked on the basis of circulating

---

[58] Ibid.   [59] Richards, *The Mughal Empire*, p. 25.   [60] Ibid.
[61] Fisher, *A Short History of the Mughal Empire*, p. 101.   [62] Ibid.   [63] Ibid., p. 102.
[64] Ibid.   [65] Richards, *The Mughal Empire*, p. 21.

nobles throughout the empire, rather than allowing them to consolidate their own local power bases. Though exceptions were sometimes made, the *mansabdari* system worked on the principle that nobles were to govern territories beyond their immediate homelands, being assigned to different parts of the empire as the emperor saw fit.[66] *Mansabs* derived much of the income necessary to supply troops to the emperor from land grants (*jagirs*).[67] But rather than concede these land grants as hereditable fiefs, *jagirs* remained revocable assignments from the emperor, which could be withdrawn at any time, and which were typically reassigned in the event of a *mansab*'s death.[68] Though it eventually fell apart as the Mughal Empire declined, this system initially worked to dislodge military and administrative elites from their local communities, while also broadening their horizons and socializing them as part of an empire-wide service nobility.[69]

The *mansabdari* system constituted a formidable institutional innovation that helped secure Indian elites' active participation in the Mughal imperial project. This assured the empire's survival and expansion well into the eighteenth century. Impressive though it was, the *mansabdari* system flourished only because Akbar and his successors were also able to overcome potentially formidable legitimation challenges. These challenges were myriad when Akbar first took power.

Among the Timurids themselves (that is, the Mughal cohort claiming direct descent from Genghis Khan and Tamerlane), there had long existed a tradition of 'collective sovereignty'.[70] This tradition theoretically invested every descendant of the original conquerors with a claim to power, rendering them averse to subordination to any one of their peers (Akbar included) claiming the mantle of universal kingship.[71] The *ulema*, the empire's Islamic scholars and jurists, meanwhile insisted that the empire strictly comport to Islamic conceptions of legitimacy. These enjoined legal discrimination against non-Muslims, and an insistence that the empire's Islamic subjects live in accordance with sharia law.[72] Such demands were necessarily at odds with the aspirations of the empire's non-Islamic majority, whose own religious affiliations inclined many to resist Islamic rule. The condescension of India's Persianate lettered elites (the *ashraf* class) towards their Timurid rulers provided an additional (if more diffuse) obstacle to entrenching the Mughal

---

[66] S. Subrahmanyam, 'A tale of three empires: Mughals, Ottomans, and Habsburgs in a comparative context', *Common Knowledge*, 12(1) (2006), 83.
[67] S. Moosvi, 'The evolution of the "Mansab" system under Akbar until 1596–7', *Journal of the Royal Asiatic Society of Great Britain and Ireland*, 2 (1981), 182.
[68] Subrahmanyam, 'A tale of three empires', 83.
[69] Richards, *The Mughal Empire*, p. 66.
[70] Streusand, *Formation of the Mughal Empire*, p. 30.   [71] *Ibid.*
[72] Richards, *The Mughal Empire*, pp. 36–7.

emperor's authority, further complicating efforts at imperial consolidation.[73] Finally, while the Mughals' Timurid genealogy elevated their prestige in Central Asia, the extreme violence that had attended the conquests of Genghis Khan and Tamerlane in north India rendered that same heritage a distinct disadvantage in the Indian context, and a significant obstacle to winning over locals' allegiance.[74]

In light of these challenges, Akbar's development of a powerful new legitimating ideology to integrate his empire's diverse fragments was arguably his greatest achievement. Previously the Mughal Empire had sustained itself with an inward-looking ideology of universal conquest, designed primarily for the Timurids' internal consumption.[75] But Mughal conceptions of legitimacy from Akbar onwards better reflected the diversity of their vast and continuously expanding domain. More precisely, Mughal ideology under Akbar and his successors was absolutist in aspiration; incorporative in its purpose; syncretic in its inspirations and expression; and decentralized in its institutional forms.

In contrast to the ideals of collective sovereignty characteristic of steppe dynasties, Mughal conceptions of rule from the mid-sixteenth century became far more absolutist. Much more than a first among equals, Akbar elevated himself to a semi-divine status, a figure uniquely possessed of the 'divine light' and therefore immune from challenge from other Timurid aspirants to the throne.[76] Not merely a change in rhetoric, the ideology of rule under Akbar also constituted a transformation in the scope and character of the imperial office. To take one example, previous Islamic rulers in India had generally accepted the *ulema*'s supremacy when it came to questions of interpreting and applying sharia law. By contrast, in 1579, Akbar arrogated to himself the supreme right of interpretation (*ijtihad*) over Islamic law, effectively usurping the *ulema*'s claims to supremacy in the religious sphere.[77] This kind of power claim was of course far from unique to Akbar's India. By the mid-sixteenth century, many Renaissance kingdoms in Europe had asserted similarly strong claims over the Church within their territory.[78] The Ottoman sultans had meanwhile also asserted their rights to make laws independent of

---

[73] Ironically, however, the Mughals would ultimately emerge as the foremost sponsors of Persephone high culture as a central means of consolidating pan-regional power. See generally M. Alam, 'The pursuit of Persian: Language in Mughal politics', *Modern Asian Studies*, 32(2) (1998), 317–49.

[74] Lefèvre, 'In the name of the fathers', 415.

[75] Jha, 'South Asia, 1400–1800', pp. 153–4.

[76] Streusand, *Formation of the Mughal Empire*, p. 136.

[77] Dale, *The Muslim Empires of the Ottomans, Safavids, and Mughals*, p. 101.

[78] G. Leff, 'Heresy and the decline of the medieval church', *Past and Present*, 20(1) (1961), 38–9.

the *ulema* – and outside the strictures of sharia law – by Akbar's time.[79] These extra-regional comparisons aside, the point remains that Akbar's reign witnessed a revolution in Mughal conceptions of authority. This revolution humbled rival claimants to power, be they steppe warlords or Islamic jurists, and established the imperial court as the solar centre of power and pinnacle of authority throughout the Empire.

Akbar's transformation of the imperial office entailed revolutionary changes in its purpose as well as its scope. Previously, Muslim conquerors in northern India had often foregrounded their Islamic credentials.[80] This had necessarily limited their capacity to reach out to non-Islamic constituencies, contributing to the notable brittleness of earlier conquest polities. To cite but one example, the Afghan warlord Sher Shah – who had successfully evicted the Mughals from India following their first conquest there – ultimately failed in his attempts to fully recruit the Rajput military elite into his own proto-empire. This failure of integration flowed from the religious inflexibility of the *ulema*, and their corresponding ability to frustrate Sher Shah's ambitious outreach efforts to non-Muslim allies.[81]

By contrast, alongside his chief ideologue Abul El Fazl, Akbar justified his rule through appeals to the ideal of *suhl e kul* (peace for all, or universal reconciliation).[82] Whereas earlier Islamic conquest dynasties had embraced religious proselytization as part of their governing mandate, Akbar recast the emperor's chief task as one of celebrating cultural and religious diversity, and safeguarding its preservation.[83] Through this lens, the emperor's possession of the 'divine effulgence' invested him with a special charisma, enabling him to bind together and reconcile otherwise irredeemably diverse and fractious ethnic and religious communities.[84] Within the Rajput case, for example, these ideological innovations enabled Akbar to do what Sher Shah had not, absorbing Rajput military manpower through appeals to a syncretic idiom of rule that transcended religious difference.[85]

Akbar's pivot to syncretism was real and enduring. The abolition of special taxes on non-Muslim subjects (the *jizya*), and prohibitions on slaves' forcible conversion to Islam, stand as but two examples of how this reimagining of the imperial office manifested itself in concrete policy.[86]

---

[79] K. Barkey, 'Political legitimacy and Islam in the Ottoman Empire: Lessons learned', *Philosophy and Social Criticism*, 40(4–5) (2014), 473.
[80] Asher and Talbot, *India Before Europe*, pp. 45–6.
[81] Kolff, *Naukar, Rajput, and Sepoy*, p. 114.
[82] Khan, 'Tracing sources of principles of Mughal governance', 51.
[83] Asher and Talbot, *India Before Europe*, pp. 130–1.   [84] Ibid., p. 50.
[85] Kolff, *Naukar, Rajput, and Sepoy*, p. 114.   [86] Jha, 'South Asia, 1400–1800', p. 155.

Likewise, Akbar famously briefly instituted a dedicated hall of religious debate (*ibadatkhanah*) to foster debate between religious leaders drawn from the empire's subject communities.[87] That said, it bears emphasis that Mughal toleration bore no resemblance to proto-Lockean ideals of individual freedom of conscience. Nor did it imply limits to the Emperor's power to intervene in religious matters, out of supposed deference to the liberties of either religious establishments or individual believers. On the contrary, Akbar's doctrine of universal reconciliation was an *incorporative* discourse that venerated the emperor as the indispensable reconciler of faith communities, imagined in irreducibly corporate and collective terms. Religion remained conceived as a 'body of believers', rather than a 'body of beliefs'.[88] Accordingly, the emperor's role was neither to relegate religion to the realm of private conscience, nor to transcend religious difference through appeals to an alternative secular ideology. Instead, his task was to guarantee the integrity of different faith traditions and to preserve inter-communal harmony, by simultaneously encompassing and embodying the different expressions of the divine that these faith traditions reflected.[89]

Above all, the empire's management of cultural diversity was geared towards shoring up the emperor's supreme authority, and incorporating subject communities under common subjection to Mughal rule. Despite superficial resemblances with modern pluralism, even practices such as the sponsorship of inter-faith debates cleaved to this broader imperative. Thus, Akbar's sponsorship of a hall of religious debate was intended at least in part as a means to undermine the authority of the *ulema*, while Mughal participation in religious debates was likewise regarded as an important expression of imperial authority.[90]

Consistent with the incorporative imperatives driving Mughal statecraft, both Mughal ideology and the accompanying diversity regime that exemplified it drew from a multitude of different traditions. It was syncretic in both its intellectual inspirations and in its modes of expression. Mughal ideology undeniably borrowed heavily from Islamic idioms of rule to shore up the emperor's authority. Thus, in a direct challenge to the

---

[87] A. Truschke, 'Dangerous debates: Jain responses to theological challenges at the Mughal court', *Modern Asian Studies*, 49(5) (2015), 1343.

[88] On the importance of this distinction in the specific context of Reformation Europe, see M. P. Holt, *The French Wars of Religion, 1562–1629* (Cambridge: Cambridge University Press, 2005), p. 2.

[89] On the core values of the Mughal ethos, which enjoined tolerance within as well as between different faith traditions, see R. Kinra, 'Handling diversity with absolute civility: The global historical legacy of Mughal *Suhl-i-Kull*', *Medieval History Journal*, 16(2) (2013), 261.

[90] Truschke, 'Dangerous Debates', 1343.

Ottomans, Akbar claimed the mantle of Caliph – Allah's 'shadow on earth', to whom all Muslims purportedly owed supreme earthly allegiance.[91] Simultaneously, however, the Mughals also drew on the pre-Islamic Persian ideal of the emperor as Padshah – a universal conqueror who secured civic and cosmic peace through the centripetal force of his divine charisma, and cultivated virtue among his subjects through pedagogical rituals.[92] When addressing his Hindu subjects, imperial propagandists meanwhile equated Akbar with Lord Ram, a deity especially revered by the Ksatriya warrior caste.[93]

These customized legitimation scripts enhanced the emperor's appeal to the empire's diverse constituencies, immeasurably enhancing the empire's ideological reach and so contributing to its longevity even after Akbar's death in 1605. That the Mughal Empire began to disintegrate once this syncretic legacy was abandoned over a century later, by Akbar's great-grandson and successor Aurangzeb, only further vindicates the wisdom of his strategy.

In his strategies of military mobilization, administration and legitimation, Akbar laid the foundations for an early modern empire surpassed in size and wealth only by China.

The Mughals' syncretic diversity regime – arguably Akbar's greatest achievement – proved particularly pivotal to their empire-building success. Arising incrementally out of alliances with local warlords, the nascent Mughal diversity regime helped Akbar to build the eclectic coalition of military specialists needed to conquer a subcontinent marked by vast environmental as well as cultural heterogeneity. Subsequently, the Mughals held the empire together through resort to a cult of emperor worship assembled from Timurid and Persianate elements, and grounded in an ethic of universal reconciliation. The ideology of *suhl e kul* sought not to eradicate communal difference, but to nourish a self-consciously hybrid court culture that bound subordinate elites in common subjection to the emperor, while simultaneously tempering but not destroying their attachments to more parochial loyalties.

The Mughal diversity regime proved extraordinarily successful in legitimizing and stabilizing Timurid rule over most of India. The incorporation and organization of cultural difference, rather than its attempted obliteration, was key to the Mughals' success as both conquerors and rulers. Nevertheless, political and military power remained highly decentralized under the Mughals. This decentralization was initially a source of

[91] Richards, *The Mughal Empire*, p. 40.
[92] Wilson, 'Early colonial India beyond empire', 956.
[93] Richards, *The Mughal Empire*, p. 23.

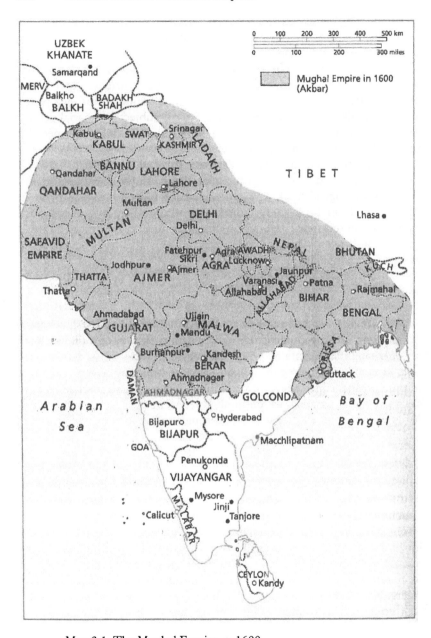

Map 3.1 The Mughal Empire, c. 1600
Source: Andrew Phillips and J. C. Sharman, *International Order in Diversity: War, trade and rule in the Indian Ocean* (Cambridge: Cambridge University Press, 2015), p. 84.

dynamism, which helped reconcile indigenous elites to life under Mughal suzerainty by enabling them to participate as junior partners within the empire. In the longer term, however, decentralization proved debilitating. Though Akbar transformed the institution of emperor and found a way to corral the Indian military labour market to Mughal purposes, the reach of Mughal power remained continuously contested, both internally and externally. An influential study of the empire in the strategically vital maritime province of Gujarat thus describes a polity in which '[i]mperial authority was established and maintained through a dynamic, ever expanding and inclusive co-sharing of sovereignty with an increasing number of local intermediaries'.[94] The Mughals' preference for incorporating rather than destroying rival power centres, and their permeability to outside cultural influences, would ultimately leave them vulnerable to infiltration and subversion once their power began to fade.[95] In this limited regard, at least, the Mughal Empire differs importantly from Qing China, the only early modern rival to eclipse it in power, wealth and size. Accordingly, it is to a consideration of the Qing Empire's rise, expansion and early institutionalization that I now turn.

The Rise of the Manchu Empire, c. 1590–1683

The Qing Empire surpassed even the Mughals as the greatest single power concentration in the world prior to the rise of the British Raj in the nineteenth century. From its tentative emergence along China's north-eastern frontier in the early 1600s (coincidentally coinciding roughly with Akbar's death), the Qing Empire eventually metamorphosed into an immense polity governing approximately 35 per cent of the world's population, and covering 10 per cent of its land surface.[96] Like the Mughals, the Manchus constituted a demographically insignificant ruling elite, who managed to remix institutions and ideological resources in conquered territories to build a vast multi-ethnic empire. Notwithstanding these similarities in the process of imperial expansion, the legitimation challenges the Manchus overcame were even more formidable than those facing the Mughals. The imperial order the Manchus constructed moreover proved bigger, tougher and less permeable to foreign infiltration than the Mughals. This disparity would have momentous consequences for the future course of Western expansion in Asia,

---

[94] Hasan, *State and Locality in Mughal India*, p. 43.
[95] On the Mughals' longstanding preference for absorbing rather than annihilating their enemies, see generally Nath, 'Through the lens of war', 249–51.
[96] L. A. Struve, 'Introduction' in L. A. Struve (ed.), *The Qing Formation in World-Historical Time* (Cambridge, MA: Harvard University Press, 2004), p. 2.

a theme I take up in Chapter 4. For now, I consider the initial evolution of the Manchu polity, sticking to the same template (emergence, expansion, institutionalization and legitimation) established earlier.

The Emergence of the Manchu Frontier Polity

To understand the Manchu polity's emergence, we must first briefly consider the larger environmental context from which it arose. Late-sixteenth-century Northeast Asia was a focal point of commercial expansion and geopolitical rivalry. Commercially, Ming China stood at this time at the centre of an emergent global economy. As mentioned previously, China's 'single whip' tax reforms had spurred huge imports of silver bullion.[97] Crucially, the economic growth these imports stimulated was highly geographically uneven, centring especially around volatile multi-ethnic frontiers along China's steppe and forest northern frontiers, as well as its southern maritime frontier.[98]

Students of European political development are already familiar with the catalytic role that the late medieval commercial revolution played in prompting the rise of new polity forms (sovereign states, city-states and city-leagues) in Latin Christendom.[99] Likewise, Asia's early modern economic efflorescence nourished a comparable wave of violent political entrepreneurship and polity formation along Ming China's frontiers. Historian Kishimoto Mio thus observes that 'Ming China was surrounded by a band of commerce and war in which people drawn by the profits of international trade congregated and engaged in violent conflict.'[100] Peter Perdue, noting the parallels between China's northern (steppe and forest) and southern (maritime) frontiers, similarly characterizes both as 'shifting zones of influence and contention' in which 'mobile rivals – nomads and seafarers – with distinct cultural and military formations challenged imperial Chinese control'.[101]

Uneven commercial growth thus churned up the social landscape along China's frontiers, injecting new resources and affording new opportunities for polity formation potentially corrosive of Ming hegemony. This destabilization moreover occurred at a time of heightened geopolitical

---

[97] Flynn and Giráldez, 'Born with a "silver spoon"', 208.

[98] K. Mio, 'The Ch'ing Dynasty and the East Asian world', *Acta Asiatica* 88 (2005), 96; Rawski, *Early Modern China and Northeast Asia*, pp. 60–1.

[99] See generally H. Spruyt, *The Sovereign State and its Competitors* (Princeton: Princeton University Press, 1994).

[100] Mio, 'The Ch'ing Dynasty and the East Asian world', 95.

[101] P. C. Perdue, 'Coercion and commerce on two Chinese frontiers' in N. di Cosmo (ed.), *Military Culture in Imperial China* (Cambridge, MA: Harvard University Press, 2009), p. 320.

competition. From 1592–8, East Asia experienced its first modern Great Power war, pitting Ming China and Yi Dynasty Korea (Choson) against the Japanese warlord, Toyotomi Hideyoshi. Hideyoshi's bid to supplant the Ming Dynasty as regional hegemon ultimately failed. But he unleashed such immense violence as to lead one historian to deem the 'Imjin War' the sixteenth century's single largest military conflict.[102] Despite its eventual victory, the war also drastically weakened Ming China. This further undermined its already tenuous grasp over its frontiers, creating space for the rise of new forms of insurgent polity – including the Manchus.[103]

The Manchus originated from a group of peoples, the Jurchen, concentrated in the frontier zone intersecting north-eastern China, Mongolia and Korea. Unlike the Timurid Mughals, the Manchus could not claim an august lineage linking them back to conquerors such as Genghis Khan or Tamerlane. Indeed, though they later legitimized themselves by tracing their origins to an earlier barbarian dynasty (the Jin) that had previously conquered parts of northern China, the Manchus initially lacked anything approximating a coherent shared collective identity.[104] Instead, the Jurchen were divided into competing clan lineages, which were resistant to any form of central organization.[105] The absence of principles of primogeniture within individual clan lineages contributed further to the Jurchens' internal division.[106]

Before the late sixteenth century, Ming Dynasty officials wrote off the Jurchen as barbarians, and successfully managed them through traditional 'barbarian management' techniques. Chinese officials conferred favoured Jurchen chieftains with Ming military titles, symbolically investing them with responsibility to help secure order along China's northern marches.[107] Besides granting them this symbolic recognition, the Ming also rewarded their clients with trading patents, which granted them exclusive privileges to trade with China.[108] These patents not only economically strengthened Jurchen clients relative to their indigenous adversaries, but also bound them in uneasy alignment with Beijing.[109] At the same time, the Ming Dynasty's capacity to withdraw or re-allocate these

---

[102] K. M. Swope, *A Dragon's Head and a Serpent's Tail: Ming China and the first great East Asian war, 1592–1598* (Norman: University of Oklahoma Press, 2009), p. 3.

[103] Rawski, *Early Modern China and Northeast Asia*, p. 65.

[104] For an excellent introduction to the literature on early Manchu identity, see R. K. Guy, 'Who were the Manchus? A review essay', *Journal of Asian Studies*, 61(1) (2002), 151–64.

[105] Rawski, *Early Modern China and Northeast Asia*, p. 65.

[106] Li, 'State building before 1644', p. 21.

[107] Rawski, *Early Modern China and Northeast Asia*, p. 65.

[108] Li, 'State building before 1644', p. 22.   [109] Ibid.

symbolic and material rewards provided them with powerful mechanisms to keep the Jurchen clans divided, supposedly foreclosing the potential rise of any supra-clan Jurchen threat to the empire.[110]

Economic dependence on the Ming, internal division and the challenges of defending against powerful and potentially predatory neighbours such as the Mongols, together kept the Jurchen clans in check down to the late sixteenth century. From 1583, however, a Jurchen chieftain named Nurhaci began to slip the imperial leash. In a manner reminiscent of the Mughal frontier polity-building discussed previously, Nurhaci exploited his strategic location at the interstices of a range of different social networks to arbitrage diverse forms of economic, military and cultural capital from these disparate sources. Braiding these resources together, Nurhaci and his successors thereafter fashioned the embryo of a later Manchu conquest state.

To see how a Manchu conquest state became possible, we must acknowledge a key initial advantage of the Jurchen clans, namely their occupation of a potentially extremely lucrative resource enclave. The Jurchen homeland was naturally richer than surrounding border territories, producing a trifecta of luxury commodities – ginseng, sable and pearls – that Chinese consumers greatly desired.[111] This demand only grew as the sixteenth-century commercial boom progressed, and imports of silver bullion further enhanced Chinese elites' appetite for hinterland luxury goods.[112]

With the growth in trade, opportunities arose for enterprising Jurchen to amass vast wealth, primarily by monopolizing brokerage between hinterland producers of luxury commodities and Chinese consumers. As we have seen, Ming officials had historically tried to pre-empt the formation of power concentrations along their frontiers, by carefully controlling the allocation of trading patents to preferred clients. With the rise of Nurhaci, this system began to break down. Nurhaci bribed corrupt border officials, first to accumulate disproportionate trading patents, and then to circumvent Ming prohibitions on the sale of iron to the Jurchens.[113] These manoeuvres respectively allowed him both to amass a sizeable war chest through enhanced control over the hinterland luxuries trade, and also to begin to construct modern weaponry from the smelted iron illegally bought through Chinese intermediaries.[114] In addition to his commercial activities, Nurhaci even undertook raiding into neighbouring territories to abduct iron workers for enslavement in his

---

[110] Ibid.   [111] Ibid., p. 40.

[112] Mio, 'The Ch'ing Dynasty and the East Asian world', 96. See also Narangoa and Cribb, *Historical Atlas of Northeast Asia*, pp. 25–7.

[113] See for example Li, 'State building before 1644', p. 40.   [114] Ibid.

smelters and armouries.[115] This combination of covert wealth accumulation and overt theft of skilled workers and dual-use technologies played a pivotal role in the genesis of a Manchu conquest state. The latter for example enabled the Manchus to replicate Ming China's success in manufacturing European-style cannons by 1631, a mere eight years after the Chinese themselves had crossed this technological threshold.[116]

Nurhaci's monopoly on the hinterland luxuries trade was never total. But his efforts to carve out a commercial monopoly were nevertheless more than sufficient to lay the material and political foundation for an emergent Manchu polity. By the early seventeenth century, the Ming may have re-exported up to 25 per cent of their New World silver reserves to Nurhaci's lineage group (the Aisin Gioro).[117] This inflow of wealth helped give Nurhaci the wherewithal to acquire more of the firearms and skilled military specialists needed to engage in large-scale conquest.[118] The frontier commercial boom in which Nurhaci participated meanwhile created a multicultural mercantile class of Jurchen and bicultural Chinese 'trans-frontiersmen'.[119] These merchants needed protection for their new-found wealth, and so emerged as a powerful potential constituency to support enterprising warlords like Nurhaci.[120]

Beyond building the material foundations for a conquest state, Nurhaci also worked hard to fashion a united pan-Jurchen collective identity, drawing freely from the cultural capital of neighbouring societies to do so. Thus, in 1599, Nurhaci commissioned local scholars to fashion for the first time a Manchu written script, adapted from the existing Mongolian alphabet.[121] Nurhaci's extensive patronage of Tibetan Buddhism, the traditional religion of the eastern Mongols, meanwhile provided further scaffolding around which a common 'Manchu' identity could gel. This patronage of Tibetan Buddhism moreover carried an additional advantage of building a point of mutual identification with the Mongols, which Nurhaci further consolidated through deft marital diplomacy.[122] Nurhaci

---

[115] D. M. Farquhar, 'Mongolian Versus Chinese Elements in the Early Manchu State', *Ch'ing-shih wen-t'i*, 2(6) (1971), 21.

[116] Ibid., 20.

[117] N. di Cosmo, 'The Manchu conquest in world-historical perspective: A note on trade and silver', *Journal of Central Eurasian Studies*, 1 (2009), 54.

[118] Ibid., p. 57. See also Li, 'State building before 1644', p. 23.

[119] On the Manchu state as a 'political rallying of frontier peoples' encompassing Mongols and Chinese as well as Jurchen, see I. Shigeki, 'China's frontier society in the sixteenth and seventeenth centuries', *Acta Asiatica*, 88 (2005), 20. On Chinese 'trans-frontiermen' as 'key brokers who synthesized the essential elements of the Manchu state from diverse roots', see Perdue, *China Marches West*, pp. 122–3.

[120] Ibid.   [121] Li, 'State building before 1644', p. 28.

[122] On the use of marital diplomacy as a key element of the statecraft of Nurhaci and his successors, see Perdue, *China Marches West*, pp. 124–5. On Nurhaci's skilful (if cynical)

eventually married nine of his fourteen daughters to Mongol princes, placing him at the centre of a sprawling web of alliances spanning Jurchen and Mongol territories.[123] The fact that it was Mongolian-speaking Korchins (rather than Jurchens) who first recognized Nurhaci as *khan* is testimony to the success of his marital diplomacy in securing his flanks from a potential Mongol challenge.[124] It also highlights the poly-glot character of the Manchu enterprise from the outset, a feature that would permanently mark the empire once it expanded to its full magni-tude under Nurhaci's successors.

The Expansion and Institutionalization of the Manchu Empire

At the time of Nurhaci's death in 1626, the Manchu polity was still far from posing an existential threat to the Ming Dynasty. Like the Mughals following Babur's demise, the Manchu polity remained weakly institu-tionalized, and rent by the tenacious egalitarianism of its upper ranks. Indeed, on this score, the Manchus were even more hamstrung than the Mughals at a comparable point in their expansion. Whereas the Mughals' Timurid heritage lent itself to grand imperial designs from the outset, Nurhaci's ambitions did not initially extend to empire-building, with his later tilt towards establishing a 'great enterprise' coming only decades into his territorial expansion.[125]

The shift towards more centralized and institutionalized rule came as an unintended and unwanted consequence of Nurhaci's territorial expan-sion in defence of his monopoly. The Manchu polity thus first congealed in a spontaneous, ad hoc and opportunistic manner. Certainly, by 1616, Nurhaci had built a powerful khanate in Manchuria, which operated increasingly beyond the control of its nominal Ming suzerains. Two years later, Nurhaci moreover formally renounced his allegiance to the Ming, later defeating a vast Ming army in the battle of Mt Sarhu in 1619.[126] But it was over fifteen years later, in 1636, that Nurhaci's son Hong Taiji declared the advent of the 'Great Qing' Empire, thereby

harnessing of Tibetan Buddhism to solidify his hold over his Mongol subjects, see D. M. Farquhar, 'Emperor as Bodhisattva in the governance of the Ch'ing Empire', *Harvard Journal of Asiatic Studies* 38(1) (1978), 22–3.
[123] Narangoa and Cribb, *Historical Atlas of Northeast* Asia, p. 25. On the centrality of marriage alliances in forging Manchu-Mongol relations – and in paving the way for Nurhaci's later dominance – see N. di Cosmo, 'From alliance to tutelage: A historical analysis of Manchu-Mongol relations before the Qing conquest', *Frontiers of History in China*, 7(2) (2012), 187.
[124] F. Wakeman, *The Great Enterprise*, 2 vols., I: *The Manchu Reconstruction of Imperial Order in Seventeenth-Century China* (Berkeley: University of California Press, 1985), p. 55.
[125] Li, 'State building before 1644', p. 39.   [126] Ibid., pp. 41–2.

directly challenging the Ming Dynasty and asserting plans for universal dominion.[127] Given the Manchus' small numbers and their cultural marginality (as barbarians at the edge of Sinic civilization), their success in toppling the Ming in 1644, and then crushing the last vestiges of Ming loyalism over the next four decades, begs explanation.

In contrast to the Mughals in South Asia, the Manchus lacked access to vast reserves of private military labour at the time of their expansion. This qualifier aside, the Manchus' echoed Mughal precedents, to the extent that they conquered their empire through extensive reliance on allies and auxiliaries drawn from beyond their immediate retinue. For the Manchus did not conquer China by themselves, but rather as ringleaders of a multi-ethnic confederacy, which encompassed Mongols, Chinese defectors and (albeit reluctantly and on a smaller scale) Koreans.[128] Consequently, their primary challenge was to mobilize, organize and channel these forces in a manner that generated the military power necessary to conquer and rule on a subcontinental scale.

We have already seen how the Mughals harnessed the Indian military labour market, and mobilized and manipulated indigenous forms of collective identity in support of empire, through the *mansabdari* system. Within the emerging Manchu Empire, the Eight Banner system performed a roughly equivalent function. The Manchu Eight Banner system was 'the most famous of all Manchu institutions'.[129] It was the primary vehicle for the Manchus' define and conquer strategy in Northeast Asia, and the eventual centrepiece of their diversity regime as their empire consolidated. The banner system mobilized military power by organizing warriors into companies (*niru*, meaning 'arrows'), grouped into battalions (*jalan*) under the larger rubric of 'banners' (*gusa*).[130] Beyond simply being fighting formations, the banners encompassed entire communities, with each soldier and his family granted a plot of land, and individual households tasked with provisioning warriors either with grain, horses and sheep, or weapons and armour.[131]

From the early seventeenth century, the banner system provided a potent means for organizing the military resources of the multi-ethnic coalition Manchu leaders mobilized to conquer China and neighbouring polities. Beyond harnessing military power, the banner system crucially also shaped the collective identities that formed the building blocks of an emerging Manchu Empire. On the one hand, it deliberately weakened

---

[127] Ibid., p. 56.
[128] Shigeki, 'China's frontier society in the sixteenth and seventeenth centuries', 20.
[129] Cited in Elliott, *The Manchu Way*, p. 39.   [130] Ibid., pp. 61–2.
[131] Chang, *A Court on Horseback*, p. 21; Burbank and Cooper, *Empires in World History*, p. 207.

older lineage loyalties among the Jurchen, the group that formed the core of the Manchu ethnicity: 'The organization of Jurchen troops with their families into separate units, each with its own distinctive flag, broke up earlier lineage groups and provided the emperor with spoke-like connections to each of his armies.'[132] This fracturing of existing lineage loyalties coincided with efforts to cultivate new group identities along what we would now recognize as modern 'ethnic' affiliations. Thus, from the 1630s, the Manchu leadership established Mongol and Han martial banners to incorporate defeated, defecting or surrendered Mongol and Han Chinese warriors into the Manchu conquest-state.[133]

By the eve of the Manchus' defeat of the Ming Dynasty in 1644, the Manchu Eight Banner system disposed of formidable military resources, comprising an estimated two million people encompassing 563 companies.[134] The banner system was the indispensable institutional innovation that made the Manchu Empire possible. Without it, the Manchus would have been unable to conquer China, simply because they lacked the numbers to do so.

The banner system's significance was not, however, limited to its military utility. Rather, an examination of its institutional DNA reveals its indisputably hybrid character. An amalgam of Jurchen, Mongol and Chinese practices, the banner system exemplified the Manchu Empire's polyglot origins, as well as powerfully conditioning the legitimating strategies and eventual diversity regime the Manchus adopted following their victory over the Ming Dynasty.

The Eight Banner system evolved from the Mongol tradition of the hunting party, which the Jurchens had earlier assimilated into their own cultural and military repertoire. Long before the Manchus' turn to conquest, the Jurchens had undertaken quarterly hunts, which were significant to them for both ritual and economic reasons.[135] As Nurhaci's ambitions grew, he conducted his first military campaigns by mobilizing these small hunting units of up to ten or twelve warriors, which typically comprised hunters related by blood or marriage.[136] From 1601, Nurhaci reorganized his hunting parties into companies comprised of 300 households of warriors and their accompanying families.[137] These companies were in turn subsumed into battalions (five companies each) and banners (comprising ten battalions each).[138]

[132] Burbank and Cooper, *Empires in World History*, p. 207.
[133] Chang, *A Court on Horseback*, pp. 21–2.
[134] Elliott, 'Ethnicity in the Qing Eight Banners', p. 30.
[135] Farquhar, 'Mongolian versus Chinese elements in the early Manchu state', 14.
[136] Wakeman, *The Great Enterprise*, p. 53.   [137] Ibid.   [138] Ibid., pp. 53–4.

The banner system thus harnessed existing hunting traditions to organize highly mobile armoured cavalry units for the purposes of plunder and conquest. Throughout Nurhaci's reign, the banners were coordinated by *beile* (chieftains). These chieftains considered the banners their own property, despite the fact that banner administration remained the responsibility of lieutenant-generals directly appointed by Nurhaci.[139] This dual structure marked a compromise between centralized control and the preservation of aristocratic privilege.[140] At least in its early incarnation, the banner system reflected the organizational form of a 'nomadic type' polity that sporadically mobilized for plunder, rather than constituting a bureaucratically organized army dedicated to large-scale conquest.[141]

In their initial probes into the Ming Empire, the Manchus relied predominantly on archery-wielding cavalry led by the chieftains, who shared equally among the spoils of war, and so possessed the means to sustain their own patronage networks. As the Manchus encountered more concerted opposition, the limits of this system became obvious. Militarily, the wave attacks of Manchu cavalry proved insufficient to conquer walled cities defended by Chinese forces equipped with modern European (mainly Portuguese) artillery.[142] Politically, the immense power the banner system left in the hands of the chieftains made it a brittle instrument for conquest, the chieftains' independence endangering the Manchus' political as well as military coherence.

What ultimately redeemed the banner system was its improvement through the incorporation of Chinese ideas, institutions, military expertise and personnel. The banner system's signal advantage was its flexible and adaptive character, which enabled the Manchus to absorb Chinese elements and synthesize them into a hybrid military and political order. Thus, as early as 1629, Nurhaci's successor, Hong Taiji, centralized power over the banners on the recommendation of Chinese advisors.[143] The chieftains were stripped of their rights and capacity to distribute feudal largesse among their underlings, and were lumbered with an increased number of advisors charged with co-supervising the banners and reporting directly to Hong Taiji.[144] These reforms tilted the balance of power in favour of the khan over the chieftains, and marked an important step towards transforming the banner system from an ad hoc host

---

[139] Ibid., p. 55.   [140] Ibid.

[141] On 'nomadic type' polities, see N. di Cosmo, 'State formation and periodization in inner Asian history', *Journal of World History*, 10(1) (1999), 30.

[142] Wakeman, *The Great Enterprise*; Di Cosmo, 'Did Guns Matter?'.

[143] Li, 'State building before 1644', p. 57.   [144] Wakeman, *The Great Enterprise*, p. 165.

geared to organized plunder, towards a centralized and bureaucratized engine of conquest.

Beyond these changes, defecting Chinese brought with them military technologies and expertise that proved indispensable to the Manchus' conquest of China. Previously, Chinese mastery of artillery had ground Manchu raids to a halt. But from 1629, the Manchus adapted the banner system to incorporate surrendering Chinese soldiers and organize them in a separate banner commanded by a senior Chinese defector.[145] This banner included gun founders and soldiers expert in the use of the latest European artillery. Chinese gunners complemented the Manchus' strengths in light cavalry, while the maintenance of separate Chinese banners enabled Chinese generals to defect to the Manchu cause, while retaining command of their own troops.[146] Most importantly, the banner system provided a ready-made institutional 'container' into which surrendering and defecting Chinese troops could be funnelled.[147] The very elasticity and adaptability of the Manchu banner system proved key in assuring the Manchus' success. It enabled the Manchus to retain their strengths in mobile cavalry warfare, while assimilating Chinese bureaucratic techniques and skills in artillery warfare. Beyond its immediate military utility, then, the banner system proved crucial as a means for attracting, organizing and synthesizing the strengths of the peoples the Manchus conquered, dramatically strengthening the Manchus' capacity for conquest.

The Legitimation of the Manchu Empire

In 1644, the Manchus triumphantly entered Beijing, displacing the Ming Dynasty as the predominant power in East Asia. This victory notwithstanding, the Manchus faced considerable and protracted opposition to their rule, stamping out the last remnants of Ming loyalism in China only following their invasion of Taiwan in 1683. The sustained opposition the Manchus confronted testifies to the considerable legitimation challenges they faced, which far surpassed those of the Mughals in South Asia. A consideration of these challenges, and the innovative legitimation strategies the Manchus developed to mitigate them, is essential to round out this portion of the inquiry.

The Manchus faced multiple challenges to their rule as they consolidated their power. First and most critically, they faced the debilitating stigma of being widely regarded as barbarians in the Sinic world. As I noted earlier, ideas of civility, and accompanying civilizing projects to

---

[145] Ibid., p. 168.   [146] Di Cosmo, 'Did Guns Matter?', p. 151.   [147] Ibid., p. 150.

pacify and subordinate warrior elites to courtly power, were common features of Eurasian societies from the late medieval period onwards. In Confucian East Asia, however, the civilized/barbarian divide had been drawn earlier and more sharply than elsewhere. From its emergence during the Axial Age, Confucianism had embodied a faith in the plastic and perfectible character of human nature, and had ascribed to rulers a special responsibility to cultivate moral virtue in their subjects.[148]

Confucianism had always structured the social world in terms of a civilized/barbarian binary, even if Confucian scholars were divided on whether 'barbarians' might be susceptible to transformation through exposure to Chinese morals, language and culture.[149] From the thirteenth century, however, the experience of Mongol invasions and the trauma of subsequent occupation (under the Yuan Dynasty) firmly etched the civilized/barbarian dichotomy as the dominant polarity in sedentary East Asia. Confucian societies (not only China, but also Korea, Vietnam and to a lesser extent, Japan) drew a sharp distinction between societies organized in accordance with Confucian norms and institutions, versus stateless barbarian polities that did not adhere to this template.[150] Barbarians were cast as dangerous moral inferiors, to be alternatively bribed, beaten back, exterminated, or assimilated into civilization, but never to be accepted as equals, much less as superiors.[151]

For the Manchus, the stigma of barbarism posed a real threat to imperial consolidation. This is because the Manchus needed the active collaboration of China's Confucian scholar-gentry to rule their new empire, as well as the public obeisance of Confucian neighbours (most especially Korea) to stabilize the empire's borders. In order to secure their rule, the Manchus needed to harness Confucianism's immense normative power for themselves. They had recognized this imperative almost a decade before conquering Beijing, with Hong Taiji's public claim to the Mandate of Heaven in 1636.[152]

Nevertheless, a wholesale appropriation of the Confucian 'civilizing mission' was by itself insufficient to secure Manchu rule. This is because of the eclecticism of the conquest coalition the Manchus drew together, as well as the radical expansion of the empire's cultural diversity that would come with further Manchu conquests in the seventeenth and eighteenth

---

[148] F. T.-S. Chen, 'The Confucian view of world order' in M. W. Janis and C. Evans (eds.), *Religion and International Law* (Leiden: Martinus Nijhoff, 2004), p. 33.

[149] Lieberman, *Strange Parallels*, pp. 591–2.

[150] Y. Wang, 'Claiming centrality in the Chinese world: Manchu–Chosŏn relations and the making of the Qing's "Zhonghou" identity, 1616–1643', *Chinese Historical Review*, 22 (2) (2015), 98.

[151] Lieberman, *Strange Parallels*, pp. 591–2.

[152] Wang, 'Claiming centrality in the Chinese world', 104.

centuries. Confucian civilization may have (eventually) rallied China's scholar-gentry in support of Manchu power. But it failed to resonate with other crucial subject populations, such as the Mongols, the Tibetans and the Uighurs. Consequently, any attempt to legitimate Manchu authority that drew exclusively from the heritage of one portion of the empire (no matter how powerful) was bound to fail.

Beyond these considerations, the Manchus also had to navigate a final challenge: developing strategies of legitimation that not only accommodated the empire's subject populations, but also preserved the distinctiveness and supremacy of the Manchu conquest elite. For while Confucian elites baulked at the prospect of barbarian rule, the Manchus themselves were seized by equally potent fears of 'Sinicization'.[153] These fears were far from groundless. Historically, barbarian dynasties had frequently lost their distinctiveness over time, as vastly outnumbered conquerors were absorbed into Sinic civilization.[154] This historical precedent was well known to Manchus and Confucian scholar-gentry alike, with many of the latter initially reassuring themselves that the same fate awaited their new conquerors.[155] The protean and newly established character of Manchu identity (Hong Taiji had only renamed the Jurchen as Manchus as late as 1635)[156] no doubt further fuelled the Manchus' assimilationist fears.

In light of these challenges, the Manchus therefore needed to develop a legitimating strategy and accompanying diversity regime that secured the collaboration of the Han Chinese scholar-bureaucrats; incorporated non-Han Chinese populations into the empire; and differentiated the Manchus as a separate conquest elite, distinct from the other peoples of the empire. These imperatives of collaboration, incorporation and differentiation yielded a correspondingly hybrid and multifaceted diversity regime, which drew freely from the ideational resources of the empire's disparate peoples.[157]

Turning first to the assimilative register of Manchu power, the Manchus worked hard to overcome the stigma of barbarism, and to deploy Confucian conceptions of legitimacy to their own advantage. This project dated from before the fall of the Ming Dynasty, when Chinese advisors convinced Hong Taiji in 1636 to substantially Sinicize his patrimony, both by asserting bureaucratic control over his banners and other key governance institutions, and also by reaffirming his exclusive claim to the Mandate of Heaven, which his father Nurhaci had already asserted two decades earlier.[158] With regard to the latter, Hong Taiji took advantage of

---

[153] Elliott, *The Manchu Way*, p. 276.   [154] Lieberman, *Strange Parallels*, p. 588.

[155] J. D. Langlois Jr, 'Chinese culturalism and the Yüan analogy: Seventeenth-century perspectives', *Harvard Journal of Asiatic Studies*, 40(2) (1980), 358.

[156] Li, 'State building before 1644', p. 63.   [157] Crossley, *A Translucent Mirror*, p. 1.

[158] Wang, 'Claiming centrality in the Chinese world', 101.

the mutability of Confucian conceptions of legitimacy. Confucianism left open the possibility that battlefield victories and other auspicious signs might disclose a shift in the Heavenly Mandate, from a declining to an ascending dynasty.[159] This possibility provided the Manchu propagandists with grounds for arguing that their victories over the Ming marked a providential sign of their fitness to rule, overriding the stigma of the Manchus' barbarian origins. Indeed, at one point during the Manchus' ascendancy, in what amounted to a form of normative ju-jitsu, defecting Chinese officials working for Hong Taiji had the audacity to damn the Ming Dynasty as barbarian and to stigmatize surrendering Chinese as 'Han Chinese barbarians', 'thereby appropriating and completely reversing the Ming's language in terms of the center of the Chinese world'.[160]

Once ensconced in Beijing, the Manchus worked hard to make Confucianism a central foundation for Qing rule. Confucianism held that the emperor was responsible for maintaining a state of cosmic and political harmony (*ping*), through a combination of pedagogical ritual and moral example.[161] Likewise, it envisioned an uncompromisingly paternalistic cosmic and social order. Ministers and gentry were to relate to the emperor as sons to fathers, while tributary kingdoms were likewise to mimic the dynamics of the patriarchal household in their submission to the emperor.[162] This vision of order served Manchu purposes, to the extent that it secured the indispensable cooperation of the scholar-gentry and key neighbouring polities. As a result, the Manchus faithfully incorporated Confucianism into their system of rule, and preserved key institutions (e.g., the imperial system of examinations domestically, the Board of Rites internationally) that upheld this order.[163] In an apparent further sign of fidelity to Confucianism, the Manchus moreover pursued policies of Confucian assimilation when dealing with barbarian peoples in the southwest, being happy to pacify these areas by imposing Confucian ideas and institutions wholesale.[164]

The Confucian face of Qing imperialism nevertheless served as but one foundation of Manchu legitimacy. Far from being passively derivative in their conceptions of political authority, the Manchus innovated distinct and customized strategies of segregated *incorporation* (not indiscriminate Confucian assimilation) when dealing with privileged non-Han Chinese

---

[159] Langlois Jr, 'Chinese culturalism and the Yüan analogy', p. 358.
[160] Wang, 'Claiming centrality in the Chinese world', 101.
[161] Chen, 'The Confucian view of world order', p. 28.
[162] J. K. Fairbank and M. Goldman, *China: A New History* (Cambridge, MA: Belknap Press, 2006), p. 19.
[163] Rawski, 'The Qing Empire during the Qianlong reign', p. 16.
[164] Elliott, *Ethnicity in the Qing Eight Banners*, p. 33.

populations. In analysing Manchu statecraft, Pamela Crossley describes an imperial ethic of 'simultaneity',[165] meaning that the Manchus self-consciously crafted different legitimating scripts to appeal to different 'imperial constituencies' throughout the empire.[166] Likewise, James Leibold observes that the Qing emperor alternatively appeared as 'a Confucian monarch among the Chinese; a "divine lord" among the Manchus; a "great khan" among the Mongols and the Manjusri, the Bodhisattva of wisdom, among the Tibetans.'[167]

Not merely a form of strategic self-presentation towards preformed communities, this ethic of imperial simultaneity and its associated practices was critically constitutive of them. Blurring the lines between internal administration and diplomacy, the Manchus established a dedicated institution (the Lifan Yuan) to govern their relations with non-Han subject peoples, such as the Mongols and the Tibetans.[168] The Qing court moreover systematically curated cultural difference through a range of strategies, from language policies and practices of religious and artistic patronage, that aimed to crystallize distinct ethnic *qua* political communities.[169]

Like the Mughals, then, the Manchus sought to make cultural diversity a source of strength rather than entropy. Unlike the Mughals, however, the Manchu ethic of imperial simultaneity did not seek to reconcile the empire's disparate fragments through an ethic of universal reconciliation. Nor did they seek – as did Akbar – to manage differences between different faith traditions, either by promoting dialogue or by sponsoring the development of syncretic religious alternatives. Rather, the Manchus instead deliberately sought to silo different imperial constituencies into mutually exclusive categories through a system of segregated – rather than syncretic – incorporation. The Manchu ideal of universal kingship and its accompanying diversity regime was 'based on the submission of divergent peoples, whose cultures would remain separate'.[170]

Finally, and again in contrast to the Mughals, the Manchu emperors fought rigorously to maintain their own distinctiveness as a separate conquest caste. Manchu 'ethnic sovereignty'[171] expressed itself in multiple ways. Most conspicuously, the Manchus crafted a highly militarized conception of collective identity. This Spartan conception of 'Manchu-ness' overtly repudiated Confucianism's denigration of military force, instead celebrating martial prowess as a defining feature of the Manchu

---

[165] Crossley, *A Translucent Mirror*, p. 12.   [166] Ibid., p. 47.
[167] Leibold, *Reconfiguring Chinese Nationalism*, p. 28.
[168] See generally di Cosmo, 'Qing colonial administration in inner Asia', pp. 287–309.
[169] Crossley, *A Translucent Mirror*, p. 1.
[170] Rawski, 'The Qing Empire During the Qianlong reign', p. 19.
[171] Elliott, *The Manchu Way*, p. 131.

people.[172] Accordingly, Qing imperial iconography reflected these values, with everything from court ceremonial to Manchu architecture stressing the military character of the empire's foundations.[173]

Not merely confined to the realm of iconography and propaganda, the imperative of maintaining the Manchus as a distinct and superior conquest caste suffused a range of Qing Dynasty governance practices. Under a system of 'Manchu apartheid',[174] the Manchus segregated themselves into walled garrisons, maintained separate court systems for Manchus and non-Manchus, and retained a separate praetorian guard of Manchu banner-men to secure the empire against the threat of internal rebellion.[175] Fearful that the 'Old Ways' of the Manchus would atrophy through immersion within Chinese civilization, the Qing court moreover promoted practices such as regular imperial hunts, as well as tours throughout southern China.[176] These practices served the dual purposes of continuously enacting, reaffirming and renewing Manchu identity, as well as intimidating subject populations into continued submission.[177]

Considered in its totality, the Manchu diversity regime was a precarious amalgam of Confucian universalism, segregated incorporation and Manchu separatism – albeit with segregated incorporation forming the dominant component of this broader constellation. This contrasted with the Mughal Empire's more comprehensively syncretic diversity regime, exemplified in Akbar's doctrine of universal reconciliation. But despite the Mughal Empire's appearance of greater ideological consistency, it was the Manchu Empire that proved more successful in the long run. Whereas the Mughal Empire began a precipitous decline from 1707 following the death of the emperor Aurangzeb, the Qing Empire continued to expand, the Manchus doubling their empire's size by the end of the eighteenth century. Similarly, by the late eighteenth century, the Mughal Empire was being rapidly dismembered by an array of local and introduced predators, ranging from the Marathas to the English East India Company. By contrast, as late as 1816, the Manchus managed to rebuff Western entreaties for greater trade privileges, without suffering any meaningful consequence. The contrasting constitutions and diverging fates of the Mughal and Manchu Empires decisively shaped the character and course of Western expansion in Asia, and so form a primary focus of Chapter 4. For now, I conclude with a brief recap of this chapter's core claims, and a restatement of their relevance for the book's larger argument.

---

[172] Elliott, 'Ethnicity in the Qing Eight Banners', p. 38.
[173] See generally J. Waley-Cohen, *The Culture of War in China: Empire and the military under the Qing Dynasty* (London: I. B. Tauris, 2006).
[174] Elliott, *The Manchu Way*, p. 98.   [175] Ibid.
[176] See generally Chang, *A Court on Horseback*.   [177] Ibid.

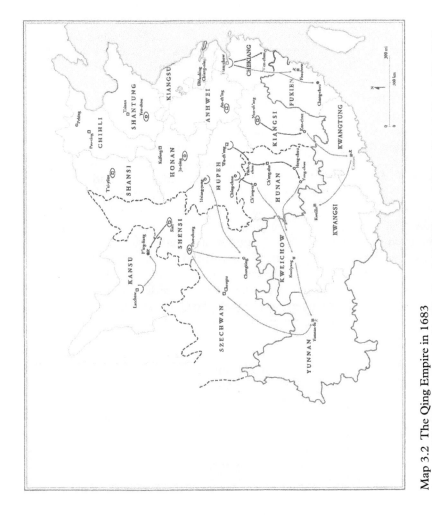

Map 3.2 The Qing Empire in 1683
Source: Willard J. Petersen (ed.), *The Cambridge History of China*, Vol. 9, Part I: *The Ch'ing Empire to 1800* (Cambridge: Cambridge University Press, 2008), p. 144.

Conclusion

This chapter has advanced three related aims.

First, proceeding from the overview of the Eurasian Transformation in Chapter 2, I have offered a comparative assessment of the rise of Asia's two largest and most populous empires, by situating them comparatively within their common Eurasian context. I have argued that the rise of the Mughal and Manchu empires formed part of a much larger process of Eurasian political consolidation. Increasing trans-regional commercial integration provided a critical precondition for the rise of more ambitious absolutist projects of imperial state-building from the late fifteenth century. These empire-building projects were themselves interwoven with large-scale processes of normative pacification, which – drawing on Eurasia-wide medieval precedents – sought to 'civilize' warrior elites, and so subordinate them more readily to central rule.

My intention in framing my inquiry through the lens of the Eurasian Transformation is to underscore a larger point: namely that it was the rise of Asian 'mega-empires'[178] (not the hesitant emergence of a proto-state system in Europe) that constituted the 'big story' of Eurasian political development in the early modern era. Acknowledging this reality, and situating the rise of these empires against the broader canvas of the Eurasian Transformation, enables us to foreground the common context out of which they emerged. And in enabling us to better recognize the similar initial conditions out of which these empires developed, it helps us also to more precisely identify both the resemblances in empire-building strategies, and the divergences in outcomes, that marked their comparative evolution.

In drawing a relatively uncommon comparison between the Mughals and the Manchus, my second aim has been to capture commonalities in these empires' genesis and early evolution, with a view to highlighting the common mechanisms through which these empires came to be. Accordingly, I have shown that the Mughal and Manchu empires both arose as new nuclei of power along Eurasia's commercially dynamic, culturally diverse and politically fragmented inner frontiers.

In the Mughal case, Babur's Timurid heritage already infused him with imperial ambitions from the outset. The distinctive resource portfolio of fifteenth-century Kabul, combining a taxable peasantry, significant pasturage for raising warhorses and ready credit facilities, meanwhile provided an indispensable springboard from which to attack wealthy and weak neighbours on the Indo-Gangetic plain. The Timurids' location at

---

[178] The concept of 'mega-empires' is taken from P. Turchin, 'A theory of formation for large empires', *Journal of Global History*, 4(2) (2009), 191–217.

the intersection of Central and South Asia also positioned them perfectly to tap into cross-regional cultural flows, priming them to later develop a uniquely powerful incorporative ethos to consolidate and sustain their empire.

Contrarily, the Manchus began with neither a common identity nor a shared imperial purpose, their aspirations only haphazardly evolving towards empire-building as they fought to preserve a lucrative militarized commercial monopoly. This crucial difference aside, the Manchus also successfully exploited the possibilities of Eurasia's booming frontiers to lay the foundations for imperial expansion. China's enormous appetite for the hinterland luxuries of ginseng, sable and fur enabled Nurhaci to build the war chest necessary to make him a pivotal player in seventeenth-century Northeast Asia. His position at the intersection of Mongolia, China, Manchuria and Korea likewise helped Nurhaci to stitch together legitimating resources from a range of disparate sources, and to develop the eclectic alliances necessary to build a multi-ethnic coalition geared to conquest.

Beyond these similarities in the initial conditions of their emergence, we have seen that the Mughals and Manchus also faced comparable challenges in institutionalizing and consolidating their rule. As vastly outnumbered parvenu conquest elites, both confronted the problem of having to mobilize, channel and control the military resources necessary to conquer and rule on a subcontinental scale. Both dynasties also had to develop diversity regimes that secured them from insurrection, while preserving the loyalties of extraordinarily heterogeneous populations. And both resorted to comparable strategies of conquest, entailing the extensive creative remixing of indigenous institutions and ideational resources, to build the coercive and ideological foundations of their empires.

These similarities in challenges and empire-building strategies are crucially important, not only in and of themselves, but also because they find important parallels in the West's subsequent pattern of expansion in Asia, a theme I take up in later chapters. These similarities aside, this chapter's third objective has been to sketch the key points of divergence in the outcomes of Mughal and Manchu empire-building.

For despite facing congruent challenges in expanding and consolidating their empires, the difficulties of Mughal and Manchu empire-building were not identical. The Mughals confronted a far more fragmented political and military landscape in their first decades of rule. Consequently, they had to mould their empire's military and administrative superstructure around these conditions, with the *mansabdari* system forming a creative (but ultimately only temporarily successful) means of doing so. Conversely, South Asian elites proved less resolutely resistant to

Mughal suzerainty than their Confucian counterparts did when facing the prospect of Manchu dominance. Despite the incongruity of Sunni Islamic Timurids ruling over a predominantly Hindu population, Akbar was able to innovate a new syncretic ideology of universal reconciliation that provided a durable foundation for Mughal power. Embracing an ideal of universal incorporative kingship, Akbar asserted dominance over Timurid courtiers and the Sunni *ulema* alike. The promotion of syncretism over dogmatism, and the embrace of a highly decentralized system of 'shared' sovereignty, yielded an imperial system flexible enough to sustain Mughal dominance well into the eighteenth century.

The Manchus did not suffer the same debilitating effects of radically dispersed political and military power when undertaking their Northeast Asian conquests. Northeast Asia had no equivalent to the Indian military labour market, while the Manchus also had the advantage of inheriting the world's most sophisticated bureaucracy following their conquest of China. China's bureaucracy constituted a ready-made extractive apparatus for milking the country's vast agricultural and commercial wealth, dispensing with the need for the Manchus to build a centralized patronage system like the *mansabdari* system.

This advantage notwithstanding, the Manchus faced far more forbidding legitimation challenges than the Mughals. In particular, as we have seen, the barbarian stigma posed a major obstacle to imperial consolidation, which the Manchus mitigated only partially by appropriating Confucianism as part of their legitimating framework. The multi-ethnic character of their conquest coalition, the Manchu Empire's expanding diversity following further conquests in the seventeenth and eighteenth centuries, and the Manchus' determination to inoculate themselves from complete Sinicization, meanwhile necessitated the adoption of incorporative and segregationist elements into the Manchus' systems of legitimation.

The differing environments into which the Mughals and Manchus expanded, the distinct assets and allies they had available for empire-building, and the discrete challenges they faced in military mobilization and ideological legitimation, thus yielded radically different imperial orders.

The Mughal Empire remained smaller, more flexible and more decentralized than its Manchu counterpart. Throughout its existence, the Mughal Empire embodied an ideal of 'galactic' suzerainty.[179] This entailed the 'co-sharing' of sovereign prerogatives with dependent subordinates, and the radical dispersal of military power among large numbers of semi-autonomous retainers.[180] The Mughals moreover promiscuously

---

[179] Tambiah, 'What did Bernier actually say?', 380.
[180] Hasan, *State and Locality in India*, p. 43.

incorporated legitimating resources from throughout their empire, braiding together myriad themes, symbols and ideals from Timurid, Persian, Central Asian, Rajput and other sources. The Mughal Empire moreover remained highly porous, its terrestrial and maritime frontiers lightly governed, and pervasively enmeshed in trans-continental networks of military, cultural and commercial exchange.

The Manchu Empire was instead bigger, tougher and more durable than that of the Mughals. Within the empire's Sinic core, suzerainty remained conceived in fractal rather than galactic terms, the imperial order reflecting in macrocosm the ideal patriarchal Confucian household. The Manchus obviously supplemented Confucian hierarchy with a looser system of colonial over-rule in non-Han Chinese territories. But even then, these tributaries were more jealously controlled than outlying portions of the Mughal Empire. In contrast to the Mughals, the Manchus also kept a far tighter rein on military power. The banner system exemplified a deliberate and systematic strategy of ethnically defined divide and rule, while the maintenance of separate praetorian Manchu banners provided a potent backstop to internal insurrection. Far from encouraging syncretism, the Manchu ethic of imperial simultaneity moreover attempted to segregate the empire into mutually exclusive constituencies, with the emperor serving as a solar focal point of loyalty, a 'grand impersonator ... controlling cultures by incarnating them'.[181] The Manchus lastly preserved far more zealous control over their inner Asian and maritime frontiers. Though hardly sealed off from the outside world, the Manchus remained wary of potential rivals building up power bases in their liminal zones, and as such tried to control their frontiers far more tightly as a consequence.

The Eurasian Transformation thus saw momentous change in both South and East Asia, as parvenu conquerors succeeded in reconciling the territorial scale of traditional steppe empires, with the population density, cultural sophistication and commercial dynamism of neighbouring sedentary societies. The Mughals and Manchus separately constructed two vast mega-empires. These achievements arguably constituted the most important political developments of early modern Eurasia. These empires together transformed Eurasia's landscape, and provided the larger system into which European maritime traders eventually infiltrated. It is to a consideration of this process of infiltration, its divergent trajectories in South versus East Asia, that I now turn.

---

[181] Crossley, *A Translucent Mirror*, p. 221.

4 European Infiltration and Asian Consolidation in Maritime Asia, 1600–1700

This chapter examines Western infiltration into maritime Asia, alongside the evolution of the Mughal and Manchu empires, over the seventeenth century. I focus on three questions. First, how was it possible for numerically insignificant Westerners, 'scurrying and worrying'[1] along Asia's littoral frontiers, to establish even minor territorial toeholds in maritime Asia? Second, why did Westerners find it so much easier to insinuate themselves into the Mughal Empire and other south and southeast Asian polities, compared to the far greater difficulties they faced in infiltrating the Qing Empire? And third, how did this process of uneven insinuation pave the way for the West's subsequent rise to at least partial dominance in Asia from the late eighteenth century?

This chapter starts from the insight that Western infiltration into maritime Asia bore important resemblances to earlier Mughal and Manchu patterns of terrestrial expansion. Like the Mughals and the Manchus, European maritime imperialists were the beneficiaries of the enhanced interregional connectivity and commercial expansion that helped comprise the Eurasian Transformation. In particular, the growth of regionally distinct economies of taste provided armed European merchants with the capacity to build empires of arbitrage, by attempting to monopolize the long-distance trade in exotic commodities, and then accumulating enhanced capacities for power and patronage from the resulting superprofits. Europeans' possession of niche military advantages – specifically superior blue water naval capabilities – moreover enabled them to muscle in on Asian markets, and carve out at least a marginal presence at the edge of Asia's terrestrial mega-empires.[2]

But while opportunities for superprofits and niche military advantages were necessary for European expansion in Asia, they were far from sufficient. Unlike the Mughals and the Manchus, Europeans did not seek

---

[1] Fernandez-Armesto, *Pathfinders*, p. 181.
[2] On Europeans' maritime military edge as an enabler of early modern expansion, see for example generally Clulow, 'European maritime violence', 72–94.

large-scale territorial rule in Asia. Nevertheless, the huge costs and risks associated with long-distance trade, the principal-agent challenges that such enterprises confronted, and the high levels of violence and physical insecurity that Europeans themselves introduced to maritime Asia demanded institutional solutions.

The joint-stock company – or company-state – proved to be the most powerful device for managing these challenges, and was integral to securing a long-term European presence in Asia. Originating in England and Holland in the early seventeenth century, company states proved effective in pooling the 'patient' capital necessary to fund the highly risky but also highly lucrative trade in Asian luxuries.[3] Company-states also proved better than their more statist European rivals (principally the Estado da India) at reconciling the interests of principals and agents.[4] Their authority to wage war independently of their sponsoring states back in Europe also allowed them to internalize their own protection costs, enhancing their competitiveness against unarmed trading diasporas already resident in Asia.[5] Perhaps most importantly, as divided sovereigns, capable of both exercising sovereign powers but also alienating their sovereignty to Asian hosts, company-states proved uniquely capable of slotting themselves into existing imperial hierarchies.[6] This frequently gave them an edge over statist European rivals such as the Portuguese, and so facilitated the companies' establishment of far-flung 'trading-post empires' across much of the Asian littoral.[7]

The company-states' adaptiveness notwithstanding, their success varied significantly depending on local conditions. This is because Asian host polities' diverse systems of legitimation and accompanying diversity regimes, the varying availability of local allies and host polities' differing frontier governance regimes decisively conditioned their receptiveness to Western insinuation. The sheer variety of local accommodations Europeans tried to negotiate with their hosts is too numerous and varied to cover below. Instead, following the book's main focus, my main

---

[3] N. Kyriazis and T. Metaxas, 'Path dependence, change and the emergence of the first joint-stock companies', *Business History*, 53(3) (2011), 365.

[4] This was especially so for the EIC. See generally E. Erikson, *Between Monopoly and Free Trade: The English East India Company, 1600–1757* (Princeton: Princeton University Press, 2014).

[5] Pearson, 'Merchants and states', p. 86.

[6] On corporations as 'bundles of hyphens' capable of customizing sovereignty arrangements in a wide range of settings, both European and non-European, see P. J. Stern, '"Bundles of hyphens": Corporations as legal communities in the early modern British Empire' in L. Benton and R. J. Ross (eds.), *Legal Pluralism and Empires, 1500–1850* (New York: New York University Press, 2013), pp. 21–48.

[7] On 'trading-post empires', see Curtin, *Cross-Cultural Trade in World History*, p. 137.

interest is in analysing the different trajectories of European insinuation in South Asia and Qing-dominated Northeast Asia.

In South Asia, the Mughal Empire proved broadly receptive to European infiltration. As we have seen, the Mughals maintained a diversity regime marked by an ethos of syncretic incorporation. This regime celebrated cultural difference, and proved flexible enough to incorporate European intruders. Though careful to forbid Europeans from developing fortified settlements, the Mughal system of decentralized rule enabled the empire's local intermediaries to build up sturdy patrimonial alliances with European company-state officials, again aiding the companies' infiltration into the empire.[8] The Mughals' indifference to blue water naval warfare finally limited the Europeans' perceived danger to imperial authority.[9] Consequently, European armed conflict with the Mughals was rare and transient, Europeans perceived as posing little threat to the Mughals' vital security or economic interests.

In the Qing Empire, by contrast, European infiltration was more limited and more strictly policed. As we have seen, the Qing emperors maintained a diversity regime predicated on the principle of segregated incorporation. This regime organized cultural difference by appealing to imperial constituencies defined primarily around categories of ethnic difference, and that were self-consciously siloed from one another into mutually exclusive categories. To preserve the distinctiveness of their diverse imperial constituencies, the Manchus accordingly customized their legitimating narratives from indigenous normative resources, and freely adapted practices for dealing with 'outsiders' from established local traditions.

In maritime southern China – a bastion of Han Chinese Ming loyalism for most of the seventeenth century – the Manchus accordingly staunchly maintained a commitment to Confucianism's assimilative ethos. This meant that European 'barbarians' were either held at a distance, or (as in the case of the Portuguese in Macau) tightly sequestered in enclaves far smaller and more contained than their cosmopolitan Mughal counterparts.[10] The Manchus' adherence to Confucian conceptions of fractal suzerainty in southern China moreover provided less room for the types of patrimonial alliance that undergirded European incorporation into Mughal port cities. Most fundamentally, for most of the late seventeenth century, the Manchus

---

[8] See generally Hasan, *State and Locality in Mughal India*.
[9] Richards, *The Mughal Empire*, p. 283.
[10] See for example generally J. Gebhardt, 'Negotiating barriers: Cross-cultural communication and the Portuguese mercantile community in Macau, 1550–1640', *Itinerario*, 38 (2) (2014), 27–50.

were fixated with crushing Ming loyalist resistance in both south-eastern China, and also in Taiwan.[11] This imperative made them hypervigilant against the threat of alternative power concentrations (either European or East Asian) congealing along their volatile maritime frontiers.[12] This further impeded European attempts to gain more direct access to Chinese markets, again contrasting with their more favourable experiences in South Asia.

The results of these regional divergences would only become clear in the eighteenth century. At this time, the Mughal Empire's decline created a power vacuum in South Asia in which multiple actors competed to maximize their wealth and power. Already firmly entrenched along the empire's maritime frontiers, the EIC eventually emerged as the most potent of these new post-imperial power concentrations. By contrast, the Qing Empire remained dynamically expansive in the eighteenth century, with the Europeans remaining a minor presence that the Manchus barely tolerated, and which would pose no meaningful threat to Qing power before 1840 at the earliest.

This chapter is organized as follows. The first section traces the gravitational pull of Asian prosperity for Europeans during the sixteenth century. Here, I chart the growth of large-scale trade between Europe and Asia, note the catalytic impact of intra-European rivalries in further pressuring Westerners to insinuate themselves into Asian political and commercial networks and sketch the basic strategies of empire by arbitrage that Westerners fashioned to advance their interests in Asia. The second section then concentrates on the emergence of the company-state as the pre-eminent institution through which Europeans forged their Asian maritime empires. The third and fourth sections then respectively contrast the varied success of European company-states in infiltrating the Mughal and Qing empires. I conclude by revisiting the larger parallels uniting the European maritime 'shadow' empires with their Asian terrestrial counterparts,[13] and the legacies of their differential integration into South versus East Asia for the West's later uneven and contested rise to global pre-eminence.

---

[11] On the Manchus' early recognition of the strategic significance of their maritime frontier and the need to defend it, see R. C. Po, *The Blue Frontier: Maritime vision and power in the Qing Empire* (Cambridge: Cambridge University Press, 2018), p. 91.

[12] See for example T. Andrade and X. Hang, 'Introduction: The East Asian maritime realm in global history, 1500–1700' in T. Andrade and X. Hang (eds.), *Sea Rovers, Silver, and Samurai: Maritime East Asia in global history, 1550–1700* (Honolulu: University of Hawaii Press, 2016), pp. 17–21.

[13] I take the phrase 'shadow empires' from Barfield, 'The shadow empires'. For an explicit comparison between steppe Asian and European 'sea nomads', see Lieberman, 'Protected rimlands and exposed zones', 721.

The Pull of Asian Prosperity and the Rise of Western Maritime Empires by Arbitrage in the Sixteenth Century

To understand the dynamics of Western infiltration into maritime Asia, we must first recall Asia's enduring commercial attraction for Europe. Though evidence of indirect trade between Western Europe and Asia dates from antiquity, it was only from the thirteenth century emergence of the *Pax Mongolica* that we see a major uptick in Europe-Asia trade.[14] From this time on, European appetite for Asian luxury goods – particularly textiles and spices – grew considerably.[15] The vast physical and cultural distances separating Europe from Asia, and the absence of any shared institutional frameworks to mediate long-distance trade and diplomacy, nevertheless posed significant challenges to the consolidation of Eurasia-wide trading networks. Consequently, unarmed ethnic trading diasporas – often Arabs, Jews or Armenians – mediated Europe-Asia trade along different portions of its primary terrestrial and maritime routes.[16] Further complicating matters, Europeans in any case produced little of value with which to entice Asian buyers. This deficiency inhibited the growth of Europe-Asia trade, as Europeans were forced to rely on their very limited supplies of specie to buy Asian luxuries.[17]

Against this backdrop, two developments in the sixteenth century together transformed the scale of European trade with Asia. Spain's conquest of the Americas – and specifically its pillaging of New World silver – enriched Europeans with vast new reserves of specie, which could be harnessed to buy their way into Asian marketplaces on an unprecedented scale.[18] At the same time, Ming China's 'single whip' rationalization of its tax system dramatically increased Chinese appetite for New World silver.[19] The resulting meeting of increased supply with increased demand laid the foundation for vastly greater Europe-Asia commerce, particularly once Habsburg Spain carved out a colony in East Asia (the Philippines – named for Philip II) through which they could directly mediate trans-Pacific trade.[20]

---

[14] See generally Abu-Lughod, *Before European Hegemony*.   [15] Ibid., p. 239.

[16] Curtin, *Cross-Cultural Trade in World History*, p. 146.

[17] On the centrality of American silver in enabling the vast increase in Europe-Asia trade in the early modern period, see K. N. Chaudhuri, 'The economic and monetary problem of European trade with Asia during the seventeenth and eighteenth centuries', *Journal of European Economic History*, 4(2) (1975), 334.

[18] Flynn and Giráldez, 'Born with a "silver spoon"', 209. The authors note that one mountain in Potosi (*cerro rico*) may have accounted for 60 per cent of all silver mined in the world in the sixteenth century, so vast were the mineral wealth reserves of Spanish America.

[19] Ibid., p. 208.   [20] Ibid., p. 201.

As we have seen, the infusion of New World silver reserves into Asia exerted profound and unanticipated effects on East Asia's geopolitics. Most notably, it nourished the rise of the Manchu commercial monopoly that ultimately toppled Ming China. This wave of early modern globalization meanwhile exerted similarly disruptive impacts on the balance of power in Europe. Engorged from the wealth it had pillaged from the New World, Habsburg Spain emerged as Latin Christendom's sole superpower during the sixteenth century. From 1580 to 1640, the union of the Spanish and Portuguese crowns further strengthened the Habsburgs, as they added the wealth of Portugal's maritime trading empire in Asia to their already massive resource portfolio. These extra-European resources enabled the Habsburgs to finance a formidable military apparatus, gravely threatening the liberty of weaker polities.[21]

Within the context of Europe's ongoing Wars of Religion, the spectre of Habsburg hegemony was particularly threatening for small Protestant polities, including England and Holland. The latter especially remained locked in an eighty-year rebellion against the Habsburgs down to 1648, and so rightly regarded the Habsburgs' access to extra-European resources as a vital threat to its aspirations for self-rule. So destabilizing was the growth in their power that the Habsburgs' enemies soon took to the seas to sever the transoceanic arteries linking Madrid to its global empire.[22] In the Americas, this strategy was most famously evident in efforts to interdict the Spanish treasure fleets, as they made their way from the Americas back to Spain.[23] In maritime Asia, however, commerce raiding quickly gave way to the construction of rival empires, as the Dutch and English especially sought to dislodge the Iberian powers and self-strengthen through extra-European trade and colonization.

The permanent pull of Asian prosperity, coupled with push factors deriving from increasingly globalized intra-European competition, thus laid the preconditions for large-scale Western infiltration into maritime Asia. A third and final enabler of European infiltration lay in the immense profits Westerners could potentially garner through controlling the interregional trade in Asian luxury commodities. Arbitrage – buying or seizing luxury goods from Asian producers to sell to European consumers at massively inflated prices – would prove foundational to the consolidation of powerful new entities such as the Dutch and English East India companies.

[21] Chaudhuri, 'The economic and monetary problem of European trade with Asia', 323–4.
[22] D. C. Peifer, 'Maritime commerce warfare: The coercive response of the weak?', *Naval War College Review*, 66(2) (2013), 86–7.
[23] Ibid.

Company-states proved especially effective in mastering the challenges of building empires by arbitrage over transcontinental distances. But we must also acknowledge the Eurasia-wide structural context that made imperial arbitrage possible. An integral part of the commercial boom that defined the Eurasian Transformation was the growth of regionally distinctive 'patterns of exotic consumption and deportment'.[24] These taste cultures were marked by political and cultural elites' increased desire to possess or consume luxury goods from distant lands, be they exotic textiles, or alternatively foodstuffs or drugs revered for their supposedly spiritual, medicinal or aphrodisiac qualities.[25]

Regardless of whether or not they were valued for their prestige value alone, or for their supposedly redemptive, curative or restorative powers, the growth in elite demand for exotic luxury commodities provided a key precondition for the rise of empires built on arbitrage. Spices and roots such as nutmeg, mace, cloves, cinnamon and ginseng could generally only be grown in certain parts of the world.[26] This placed a natural limit on supply. At the same time, regionally distinctive religious and medicinal beliefs and canons of taste generated pockets of high demand for exotic commodities far from their places of origin.[27] The fact that luxury commodities were moreover typically low volume and high value in character moreover made them easy to transport across long distances.

Restricted supply, rapidly growing elite demand, a significant geographic separation between centres of production and consumption, and the relative ease of physically transporting them made control over the exotic luxuries trade a potentially potent source of financial and political aggrandizement. This was evident not only in the case of the spices that gave rise to the European maritime empires in Asia, but also for the luxuries (principally ginseng and sable) that had formed the root of Manchu power. Control of the trade in luxuries was by no means the only pathway to empire formation in the early modern era. Indeed, down to the nineteenth century, control over agrarian surplus provided the foundation for most Eurasian empires, including the Mughal, Manchu and British empires in their mature phase.[28] This qualifier aside, arbitrage did form a critically powerful mechanism through which the nuclei of empires could form along Eurasia's terrestrial and maritime frontiers. We will revisit the parallels between Asian and European patterns of imperial

---

[24] Bayly, '"Archaic" and "modern" globalization', p. 51.   [25] Ibid.
[26] Chaudhuri, *Trade and Civilization in the Indian Ocean*, p. 21.
[27] Bayly, '"Archaic" and "modern" globalization', pp. 51–2.
[28] K. Roy, 'Horses, guns and governments: A comparative study of the military transition in the Manchu, Mughal, Ottoman and Safavid empires, circa 1400 to circa 1750', *International Area Studies Review*, 15(2) (2012), 112.

arbitrage in this chapter's conclusion. First, however, a more sustained consideration of the European company-states – as the vanguards of European insinuation into maritime Asia – is essential.

European Company-States as Vehicles for Insinuation into Asian Empires

It bears repeating that Western imperialism in early modern Asia was a form of *insinuation* into existing Asian networks, rather than a process of relentless *expansion* and *imposition* onto supine local societies. Despite an excellent wave of revisionist scholarship seeking to correct this misperception, tropes of European 'expansion' still dominate characterizations of European incorporation into early modern Asia.[29] The expansion trope obscures the fact that before the mid-eighteenth century, Westerners were generally no more than a minor irritant to Asian rulers. Certainly, Western niche capabilities in blue water warfare enabled them to sometimes extort commercial privileges from Asian traders.[30] But more often than not, Westerners were supplicants rather than superiors, who had to win local rulers' favour to gain permanent access to Asian markets, and to eke out the territorial toeholds from which their commercial activities could be coordinated.[31] Accordingly, my focus here is not on how Westerners eventually built imperial hierarchies in Asia, but rather on how they first tried with varying success to ingratiate their way into existing Asian hierarchies.

'Maritime Asia' is a deceptively expansive category, encompassing two distinct environments: the Indian Ocean, where no maritime power predominated before the sixteenth century, and littoral East Asia, where China had historically asserted regional hegemony, however fitfully and incompletely. Before Portugal's arrival in December 1497, local rulers saw the Indian Ocean as an 'asocial space', a medium for trade rather than a domain where one could meaningfully assert political claims to authority or control.[32] In contrast to Western practices of asserting custodianship over maritime spaces, Indian Ocean polities possessed nothing approaching the Roman ideal of *Mare Nostrum*. Traditions of large-scale naval warfare were absent, with most rulers absorbed by terrestrial

---

[29] For an excellent recent exception to this generalization, see S. Suzuki, Y. Zhang and J. Quirk (eds.), *International Orders in the Early Modern World: Before the rise of the West* (London: Routledge, 2013).

[30] Clulow, 'European maritime violence', 73.

[31] See for example L. Benton and A. Clulow, 'Empires and protection: Making interpolity law in the early modern world', *Journal of Global History*, 12(1) (2017), 88.

[32] Steinberg, *The Social Construction of the Ocean*, p. 41.

competition, especially along the junction between the Middle East, Central Asia and South Asia.[33] Preoccupied with extracting agricultural surpluses from the peasantry, rulers in South Asia and elsewhere paid only minimal attention to managing maritime trade.[34] Instead, resident trading diasporas mediated trade across a transoceanic circuit of largely autonomous port cities, contributing to the customs revenues of host societies in exchange for rights of limited self-government.[35]

In contrast to the Indian Ocean, the East Asian littoral undeniably bore the imprint of Chinese hegemony. Certainly, the Asian steppe frontier remained rulers' primary focus of concern, being the vector from which existential threats to Chinese dynasties had historically emerged.[36] Barring a transient exception under the Ming Dynasty, when Chinese treasure fleets had voyaged as far as East Africa, China also lacked a history of blue water power projection.[37] These qualifiers aside, China did maintain a loose set of suzerain claims over neighbouring East Asian polities, and sought – with admittedly limited success – to channel regional trade through the tributary system.[38] China's consistent efforts to suppress 'pirates', the Ming Dynasty's extremely costly effort to repel an amphibious Japanese invasion of Korea, and China's efforts to segregate and quarantine foreign traders in strictly regulated trading entrepots further distinguished East Asia from the *laissez-faire* environment of the Indian Ocean.[39]

The regional differences between the Indian Ocean and East Asian halves of maritime Asia are important, for they meaningfully shaped patterns of European insinuation into South and East Asia. For now, though, it is sufficient to note that Asia's maritime frontier was as a whole less contested and less consistently controlled than its steppe counterpart. This left it permeable to Western infiltration, beginning with the Portuguese foray into the Indian Ocean region from 1497.

---

[33] Roy, 'Horses, guns and governments', 112.   [34] Ibid.

[35] J. Fisch, 'Law as a means and as an end: Some remarks on the function of European and non-European law in the process of European expansion' in W. J. Mommsen and J. A. de Moor (eds.), *European Expansion and Law: The encounter of European and indigenous law in 19th- and 20th-century Asia and Africa* (Oxford: Berg Publishers, 1992), p. 23.

[36] On the centrality of the steppe for the Qing Empire, the largest and last of the dynasties to have ruled China, see generally Perdue, *China Marches West*.

[37] J. Mackay, 'Pirate nations: Maritime pirates as escape societies in late Imperial China', *Social Science History*, 37(4) (2013), 556.

[38] On the tributary system, see generally Kang, 'Hierarchy and legitimacy in international systems'. For a more critical view of the tributary system as a construct for understanding East Asian international relations, however, see P. C. Perdue, 'The tenacious tributary system', *Journal of Contemporary China*, 24(96) (2015), 1002–14.

[39] D. C. Kang, 'Hierarchy in Asian international relations: 1300–1900', *Asian Security*, 1(1) (2005), 59.

From the late fifteenth century, the Portuguese negotiated, cajoled, bullied and bought their way into maritime Asia's regional commercial networks. Originally driven at least in part by the search for non-Muslim allies to support them in Christendom's conflicts with the 'Moors', the Portuguese soon sought to carve out a pan-regional trading empire in Asia.[40] Having seized a series of strategic strongholds (most notably Hormuz, Goa and Malacca), the newly established Estado da India used its superior naval power to attempt to establish a protection racket for maritime commerce throughout the Indian Ocean.[41] Further afield, the Portuguese also managed to establish toeholds in China and Japan, albeit largely under the sufferance of local rulers.[42]

The Portuguese established a critical precedent for other European powers, most notably the English and the Dutch. In militarizing ocean-going trade in the Indian Ocean, and skimming the profits of the region's vast commerce, the Estado da India demonstrated the potentially vast wealth that could come from pursuing arbitrage opportunities at gun-point in maritime Asia. That the Portuguese were also able to internalize their protection costs at sea also distinguished them from local commercial rivals.[43] This enabled them to lord over the unarmed trading diasporas that had formerly mediated the region's commerce.[44]

Simultaneously, however, the Portuguese precedent also illustrated the formidable challenges of pursuing armed trade in Asia. The Estado da India's initially stubborn insistence on engaging the Chinese emperor as an equal had for example seen its envoys unceremoniously beheaded during their initial foray into Chinese waters.[45] This dramatized the need for Westerners to develop a more flexible means of negotiating with Asian host polities, in terms that reflected deference rather than either equality or (Western) domination. The enormous expenses entailed in maintaining a pan-Asian trading empire also proved daunting, requiring large amounts of patient capital to sustain such an edifice.[46] The principal-agent challenges involved in transoceanic trade and colonization were also forbidding. Indeed, the Estado da India's rigid insistence on attempting to arrogate all trade for the king soon bred corruption of

---

[40] A. R. Disney, *A History of Portugal and the Portuguese Empire: From beginnings to 1807*, 2 vols., II: *The Portuguese Empire* (Cambridge: Cambridge University Press, 2009), p. 126.

[41] L. Benton, 'Legal spaces of empire: Piracy and the origins of ocean regionalism', *Comparative Studies in Society and History*, 47(4) (2005), 713.

[42] On Portugal's presence in East Asia, see generally G. B. Souza, *The Survival of Empire: Portuguese trade and society in China and the South China Sea 1630–1754* (Cambridge: Cambridge University Press, 2004).

[43] Benton, 'Legal spaces of empire', 713.   [44] Ibid.

[45] Disney, *A History of Portugal*, p. 127.

[46] Kyriazis and Metaxas, 'Path dependence', 365.

such a magnitude as to eventually cripple it as a profit-making enterprise.[47]

The foregoing observations should not detract from the adaptiveness of the Portuguese Estado da India. Across an arc stretching from Mozambique to Japan, the Portuguese empire reflected an enormous diversity in its accommodations with local rulers.[48] Theoretically, invoking the 1494 Treaty of Tordesillas, the Portuguese asserted a right to universal conquest in the East. In practice, however, the Portuguese imperial network rested on links of 'friendship' (*amizade*) or even indirect submission (*vassalagem*) to indigenous hosts.[49] The Portuguese moreover skilfully underwrote this network of allegiances through practices of gift exchange that were carefully calibrated to leverage local conceptions of legitimacy.[50] But even taking this adaptiveness into consideration, the Estado da India was from the seventeenth century eclipsed by a new species of polity: the chartered company-state.

The company-state constituted one of the most important institutional innovations in the early modern world. From the late fifteenth century, Europeans resorted to a host of different expedients to project power over transcontinental distances. In addition to more conventionally state-led enterprises, such as the Estado da India, Europeans also relied on a host of different non-state actors to extend their power into the New World and Afro-Asia. In the Americas, for example, proprietary grants provided one of the main mechanisms through which Europeans 'planted' colonies, as evidenced by their extensive use by England to colonize Maryland, New York, New Jersey and the Carolinas.[51] In Asia, however, it was the company-state – combining features of the joint-stock company with the sovereign state – that formed the chief means through which Europeans sought to inveigle their way into local imperial hierarchies.

Company-states possessed several advantages over more conventionally statist vehicles for long-distance trade and colonization. Most obviously, company states' combination of monopoly trading privileges, limited liability and separation of the means of ownership from corporate control granted them the ability to mobilize the large reserves of patient

---

[47] N. Steensgaard, *Caravans, Carracks and Companies: The structural crisis in the European-Asia trade in the early 17th century* (Lund: Studenliterratur, 1973), p. 67.

[48] Z. Biedermann, 'Portuguese diplomacy in Asia in the sixteenth century: A preliminary overview', *Itinerario*, 29(2) (2005), 14.

[49] Ibid., p. 13.

[50] See generally J. V. Melo, 'Seeking prestige and survival: Gift exchange practices between the Portuguese Estado da India and Asian rulers', *Journal of the Economic and Social History of the Orient*, 56(4–5) (2013), 672–95.

[51] W. A. Pettigrew, 'Corporate constitutionalism and the dialogue between the global and local in seventeenth-century English history', *Itinerario*, 39(3) (2015), 490.

capital necessary to finance highly speculative commercial ventures.[52] As we have seen in the case of the Portuguese, transcontinental trade and colonization was hugely expensive, even when undertaken on a relatively small scale. And though the Portuguese enjoyed a first mover advantage in leading the European thrust into maritime Asia, the Portuguese king's limited fiscal strength necessarily constrained the Estado da India's ability to assert and defend its claims in Asia in the longer-term.[53]

By contrast, the Dutch and English East India companies in particular soon managed to mobilize the wealth necessary to sustain formidably competitive maritime empires. In contrast to the Estado da India, the company-states were also at least marginally better suited to overcoming principal-agent challenges, and so limiting the corrosive effects of internal corruption on their commercial monopolies. The conduct of private trade outside of the structure of the Estado da India was expressly forbidden, but also widely practiced by the Portuguese king's servants in Asia.[54] Consequently, the Estado da India bore the costs of sustaining the Portuguese presence in Asia, but captured disproportionately small commercial dividends from doing so.[55] Conversely, while hardly free from the curse of corruption, the EIC (and eventually also the Dutch) permitted employees to partake in limited private trade, thereby mitigating the principal-agent challenges that proved so debilitating for the Portuguese.[56]

More fundamental than these advantages, however, was the unique constitutional character of company-states. As chartered entities that exemplified a form of delegated sovereignty, companies often proved more immediately well-suited than their statist counterparts to winning acceptance into foreign hierarchies. On this point, William Pettigrew observes:

Trading corporations proved more agile transnational interlocutors than the states who authorised them because of their ability to become willing tributaries to foreign states ... As a subordinate constitutional entity, a corporation was in a position to submit itself to a foreign state and ... could offer obeisance to foreign states in support of its commercial activities and territorial holdings.[57]

---

[52] Kyriazis and Metaxas, 'Path dependence', 365.
[53] G. D. Winius, *The Fatal History of Portuguese Ceylon: Transition to Dutch rule* (Cambridge, MA: Harvard University Press, 1971), xiv.
[54] Steensgaard, *Caravans, Carracks and Companies*, p. 67.   [55] Ibid.
[56] On the EIC, see generally Erickson, *Between Monopoly and Free Trade*. On the Dutch East India company's limited and later moves to tolerate some private trade from its employees, see S. V. Sgourev and W. van Lent, 'Balancing permission and prohibition: Private trade and adaptation at the VOC', *Social Forces*, 93(3) (2015), p. 944.
[57] Pettigrew, 'Corporate constitutionalism', 490.

As the Dutch and English East India companies infiltrated Asia, they repeatedly took advantage of their corporate form to strike bespoke bargains with local rulers. This enabled them to rapidly establish a series of territorially non-contiguous outposts throughout maritime Asia.[58] These outposts were very loosely governed from Amsterdam and London respectively. But each outpost was just as importantly incorporated into local polities through charters or treaties painstakingly negotiated between company representatives and indigenous rulers.[59] From sponsoring polities (Holland and England), company-states derived specific constitutional rights, such as rights to conduct diplomacy, wage war, mint currency and administer civil and criminal justice.[60] But the *exercise* of these rights depended on the terms and conditions negotiated with Asian host polity rulers and their local intermediaries.[61] In this respect, then, company states shared the 'hermit crab' character historian Felipe Fernandez-Armesto has elsewhere attributed to trading post empires (e.g., the Genoese) in the medieval Mediterranean – in dealing with powerful foreign suzerains, companies could partially incorporate themselves into the protective shell of Asian hosts, without relinquishing their identity as distinct (if territorially non-contiguous) corporate polities.[62]

The company-states' structure – as corporations that could alienate portions of their sovereignty in exchange for trading privileges in host polities – gave them an important advantage for ingratiating their way into Asian imperial hierarchies. But the companies' capacity to be incorporated into Asian polities also depended on enabling local conditions. In particular, permissive traditions of commercial extraterritoriality, the relative availability of local allies of convenience, and the presence of commensurable conceptions of political legitimacy decisively conditioned host polities' receptivity to European infiltration.

Composed of networks of non-contiguous littoral outposts, Europe's Asian maritime empires were parasitically dependent on Asian traditions of commercial extraterritoriality. Despite their dominance on the high seas, European imperialists almost always lacked the military strength on land to dictate terms to Asian sovereigns, at least prior to the mid-

---

[58] See for example P. J. Stern, *The Company-State: Corporate sovereignty and the early modern foundations of the British Empire in India* (Oxford: Oxford University Press, 2011), and K. Ward, *Networks of Empire: Forced migration in the Dutch East India Company* (Cambridge: Cambridge University Press, 2009).
[59] Stern, *The Company-State*, p. 13.   [60] Ibid., p. 12.
[61] Pettigrew, 'Corporate constitutionalism', 491.
[62] F. Fernando-Armesto, *Before Columbus: Exploration and colonization from the Mediterranean to the Atlantic, 1229–1492* (Philadelphia: University of Pennsylvania Press, 1987), p. 96.

eighteenth century. Instead, a 'balance of blackmail' typically mediated European-Asian relations.[63] At sea, Europeans could generally best their Asian counterparts, who in any case rarely contested European maritime supremacy.[64] But Europeans nevertheless needed territorial toeholds onshore to conduct their commercial operations. This left them beholden to host rulers' hospitality. In some instances, established customs of commercial extraterritoriality were permissive enough to make it straight-forward for European guests and Asian hosts to negotiate mutually prof-itable accommodations.[65] In others, however, customs of commercial extraterritoriality and accompanying maritime frontier governance regimes were much more restrictive, significantly impeding European incorporation into host polities.

Beyond needing physical space in which to base their factories, Europeans also required local collaborators, both as political and com-mercial allies. In some instances, the treaties and grants guaranteeing them commercial privileges were so restrictive that Europeans had to depend on local sub-rulers for physical protection. To cite one example, the Mughal emperor routinely forbade Europeans from maintaining large-scale fortifications in their territorial concessions.[66] This left them reliant on local officials, most notably the resident fort com-mander, for physical protection.[67] Equally, Europeans also depended on indigenous commercial allies for a host of services, ranging from commercial intelligence, through to credit facilities and local transportation.[68]

The commercial durability of both the Estado da India and the com-pany-states depended on striking deep social roots into local societies, via the mediation of indigenous allies.[69] The relative availability of these allies varied significantly across maritime Asia. In patrimonial polities such as the Mughal empire, the Emperor loosely shared sovereign

---

[63] Clulow, 'European maritime violence', 73.

[64] It is nevertheless worth noting that Asian indifference to maritime affairs was far from universal, with powers such as the Omani sultanate, the Maratha Empire and the Chinese Zheng state in Taiwan bucking this general rule. See Andrade, 'Beyond guns, germs, and steel'.

[65] See for example the partnership between EIC agents and the local ruler of Madraspatnam that yielded the Fort St George settlement that later became Madras, in D. Vigneswaran, 'A corrupt international society: How Britain was duped into its first imperial conquest' in S. Suzuki, Y. Zhang and J. Quirk (eds.), *International Orders in the Early Modern World*, pp. 94–117.

[66] G. A. Nadri, *Eighteenth Century Gujarat: The dynamics of its political economy, 1750–1800* (Leiden: Brill, 2009), p. 11.

[67] Ibid.

[68] See for example R. Maloni, 'Europeans in seventeenth century Gujarat: Presence and response', *Social Scientist*, 36(3–4) (2008), 64–99.

[69] Pettigrew, 'Corporate constitutionalism', 495.

prerogatives with quasi-autonomous *mansabdars* and lesser princelings.[70] Consequently, though the Western presence still required the emperor's imprimatur, Europeans were able to forge durable political and commercial alliances with a range of indigenous intermediaries.[71] The search for local partners proved even easier in smaller south and southeast Asian polities outside the Mughal orbit, where indigenous rulers were often more than happy to trade commercial privileges in exchange for the increased customs revenue the European presence stimulated.[72] By contrast, the more direct system of bureaucratic rule the Manchus imposed on their militarized coastal periphery limited the availability of local collaborators, significantly constraining European infiltration.[73]

Finally, in addition to requiring territorial toeholds and local political and commercial allies, Europeans also needed to win acceptance as legitimate participants within Asian hierarchies, whether as vassals, 'friends', or (in some instances) suzerain 'stranger kings'.[74] This in turn required a sufficient correspondence between European and local conceptions of political authority, in order to lubricate the formers' incorporation into established power networks. As with the availability of local allies, the degree of congruence between European and local conceptions of legitimacy varied significantly, especially between the Indian Ocean region and East Asia. In the former, the presence of 'quasi-commensurable political imaginations'[75] between Western intruders and local hosts significantly aided European efforts to infiltrate indigenous hierarchies. Despite their differences, for example, Europeans and Indians both clearly distinguished sacred and profane functions in society, represented for example in the respective dichotomies they drew between their priestly (*Oratores* and *Brahmins*) and warrior (*Bellatores* and *Kshatriyas*) classes.[76] However rudimentary and approximate, such correspondences aided early efforts at

---

[70] Tambiah, 'What did Bernier actually say?', 380.
[71] See for example Maloni, 'Europeans in seventeenth century Gujarat', 77–80.
[72] F. Hasan, 'Conflict and cooperation in Anglo-Mughal trade relations during the reign of Aurangzeb', *Journal of the Economic and Social History of the Orient*, 34(4) (1991), 360.
[73] On the predominance of strategic over commercial considerations in the Qing Dynasty's early approach to maritime frontier governance, see A. Schottenhammer, 'Characteristics of Qing China's maritime trade politics, *Shunzhi* through *Qianlong* reigns' in A. Schottenhammer (ed.), *Trading Networks in Early Modern East Asia* (Wiesbaden: Harrassowitz Verlag, 2010), p. 103.
[74] On the 'stranger king' tradition as an important enabler of European infiltration into Southeast Asia, see, for example, generally D. Henley, 'Conflict, justice, and the stranger-king roots of colonial rule in Indonesia and elsewhere', *Modern Asian Studies*, 38(1) (2004), pp. 85–144.
[75] Z. Biedermann, 'The matrioshka principle and how it was overcome: Portuguese and Habsburg imperial attitudes in Sri Lanka and the responses of the rulers of Kotte (1506–1598)', *Journal of Early Modern History*, 13(4) (2009), 266–7.
[76] Biedermann, 'Portuguese diplomacy in Asia in the sixteenth century', 21–2.

cross-cultural diplomacy and European incorporation. By contrast, Confucian ideas of sacred kingship contrasted radically with Western conceptions of political legitimacy.[77] The resulting mismatch sharply increased tension between Confucian hosts and European infiltrators. Through Confucian eyes, Western diplomatic gaffes were tantamount to sacrilege, and thus an intolerable affront to local sensibilities.[78]

I have outlined above the structural properties of Western polities that enabled long-distance trade and colonization in maritime Asia from the late fifteenth century. I have also discussed in general terms the local preconditions influencing Western success in insinuating their way into Asian hierarchies. Much like the vast territorial empires they tried to infiltrate, the Western maritime empires depended for their success on local partners. Like their Asian counterparts, Western empires were also forged from a creative remixing of local practices, institutions and ideas, and so were dependent on conducive local circumstances for their establishment and perpetuation. Critically, this variation in local circumstances helps explain the divergent trajectories of Western 'shadow' imperialism in South and East Asia – a fateful divergence that forms the focus of the rest of this chapter.

A Great Divergence: Western Infiltration into Early Modern South and East Asia

Western Infiltration into the Mughal Empire

Turning first to South Asia, it is worth recalling the scale and sophistication of the Mughal Empire, the region's most powerful polity, and together with China the main magnet pulling Western commercial interest eastwards in the early modern period. Following Akbar's death in 1605, the Mughal Empire continued to grow in size and wealth. Under succeeding emperors Jahangir and Shah Jahan, the empire retained its distinctive commitment to syncretism, embracing a diversity regime stressing the incorporation of communal difference, rather than a programme of coercive cultural assimilation. As the empire continued to expand, the Mughals doubled down in their reliance on the *mansabdari* system of centralized elite patronage, and on a loose system of suzerainty that shared sovereign prerogatives with dependent rulers.[79] Following Akbar's conquests of the rich maritime provinces of Gujarat and Bengal, the Mughal Empire had assumed a commanding position of centrality within pan-regional Indian Ocean trading networks.[80] But

---

[77] Ibid., p. 22.   [78] Ibid.   [79] Tambiah, 'What did Bernier actually say?', 385.
[80] Richards, *The Mughal Empire*, p. 31.

imperial elites remained primarily landward in their orientation, focusing mostly on terrestrial opportunities for wealth and conquest, while leaving in place the *laissez-faire* frontier governance regime that had traditionally prevailed in maritime South Asia.[81]

As we saw in Chapter 3, the Mughals' commitment to syncretism, their 'galactic' model of loose suzerain over-rule, and their embrace of a *laissez-faire* maritime frontier governance model all arose out of the distinct challenges and opportunities the Mughals first confronted when carving out their own empire in the sixteenth century. Serendipitously, however, these characteristics greatly aided Western infiltration into the subcontinent.

The first meaningful European encroachment in South Asia came with the Portuguese conquest of Goa in 1510. Once ensconced in Goa, the Portuguese cultivated an elaborate network of alliances with neighbouring rulers. Dominant only at sea and surrounded by potentially hostile powers, the Portuguese worked hard to master locally dominant norms and diplomatic practices. This involved maintaining extensive diplomatic correspondence with the region's 'petty kings', as well as Portugal's early adoption of locally prevalent practices of reciprocal gift exchange.[82] In securing their position, the Portuguese often struggled to credibly assert the prestige of their distant king to indigenous audiences. Nevertheless, their great distance from the Mughal Empire (which arose only after Portuguese Goa's establishment) afforded the Portuguese the benefit of participating in Indian Ocean trading networks, without having to potentially compromise the honour the Portuguese king by symbolically submitting to Mughal suzerainty.[83]

By the time the English and Dutch company-states made it to the subcontinent a century later, the Mughal Empire was well-established, its reach extending deep into South and Central Asia. Consequently, whereas the Portuguese could still deploy skilful diplomacy to maintain a respectful distance from the Mughals, neither the EIC nor the VOC could be so aloof. Instead, in order to eke out a commercially viable niche in Indian Ocean trading networks, Europe's company-states had to forge a working relationship with the emperor and his intermediaries. In practice, this entailed lobbying for incorporation into the Mughal Empire, accepting imperial 'protection', and assuming the rights and responsibilities that came with being one of the Mughal Emperor's loyal vassals.[84]

---

[81] Gommans, *Mughal Warfare*, p. 164.

[82] See generally J. V. Melo, 'In search of a shared language: The Goan diplomatic protocol', *Journal of Early Modern History*, 20(4) (2016), 390–407.

[83] Ibid., pp. 394–5.

[84] On the centrality of Mughal protection as the legitimating formula enabling the EIC's incorporation into the Mughal Empire, see Benton and Clulow, 'Empires and protection', 88.

A consideration of the EIC's incorporation into the Mughal Empire helps illustrate both the challenges accompanying this process, and the structural preconditions that made it possible.

The EIC first sought trading privileges from the Mughal Emperor Jahangir in the early 1600s, shortly after the latter's ascension to the imperial throne. A first priority for the EIC was to secure a toehold in Surat, then the principal port in Gujarat, and a key hub connecting maritime trading networks in the western Indian Ocean with caravan networks conveying goods from the Silk Road.[85] Given the region's longstanding traditions of commercial extraterritoriality, company officials naturally hoped to establish a network of trading factories in Mughal territory. To do so, however, required that the EIC receive an official charter of privileges (a *farman*) from the emperor.[86] This in turn necessitated that the EIC first be recognized as a 'slave' of the emperor – a status that could only be conferred through company officials' participation in the ritual diplomacy of the Mughal court.[87]

As we have seen, the Mughals under Akbar innovated a powerful legitimating ideology of universal reconciliation, which empowered the emperor as the centripetal force binding together the empire's otherwise irredeemably diverse communities. This ideology both reflected and celebrated the immense cosmopolitanism of the Mughal court, and meant that the EIC's status as white Christian 'Franks' did not disqualify them from potential incorporation within the empire. What it did mean, however, was that EIC officials had to conform to local standards of legitimacy, and participate in the practices that ritually enacted these standards, to successfully slot into the Mughal hierarchy. Characteristic of many early modern polities, the Mughal Empire was constituted by networks of allegiances – and more specifically 'webs of protection'[88] – rather than by rigidly delineated notions of territorial exclusivity or categorically exclusive forms of collective identity. Outsiders – 'Franks' included – could therefore be accepted within Mughal networks of protection, and win trading privileges and territorial rights of self-government. But they could become eligible for Mughal protection only as acknowledged servants of the emperor. Ritual incorporation was a necessary antecedent to commercial integration into the Mughal world.[89]

---

[85] On Surat's commercial importance, see K. N. Chaudhuri, *The Trading World of Asia and the East India Company, 1660–1760* (Cambridge: Cambridge University Press, 1978), p. 49.

[86] R. Barbour, 'Power and distant display: Early English "ambassadors" in Mughal India', *Huntington Library Quarterly*, 61(3–4) (1998), 361.

[87] Ibid.   [88] Benton and Clulow, 'Empires and protection', 76.

[89] M. Siddiqi, *The British Historical Context and Petitioning in India* (New Delhi: Aakar Books, 2005), p. 11.

Of the ritual practices that helped constitute the Mughal Empire, the rite of *arzdasht* (petitioning) was the most important for would-be suppliants to the imperial court. Like much of Mughal court ceremonial, *arzdasht* was adapted from the Mughals' Persian cultural inheritance. It entailed the ceremonial exchange of gifts between the emperor and favoured subjects, and aimed to establish lasting personal ties of benevolence and obedience between suzerains and vassals.[90] A central feature of this practice was the emperor's conferral of special robes (*khilat*) to imperial subjects, in exchange for gifts of gold or silver (*nazr*).[91]

By itself, gift exchange was hardly a novel feature of Mughal hierarchy, being rather a common feature of diplomatic and court ceremonial in the early modern world.[92] Nevertheless, the rite of *arzdasht* was saturated with a highly distinctive structure of meaning. For example, the robes the emperor granted to petitioners were meant to have been worn by the emperor himself.[93] Consequently, gifting these robes to vassals signified the establishment of an intimate and personal corporeal bond between sovereign and subject, marking the latter's symbolic incorporation into the imperial household.[94] Likewise, contrary to early English interpretations, gifts of money to the emperor did not constitute mere bribery.[95] Rather than being of primarily commercial significance, the *nazr* symbolically represented the gratitude of loyal vassals to benevolent suzerains, again affirming the personal bonds of fealty linking the emperor to his vassals.[96] That the imperial *farman* had to be renegotiated and reconfirmed under each successive emperor further affirms the personalistic character of the allegiance underwriting the EIC's presence in the Mughal Empire, and the importance of ritual supplication as a practical means of enacting and affirming this allegiance.[97]

The flexible and syncretic character of Mughal ideology was indispensable in enabling European incorporation into the empire. Equally, the ready availability of local allies of convenience in the Mughal Empire also aided Europeans' insinuation into indigenous hierarchies. On this point, the Mughal Empire's dispersion of sovereign powers among its various

[90] Ibid. [91] Hasan, *State and Locality in Mughal India*, p. 37.
[92] K. Siebenhüner, 'Approaching diplomatic and courtly gift-giving in Europe and Mughal India: Shared practices and cultural diversity', *Medieval History Journal*, 16(2) (2013), 532.
[93] Hasan, *State and Locality in Mughal India*, p. 37. [94] Ibid.
[95] Siebenhüner, 'Approaching diplomatic and courtly gift-giving', 533.
[96] Ibid., p. 539. Indeed, Siebenhüner notes that Mughal practices of gift-giving between the Mughal emperor and his *mansabs* systematically blurred the line between 'gift' and 'tribute' to a degree that finds no precise analogue in European cultures.
[97] Hasan, 'Conflict and cooperation in Anglo-Mughal trade relations under Aurangzeb', 354.

vassals made it imperative for Europeans to negotiate accommodations with local authorities, if the trade privileges won through imperial petitioning were to yield practical commercial benefits. Local officials, from provincial governors, through to the harbour master and municipal fort commanders, were themselves typically deeply enmeshed in regional commerce.[98] The European presence first boosted the wealth of local officials by increasing commercial activity, and thereby enhancing local customs revenues.[99] Over time, the enhanced intercontinental trade Europeans stimulated moreover brought more diffuse benefits. European payments for Indian textiles in American gold and silver spurred the further monetization of local economies.[100] Europeans also brokered the importation of New World crops, including chilli peppers, maize, tomatoes and tobacco.[101] These imports not only transformed local cuisines, but also (in the case of tobacco) provided indigenous entrepreneurs with access to a lucrative new cash crop.

The European presence in Mughal India thus rested on parallel and mutually reinforcing systems of imperial and provincial patronage. Mughal syncretism, combined with a Mughal willingness to maintain a *laissez-faire* attitude to maritime frontier governance, made it possible for Europeans to establish a foothold in the empire in the first place. But the patronage and protection of commercially extraverted and engaged local officials remained essential for Europeans to practically realize their ambitions. To characterize European patterns of incorporation in this way should not mislead us into imagining a frictionless harmony of interests between Mughal suzerains, provincial patrons and European vassals. Europeans frequently complained to the emperor that local officials were dishonouring the terms of the *farman*, even as they self-servingly interpreted its terms to exaggerate the scope and character of the privileges that it conferred.[102] In its mature phase, the empire under Aurangzeb moreover demanded an increasing cut in maritime trading revenues. This newfound appetite for customs revenues put fiscal pressure on provincial officials, increasing in turn their exactions on European and indigenous traders.[103]

The Mughal model of accommodating Europeans was far from universal, even within South Asia. In southern India, beyond the Mughal Empire's reach, Europeans struck bargains on more even terms with the local rulers (*nayakas*) that succeeded the Hindu empire of Vijayanagar once it began to fragment after 1565. In Madras, for example, the EIC

---

[98] Ibid., p. 356.   [99] Ibid.   [100] Fisher, *A Short History of the Mughal Empire*, p. 155.
[101] Ibid., p. 155.
[102] Hasan, 'Cooperation and conflict in Anglo-Mughal trade relations', 353.
[103] Ibid., p. 357.

founded its first fortified settlement in South Asia in 1644, having been tricked by the indigenous ruler into assuming full costs for the establishment of a fortified trading settlement, and despite an initial agreement that such costs would be shared between the EIC and its local hosts.[104] Elsewhere, on Madurai, the Dutch East India Company (Vereenigde Oostindische Compagnie, or VOC) likewise established a settlement from 1645 at the encouragement of local rulers, albeit initially on the proviso that the VOC was forbidden from building fortifications.[105]

As was the case with the Mughals, South Asian rulers benefited from the enhanced commerce the European presence helped catalyse. They also welcomed the prestige that came with their accumulation of exotic 'curiosities', either gifted or bought from their European guests.[106] In contrast to the Mughals' open syncretism, however, the Hindu *nayakas'* view of Europeans as 'low caste' traders significantly complicated European efforts at incorporation. Stigmatized for their consumption of beef and alcohol, their poor sanitary practices and their interaction with lower caste Indians, Europeans in South India frequently had to rely on high caste indigenous intermediaries to conduct their diplomacy with local rulers.[107] The difficulties Europeans encountered in negotiating with the *nayaka* kingdoms, despite the proportionately greater economic benefits they could bring to local rulers, illustrate again the central role that indigenous conceptions of legitimacy played in conditioning European incorporation into maritime Asia. This observation holds with even greater force when we contrast the European experience of successful incorporation in South Asia, against the far cooler reception Europeans received in their attempts to infiltrate East Asia.

European Incorporation into Maritime East Asia

In East as well as South Asia, Europeans' capacity to infiltrate local hierarches was shaped by prevailing diversity regimes, the availability of local commercial and political allies, and the character (more or less permissive) of maritime frontier governance regimes. Over the Ming and early-mid Qing periods, China maintained a far tighter control over its maritime periphery than either the Mughals or other Indian Ocean

---

[104] Vigneswaran, 'A corrupt international society', pp. 109–11.
[105] M. P. M. Vink, 'Images and ideologies of Dutch-South Asian contact: Cross-cultural encounters between the Nayaka state of Madurai and the Dutch East India Company in the seventeenth century', *Itinerario*, 21(2) (1997), 94. See also M. P. M. Vink, *Encounters on the Opposite Coast: The Dutch East India Company and the Nayaka state of Madurai in the seventeenth century* (Leiden: Brill, 2015), p. 296.
[106] Vink, 'Images and ideologies of Dutch-South Asian contact', 84–5.
[107] Ibid., pp. 85–6.

powers. A diversity regime in the Han-dominated southeast stressed Confucian assimilation over incorporation, and China's stricter policing of contacts between its subjects and European infiltrators, also limited Westerners' room for manoeuvre. Finally, the fact that the East Asian littoral remained militarily highly contested in the early Qing period further curtailed the scope for European infiltration. European designs to extend their commercial reach into East Asia were frustrated in the mid-late seventeenth century, victims to the Qing Dynasty's determination to consolidate its power and ruthlessly crush any nascent challengers forming on its open maritime flank.

The first noteworthy contrast between the Indian Ocean and littoral East Asia lay in the latter's far more contested and politicized character. From the Ming Dynasty onwards, successive imperial regimes oscillated in their strategies for managing China's maritime frontier. At times, the Ming and later also the Qing dynasties adopted a policy of hypervigilant defensiveness and even outright hostility to maritime trade, imposing draconian (if mostly unsuccessful) bans on seaborne traffic taking place outside the bonds of its tribute trade system.[108] This contrasted with periods of greater openness, in which both the regime and local officials allowed greater commerce, and acquiesced to foreigners' establishment of temporary offshore settlements in the islands and atolls immediately adjacent to the Pearl River delta.[109]

These variations notwithstanding, at no time did Chinese authorities embrace the *laissez-faire* attitude towards maritime affairs seen in major Indian Ocean polities. On the contrary, control of China's littoral frontier and surrounding seas remained an important goal for successive dynasties.[110] Imperial bans on maritime traffic ensured the rise of often heavily armed pirates and smuggling networks on China's maritime periphery. The resulting violence and insecurity prompted Chinese authorities to maintain a stance of watchful wariness towards potential threats and challengers from the sea, and to dedicate significant resources to suppressing 'pirates' and others conducting officially unsanctioned trade.[111] Not merely a Chinese preoccupation, the Japanese Tokugawa Shogunate likewise aimed to police its maritime affairs.[112] This went so

---

[108] Wills Jr, 'Introduction', p. 4.   [109] Ibid., p. 12.

[110] On the increased importance the Qing Empire attached to mapping its maritime frontiers and asserting suzerainty over its 'near seas', see generally R. C. Po, 'Mapping maritime power and control: A study of the late eighteenth century *Qisheng yanhai tu* (a coastal map of the seven provinces)', *Late Imperial China*, 37(2) (2016), 93–136.

[111] Wills Jr, 'Introduction', p. 8.

[112] L. Benton and A. Clulow, 'Webs of protection and interpolity zones in the early modern world' in L. Benton, A. Clulow and B. Attwood (eds.), *Empires and Protection: A global history* (Cambridge: Cambridge University Press, 2017), p. 53.

far as to extending Edo's nominal protection to all merchants trading in Japanese coastal waters, as well as to Chinese merchants bound for Japan, even if they were located thousands of miles from the home islands.[113]

East Asian waters were thus more politicized and policed by regional powers at the time of European infiltration than elsewhere. East Asian vigilance towards potential maritime threats moreover extended towards far tighter control of coastal territories, constraining European opportunities for incorporation into local political and economic networks. Certainly, some customs of very limited commercial extraterritoriality existed in China, as they did in more expansive forms throughout the Old World in the early modern period.[114] But Europeans' scope for carving out meaningful enclaves in China remained minimal compared to their expansive trading post empires in Southeast Asia and southern India, or even their unfortified settlements in the Mughal Empire. Under both the Ming and Qing empires, Europeans were held at arms' length. Imperial officials conceded Europeans' short-term settlement of offshore islands. But even then, they remained apprehensive of European efforts to fortify these settlements, expelling an early Portuguese mission when they deemed its fortifications too formidable for the empire's comfort.[115]

In time, some European powers were able to establish limited enclaves in China, most notably the Portuguese, who established a permanent settlement in Macau from the 1550s.[116] But even then, they depended on the sufferance of Chinese authorities, paid regular tribute to the local authorities, and were denied anything more than the most limited and revocable rights of resident self-government.[117] This treatment again contrasts sharply with the more generous arrangements Europeans negotiated with various Indian Ocean polities, and reflects in part the difficulty Europeans faced in being assimilated into the legitimating frameworks that constituted Sinocentric (and later Manchu-centric) hierarchy.

Under both the Ming and Qing dynasties, imperial rule in Han-dominated southern China rested on resolutely Confucian ideological foundations.[118] As 'barbarians', Europeans by definition stood outside Confucian civilizational boundaries. According to Confucian precepts, barbarians could potentially be civilized through acculturation and

---

[113] Ibid., p. 54.

[114] J. E. Wills Jr, 'Maritime Europe and the Ming' in J. E. Wills Jr (ed.), *China and Maritime Europe, 1500–1800: Trade, settlement, diplomacy, and missions* (Cambridge: Cambridge University Press, 2010), pp. 42–3.

[115] Gebhardt, 'Negotiating barriers', 38–9.

[116] Wills Jr, 'Maritime Europe and the Ming', p. 35.   [117] Ibid., p. 42.

[118] Wills Jr, 'Introduction', p. 3.

exposure to Chinese language and Confucian rites and norms.[119] In practice, however, the empire forbade all but the most limited contact between its subjects and European traders, sought to channel all contacts with Westerners through officially sanctioned channels, and even forbade Chinese from teaching Europeans the Chinese language, reputedly on pain of death.[120] Segregation and containment, rather than acculturation and assimilation, predominated in Chinese efforts to manage the European barbarians on their maritime frontiers.

Critically, the preference for strategies of containment over incorporation or assimilation persisted in maritime China over the Ming-Qing transition. Under the Han Ming Dynasty, a genuine correspondence in legitimating beliefs linked the emperor to the locally dominant Confucian scholar-literati. Imperial legitimacy rested on the conception of the emperor as the Son of Heaven, to whom imperial subjects and barbarians alike owed unquestioned submission.[121] Consequently – and despite their own misgivings – Europeans had to conform to Confucian tributary practices of ritual subordination to win trading concessions from the Ming emperor, and to grudgingly accept whichever strategies of geographical containment that accompanied them.[122]

This requirement of conformity to Confucian precepts and practices endured and perhaps even intensified under the Manchus. As a barbarian dynasty, the Manchus for decades faced fierce resistance to their rule, especially in southern China. Residual Ming loyalism among local elites simmered there throughout the late seventeenth century, abetted from 1661 to 1683 by a powerful Ming loyalist proto-state ensconced in Taiwan.[123] Though the Qing Dynasty used violence unsparingly to destroy Ming loyalist opposition, the duration and intensity of this resistance also compelled the Manchus to double down in their own adherence to Confucian orthodoxy, in order to secure the support of the local Han scholar-literati.

What this meant in practice for European infiltrators was that access to Chinese markets remained strictly regulated despite the otherwise

---

[119] On the theoretical possibility of 'barbarians' being 'civilized' through exposure to Sinic culture, see Langlois Jr, 'Chinese culturalism and the Yüan analogy', 358.

[120] Gebhardt, 'Negotiating barriers', 47.

[121] J. L. Cranmer-Byng and J. E. Wills Jr, 'Trade and diplomacy with maritime Europe, 1644–c. 1800' in J. E. Wills Jr (ed.), *China and Maritime Europe, 1500–1800: Trade, settlement, diplomacy, and missions* (Cambridge: Cambridge University Press, 2010), p. 185.

[122] Ibid., p. 251. Notwithstanding their pragmatic submission, the authors stress that no Europeans ever felt that they were genuinely presenting tribute from their sovereign to the Son of Heaven.

[123] Wills Jr., 'Introduction', p 17.

tectonic transformation in East Asia that accompanied the Ming-Qing power transition. Incongruous though it may first seem, the Manchus' very status as barbarians in the eyes of the Han scholar-literati compelled the former to cleave even more dogmatically to norms of imperial Confucianism in governing their southern maritime provinces, even as the Manchus themselves retained a lingering suspicion towards maritime China as a whole.[124] This dogmatism was not limited to insistence that Europeans conform to the norms of tributary diplomacy. Rather, it extended also to a continuation of the Ming Dynasty's practice of vigorously seeking to geographically contain the European presence to tiny offshore enclaves, and to channel European interactions through officially sanctioned channels.[125]

Regardless of whether they were government officials or licensed private traders, the Manchus kept a tight rein on any local intermediaries interacting with Europeans. Imperial policy expressly sought to stop Europeans from forging meaningful long-term partnerships with local allies, prioritizing security and the preservation of social order over expanded trade whenever these imperatives came into conflict.[126] This policy pre-empted the emergence of indigenous constituencies favouring an expanded European presence, as well as frustrating European efforts to strike deeper social roots within the Qing Empire. In the Indian Ocean region, the resident Mughal superpower had fostered European infiltration, not only by embracing an incorporative rather than an assimilative ideology, but also by farming out sovereign prerogatives to local elites, who in turn embraced lucrative alliances of convenience with European (and non-European) resident commercial communities.[127] The Manchus by contrast retained a more absolutist conception of imperial suzerainty, which granted less autonomy to local intermediaries, and deliberately tried to foster estrangement between these intermediaries and European infiltrators.[128]

---

[124] Ibid., p. 18.

[125] Cranmer-Byng and Wills Jr, 'Trade and diplomacy with maritime Europe', p. 185. Admittedly, the Qing Dynasty significantly lifted trade restrictions following the seizure of Taiwan in 1683, but security considerations and accompanying restrictions on foreigners remained a feature of Qing maritime governance throughout the dynasty's existence.

[126] N. Chin-Keong, 'Information and knowledge: Qing China's perceptions of the maritime world in the eighteenth century' in A. Schottenhammer (ed.), *The East Asian Maritime World 1400–1800: Its fabrics of power and dynamics of exchanges* (Wiesbaden: Harrassowitz Verlag, 2007), p. 96.

[127] Hasan, 'Conflict and cooperation in Anglo-Mughal trade relations under Aurangzeb', 360. See also more generally J. Flores, 'The sea world of the *Mutasaddi*: A profile of port officials from Mughal Gujarat (c. 1600–1650)', *Journal of the Royal Asiatic Society*, 21(1) (2011), 55–71.

[128] That said, like their Mughal counterparts, Qing officials – and even the emperor himself often later profited from covert trade with Europeans, even while publicly declaiming

We can explain continuities in maritime frontier governance across the Ming-Qing transition in part due to the Manchus' dependence on Confucian local elites for political support, and their ensuing adherence to Confucian norms and practices to govern the southern provinces' interactions with the outside world. To these considerations, however, we must also add a final crucial (albeit more temporary) grand strategic motivation shaping Manchu frontier policy – specifically the need to isolate, financially cripple and eventually destroy the Zheng maritime confederacy, which to its demise in 1683 constituted the main threat to Manchu consolidation in the southern provinces.

The Zheng confederacy first emerged in the 1620s, under the leadership of Zheng Zhilong, a charismatic trader, entrepreneur and pirate who leveraged his clan connections and commercial wealth to build an organization that at its height controlled 90 per cent of China's commercial shipping in maritime East Asia.[129] Originating as a clandestine armed trading enterprise, the Zheng confederacy accumulated immense wealth in the waning years of the Ming Dynasty, eventually disposing of annual revenues equal or even greater than both the Dutch and English East India Companies.[130] With great wealth came correspondingly enormous political power, the declining Ming Dynasty eventually formally deputizing Zheng Zhilong to suppress piracy and smuggling as it confronted the existential Manchu threat on its North-eastern frontier.[131]

Following the Ming Dynasty's defeat, the Zheng confederacy retained its loyalty to the old order, while simultaneously pursuing a full-fledged maritime state-building project through its defeat of the VOC and capture of Taiwan from the Dutch in 1662.[132] Thereafter, the emergent Zheng protopolity remained a thorn in the side of the new Manchu regime, proving a magnet for Ming loyalists and a commercial and military threat to the Manchus' control of their maritime periphery until 1683, when the Manchus invaded Taiwan and so brought an end to the Zheng enterprise.[133]

The Zheng confederacy's rise and fall is important first because it shows that Europeans were far from alone in building militarized maritime

---

a direct financial interest in overseas commerce. See J. K. Fairbank, 'The canton trade and the Opium War' in J. K. Fairbank (ed.), *The Cambridge History of China*, 15 vols., X: *Late Ch'ing, 1800–1911*, Pt. I (Cambridge: Cambridge University Press, 1978), p. 164.

[129] Andrade and Hang, 'Introduction: The East Asian maritime realm in global history', p. 11.

[130] Ibid., p. 12.   [131] Ibid.

[132] T. Andrade, 'The rise and fall of Dutch Taiwan, 1624–1662: Cooperative colonization and the statist model of European expansion', *Journal of World History*, 17(4) (2006), 431. For a more comprehensive account, see T. Andrade, *Lost Colony*.

[133] X. Hang, *Conflict and Commerce in Maritime Asia: The Zheng family and the shaping of the modern world, c. 1620–1720* (Cambridge: Cambridge University Press, 2015), p. 234.

commercial entities with the potential to evolve into viable political units. That the Zheng confederacy matched or even exceeded the wealth of the VOC and the EIC, and that it was able to best the former in battle, further offsets accounts of European infiltration into maritime Asia that stress the unbeatable supremacy of Western arms and institutions in driving this process.[134] Beyond these observations, the Zheng confederacy is relevant to this inquiry for its impact on Manchu governance strategies on their maritime frontier, and thus on Manchu receptivity to European infiltration.

As we have seen, the Manchus faced a major legitimation deficit in southern China in the decades following their rise to power. Having themselves originated as a militarized commercial monopoly on China's northern flanks, the Manchus were also well aware of the great threat a hybrid frontier organization such as the Zheng confederacy posed to their power. Consequently, as they consolidated their power in the south, the Manchus sought the Zheng polity's elimination. Lacking any maritime military experience or capabilities, the Manchus were at first ill-equipped to confront the Zheng confederacy at sea. Instead, to dislodge the Zheng presence on the mainland, the Manchus had to augment their offensives on land with Dutch naval assistance, in the form of an alliance of convenience with the Dutch East Indies Company.[135] Having eliminated Zheng footholds on the Chinese mainland, the Manchus then pursued an enormously destructive policy of economic blockade from 1661 to 1683, entailing the forced evacuation and razing of all settlements within ten kilometres from the sea along a 1,000-mile stretch of the Chinese coast.[136] But though it wrought untold devastation on targeted communities, even the Coastal Exclusion Policy, recalled by historians as 'the most draconian – and devastating – maritime prohibition the world has ever known', failed in its objective of financially strangling the Zheng confederacy.[137] Ultimately, the Manchus had to entice a defecting Zheng admiral, Shi Lang, to lead an amphibious invasion to totally destroy the confederacy in its Taiwanese stronghold.[138] The failures of the Coastal Exclusion Policy notwithstanding, that the Manchus were willing and able to oversee mass destruction and displacement in their most lucrative

---

[134] Andrade, 'The rise and fall of Dutch Taiwan', 447.
[135] Andrade and Hang, 'Introduction: The East Asian maritime realm in global history', p. 16.
[136] This is described in detail in D. D. Ho, 'The burning shore: Fujian and the coastal depopulation, 1661–1683' in T. Andrade and X. Hang (eds.), *Sea Rovers, Silver, and Samurai: Maritime East Asia in global history, 1550–1700* (Honolulu: University of Hawaii Press, 2016), pp. 260–89.
[137] Andrade and Hang, 'Introduction: The East Asian maritime realm in world history', p. 17.
[138] Hang, *Conflict and Commerce in Maritime Asia*, p. 234.

provinces, and to do so for over two decades, illustrates the magnitude of the danger they saw in the Zheng threat. More fundamentally, it also dramatizes a deeper reality – that the Manchus at least initially saw their maritime frontier as a source of peril as much as profit, where extreme measures – up to and including 'scorched earth' policies – might be warranted to fend off threats to the new dynasty's survival. Though the Manchus would later relax their policies, this vigilance against maritime threats persisted for the dynasty's duration, severely limiting European efforts at infiltration and insinuation before the mid-nineteenth century.

Conclusion

This chapter has examined the first phase of European infiltration into maritime Asia, and European efforts at this time to insinuate themselves into hierarchical regional orders respectively dominated by the Mughal and Qing empires. My purposes have been to gain a better purchase on the nature, origins and limits of Europe's maritime empires in Asia; to explain how Europeans were able to insinuate themselves into local hierarchies; and to account for the meaningful variance in European patterns of infiltration in South and East Asia.

The discussion began by foregrounding an underappreciated parallel between European maritime empires and the terrestrial Asian empires on which they were parasitically grafted. Like the Mughals and the Manchus, the European maritime empires were products of the enhanced interregional interconnectivity and commercial dynamism that defined the Eurasian Transformation. As we saw in Chapter 3, the Mughal and Manchu empires had originated on Eurasia's steppe and forest frontiers, as entrepreneurial elites leveraged niche military advantages (primarily in cavalry warfare) and profits from the long-distance luxury trade to conquer large-scale terrestrial agrarian empires. Similarly, Europeans likewise carved out a space for themselves in Asia by exploiting their own niche military advantages (this time in blue water naval warfare) to forcefully intermediate Eurasian maritime trading networks and accumulate superprofits by arbitraging the Europe-Asia trade in precious spices.

The commercial dynamism of the Eurasian Transformation made it possible and profitable for Europeans to pursue projects of transcontinental trade and colonization. So too did the political stability that came with the growth of new terrestrial mega-empires in South and East Asia. Europe's outward thrust was thus thoroughly entwined with, and dependent on, projects of Asian imperial consolidation. Asian prosperity and power exerted a gravitational pull on Europeans. Chinese (and to a lesser extent, Indian) demand for New World silver provided Europeans with a means of buying their way into Asian marketplaces on a far grander scale than ever before. And institutional innovations – most notably the company-state – provided formerly marginal northern European powers with a more reliable means of mobilizing capital and coercion over trans-continental distances. In their corporate structure, company states also proved both strong enough to compete with indigenous and Iberian maritime rivals, and supple enough to potentially negotiate their way into acceptance as either partners or clients of Asian host polities.

Notwithstanding the extreme (sometimes even genocidal) violence that attended European interactions with some smaller Southeast Asian polities, ingratiation rather than imposition predominated as the West's dominant mode of interaction with Asian hosts during the seventeenth century. On land at least, power asymmetries typically favoured locals, forcing Europeans to seek accommodations on local terms. The Eurasia-wide prevalence of cus-toms of commercial extraterritoriality provided Europeans with the potential to establish non-contiguous networks of trading posts throughout maritime Asia. But prevailing systems of legitimation and accompanying diversity regimes, the varying availability of local political and commercial allies, and the existence of more or less restrictive maritime frontier governance regimes together decisively shoved and shaped patterns of European infiltration.

The contrasting examples of European infiltration into Mughal India and Qing-dominated East Asia sharply illustrated this observation. The Mughals' subscription to an ideology and diversity regime defined by syncretic incorporation, their co-sharing of sovereign prerogatives with powerful and partially autonomous local intermediaries, and their *laissez-faire* approach to maritime frontier governance together provided a highly conducive environment for European infiltration. Practices of ritual sub-ordination, centred around elaborate court ceremonial and reciprocal gift exchange, provided a point of traction for Europeans seeking to ingratiate themselves into the Mughal emperor's good graces. Confounding tropes of intractable Christian-Muslim hostility, the different religious affili-ations and customs of the 'Franks' also proved no barrier to their incorp-oration into the Mughal hierarchy, which remained grounded in a syncretic ideology of universal reconciliation. This contrasted with the ostensibly more accommodating context of the smaller Hindu polities in southern India, where perceptions of Europeans as low caste 'sea nomads' or 'bandit-kings' significantly impeded (though did not entirely frustrate) Western efforts to forge viable alliances with local partners.[139]

---

[139] M. P. M. Vink, 'From port-city to world-system: Spatial constructs of Dutch Indian Ocean studies, 1500–1800', *Itinerario*, 28(2) (2004), 57; and Vink, *Encounters on the Opposite Coast*, p. 15.

In contrast to the Mughals, the Manchus' opportunistic embrace of imperial Confucianism, their retention of Ming practices mandating the segregation of Europeans from potential local partners and their security-driven preoccupation with dominating their maritime frontier each significantly restricted European opportunities for ingratiation into the Manchu hierarchy. As barbarian occupiers themselves, the Manchus could ill afford to alienate the local Han scholar-literati. Consequently, at least in the first phase of imperial consolidation, they largely retained Ming traditions that coded Europeans as barbarians unworthy of assimilation and best kept at a safe distance. The powerful threat of the Zheng confederacy to Manchu power in the south further mandated a militarization of maritime frontier governance, further inhibiting European efforts at ingratiation.

The consequences of this regional variability in European patterns of infiltration into Asian hierarchies were far-reaching. By the turn of the eighteenth century, India played host to resident trading communities from multiple Western powers, with the English especially having established extensive networks of settlements throughout the Indian subcontinent. By this time, the EIC had founded major settlements in Bombay, Madras and Calcutta – the future company presidencies around which the EIC's Indian Empire would later congeal. The EIC was still a vassal of the Mughal emperor in the late 1600s, and would indeed remain so down to the Mughal emperor's official overthrow following the Indian 'Mutiny' of 1857–8. The terrestrial military capabilities of the EIC and other Europeans meanwhile remained laughably puny, their predation at sea little more than a bearable nuisance for Indian rulers and merchants.

These disclaimers aside, Europeans were firmly entrenched in India by the end of the 1600s, in ways that differed markedly from their far more tentative and fragile footprint in littoral East Asia. In Southeast Asia, to be sure, Dutch Batavia and the Spanish Philippines stood as valuable colonies in their own right, and potential platforms for further regional expansion. Elsewhere, however, Europeans remained firmly subordinate to local powers, either completely excluded or otherwise barely tolerated at the fringes of established hierarchies. Having been thrown out of Taiwan by the Zheng confederacy, the VOC retained only a token presence on Deshima Island in Nagasaki from which to coordinate its Northeast Asian commerce. On mainland China, meanwhile, the Portuguese had in Macao managed to cling on to their status as tenants and tributaries of the emperor following the Ming-Qing transition, but even then were anomalous in the extent of their (comparatively meagre) trading privileges.

By 1700, the Mughal Empire and the Qing Empire still reigned supreme in their respective regions. But whereas Europeans had by then extensively infiltrated the former's maritime fringe, they remained a comparatively trivial presence along the Manchus' militarized littoral frontier. This contrast is key to understanding the radically divergent evolution of regional imperial orders in South versus East Asia from this time on. For in South Asia, the early eighteenth century would see the Mughal Empire's rapid decline, following Emperor Aurangzeb's abandonment of syncretism for sectarian exclusion, and a disastrous overextension into the Deccan. Thereafter, the Mughal Empire's implosion would pave the way for the rise of competing European and Asian polities, culminating in the EIC's ascent to regional hegemony by century's end. By contrast, Europeans would remain largely excluded from the Manchu Empire, as it not only maintained but extended its regional hegemony throughout the eighteenth century. This great divergence, marked by Mughal decline, Manchu expansion and the West's uneven ascent at the interstices of both trends, forms the subject of Chapter 5.

5 The Great Asian Divergence
Mughal Decline and Manchu Expansion in the Eighteenth Century

Introduction

This chapter examines and explains the diverging fates of the Mughal and Qing empires over the eighteenth century. In 1700, the Mughal and Qing empires dominated their respective regions. In South Asia, the Mughals had reached their greatest territorial extent by Emperor Aurangzeb's death in 1707. And while Aurangzeb had failed to suppress a decades-long Maratha insurgency in south India, no immediate peer competitor seemed likely to threaten Mughal regional hegemony at the time of the emperor's demise. Likewise, having destroyed the Zheng Confederacy in 1683, the Qing Dynasty in the early 1700s consolidated its supremacy over China's Confucian core, having by now also seen off the last remnants of Ming loyalism on the mainland.

From this starting point of apparent parity, however, the Mughal and Qing empires spectacularly diverged. For the Mughals, Aurangzeb would be the dynasty's last strong emperor. Dying at the age of nearly ninety, Aurangzeb left behind him an empire that was militarily over-extended and increasingly polarized along regional and cultural lines.[1] The Mughals' lack of clear rules governing imperial succession already guaranteed a violent struggle between the Timurid princes after 1707.[2] But the post-Aurangzeb succession contest yielded a sequence of increasingly weak and lacklustre rulers, who failed to assert their authority against a backdrop of rising noble disaffection and regional rebellion.[3] The Mughals' inability to preserve public order – especially in the empire's chaotic south – meanwhile encouraged provincial governors to hoard tribute rather than remit it to the imperial capital. This simultaneously laid the foundation for the emergence of more territorially compact regional successor states, while gutting the empire's fiscal

[1] Richards, *The Mughal Empire*, p. 253.   [2] Ibid.
[3] Fisher, *A Short History of the Mughal Empire*, p. 212.

158

foundations.[4] Facing a downward spiral of legitimacy, military strength and fiscal capacity, the Mughals became ever more vulnerable to internal rebellion and external predation. In 1739, the Persian warlord Nadir Shah's sack of Delhi and looting of the imperial treasury dramatized Mughal impotence.[5] This catastrophe marked the empire's end as a viable regional hierarchy, and heralded a bloody and protracted decades-long interregnum culminating in the rise of the British Raj.

The contrasting fate of the Manchu Empire could not have been more stark. Having seen off the last of their internal rivals, the Manchus embarked on a series of successful military campaigns, which doubled the empire's size by the end of the eighteenth century. Vast new territories, including Tibet and Xinjiang, fell under the Manchu yoke during this time, while the Manchus simultaneously consolidated Qing dominance in the ethnically diverse borderlands in the southwest.[6] Despite their initial hostility to 'barbarian' suzerainty, Confucian satellites and traditional Ming tributaries Korea and Vietnam also eventually accommodated themselves to the new order, shoring up the Manchus' dominance in littoral East Asia.[7] Exceeding the achievements of all previous dynasties, the Manchus meanwhile also achieved the unique feat of pacifying the eastern Eurasian steppe, while retaining and fortifying their control over China's sedentary heartland.[8] Through a combination of skilful diplomacy, military-logistical innovations and genocidal violence, the Manchus annihilated their last competitor on the steppe (the Zunghar Confederacy), consolidating their supremacy across steppe and coastal eastern Eurasia.[9]

Both the Mughals and the Manchus had embarked on ambitious projects of territorial expansion in the seventeenth and eighteenth centuries. In the former case, these exertions helped unleash centrifugal forces that proved fatal for the Mughals, and cleared the path for the West's later rise to subcontinental dominance. Conversely, judging them by the great size of their conquests, as well as their total destruction of neighbouring peer competitors, the Manchus were clearly not merely Asia's – but the world's – most successful expansionist regime for the period under review. Why did the Manchus succeed where the Mughals failed? What can the contrasting fates of these empires tell us about the respective dynamics of imperial hierarchies' collapse or consolidation?

[4] R. P. Sana, 'Was there an agrarian crisis in Mughal north India in the late-seventeenth and early-eighteenth centuries?', *Social Scientist*, 34(11–12) (2006), 20.
[5] M. Axworthy, *The Sword of Persia: Nader Shah, from tribal warrior to conquering tyrant* (London: I. B. Tauris, 2009), p. 213.
[6] Di Cosmo, 'Qing colonial administration in inner Asia', p. 288.
[7] See generally J.-Y. Lee, *China's Hegemony: Four hundred years of East Asian domination* (New York: Columbia University Press, 2016), chapter 5.
[8] See generally Perdue, *China Marches West*.   [9] Ibid.

And how did this great divergence shape the subsequent course of Western imperial expansion in Asia? These are the questions this chapter engages.

I argue below that we can explain the Mughal and Manchu empires' diverging fates primarily by reference to variations in their ability to continue to accommodate cultural diversity over the course of territorial expansion. Revisiting my earlier account of these empires' emergence, I argued that both depended for their success on two overriding considerations. First, rulers needed to *mobilize* coalitions from broad multicultural alliances to conquer on a subcontinental scale. Second, to then *stabilize* their rule, they needed to articulate legitimizing ideologies and diversity regimes capable of accommodating the immense cultural heterogeneity of the populations they encompassed.

Beneath the common umbrella of systems grounded in universal kingship, the Mughals and Manchus developed distinctive models of empire to address these challenges.

As we have seen, the Mughals crafted an imperial model grounded in three core components: a legitimizing ideology and accompanying diversity regime marked by incorporative syncretism; the sharing of sovereign powers with client rulers through a system of 'galactic' suzerainty; and the maintenance of a *laissez-faire* open maritime frontier governance regime. By contrast, the Manchus instead sought to embody and segregate their diverse constituencies through a model of imperial simultaneity. They also maintained a system of fractal suzerainty mandating far more direct rule in the Han heartland, and enforced a militarized and 'closed' governance regime on their maritime frontier.

With this background in mind, the main cause for Mughal decline lay in Aurangzeb's abandonment of syncretism for a more strictly sectarian vision of empire. Though polemicists have undeniably dramatically exaggerated Aurangzeb's zealotry and downplayed his pragmatism,[10] there can be no doubt that Aurangzeb recast the empire on more explicitly Sunni Islamic lines. Measures such as the reintroduction of head taxes (the *jizya*) and pilgrimage taxes for non-Muslims, as well as Aurangzeb's pressures for non-Muslim nobles and client rulers to convert to Islam, fomented resentment and rebellion that seriously threatened the empire's stability.[11] Later, Aurangzeb failed to translate battlefield victories in the

---

[10] For an excellent critique of traditional stereotypes of Aurangzeb as a one-dimensional Islamic zealot, see generally A. Truschke, *Aurangzeb: The man and the myth* (Gurgaon: Penguin Random House India, 2017).

[11] On Aurangzeb's motives for reintroducing the *jizya*, see S. Chandra, '*Jizya* and the state in India during the 17th century', *Economic and Social History of the Orient*, 12(3) (1969), 322–40.

Deccan into enduring political success. Instead, he proved incapable of assimilating south Indian (especially Maratha) political elites into the empire's dominant Indo-Persian court culture, despite gifting generous imperial honours and land grants to defeated adversaries.[12] Rather, the emperor's sectarianism alienated established and prospective clients. The resulting processes of religious confessionalization fuelled armed resistance from constituencies (e.g., the Rajputs) that had long been loyal to the empire, while rendering indigestible the empire's newly conquered southern territories.[13] These failures sparked the downward spiral of violence, fiscal crisis and decentralization that propelled the empire's decomposition in the post-Aurangzeb era.

The Manchus' contrasting experience – of resilience over the course of large-scale territorial expansion – is instructive. Already familiar with the cultures of the Eurasian steppe, the Manchus readily adapted their model of segregated incorporation to integrate new clients into their expanding imperium, and so accommodate the expanded cultural diversity that came with further conquest. Harnessing a repertoire combining religious patronage, marital alliances and tributary gift exchange, the Manchus braided together a loose system of suzerainty over newly incorporated territories, in the process inducting new clients into the imperial service elite.[14] At the same time, the Manchus also innovated logistical systems to support enlarged terrestrial lines of communication and supply well beyond China's traditional limits.[15] This enabled the Manchus to overcome rivals' ability to retreat into the vastness of the steppe when confronted with superior military strength.[16] When necessary, this then enabled the Manchus to destroy rival polities, such as the Zunghar confederacy, that they could not accommodate. Alone among China's dynasties, this helped the Manchus to permanently pacify the steppe frontier, by pursuing and eliminating alternative gravitational centres of power and loyalty.

This chapter proceeds as follows. The first section sketches the Mughal Empire's fall, canvassing existing explanations for its decline before advancing my own alternative account in the second section. The third and fourth sections then respectively narrate and explain the Manchu Empire's further expansion during the eighteenth century. I conclude in the fifth section by reviewing the legacies of these empires' divergent

---

[12] J. F. Richards, 'The imperial crisis in the Deccan', *Journal of Asian Studies*, 35(2) (1976), 256.
[13] Ibid. See also Richards, *The Mughal Empire*, pp. 179–82.
[14] See generally di Cosmo, 'Qing colonial administration in inner Asia'.
[15] Perdue, *China Marches West*, pp. 522–3.   [16] Ibid.

trajectories in shaping their respective regions, and thereby conditioning the environment out of which Western dominance later arose.

Existing Explanations for the Decline of the Mughal Empire

A Brief Overview of Mughal Decline

In surveying the Mughals' decline, we must begin by recognizing distinctive features of Mughal succession practices that left the empire vulnerable to fragmentation. Consistent with their steppe forefathers' insistent egalitarianism, the Mughals firmly rejected principles of primogeniture.[17] Instead, they saw princely claimants to the throne as being equally eligible to rule, and believed that the best claimant would emerge triumphant from fraternal armed struggle following the death of the reigning emperor.[18] Mughal succession practices encouraged Timurid princes to cast a wide net for allies on the empire's volatile marchlands, as they cultivated constituencies to support their bid for power.[19] In this way, the lead-up to succession struggles propelled the empire's continuous territorial expansion.[20] It also enabled princely claimants to hone their skills in diplomacy and governance in their own fiefdoms – an apprenticeship of sorts for the greater responsibilities of imperial rule.[21] Summed up in a suitably sanguinary Persian aphorism – 'Either the throne or the tomb'[22] – the Darwinian logic of Mughal succession finally presumed that only the strongest and most ruthless prince would rise to absolute power, providing the best guarantee for the empire's security and prosperity.

The Mughals were not alone in embracing bloody meritocracy over firstborn privilege to manage imperial succession. But unlike contemporaries such as the Ottoman and the Safavid dynasties, which eventually instituted more ordered rules of succession,[23] the Mughals held fast to determining succession on the battlefield. Mughal court politics thus remained marked by lethal struggles for power, justified on grounds of fraternal egalitarianism and meritocratic pragmatism. Despite norms prohibiting it, even princely rebellion against the reigning emperor was not uncommon. Even against this backdrop, however, Aurangzeb's ouster and

---

[17] Balabanlilar, *Imperial Identity in the Mughal Empire*, p. 139.   [18] Ibid.

[19] M. D. Faruqi, *The Princes of the Mughal Empire, 1504–1719* (Cambridge: Cambridge University Press, 2012), p. 2.

[20] Ibid., p. 9.   [21] Ibid., p. 10.

[22] Cited in M. D. Faruqi, 'At empire's end: The Nizam, Hyderabad, and eighteenth-century India', *Modern Asian Studies*, 43(1) (2009), 10.

[23] Dale, *The Muslim Empires of the Ottomans, Safavids, and Mughals*, p. 271.

imprisonment of his father Shah Jahan in 1658 was unprecedented.[24] During Aurangzeb's near fifty-year reign, the empire reached its largest territorial extent. But the traumatic circumstances of Aurangzeb's rise troubled the early years of his reign, nudging him to adopt an increasingly narrow Islamic legitimizing ideology to rule over an ever more diverse empire.[25] Mindful of the precedent he had set, Aurangzeb also remained hypervigilant against possible challenges from his sons – a consideration which would prove crucial in shaping Aurangzeb's approach to rule, and with it, the empire's subsequent trajectory.[26]

Piety and conquest stand out as the two master themes of Aurangzeb's rule. Turning first to considerations of piety, both Aurangzeb's champions and his critics stressed his religious dedication as an orthodox Hanafi Muslim, both personally and in his capacity as emperor. In contrast to his great-grandfather Akbar's famed syncretism, under Aurangzeb, '[i]ncreasingly, the political culture of the empire would be defined in exclusive Muslim terms'.[27] Given that he had violated both the Sharia and norms of filial piety in deposing his father, Aurangzeb was quick to signal his Islamic credentials to relevant constituencies both inside the empire and beyond.[28] Accordingly, Aurangzeb bestowed lavish gifts on Sharif Zaid, ruler of Mecca and Medina, to win international recognition of his right to rule.[29]

Having justified his war against his more religiously tolerant older brother as necessary to 'uproot the bramble of idolatry and infidelity from the realm of Islam',[30] Aurangzeb worked hard to recast the empire on a more Islamic basis. This imperative prompted him to impose a range of discriminatory measures against non-Muslim subjects, ranging from pilgrimage taxes through to the reintroduction of the *jizya*.[31] Aurangzeb furthermore mandated the destruction of several major Hindu temples, as well as endorsing policies of preferment for Islamic candidates in local succession disputes, and for recruitment into the imperial bureaucracy.[32] While innocent of the notorious slander of having banned music within the empire, Aurangzeb did cease the emperor's traditional patronage of Hindustani musicians at court, while also slashing investments in the monumental architecture for

---

[24] Truschke, *Aurangzeb*, pp. 43–4.
[25] On Aurangzeb's public piety being motivated in part out of a desire to whitewash the controversial circumstances of his succession, see Asher and Talbot, *India Before Europe*, p. 227.
[26] Faruqi, *The Princes of the Mughal Empire*, p. 274.
[27] Richards, *The Mughal Empire*, p. 172.   [28] Ibid.   [29] Ibid.   [30] Ibid., p. 164.
[31] See generally Chandra, 'Jizya and the state in India'.
[32] Asher and Talbot, *India Before Europe*, p. 231.

which the Mughals were famous.[33] These efforts formed part of a broader effort to partially dismantle the syncretic culture Akbar and his successors had nurtured, in favour of an ascetic courtly ethos more appropriate for a pious Islamic ruler.

Besides recasting the Mughals' ruling ideology on more firmly Islamic lines, Aurangzeb's reign was also defined by continuous territorial expansion, most notably in the Deccan. Having honed his skills as commander and administrator during Shah Jahan's efforts to subdue the Deccan, Aurangzeb was familiar with the difficulties the frontier region posed for would-be conquerors. Nevertheless, Aurangzeb spent most of the latter part of his rule campaigning there, and unsuccessfully seeking to incorporate regional polities into the empire. In addition to maintaining the Mughals' longstanding policy of seeking to extend their southern frontier, Aurangzeb was also drawn into the Deccan once his rebellious son Akbar fled there following his failed ouster of his father.[34]

While Aurangzeb eventually subdued his son, and repeatedly bested local rulers on the battlefield, the Deccan proved a quagmire, where an enduring political victory remained elusive. Indeed, despite ongoing debate among historians regarding the causes of Mughal decline, there remains general agreement on the catalytic role of the Deccan wars in driving this process. The Deccan wars saw in the Maratha confederacy the emergence of a dynamic and highly decentralized new polity, which proved a rallying point for many Hindus unreconciled to Aurangzeb's rule.[35] The Marathas' decentralized political structure, their military organization around irregular light cavalry and their preference for guerrilla warfare over pitched battle made them extremely difficult for the slow-moving Mughal armies to defeat.[36] Additionally, the vast insecurity that Maratha raiding generated meanwhile corroded public order and disrupted local commerce and agriculture.[37] Coupled with the great economic costs of continuous campaigning, this additional disruption undermined the Mughal Empire's fiscal strength. Aurangzeb demanded escalating military and financial contributions from subordinate nobles, at a time when the rewards of imperial service seemed increasingly tenuous.[38]

Facing an unwinnable war that increasingly monopolized the emperor's attention, Mughal nobles and regional grandees increasingly hoarded

---

[33] See generally K. B. Brown, 'Did Aurangzeb ban music? Questions for the historiography of his reign', *Modern Asian Studies*, 41(1) (2007), 77–120.

[34] Fisher, *A Short History of the Mughal Empire*, pp. 198–9.

[35] See generally S. Gordon, *The Marathas, 1600–1818* (Cambridge: Cambridge University Press, 1993).

[36] Asher and Talbot, *India Before Europe*, p. 237.

[37] Richards, *The Mughal Empire*, p. 245.

[38] Asher and Talbot, *India Before Europe*, p. 236.

imperial revenues as they consolidated their own local alliances, and hedged against the violence that would inevitably come upon the ageing emperor's death.[39] Aurangzeb had meanwhile sought to politically neuter his sons to prevent further challenges to his rule. He had done so mainly by denying them the opportunities for military command and experience in government that had until then constituted a necessary apprenticeship for imperial aspirants.[40] As a result, when Aurangzeb died in 1707 at the age of eighty-nine, he left no strong and experienced potential heirs to succeed him. The inevitable wars of succession that followed predictably failed to produce rulers as capable as preceding Mughal emperors, with the Mughal court steadily descending into factional intrigue thereafter. This weakness in the centre – coupled with accelerating ethnic and religious polarization and military and fiscal decentralization – paved the way for the Mughals' relatively rapid subsequent decline.

Existing Explanations for Mughal Decline

Why did the Mughal Empire decline so swiftly and spectacularly following Aurangzeb's death? Dominant explanations for the empire's weakening typically cleave to two models. These stress respectively the priority of imperial overstretch and agrarian-fiscal crisis, versus top-down religious polarization and a crisis of imperial legitimacy, to explain Mughal disintegration.

Marxist historians and political scientists have long attributed Mughal India's decline mainly to fiscal crisis, arising from the intersection of geopolitical pressures with the institutional imperfections of the empire's revenue system.[41] Proponents of this view argue that the Mughal revenue system contained potentially fatal tensions, which the pressures of the Deccan campaigns eventually exposed. Recall that the *mansabdari* system sought to avoid the centrifugal tendencies endemic in feudal systems of hereditary tenure. By periodically circulating *mansabdars* throughout different land assignments, the Mughals aimed to prevent their service nobility from consolidating a permanent power base within any particular territory.[42] Instead, *mansabdars* were temporarily assigned territories,

---

[39] Sana, 'Was there an agrarian crisis in Mughal north India', 20.

[40] Faruqi, *The Princes of the Mughal Empire*, p. 274.

[41] See for example I. Habib, *The Agrarian System of Mughal India, 1556–1707* (Oxford: Oxford University Press, 1963); and more recently the discussion of Mughal decline in Anievas and Nişancioğlu, 'How did the West usurp the rest?', 34–67.

[42] R. D'Souza, 'Crisis before the fall: Some speculations on the decline of the Ottomans, Safavids and Mughals', *Social Scientist*, 30(9–10) (2002), 10.

from which they were expected to raise an allotted number of military forces to support the empire.[43]

The *mansabdari* system worked well for the first century of its operation. The system not only constrained its warrior nobility from becoming too independently powerful. It also broadened their geographical and social horizons by mandating periods of service and administration outside nobles' original localities.[44] In this way, more than simply meeting the empire's fiscal and military needs, it also aided aristocratic elites' socialization into an empire-wide imperial service culture.[45] These benefits aside, the Mughal revenue system also embodied a dangerous tension between the needs of the empire as a whole, versus the short-term interests of individual *mansabdars*. From the emperor's vantage point, the imperatives of productivity and sustainability were paramount for territorial administration. Rather than subjecting the peasantry to ruinous taxation, the empire's fiscal and military needs were best met through more moderate exactions.[46] This would encourage greater agricultural productivity and commercial dynamism over time, thereby maximizing the surplus from which the Mughals could generate military power.[47] By contrast, individual *mansabdars* confronted different incentives. As they were only temporarily assigned to particular territories, *mansabdars* were tempted to enrich themselves by maximizing short-term revenue extraction, regardless of long-term considerations of productivity or sustainability.[48]

This latent misalignment of incentives between emperor and nobility was manageable during the empire's ascendant phase. This is because the long-term prospect of promotion or demotion within the *mansabdari* system worked as a powerful check on nobles' short-term temptations to engage in ruinous taxation. For Marxist analysts of Mughal decline, however, the empire's over-extension into the Deccan brought the revenue system's contradictions to the fore. Specifically, they argue that increased imperial revenue demands to finance Aurangzeb's wars triggered a downward spiral of predatory taxation, peasant rebellion, military-fiscal atrophy and political disintegration.[49] As the costs of wars of conquest increased relative to the often negligible returns of territorial expansion, the empire demanded greater revenue and larger military contributions from its *mansabdars*.[50] This squeezed the service nobility, encouraging them to abandon any earlier restraints that had previously moderated their taxation of peasant agriculture. The popular distress that

[43] Ibid.   [44] Subrahmanyam, 'A tale of three empires', 83.   [45] Ibid.
[46] D'Souza, 'Crisis before the fall', 11–12.   [47] Ibid.   [48] Ibid., p. 12.
[49] See for example Habib, *The Agrarian System of Mughal India*, pp. 367–8.
[50] Anievas and Nişancioğlu, *How the West Came to Rule*, p. 268.

rapacious taxation engendered then supposedly induced a larger agrarian crisis in the Mughal economy, marked by widespread peasant flight and rebellion.[51] This crisis – which was aggravated by the already pronounced commercial disruption induced by the Deccan campaigns – fatally undermined the empire's economic foundations, eventually crippling the centre's capacity to project power and deter elite defection throughout the subcontinent.[52]

Marxist interpretations of Mughal decline have been criticized on multiple fronts. Pointing to evidence of sustained commercial dynamism and agricultural growth in the late seventeenth and early eighteenth centuries, critics have questioned either the existence or magnitude of widespread agrarian crisis within the late Mughal economy.[53] Others have meanwhile challenged the supposedly deterministic causal nexus linking war-fighting, revenue extraction and peasant rebellion. John Richards thus argues that conscious policy choices – rather than flaws inherent to its revenue system – best explain Mughal decline.[54] Specifically, he posits that Aurangzeb's decision to hoard newly conquered territories in the Deccan as crown lands – rather than assigning them to local *mansabdars* – was critical in starving intermediaries of the resources they needed to preserve order on the frontier.[55] This mistake was supposedly symptomatic of Aurangzeb's larger failure to integrate diverse local leaders into his expanding empire.[56]

Besides Marxist interpretations, the literature on Mughal decline has also historically been dominated by accounts stressing the fatal impact of Aurangzeb's supposed religious fanaticism on the empire's constitution.[57] The Mughal Empire was alone of the great early modern Islamic 'gunpowder empires' in being a Muslim-minority regime. Consequently, the emperor's conciliation of local intermediaries, through adherence to policies of religious accommodation and toleration, was especially critical for the empire's internal stability and ongoing expansion. Through this lens, Aurangzeb's rejection of Akbar-style syncretism for Sunni orthodoxy wrecked the legitimating formula that had previously held the Mughal Empire together. In cleaving to a more exclusively Sunni Islamic conception of empire, Aurangzeb weakened the ties of loyalty that had tethered critical non-Muslim imperial constituencies, such as the Rajput warrior

---

[51] Ibid.   [52] Ibid.
[53] S. Alavi (ed.), *The Eighteenth Century in India* (Oxford: Oxford University Press, 2002), pp. 1–56.
[54] Richards, 'The imperial crisis in the Deccan', 239.   [55] Ibid.   [56] Ibid., p. 256.
[57] Though now long since discredited, Jadunath Sarkar's biography of Aurangzeb remains a seminal statement of this position. See J. Sarkar, *A Short History of Aurangzib* (London: Orient Longman, 2009).

lineages, into the Mughal order.[58] Besides alienating old allies, scholars have also blamed Aurangzeb's orthodoxy for his failure to conciliate the Hindu Marathas to Mughal dominance, preventing him from pacifying the Deccan.[59] Elsewhere within the empire, the coterminous consolidation of an increasingly militant and territorialized Sikh identity appears to at least partially corroborate claims that Aurangzeb's more narrowly Islamic conception of empire estranged and energized imperial subjects besides Hindus, further weakening the Mughal order.[60]

Claims that Aurangzeb's abandonment of syncretism was primary in undermining the Mughal Empire have much to commend them. In particular, this approach acknowledges that the late Mughal imperial crisis was not confined to the Deccan, and that Aurangzeb's empire was weakened by a succession of rebellions from multiple imperial constituencies right across the empire, rather than being confined to southern India and the Marathas alone. Nevertheless, several deficiencies in this position demand modification. First, such accounts have traditionally exaggerated Aurangzeb's zealotry, and overstated the importance of personality over politics in shaping his approach to rule.[61] To correct this bias, a consideration of the pragmatic political imperatives that compelled Aurangzeb to embrace a more Islamic idea of empire is necessary to understand Mughal decline. Second, explanations stressing religious polarization as the cause of Mughal decline run the risk of imposing current understandings of communal identity onto the past.[62] This carries the danger of distorting our appreciation of how actors perceived, negotiated and mobilized these collective identities when pursuing their political objectives. We must be especially mindful to avoid reifying categories of identity – most notably the Hindu-Muslim binary – that were at the time more fluid, permeable, contested and internally diverse. Third and most importantly, existing explanations for Mughal decline remain underspecified in teasing out the causal mechanisms linking religious chauvinism to imperial fragmentation.

The demonization of Aurangzeb – in British imperial as well as Indian nationalist historiography – has had the unfortunate consequence of

---

[58] Richards, *The Mughal Empire*, pp. 183–4.

[59] See for example Gordon, *The Marathas*, p. 79.

[60] J. S. Grewal, *The Sikhs of the Punjab* (Cambridge: Cambridge University Press, 1991), p.72.

[61] On this score, Audrey Truschke's excellent biography of Aurangzeb constitutes a powerful rejoinder to earlier type-castings of Aurangzeb as a one-dimensional Islamic zealot. See generally Truschke, *Aurangzeb*.

[62] On the dangers of projecting back contemporary understandings of communal identity onto the pre-colonial past, see generally C. A. Bayly, 'The pre-history of "communalism"? Religious conflict in India, 1700–1860', *Modern Asian Studies*, 19(2) (1985), 177–203.

personalizing the causes of Mughal ruin. Conversely, the account I advance in the following section remedies this defect by focusing on the institutional dimensions of Mughal crisis. In particular, it teases out the specific ways that changing imperial conceptions of legitimacy undermined the social ties linking the emperor to his intermediaries, paving the way for the empire's decentralization and disintegration following Aurangzeb's death.

The Decline of the Mughal Empire: An Alternative Explanation

To understand the root causes of Mughal decline, we must first revisit the sources of their success. As a numerically tiny war-band originating from beyond Hindustan, the Mughals won their empire because of their great skill in mobilizing diverse multi-ethnic coalitions during their conquest campaigns. Second, the Mughals solidified their rule by integrating local intermediaries into an even more heterogeneous ruling elite as the empire expanded and consolidated during Akbar's reign. We have seen that Akbar's development of a syncretic legitimizing ideology (*suhl I kul*: universal reconciliation) was critical to this success. In concentrating supreme power within the body of the emperor, Akbar neutralized the *ulemas*' claims to supremacy in Islamic jurisprudence, while also taming the egalitarianism within the Timurid elite that had condemned previous steppe dynasties to rapid disintegration.[63] Akbar's sponsorship of an incorporative and syncretic ethic of rule manifested itself in highly ritualized practices of gift exchange and investiture, reflecting 'a highly embodied notion of sacrality' centred on the body of the emperor.[64] These practices were undertaken in a mobile imperial court that frequently circulated throughout the empire.[65] And they provided the key means through which the empire's warrior elites were socialized into conformity with a common Indo-Persian culture, and partially pacified through induction into a cosmopolitan imperial service elite.

The Mughal Empire therefore depended on inclusivity as the basis of its success. This dependence only increased as successive waves of conquest merely added to the empire's internal diversity. Despite its centrality to the Mughals' success, however, incorporative syncretism constituted only one vision of order among several. Hegemonic though it was for the century following Akbar's ascent, Mughal syncretism

---

[63] A. Ahmed, 'The role of *ulema* in Indo-Muslim history', *Studia Islamica*, 31 (1970), 6–7.

[64] A. A. Moin, *Islam and the Millennium: Sacred kingship and popular imagination in early modern India and Iran* (PhD diss., University of Michigan, 2010), p. 210.

[65] Gommans, 'Warhorse and post-nomadic empire in Asia', 14–15.

competed with more particularistic conceptions of empire. Most notably, sections of the Mughal court and their *ulema* supporters throughout the empire favoured more narrowly legalistic Sunni Islamic imperial ideas – ideas that would prove highly influential in shaping Aurangzeb's conception and practice of imperial rule.[66]

Historians and polemicists have made much of Aurangzeb's personal piety in explaining his abandonment of Mughal syncretism. But the practical challenges of consolidating political power provide a more plausible basis for explaining Aurangzeb's sectarian turn. In overthrowing and imprisoning his father, Aurangzeb violated norms of filial piety, as well as Islamic imperatives that enjoined submission to authority – even to a tyrannical ruler – as being ethically superior to rebellion (*fitna*).[67] In the war of succession that brought him to power, Aurangzeb was moreover forced to fight his three brothers for the throne. These rivals included Dara Shukoh, Shah Jahan's favoured successor.[68] The favourite of most Mughal courtiers, Prince Dara was also a conspicuous champion of Mughal syncretism.[69] He therefore presented a formidable ideological as well as political and military threat to Aurangzeb's ambitions.

In legitimizing his seizure of power, Aurangzeb thus had to excuse his rebellion against his father, as well as neutralize the appeal of his most threatening fraternal rival. Though it undoubtedly dovetailed neatly with his personal religious convictions, Aurangzeb's embrace of Sunni Islamic sectarianism crucially served both of these political imperatives.[70] In his generous patronage of Mecca and Medina, as well as his enforcement of Islamic orthodoxy within his empire, Aurangzeb did much to prove his credentials as a legitimate Muslim ruler.[71] More importantly and enduringly, Aurangzeb took the unusual step of delegitimizing Prince Dara's faction by accusing, trying and eventually executing his brother on the charge of apostasy.[72] In so positioning himself as Islam's champion and the scourge of apostasy, Aurangzeb thus tied the legitimacy of his reign to the cause of Sunni orthodoxy. This legitimation strategy would prove enduring. Indeed, Aurangzeb doubled down on it decades later, when his more liberal son Akbar challenged him for the throne, and even when this policy inevitably strained relations with important non-Muslim clients and collaborators such as the Rajput kings, which had long been crucial

---

[66] On Aurangzeb's early collaboration with orthodox Sunni *ulema* to suppress heterodox Islamic sects in the strategically vital province of Gujarat, see S. Sheikh, 'Aurangzeb as seen from Gujarat: Shi'i and millenarian challenges to Mughal sovereignty', *Journal of the Royal Asiatic Society*, 28(3) (2018), 566.
[67] Richards, *The Mughal Empire*, p. 172.   [68] Ibid., p. 151.   [69] Ibid., p. 152.
[70] Asher and Talbot, *India Before Europe*, p. 227.
[71] Fisher, *A Short History of the Mughal Empire*, p. 188.
[72] Richards, *The Mughal Empire*, p. 161.

lynchpins of Mughal power.[73] Indeed, Aurangzeb's shift towards a more sectarian mode of legitimation would prove supremely consequential in shaping the dynamics of contention between the emperor and local inter- mediaries, undermining the empire's integrity in three ways that hastened its decline.

Aurangzeb's sectarian turn weakened the empire first because it hol- lowed out the empire's centre, specifically by diminishing the Mughal court's status as a focal point for elite socialization into a common syn- cretic service culture. Though they played an outsize role within the empire, the *mansabdari* elite constituted a tiny portion of its population.[74] Historian Michael Pearson estimates that the *mansabdars* during Aurangzeb's time numbered at a maximum 8,000, with a true figure for the 'core Mughal nobility' closer to 1,000.[75] Linked directly to the emperor through dense webs of patronage, these nobles '*were* the empire ... the only people in whom it was possible that the concept of the Mughal Empire outweighed primordial attachments'.[76]

Given their centrality to the empire, the emperor's effectiveness as a ruler rested on his ability to sustain their loyalty, and keep them tightly integrated within an overarching trans-local Mughal politico-cultural order. The Mughal elite's great heterogeneity merely reinforced this imperative. In this context, Mughal syncretism formed the ideological glue binding the nobility together as a cohesive ruling service elite. Aurangzeb's sectarianism thus weakened the empire first because it marked an abandonment of the legitimating formula that had formerly sustained elites' attachments to both the emperor and the larger Mughal imperial enterprise.

Mughal syncretism was articulated through a distinct Indo-Persian high culture, which was spread among the empire's elite through rituals centred on the imperial court, and on the body of the emperor in particu- lar. Following Aurangzeb's embrace of Islamic orthodoxy, however, imperial sponsorship of Indo-Persian high culture drastically declined. As part of this ideological renovation, Aurangzeb downplayed the Mughals' traditional emphasis on the emperor's semi-divine character, and charismatic status as the great reconciler binding the empire's other- wise disparate communities together.[77] Instead, Aurangzeb favoured more traditionally Islamic conceptions of imperial authority. These con- ceptions invested the emperor with less independent charismatic author- ity, instead grounding his legitimacy on his status as a ruler righteously

[73] Ibid., pp. 183–4.
[74] M. N. Pearson, 'Shivaji and the decline of the Mughal Empire', *Journal of Asian Studies*, 35(2) (1976), 223–4.
[75] Ibid.   [76] Ibid., p. 223.   [77] Sheikh, 'Aurangzeb as seen from Gujarat', 559.

governing in accordance with the precepts of Islam.[78] Naturally, this conception of legitimacy had limited appeal among the largely non-Muslim *mansabdari* elite, and Aurangzeb's growing reliance on it frayed the ties of fealty linking him to his most important collaborators.

In challenging the Mughal Empire's ideological basis, Aurangzeb inadvertently diminished the authority of the imperial office. Indeed, in abandoning broadly accepted conceptions of imperial authority for more orthodox Islamic alternatives, Aurangzeb 'was effectively sawing off the branch on which he sat, for his authority rested on being a sacred king'.[79] The largely absentee character of Aurangzeb's rule in the empire's northern heartland compounded this error. For much of his rule, Aurangzeb was thoroughly preoccupied with personally leading campaigns to suppress the Deccan insurgency. As the emperor's court travelled with him, this meant that much of the personal contact and ritual reaffirmation of loyalties that had sustained the emperor's relations with the nobility weakened. At the empire's height, the imperial court had been mainly based in great cities such as Delhi or Agra, and had been the primary focal point for elite socialization. But under the pressure of continuous war in the Deccan, the Mughal court partially reverted to its origins, as a mobile armed camp rather than a site for inculcating warrior elites into a shared ethic of imperial service.[80] This return to a more permanently peripatetic form of rule – and the emperor's relocation to a war-torn frontier far from most of the empire's great cities – was profoundly corrosive of the empire's integrity. For it effectively robbed the empire of the chief forum where its elites could perform the rituals of deference affirming the emperor's authority, thereby jeopardizing the empire's very viability as a political community.[81]

Besides corroding elite solidarity, a second key way in which Aurangzeb's sectarianism weakened the empire lay in the difficulties it presented for absorbing and integrating newly conquered territories into the empire. Historians agree on the Deccan campaigns' centrality in sapping the Mughal Empire's strength. But it is essential that we examine the precise nature of Aurangzeb's failures in the Deccan to understand how the Deccan wars came to be such a debilitating drain on the empire.

The rise of the Marathas under Shivaji and his successors is rightly seen as a key contributor to the Mughal Empire's decay. With their reliance on

---

[78] Ibid.   [79] Ibid.

[80] Gommans estimates that Aurangzeb spent about 35 per cent of his rule in circulation throughout the empire, roughly equivalent to that of his predecessors. He nevertheless notes that this circulation was mainly concentrated in the second half of Aurangzeb's rule, contributing strongly to the centrifugal dynamics jeopardizing the empire during this time. See Gommans, *Mughal Warfare*, pp. 101–3.

[81] Ibid., p. 103.

light irregular cavalry, alongside the defensive advantages they enjoyed in the widely dispersed networks of mountain forts that pock-marked the Deccan, the Marathas constituted a formidably effective insurgent threat to Mughal dominance.[82] Later, once the Mughal Empire had faded, the Marathas also emerged as arguably India's most potent indigenous polity, and the last major threat to the EIC's empire-building by the early nineteenth century.[83] But during Aurangzeb's time, the Mughals repeatedly bested the Marathas in battle. Despite humiliating and politically demoralizing Maratha assaults on key Mughal cities (including two assaults on Surat, the empire's foremost port city), the Marathas at no time posed an existential military threat to the Mughal Empire.[84] Instead, the threat they posed was more insidious, in the form of the pervasive insecurity they inflicted on the empire's southern frontier. This insecurity in turn reflected Aurangzeb's political failures to subdue the Marathas politically, by integrating their defeated leaders into the Mughal Empire. And once again, this failure importantly derived in part from Aurangzeb's more narrowly sectarian vision of empire, which alienated the very intermediaries he would have needed to consolidate a favourable peace in the Deccan.

Historically, the Mughals had proved exceptionally adept at inducing culturally dissimilar local elites into imperial service following their defeat. As we saw in earlier chapters, one of Akbar's greatest achievements was his incorporation of Rajput chieftains into the Mughal polity. Rather than relying simply on military strength to overawe them, Akbar had assiduously cultivated ties with the Rajputs to draw them into the Mughal web. A combination of marital diplomacy and ideological innovation, including customized appeals to the Rajputs' dharma as warrior elites, helped win over a key element of the Rajput nobility.[85] This enabled them to reconcile imperial service with the demands of their warrior identity, aiding their induction as vital pillars of the Mughal service elite.[86]

The contrast with Aurangzeb's failure to tie Maratha and other Deccani elites to the Mughal Empire could not be more stark. This failure was not for want of providing material inducements to these potential partners. On the contrary, Aurangzeb employed the well-practiced Mughal technique of bringing local collaborators into the *mansabdari*

---

[82] Gordon, *The Marathas*, p. 75.
[83] R. G. S. Cooper, *The Anglo-Maratha Campaigns and the Contest for India: The struggle for control of the South Asian military economy* (Cambridge: Cambridge University Press, 2003), p. 3.
[84] Gordon, *The Marathas*, p. 71.
[85] See for example Richards, *The Mughal Empire*, pp. 20–3.   [86] Ibid.

system of privilege.[87] But he failed to effectively incorporate Deccani elites ideologically into the empire. On this point, historian John Richards observes: 'the failure of the empire of the south (and perhaps of the north) lay in the inability of Aurangzeb to initiate or continue this process of assimilation of the rural aristocracies'.[88]

Aurangzeb's failures on this front were most conspicuous in his mishandling of Shivaji, the father of the Maratha polity. In May 1666, Shivaji and his entourage proceeded to Agra to seek a peace with the emperor. At this time, Shivaji's polity was still in its most primitive and protean form, and Aurangzeb's rule had yet to be diverted by the decades-long anti-Maratha wars that were to dominate the last half of his reign. Shiavji's fortunes were moreover at a low ebb.[89] These conditions ostensibly favoured a Mughal policy of post-conquest conciliation – 'to beat enemies and then buy them', consistent with the Mughal tradition of subduing adversaries through incorporation.[90] Aurangzeb was moreover predisposed to seek an accommodation with Shivaji – albeit not on terms sufficiently generous that Shivaji was likely to accept.[91] But Aurangzeb squandered his first (and as it turned out, only realistic) opportunity to bring Shivaji into the Mughal fold. This was in part because of the emperor's condescension to a leader he saw as little more than a rebel feudal lord, a 'mountain rat' whose pretensions towards kingship Aurangzeb viewed with contempt.[92] But it was also because of the 'cultural gulf' between the Mughal court and the Marathas – a gulf exacerbated by Aurangzeb's turn towards sectarianism.[93]

Following a disastrous reception at Aurangzeb's court – in which he was treated as a low-born noble and deliberately humiliated by the emperor – Shivaji contrived his escape from Agra. He then resumed his predations against Mughal territories. Following a brief rapprochement, in June 1674 Shivaji took the extraordinary step of having himself crowned as an independent Hindu monarch, having contrived a legitimating genealogy tracing his ancestry back to a line of Rajput warriors that had migrated to Maharashtra in the thirteenth century.[94] In doing so, Shivaji created 'a militantly Hindu monarchy', as well as violently asserting his independence of both the Mughal emperor and of Indo-Muslim political culture and authority more generally.[95] Subsequent generations of Hindu Indian nationalists have undeniably mischaracterized Shivaji's state-building as proto-nationalist.[96] This

---

[87] Pearson, 'Shivaji and the decline of the Mughal Empire', 229.
[88] Richards, 'The imperial crisis in the Deccan', 256.
[89] Pearson, 'Shivaji and the decline of the Mughal Empire', 229.   [90] Ibid.   [91] Ibid.
[92] Gordon, *The Marathas*, p. 84.   [93] Ibid., p. 79.   [94] Ibid., p. 88.
[95] Richards, *The Mughal Empire*, p. 213.   [96] Gordon, *The Marathas*, p. 80.

caveat aside, Shivaji's coronation was profoundly consequential, for it marked the first time in generations that a regional ruler had effectively declared themselves independent – and positioned themselves as a competing point of authority – to the Mughal emperor.[97] In this respect, Shivaji's labours cemented the Marathas' estrangement from the Mughals, and dramatized the failure of the latter's efforts to integrate new intermediaries into the Mughal service elite.

Aurangzeb's mishandling of the Maratha leadership marked the single most serious failure to integrate newly conquered local elites into the Mughal Empire. But it was hardly exceptional. On the contrary, similar errors with other potential intermediaries compromised Aurangzeb's entire effort to subdue southern India. As Aurangzeb extended his empire further south from the empire's heartland in the northern Indo-Gangetic provinces, the distance between Mughal court culture and that of newly conquered territories grew. This made the task of assimilating intermediaries into the Mughal imperial project increasingly difficult.

Aurangzeb's attempt in 1688 to incorporate Pam Nayak, leader of the Bedars and ruler of a strategically important territory between Bijapur and Golconda, sharply illustrates these difficulties of assimilation. Though Aurangzeb inducted Pam Nayak into the *mansabdari* system at a high rank, other *mansabs* refused to countenance him as a peer.[98] This owed in part to his unfamiliarity with the urbane Indo-Persian court culture of the Mughal elite, as well as to established *mansabs'* more venal jealousies at the rank Aurangzeb had accorded him to bind him into the imperial system.[99] But in addition to these considerations, both Muslim and Hindu *mansabs* were contemptuous of Pam Nayak owing to 'a sense of ritual pollution and colour prejudice' towards their new ostensible colleague.[100] Contemporary sources derided Pam Nayak for his 'pot-black' and 'hideous' appearance, as well as ridiculing him for belonging to a tribe of 'indiscriminate carrion-eaters'.[101] Given this poor reception, it is unsurprising that the Bedar leadership were never effectively brought into the Mughal order, but developed as another inveterate insurgent enemy to the Timurid project of southern conquest.

The prejudices that stopped established Mughal elites from accepting Pam Nayak into the empire hint strongly that the Mughals' famed Indo-Persian syncretism was not infinitely elastic, and that the empire was perhaps inherently restricted in its ability to accommodate cultural diversity once it expanded beyond northern India. But even keeping these

---

[97] Richards, *The Mughal Empire*, p. 213.
[98] Richards, 'The imperial crisis in the Deccan', 245.   [99] Ibid.   [100] Ibid., p. 246.
[101] Ibid.

limits in mind, Aurangzeb's sectarianism further aggravated these limitations. John Richards thus notes that Pam Nayak's refusal to convert to Islam denied him the protection the emperor might otherwise have afforded him against the hostility of established *mansabs*.[102] More generally, as the empire expanded, Aurangzeb exerted meaningful pressure on defeated elites – Marathas, Bedars and others – to convert to Islam.[103] These pressures were rarely successful. But they did work to compound potential collaborators' estrangement from what they saw as an ideological as well as military assault. This in turn increased their resistance to Mughal expansion, made newly conquered territories ungovernable and fed into a growing insecurity that corroded the empire's ability to reliably project power and authority.

The final way in which Aurangzeb's sectarianism weakened the Mughal Empire lay in the fillip it provided to the consolidation of powerful new regional polities that harnessed popular religious movements in opposition to the empire. A conspicuous example of this was the consolidation and militarization of Sikhism during Aurangzeb's rule. The Sikh community had periodically suffered Mughal persecution from Jahangir's reign onwards, though more for political reasons than because of sectarian hostility.[104] Under Aurangzeb's reign, however, Mughal persecution of the Sikhs increased, and acquired a more overtly religious tincture. Concerned at the Sikhs' growing political influence in the Punjab, and enraged at reports of their efforts to convert Muslims to Sikhism, Aurangzeb pursued 'a relentless policy of repression' against the Sikhs.[105] This repression extended to the execution of the Sikhs' pre-eminent leader, Guru Tej Bahadur, after he had refused to accept Islam, as well as the demolition of Sikh Gurdwaras.[106] Guru Bahadur's martyrdom, and the desecration of Sikh places of worship, had the predictable effect of instilling in the Sikhs a fierce desire for vengeance in their subsequent relations with the Mughals.[107] This weakened the empire's grasp on the Punjab, one of its most fertile provinces, further sapping the Mughals' strength.

Beyond simply weakening the Mughals' control over the Punjab, however, Aurangzeb's persecution accelerated internal transformations in the Sikh community, which prefigured its emergence as a powerful regional polity in its own right following the Mughals' decline. Following a pattern

---

[102] Ibid.   [103] Ibid.
[104] Richards, *The Mughal Empire*, p. 98. See also Grewal, *The Sikhs of the Punjab*, p. 62.
[105] Bayly, 'The pre-history of "communalism"?', 188.
[106] Ibid. See also Grewal, *The Sikhs of the Punjab*, p. 72; and Richards, *The Mughal Empire*, p. 178.
[107] Bayly, 'The pre-history of "communalism"?', 199.

common throughout the empire, Punjab had seen a significant growth in agricultural productivity and trade under the *Pax Mughalica*.[108] Instability in this province under Aurangzeb's reign admittedly temporarily disrupted this prosperity.[109] But the secular growth of the Punjab laid the commercial foundations for Sikh state-building efforts as Mughal power waned. In the meantime, the social upheavals associated with Aurangzeb's reign provided propitious circumstances for the Sikhs to proselytize and expand their numbers.

Under the pressure of persecution, Guru Gobind Singh, Guru Bahadur's successor, meanwhile began concerted efforts to strengthen Sikh capacities for governance and self-defence. Thus in 1699, Guru Gobind Singh reorganized the Sikhs into a more centralized, militarized and egalitarian community. This reformation included the proscription of the *masands* (deputies), Sikh ministers who had formerly proselytized, ministered to the guru's followers and collected tithes for the community.[110] In their place, he insisted that all true Sikhs be directly subordinate to the guru's leadership. To cement this tie, the guru formulated a new baptismal ceremony (*khande ki pauhl*) to mark initiates' entry into the Sikh community.[111] This was accompanied by a range of new requirements (e.g., that initiates keep their hair unshorn, bear arms and adopt the name 'Singh') that together constituted a binding code of conduct (the *rahit*) which consolidated a far more coherent Sikh collective identity than before.[112] Perhaps most importantly, the guru organized initiates into the *Khalsa* (literally: 'pure'), an armed order of 'saint-soldiers' charged with both embodying Sikh spiritual virtues while defending Sikhs from their temporal enemies.[113] The establishment of the Order of the *Khalsa* not only 'visibly sharpened' Sikh identity.[114] It also forged the nucleus of a fighting force that would successfully repel Mughal and Afghan armies in the eighteenth century, and form the military foundation for the Sikh kingdom that later emerged under Ranjit Singh's leadership.[115]

The causes of Mughal decline were undoubtedly complex. Nevertheless, I have argued that a decisive driver of decline was Aurangzeb's abandonment of the Mughal model of syncretic incorporation that had formerly bound the empire's disparate fragments together.

---

[108] Grewal, *The Sikhs of the Punjab*, pp. 69–70.   [109] Ibid., p. 70.   [110] Ibid., p. 77.
[111] Ibid.   [112] Ibid.
[113] L. E. Fenech, 'The Khalsa and the Rahit' in P. Singh and L. E. Fenech (eds.), *The Oxford Handbook of Sikh Studies* (Oxford: Oxford University Press, 2014), p. 240.
[114] P. Singh, 'An overview of Sikh history' in P. Singh and L. E. Fenech (eds.), *Oxford Handbook of Sikh Studies* (Oxford: Oxford University Press, 2014), p. 26.
[115] Ibid., p. 27.

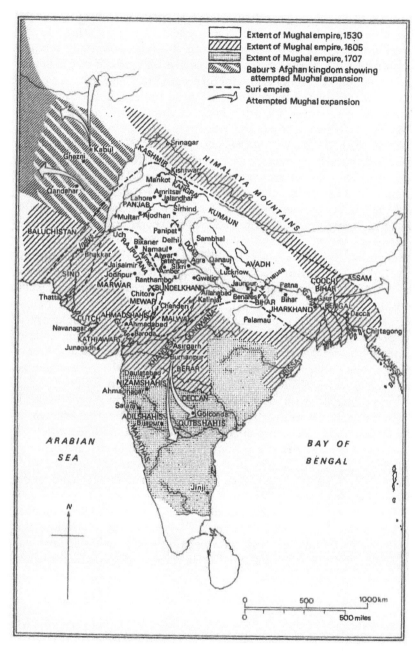

Map 5.1 The Mughal Empire at its greatest territorial extent
Source: John Richards, *The Mughal Empire* (Cambridge University Press, 1995), frontispiece.

In ditching syncretism for sectarianism, Aurangzeb diminished the Mughal court's acculturative function as a venue for socializing the empire's warrior elites into a common service culture. He also weakened the empire's capacity to absorb and integrate potential intermediaries from newly conquered territories into the Mughal elite. This effectively made these new conquests ungovernable, and ensured that Aurangzeb would be ensnared in unwinnable wars of pacification that drained the empire's fiscal strength, and corroded the emperor's authority. Religious persecution finally played an important role in driving counter-hegemonic projects of regional polity formation, as warlords and religious leaders from the Deccan to the Punjab selectively refashioned communal identities and hoarded military and economic power to resist Aurangzeb's sectarian turn.

That Aurangzeb's sectarianism was disastrous for the Mughal Empire is further evidenced by the fact that his immediate successors tried vainly to restore the old syncretic order, in a futile effort to reverse the damage Aurangzeb had done. Most notably, Aurangzeb's successors abolished the *jizya* in 1712–13, and then successfully resisted proposals for its reimposition in 1719.[116] The Mughals' syncretic vision of empire more-over continued to attract the loyalty of imperial elites such as Rajput nobles, at least until Nadir Shah's 1739 sack of Delhi confirmed the empire's *de facto* end as a viable supra-regional polity.[117] Indeed, so tenaciously appealing and powerful was the old Mughal vision of empire that even decades after the collapse of Mughal power, '[the] memory of the Great Emperors hung over north India in the eighteenth and nine-teenth centuries as the name and institutions of Imperial Rome domin-ated Christendom in the European Middle Ages'.[118] Across the breadth of the subcontinent, regional rulers meanwhile sought to imitate Mughal syncretism in their own state-building efforts, with many (including eventually the EIC) at least nominally swearing fealty as vassals to the Mughal emperor long after his power had ebbed away. From the mid-eighteenth century, however, the Mughals were spent as a real political force. With the empire practically dead by the mid-1700s, an exotic menagerie of indigenous and European polities struggled for supremacy. It would be out of this protean state system, still yoked under the nominal umbrella of a now-fictitious Mughal suzerainty, that the EIC would later emerge as the next victorious empire-builder in India.

---

[116] I. A. Khan, 'State in the Mughal India: Re-examining the myths of a counter-vision', *Social Scientist*, 29(1–2) (2001), 23.

[117] Ibid., p. 32.

[118] C. A. Bayly, *Rulers, Townsmen and Bazaars: North Indian society in the age of British expansion 1770–1870* (Oxford: Oxford University Press, 1983), p. 9.

Segregated Incorporation and the Consolidation and Expansion of Manchu Imperialism

In contrast to the Mughals, the Qing Empire went from strength to strength in the eighteenth century. Having stamped out the cinders of Ming loyalism on the mainland and crushed their last major rival in littoral East Asia (the Zheng confederacy), the Manchus then embarked on a series of largely successful conquest campaigns. These wars of conquest doubled the empire's size and amplified its already marked heterogeneity. At least as important, the Manchus extended their reach deep into the Eurasian steppe. There, they encircled and destroyed a rival steppe confederacy, the Zunghars, that had at one point begun to imitate the Manchus' model of multi-ethnic empire building.[119] By the end of the eighteenth century, while the Mughals had declined into irrelevance, the Manchus had confirmed their seemingly uncontested supremacy throughout eastern Eurasia.

Consistent with this book's larger argument, I maintain that the Manchus' success can be mainly credited to their successful management of cultural diversity. Specifically, the Manchus succeeded as conquerors because they managed to extend their system of segregated incorporation into new territories following battlefield victories. The Manchu model of ethnic governance, so crucial to binding together the motley coalition that had toppled the Ming Dynasty, proved elastic enough to also later encompass new intermediaries as the empire extended its reach into Tibet, Xinjiang and beyond. The Manchus' systematic cultivation of protégés in these territories in most cases laid the political foundations for durable collaboration and thus stable imperial rule. Meanwhile, the curation of customized idioms of legitimacy for each of these imperial segments bound local partners to the centre, while foreclosing the possibility of widespread anti-imperial mobilization between them.

In those rare instances where Manchu strategies of enticement and incorporation proved insufficient to achieve their aims, the Manchus lastly developed the logistical and power projection capabilities necessary to defeat insurgent threats to their rule, and pre-emptively break apart potential counter-hegemonic coalitions. We have seen how, when confronting a decentralized Maratha insurgency in the hilly terrain of the Deccan, the Mughals became ensnared in a decades-long quagmire.[120]

---

[119] See generally P. C. Perdue, 'Military mobilization in seventeenth and eighteenth-century China, Russia, and Mongolia', *Modern Asian Studies*, 30(4) (1996), 757–93.

[120] See generally Pearson, 'Shivaji and the decline of the Mughal Empire'; and Richards, 'The imperial crisis in the Deccan'.

The Manchus conversely undertook extensive logistical, military and ideological innovations to pre-emptively crush the Zunghar state-building project, prevailing over a potentially lethal asymmetric adversary, and effectively solving the 'steppe problem' that had plagued all previous dynasties.[121]

The discussion follows the same structure as my appraisal of the Mughals. I begin with a survey of the Manchus' trajectory from the late 1600s onwards, before proceeding to an explanation for their experience of imperial expansion. The chapter then concludes by reprising the argument, and considering the consequences of the Mughal-Manchu divergence for the trajectory of Western expansion in Asia from the late 1700s.

The Consolidation and Expansion of the 'Manchu Raj', 1683–1759

In 1683, the admiral Shi Lang, a defector from the Zheng Confederacy, spearheaded the Manchus' invasion and subjugation of Taiwan. With the destruction of the Zheng Confederacy, the Manchus confirmed their dominance throughout littoral East Asia, and extinguished a dangerous rival that had by dint of its stubborn survival sustained the hopes of remnant Ming loyalists on the mainland.[122] Coming in the aftermath of the War of the Three Feudatories (1673–81), which had consolidated the Manchus' hold on southern China, the capture of Taiwan closed the first era of Manchu conquest that had begun almost a century earlier in the Jurchen homeland. Under the dynamic leadership of the Qianlong emperor, however, the eighteenth century would see vast new conquests, and the consolidation of a hugely expanded empire that would eventually bequeath its prodigious territorial boundaries to the modern Chinese state.

Considering the Manchus' success in its totality, three achievements merit particularly close attention. These were: the successful maintenance of Manchu 'alien' rule over the empire they had wrested from the Ming Dynasty; the empire's extension to encompass huge new territories beyond its Sinic core; and the confirmation of Manchu unipolarity in eastern Eurasia, through the destruction of potential peer competitors, and the clearer demarcation of the empire's terrestrial and maritime boundaries.

Turning first to the Manchus' preservation of power, we must acknowledge the Manchu achievement of simply holding on to power following

---

[121] On the 'steppe problem' as a perennial challenge for China-based empire-builders, see O. Lattimore, 'Inner Asian frontiers: Chinese and Russian margins of expansion', *Journal of Economic History*, 7(1) (1947), 36.

[122] T. Andrade, *How Taiwan became Chinese: Dutch, Spanish and Han colonization in the seventeenth century* (New York: Columbia University Press, 2008), p. 260.

their victory over the Ming, and doing so in a way that preserved the Manchus' distinctiveness as a conquest elite. Throughout Eurasia generally and China in particular, the historical norm had been for barbarian dynasties from the steppe and forest frontiers to become rapidly assimilated into the sedentary societies they had conquered.[123] Within China especially, at the outset of Qing rule, the Confucian scholar-gentry had a strong historical basis for believing that they could play 'Greeks' to the Manchu 'Romans', 'civilizing' the latter through Sinicization until they became indistinguishable from their Chinese subjects.[124]

Confounding these expectations, the Manchus perfected their system of 'ethnic sovereignty',[125] and its accompanying model of segregated incorporation, over the first century of their rule. Recall that one of the Jurchen chieftains' earliest challenges was the forging and institutionalization of a pan-tribal 'Manchu' identity, and the extension of the resulting banner system to encompass Mongol and Han Chinese allies.[126] Coalition-building – first among the Jurchen and later with non-Manchu allies – formed the bedrock of the nascent Qing Empire. This process entailed navigating two potentially contradictory imperatives – winning the collaboration of non-Manchu intermediaries, while differentiating and elevating the Manchus as a separate and superior conquest elite.

Once they had won power, the Manchus remained hypervigilant to the threat of Sinicization. This hypervigilance took shape in numerous policies aimed at preserving the 'Manchu way',[127] and sequestering and distinguishing the Manchu elite from imperial subjects. Manchu 'apartheid' thus saw the Manchus fortify themselves in walled garrisons in Beijing and other strategically located cities and towns, separate from the Chinese majority.[128] The Manchus also maintained a range of sumptuary laws and other embodied practices (e.g., Manchu women did not submit to foot-binding) to physically differentiate themselves from the non-Manchu majority.[129] Manchu men were admonished to maintain their 'manly virtue' by favouring horseback riding and archery over literary pursuits, and to be forever vigilant against the dangers of 'softening' associated with Han Chinese 'decadence'.[130] To guard against assimilation, the Manchus also worked hard to maintain the Manchu language,

---

[123] Lieberman, *Strange Parallels*, p. 591.   [124] Ibid.   [125] Elliott, *The Manchu Way*, p. 4.
[126] Mark Elliott, 'Ethnicity in the Qing Eight Banners', p. 29.
[127] Elliott, *The Manchu Way*, p. 8.
[128] Rawski, 'The Qing Empire during the Qianlong reign', p. 16.
[129] M. C. Elliott, 'Manchu widows and ethnicity in Qing China', *Comparative Studies in Society and History*, 41(1) (1999), 66.
[130] Ibid., p. 64.

which remained down to 1750 a 'security language for the rulers' that was often the sole medium for communication on sensitive military matters.[131] Finally, at the apex of imperial governance – the Grand Council – successive Qing rulers ensured that Manchus rather than Han Chinese remained in the majority, at least for most of the Qianlong emperor's reign.[132]

Notwithstanding their precautions against Sinicization, the Manchus consolidated their power precisely because they were able to deftly balance 'ethnic' and 'cosmopolitan' modes of rulership.[133] The latter entailed a necessary embrace of Confucianism, and an accompanying mastery of Chinese language, culture and practices of rule and diplomacy. In courting the Chinese scholar-literati, the Manchus diligently 'studied the Confucian canon and patronized Chinese art and literature',[134] as well as embracing Confucian idioms of legitimate rule, centred on sacerdotal universal kingship. Internationally, the Manchus had meanwhile already browbeaten the Yi Dynasty in Korea – the Ming Dynasty's most loyal Confucian tributary – into sullen submission to Qing suzerainty even prior to conquering China.[135] Thereafter, for nearly the full duration of Qing rule, the Manchus maintained the Ming Dynasty's system of tributary diplomacy when interacting with Confucian monarchies, even while relying on a radically different parallel mixture of diplomatic and military expedients in their dealings with non-Confucian neighbours. The ensuing 'Confucian peace' not only stabilized the Qing Empire's borders with Confucian polities; rather, the public supplication and ritual tribute these neighbours rendered reinforced the Manchus' status and prestige, further strengthening their hold on power.[136]

Beyond maintaining their distinctiveness and their hold on power – impressive achievements in and of themselves – the Manchus also hugely expanded their empire's size and internal diversity. Under the Kangxi (1662–1722), Yongzheng (1723–35) and Qianlong (1736–95) emperors, the Manchus waged a series of wars of conquest that carved out an empire stretching 'from the Pacific Ocean to the gateway of Central Asia'.[137] During the reign of the Qianlong emperor in particular, 'a man obsessed

---

[131] Rawski, 'The Qing Empire during the Qianlong reign', p. 17. More generally, Peter Perdue observes of successive non-Han efforts to develop and preserve their own written scripts: 'The goal of writing Central Asian languages was not to become more Chinese, but to enforce the boundary [between Han Chinese and non-Han].' See Perdue, 'Military mobilization', 784.
[132] Ibid.   [133] Elliott, 'Manchu widows', 37.
[134] Rawski, 'The Qing Empire during the Qianlong reign', p. 16.
[135] See for example Lee, *China's Hegemony*, pp. 135–6.
[136] See generally ibid., chapter 5.
[137] Rawski, 'The Qing Empire during the Qianlong reign', p. 15.

by empire and the military power necessary to attain it',[138] the empire reached historically unprecedented dimensions. At its height, the Qing Empire encompassed not only the territories of today's People's Republic of China, but also Mongolia, the Ili Valley in present-day Kazakhstan, part of Khirghizia and large swathes of Siberia north of the Amur river.[139] The Qing Dynasty also marked the longest period in Chinese history during which one empire simultaneously ruled over both China and the Central Asian steppe.[140] This was a remarkable accomplishment, which contrasted with Sinic dynasties' historic inability to permanently control or contain predation from the steppe, and steppe dynasties' countervailing tendency to rapidly fragment, most often following the death of charismatic founders.

The Qing Dynasty's cultural heterogeneity correspondingly increased over the course of its prodigious territorial expansion. As they extended their reach beyond the 'core' eighteen provinces of Sinic China, the Manchus brought a diverse range of peoples – including Mongols, Tibetans, Uighur Muslims and others – under the umbrella of Qing rule. The Manchus' model of segregated incorporation proved elastic enough to accommodate and integrate diverse intermediaries from the empire's frontiers into a Qing-centred network of allegiances. This 'unification' of peoples within the 'one family' of the Qing Empire[141] contrasted significantly with Aurangzeb's failure to incorporate conquered elites from the Deccan and elsewhere, following his abandonment of the Mughals' model of syncretic incorporation. These contrasting experiences of accommodating cultural diversity over the course of imperial expansion constitute a key cause of the Manchu and Mughal empires' contrasting fates, which I engage in greater detail below.

In addition to maintaining their hold on power and significantly expanding their empire, the Manchus finally succeeded in either subordinating, containing, or eliminating potential peer competitors, ensuring the Qing Dynasty's unassailable supremacy in East and Central Asia. In littoral East Asia, Confucian monarchies either submitted to Qing suzerainty with varying degrees of enthusiasm (Korea and Vietnam), or alternatively withdrew into self-imposed diplomatic – though not necessarily commercial – seclusion (Japan).[142] To the Qing Empire's immediate

---

[138] J. Waley-Cohen, 'Changing spaces of empire in eighteenth century China' in N. di Cosmo and D. J. Wyatt (eds.), *Political Frontiers, Ethnic Boundaries and Human Geographies in Chinese History* (London: Routledge Curzon, 2003), p. 325.

[139] Perdue, 'Military mobilization', 759.   [140] Ibid.

[141] M. C. Elliott and N. Chia, 'The Qing hunt at Mulan' in R. W. Dunnell, M. C. Elliott, P. Foret and J. A. Millward (eds.), *New Qing Imperial History: The making of inner Asian empire at Qing Chengde* (London: Routledge, 2004), pp. 76–7.

[142] On the subtleties of Japan's policy of seclusion (*sakoku*) during the Qing Dynasty, see generally M. S. Laver, *The Sakoku Edicts and the Politics of Tokugawa Hegemony*

north, successive treaties (Nerchinsk in 1689 and Kiakhta in 1727) regulated trade and formally delimited the Manchus' border with tsarist Russia.[143] With a separate 'Confucian peace'[144] stabilizing its littoral frontier, and a wary accommodation securing its borders with Russia, the Qing Empire directed its energies towards neutralizing its last remaining threat – the emergence of a rival Mongol steppe polity, in the form of the Zunghar confederacy, to the empire's northwest.

The Zunghar confederacy's containment and destruction at one level signified the limits of Manchu capacities for incorporation. A succession of conflicts from the late seventeenth century failed to subdue the Zunghars, culminating in their total destruction and dispersal following their 1759 defeat in the last Manchu-Zunghar war. The Manchus' inability to integrate the Zunghars undeniably reveals the limits to even their formidable capacities for incorporation. From a world-historical standpoint, however, the Zunghars' defeat is significant in that it marked the end of a protracted era in which steppe and sedentary polities co-existed as 'equal, autonomous presences'.[145] Before the Zunghar wars – and indeed for most of their duration – steppe warriors could retreat into the vast interior of the Central Asia when confronting determined opposition from sedentary societies. The great size of the steppe and its mostly uncultivated nature historically ensured that sedentary forces' supply lines were overstretched before they could land a decisive blow on their enemies. Conversely, a cultural familiarity with the Mongols enabled the Manchus to employ 'divide and rule' strategies to disrupt and weaken steppe coalitions, reducing their threat to the Qing Empire. Even more significantly, the Manchus systematically cultivated a network of magazine stores, and encouraged the commercialization of agriculture in the empire's north-west, to provide the logistical means of overcoming the historic limits of sedentary imperial expansion.[146] These innovations eventually enabled the Qing to launch years-long expeditions into the northwest that 'exceeded the distance of Napoleon's march on Russia',[147] eventually enabling them to destroy the last of their enemies that they could otherwise neither absorb nor subdue.

(New York: Cambria Press, 2011). Japan was of course far from hermetically sealed from maritime East Asia or the wider world from this time, frequently relying on unorthodox partners such as the Zheng maritime confederacy to help mediate its engagement with the wider world. See for example X. Hang, 'The shogun's Chinese partners: The alliance between Tokugawa Japan and the Zheng family in seventeenth-century maritime East Asia', *Journal of Asian Studies*, 75(1) (2016), 111–36.

[143] Perdue, 'Military mobilization', 758.

[144] R. E. Kelly, 'A "Confucian long peace" in pre-Western East Asia?', *European Journal of International Relations*, 18(3) (2012), 407–30.

[145] Perdue, 'Military mobilization', 760.   [146] Ibid., pp. 777–9.   [147] Ibid., p. 763.

The preservation of Manchu hegemony over a Han Chinese majority that vastly outnumbered them; the incorporation of a diverse coalition of intermediaries from newly conquered territories; the destruction and dissolution of the Manchus' last remaining peer competitor – these constitute the foundational achievements that together upheld and prolonged the Qing Empire's unipolar dominance of eastern Eurasia well into the nineteenth century. It is towards a more sustained explanation of the sources of Manchu success that I now turn.

Explaining the Success of the Pax Manjurica, I: Reinventing Confucian Tradition for the Expanding Sinic Core

As previously established, the success of the Manchu imperial enterprise depended fundamentally on their capacity to exploit China Proper's immense agricultural and commercial wealth. This in turn demanded the cooperation of the Confucian scholar-gentry, both as civil administrators and in their capacity as the Han majority's political and cultural elite. A consideration of Confucianism's properties as a legitimating ideology is necessary for us to establish precisely how the Manchus were able to customize their claims to legitimacy, and so bind the scholar-gentry as collaborators and participants in the Manchu project.

Central to imperial Confucianism was the role of the emperor as the pivot linking the sacred and temporal worlds. For the scholar-gentry, the social and cosmic orders were inseparable from one another, and the emperor, as Son of Heaven, provided the necessary link between these two domains. The emperor's jurisdiction was universal, encompassing 'all under heaven' (*tianxia*), and his purpose was to promote a state of *ping* (understood as a condition of universal harmony) throughout his patrimony.[148] Consequently, the emperor's responsibilities entailed both spiritual as well as temporal functions. Besides the routine tasks of governance, such as preserving the peace and providing for his subjects' material welfare, the emperor was also expected to lead by moral example, and to perform the mystical rites (*li*) necessary to preserve a state of social and cosmic harmony.[149]

Confucianism thus rested on an immanent conception of the divine, investing supreme spiritual as well as temporal power in the office of an omni-competent emperor. It moreover embraced a pervasively paternalistic vision of social order. At the core of Confucianism was the patriarchal

---

[148] Chen, 'The Confucian view of world order', p. 28.

[149] Fairbank and Goldman, *China: A New History*, pp. 52–3. On the Manchus' appropriation and repurposing of *li* to rule a multi-ethnic empire, see generally M. Keliher, *The Manchu Transformation of Li: Ritual, politics, and law in the making of Qing China, 1631–1690* (PhD diss., Harvard University, 2015).

family, in which husbands dominated wives and children, their relations conceived as a divinely ordained system of bonds of asymmetric benevolence and obedience. The Confucian political order, moreover, was simply the Confucian familial order writ large. Accordingly, the emperor related to his subjects as a father to his children and a husband to his wife, as a benevolent patriarch to whom subjects owed unquestioning obedience.[150] This pattern of nested hierarchies repeated itself internationally, in the tributary diplomacy system successive Chinese emperors maintained with their Confucian satellites.

Finally, and most importantly, Confucianism stressed civilizational identity over imagined ties of consanguinity as the basis of imperial legitimacy. In particular, the Chinese concept *wen-hua* ('to civilize') stressed the transformative power of Chinese rites, language and culture upon all who were exposed to them.[151] For the Confucian literati, it was largely irrelevant whether or not a ruling dynasty was Han Chinese in origin. Dynastic genealogy did not by itself confer legitimacy upon aspirants to the imperial throne. Rather, the Mandate of Heaven was available to any aspirant capable of most effectively discharging the ritual and temporal functions of emperorship. By implication, this demanded that 'barbarians' transform themselves through exposure to 'civilization' (*wen-ming*), by steeping themselves in Chinese language and culture, and Confucian values.[152] The point remains, however, that 'civilization' was something that could be learned, even by conquest elites originating beyond China's Sinic core.

To sum up: the Confucian civilizational imaginary was *immanent* in its conception of the divine; *integrative* in its assumption of a basic homology linking the nested hierarchies of Confucian family, empire and cosmos; and *inclusive* in its ostensible renunciation of ethnic chauvinism for the ideal that non-Han 'barbarians' were indeed susceptible to civilization.

These features of Confucianism made it extremely attractive as a ruling ideology for the Manchus. In combining supreme temporal and spiritual power in the office of emperor (the Son of Heaven), Confucianism theoretically minimized religious challenges to the emperor. Chinese history of course abounds with millenarian challenges to incumbent dynasties. But the *structural* vulnerability of a Chinese emperor to religious challenge, for example, was much less than that faced by kings and emperors in Latin Christendom, who for centuries chafed against the

---

[150] K.-W. Chow, *The Rise of Confucian Ritualism in Late Imperial China: Ethics, classics, and lineage discourse* (Stanford: Stanford University Press, 1994), p. 10.
[151] Gungwu, 'The Chinese urge to civilize', 22–3.
[152] See for example Lieberman, *Strange Parallels*, p. 591.

papal monarchy's countervailing power. Likewise, Confucianism's integrative character bound local elites tightly into the imperial political order, again contrasting with traditions of municipal liberty that complicated central rule in other international systems, from Christendom to the Indian Ocean littoral. Lastly, Confucianism's ethnic inclusivity potentially removed a major nativist barrier to the Manchus' consolidation of power. Elsewhere in the early modern world, nascent 'vernacular' identities were already complicating rulers' efforts to maintain power over multi-ethnic empires.[153] But in seventeenth-century China, Confucianism contained to privilege civilization over '*ethnie*' as the prime source of lettered elites' social identity, leaving the door open for non-Han dynasties to rule.[154]

Imperial Confucianism thus represented a powerful form of symbolic capital for the Manchus. Successfully appropriated and adapted, Confucianism could win over the local lettered elites, as well as forestalling religious and nativist challenges to Manchu rule.[155] Additionally, at least among the Manchus' Confucian satellites, embrace of imperial Confucianism provided a potential mechanism for perpetuating the tributary hierarchy that had historically mediated China's relationships with its immediate neighbours.

Consequently, the Manchus worked diligently to incorporate Confucianism as a central element of their ruling ideology. Successive Manchu emperors strove to master Chinese language and culture, and to uphold the ritual responsibilities vested in them as Son of Heaven. Confucian ideology was sufficiently flexible to accommodate alien (i.e., non-Han) rule in China, precisely because it placed little store in rulers' ethnic origins, provided they assimilated to Confucian civilizational standards.[156]

At the same time that they were able to exploit Confucianism's cultural malleability, the Manchus also benefited from the peculiar circumstances and needs of the scholar-gentry following the conquest. Traditional accounts of the Manchu conquest stressed the Manchus' rapid Sinicization, affirming Confucianism's supposedly enduring capacity to capture and assimilate conquest elites throughout Chinese history.[157] But the reality was that the specific variety of Confucianism

---

[153] See for example generally the discussion in S. Pollock, 'The vernacular millennium: Literary culture and polity, 1000–1500', *Daedalus*, 127(3) (1998), 41–74.
[154] Lieberman, *Strange Parallels*, p. 591.
[155] Chow, *The Rise of Confucian Ritualism in Late Imperial China*, p. 45.   [156] Ibid.
[157] For a recent statement of this perspective, see P.-T. Ho, 'In defence of Sinicization: A rebuttal of Evelyn Rawski's "reenvisioning the Qing"', *Journal of Asian Studies*, 57(1) (1998), 123–55.

the Manchus embraced – ideologically purist, fixated on ritual and profoundly conservative – was in fact relatively new to China.

As we have seen, the Ming Dynasty's chaotic last decades had been marked by a volatile combination of war, commercialization, social upheaval and ideological ferment. Even before the Manchu conquest, this instability had sparked a turn towards extreme conservatism among sections of the scholar-gentry. In the Ming Dynasty's last decades, and in the first decades of its Qing successor, this conservative reaction ripened into an intellectual movement that spurred an effective reinvention of Confucianism. This reinvention aimed first to shore up the scholar-gentry's authority at the local level, both from heterodox challenges from below, and also from the encroachment of a new and alien Manchu administration.[158]

Following the Manchu conquest, then, the Manchus and the majority of the scholar-gentry forged an uneasy alliance of convenience, cemented by their commitment to a profoundly conservative reinterpretation of Confucian tradition. From a top-down vantage point, this manifested itself in diverse ways under different emperors, depending on the incumbent's intellectual and ideological proclivities, as well the political needs of the moment. The Yongzheng emperor (who ruled from 1723–35), for example, ascended the throne amid controversy over the circumstances of his succession, having been accused of parricide, and so faced similar legitimation challenges to those that had earlier confronted his Mughal counterpart, Aurangzeb.[159] Much like Aurangzeb, though with much greater success, the Yongzheng emperor responded by stressing his fidelity to orthodoxy as a key qualification for his right to rule. Consistent with a dynasty-defining Manchu effort to detach Confucianism from any notion of 'ethnic proprietorship',[160] the Yongzheng moreover placed great stress on those aspects of the tradition that emphasized the irrelevance of ethnic heritage to a ruler's legitimacy, provided that they ruled in accordance with civilized Confucian precepts.[161] This enabled him to fend off the stigma of barbarism, which a minority of Han scholar-gentry still vigorously sought to mobilize to discredit the Qing Dynasty.[162]

---

[158] See generally Chow, *The Rise of Confucian Ritualism in Late Imperial China.*

[159] On the controversies surrounding the Yongzheng emperor's accession to the dragon throne, see M. Zelin, 'The Yung-Cheng reign' in W. J. Peterson (ed.), *The Cambridge History of China*, 15 vols., IX: *The Ch'ing Empire to 1800*, Pt. I (Cambridge: Cambridge University Press, 2002), pp. 183–9.

[160] A. Woodside, 'The Ch'ien-lung reign' in W. J. Peterson (ed.), *The Cambridge History of China*, 15 vols., IX: *The Ch'ing Empire to 1800*, Pt. I (Cambridge: Cambridge University Press, 2002), p. 244.

[161] Zelin, 'The Yung-Cheng reign', p. 192.   [162] Ibid.

Conversely, the Qianlong emperor (1736–95) made more of an effort to differentiate the Manchus as a separate conquest elite, and in particular to enforce preservation of the 'Manchu way' as a collective responsibility of the conquest elite.[163] Nevertheless, even with his more systematic dedication to preserving 'Manchu-ness', the Qianlong emperor likewise also invested immense resources in venerating a state-sponsored cult of Confucius, and in inculcating and enforcing 'traditional' Confucian values of hierarchy and filial piety among the scholar-gentry. This 'micromanaging fundamentalism' sought to cement this critical constituency's allegiance and subordination to the Qing Dynasty.[164] More than this, the Manchus' embrace of a highly orthodox form of Confucianism also aimed to legitimate an increasing centralization of state power. This paradoxically weakened the autonomy of the scholar-gentry within their local communities, even while purportedly celebrating the values that helped constitute them as a lettered service elite.[165]

Rather than simply adopting Confucianism wholesale, then, the Manchus actively adapted it as a legitimating code, and modified it to suit their own purposes. This involved both reinforcing its ideological conservatism, as well as extending the depth and breadth of its reach throughout the empire. In the former case, this entailed a largely successful effort to spread the Confucian ideal of the traditional family, and its accompanying veneration of norms of filial piety and lineage-based loyalties, from the lettered elites towards commoner households.[166] Historian Susan Mann thus notes that supposedly timeless markers of the 'traditional' Chinese family – the 'spread of footbinding, the strict confinement of women to the home, the widow chastity cult, the touting of female labour for household-based spinning and weaving' – in fact took popular purchase beyond the literati only during the Qing Dynasty, and in no small part due to Qing state sponsorship.[167]

Geographically, meanwhile, Qing rule was also marked by zealous efforts to advance the Confucian 'civilizing mission' through the consolidation and bureaucratization of imperial dominion over the empire's mainly non-Sinic south-western territories (the provinces of Yunnan, Guizhou and Sichuan). We have seen that the Manchus generally preferred to manage cultural diversity through practices of segregated

---

[163] Elliott, *The Manchu Way*, p. 171.

[164] Woodside, 'The Ch'ien-lung reign', pp. 248–9.

[165] Zelin, 'The Yung-Cheng reign', pp. 193–4.

[166] S. Mann, 'Women, families, and gender relations' in W. J. Peterson (ed.), *The Cambridge History of China*, 15 vols., IX: *The Ch'ing Empire to 1800*, Pt. I (Cambridge: Cambridge University Press, 2002), p. 453.

[167] Ibid., p. 471.

incorporation. But in the southwest during the eighteenth century they departed from this general pattern, choosing instead to assimilate indigenous populations through forced Sinicization. The reasons the Manchus departed from their traditional preference for incorporation over assimilation were both strategic and ideational. Strategically, the impulse to impose direct rule on the southwest stemmed from the need to secure and exploit the region's extensive copper reserves, then located predominantly on hereditary lands overseen by indigenous native officials (*tusi*).[168] This imperative became especially urgent following Tokugawa Japan's decision to restrict exports of copper to the Qing Empire, which endangered continued supply of a metal essential for the production of the specie currency most imperial subjects used to conduct everyday commercial transactions.[169] The need to strengthen control over the region's northern boundaries, to secure the Manchus' flanks as they struggled with the Zunghars for supremacy in Tibet and the northwest, provided further grounds for strengthening imperial control further south.

From an ideational standpoint, meanwhile, the Manchus largely internalized Han Chinese conceptions of south-western indigenes as 'raw' peoples, potentially susceptible to and in need of civilization through Sinicization.[170] But whereas the Ming Dynasty had moderated this prejudice in practice, preferring indirect rule via native officials to central rule, the Qing instead zealously pursued parallel projects of 'defeudalization' and 'civilization' in the southwest, aimed at bureaucratizing and Sinicizing imperial domination there.[171] Largely lacking centralized structures of rule and codified civil and religious hierarchies, indigenous south-western peoples proved harder to insert into Qing-centric structures of rule than other subject peoples.[172] Having played no part in the Qing conquests, neither were their leaders attached to the Manchus through shared history. Much less did they enjoy ties of kinship, marriage or cultural affinity such as those that underwrote the more generous accommodations extended to other imperial constituencies, such as the Mongols.

Consequently, even in the face of pragmatic objections from elements of the imperial bureaucracy, and notwithstanding bouts of introspection and backsliding, successive Qing emperors generally pursued highly coercive assimilationist strategies in the southwest. These strategies have been

---

[168] J. Herman, 'Collaboration and resistance on the southwest frontier: Early eighteenth-century Qing expansion on two fronts', *Late Imperial China*, 35(1) (2014), 78.
[169] Ibid.   [170] Rawski, 'The Qing Empire during the Qianlong reign', p. 17.
[171] Woodside, 'The Ch'ien-lung reign', pp. 253–4.   [172] Ibid.

likened by at least one eminent historian to the United States' colonization and conquest of its western territories.[173] For they encompassed the
full gamut of practices traditionally associated with Western settler colonialism, including appropriation of indigenous lands, the dismantling of
local authority structures and disempowerment of traditional elders,
forcible suppression of indigenous languages and customs, state sponsorship of (Han) settler colonization, and the encouragement of intermar-
riage between Han settlers and locals as a means of acculturating the latter
and subsuming them within civilization.[174] Though scrupulous themselves in never submerging their Manchu identity within a Sinic
Confucian frame, the Qing proved adept at harnessing the 'Confucian
man's burden'[175] for purposes of centralized state-building, to a degree
that exceeded even that of the Sinic dynasty they had earlier displaced.

Explaining the Success of the Pax Manjurica, II: Segregated Incorporation and Indirect Rule on the Northwestern Frontier

The coercive Sinicization of the southwest marked a particularly brutal
demonstration of the Manchus' capacity to harness Confucianism for
their own purposes. But assimilation did not form the major key of
Manchu territorial expansion and colonial administration. Instead, segregated incorporation remained the dominant feature of the Manchu
diversity regime, and it was the elasticity of this system that enabled the
Manchus to expand their empire to a degree that eluded both their Ming
predecessors and their Mughal counterparts. The Manchus' consolidation of control over the Mongols provides an especially powerful illustration of this model of segregated incorporation in action.

The Mongols constituted a particularly important constituency within
the Qing Empire. As part of the initial Manchu conquest elite, they were
nominally privileged within the Qing order. Mongol allegiance afforded the
Qing emperor valuable symbolic capital, in that it represented the channel
through which he could claim the mantle of Genghis Khan, and so assert
his claims to primacy throughout the Eurasian steppe.[176] The Mongols
also provided a crucial reservoir of military labour, especially as light
cavalry shock troops for the empire.[177] Their indispensability notwithstanding, the Mongols also represented a vexing challenge for the Qing.
Their traditions of fierce egalitarianism, decentralized organization and

---

[173] Di Cosmo, 'Qing colonial administration in inner Asia', p. 308.
[174] Ibid. See also Woodside, 'The Ch'ien-lung reign', p. 257.
[175] Elliott, 'Ethnicity in the Qing Eight Banners', p. 33.
[176] Crossley, 'Making Mongols', p. 72.
[177] Di Cosmo, 'Qing colonial administration in inner Asia', p. 292.

tendencies towards fragmentation and feuding gave the Mongols a protean character. Indeed, the category of 'Mongol' overstates their coherence and unity, both at the time and for at least the century following the Ming-Qing transition. The Mongols' location on the Eurasian steppe moreover gave them a ready 'exit' option from external efforts to impose central rule, as they could withdraw into the interior and form countervailing coalitions to frustrate or even overwhelm would-be empire-builders.[178]

For a host of reasons, then, the Manchus needed to graft the Mongols firmly into a Qing-centric imperial order. Doing so however required that the Mongols be fixed in place, both spatially and ontologically. This necessitated that the Manchus develop an institutional architecture that could enfold the Mongols administratively, and mitigate the risks of separatism, rebellion, or defection to rival polities (most notably Romanov Russia). As importantly, it also entailed the curation and entrenchment of 'Mongols' as a coherent and controllable community within the larger 'state-family' of the Qing. For this reason, the imperative of define and conquer[179] was integral to the Qing colonial enterprise. A consideration of this dimension of Qing expansion illuminates the dynamics of Manchu imperial statecraft, and showcases the institutional practices that underwrote their regime of segregated incorporation.

The Lifan Yuan constituted the pre-eminent institution through which the Manchus established and maintained indirect rule throughout not only Mongolia, but also the other 'outer provinces' of Qinghai, Tibet and Xinjiang.[180] Established as both a colonial authority and diplomatic office, the Lifan Yuan aimed to establish a cost-effective system of indirect rule over subject peoples in the steppe provinces, while controlling and if possible minimizing their contacts with outside polities.[181] Superintended by Manchus and Mongols (Han Chinese were excluded from all ranks above clerk-translator), the Lifan Yuan performed a host of functions, ranging from regulating the treatment of local elites, through to supervision of Mongol princes' tributary embassies to the Qing court, to the codification and administration of the Mongol legal code.[182] Beneath the Lifan Yuan, and answering directly to it, a network of civil and military residents (eventually augmented by an administrative cadre of 'frontier specialists') provided the main means through which the Qing enforced their writ throughout the outer provinces, especially beyond the main urban centres.[183] Finally, a layer of local intermediaries – of which

---

[178] Perdue, *China Marches West*, pp. 527–8.   [179] Crossley, 'Making Mongols', p. 72.
[180] Di Cosmo, 'Qing colonial administration in inner Asia', p. 294.
[181] Ibid., pp. 292–3.   [182] Ibid., pp. 295–6.   [183] Ibid., p. 296.

the Mongol banner chiefs (*jasaghs*) were the most critical – plugged the Qing colonial apparatus into indigenous power networks, and elicited the collaboration necessary to perpetuate Manchu hegemony.[184]

Taken together, the Lifan Yuan, the network of civil and military residents and the local Mongol nobility constituted an immensely durable hybrid 'frontier governance system'[185] that in one form or another survived the end of Qing rule, dissolving only with Mongolia's secession from republican China in 1921. Central though these institutional innovations were to the consolidation of Manchu rule, however, their success rested on their essential congruence with Mongol conceptions of collective identity. Qing suzerainty presupposed a level of stable affective connection between Mongols and the Qing state, at least at the elite level.[186] Given the strength of Mongols' traditional resistance to outside rule, then, the reshaping of Mongol subjectivities in ways supportive of Qing rule thus proved a critical part of the Manchu imperial enterprise. Indeed, so central was this process of refashioning Mongol identity that historian John Elverskog has observed: '[The] success of the Qing model [of imperial governance] resided less in brute military power and intimidation than within this process whereby they were able to redefine what it meant to be Mongol.'[187]

The Manchu project of define and rule encompassed multiple dimensions, including the then unprecedented entrenchment of linguistic unity and standardization as an essential criterion of Mongol identity.[188] Nevertheless, it was the manipulation of religious affiliation – and specifically the establishment of adherence to a particular form of Tibetan Buddhism – that arguably was most critical in tethering Mongol allegiances to the Manchu imperial state. The Manchus' harnessing of Tibetan Buddhism marks a classic example of a larger process of imperial consolidation – customization – that constitutes one of the key mechanisms underpinning projects of empire formation that I foreground in this inquiry. More specifically, three features of Qing customization with respect to the consolidation of rule over the Mongols warrant our attention here, respectively centralization, rationalization and negotiation.

Centralization refers to the Manchus' deliberate strategy of centralizing and appropriating the symbolic and sacred powers enjoyed by the Tibetan

---

[184] Ibid., p. 300.
[185] L. Wang, 'From masterly brokers to compliant protégées: The frontier governance system and the rise of ethnic confrontation in China-Inner Mongolia, 1900–1930', *American Journal of Sociology*, 120(6) (2015), 1653.
[186] Crossley, 'Making Mongols', p. 58.
[187] J. Elverskog, *Our Great Qing: The Mongols, Buddhism and the state in late Imperial China* (Honolulu: University of Hawaii Press, 2006), p. 27.
[188] Crossley, 'Making Mongols', p. 79.

Buddhist religious hierarchy, incorporating them as a key aspect of Manchu suzerainty. In particular, the Manchus carefully co-opted the Dalai Lama – as the pre-eminent authority figure within the Tibetan Buddhist hierarchy – as a key locus of authority and a critical partner in Qing domination over the Mongols. The Dalai Lama had only recently established a tentative supremacy over rival lamas within Tibetan Buddhism, and consolidated his hold as both temporal and spiritual ruler of Tibet, in the decades immediately preceding Manchu expansion in the northwest. Given the tenuousness of his hold on power, the Manchus were able to secure the Dalai Lama's allegiance in a patron-client relationship that has been described as 'Lamaist-Caesero-papist' in its essential character.[189] Following their first meeting in 1652, the Qing emperor thus recognized the Dalai Lama as Tibetan Buddhism's supreme spiritual arbiter. In exchange, the Dalai Lama submitted to perform regular tribute missions to the Qing capital, symbolically affirming the emperor's suzerainty.[190] At least as important, the Dalai Lama also acknowledged the Qing emperor and his successors as an embodiment of *Manjusri*, the personification of the Buddha's intellect.[191] This invested the emperor with a sacred charisma within Tibetan Buddhism, providing a powerful additional resource for cementing the allegiance of Tibetan Buddhists, including the Mongol elites the emperor needed to win over in the empire's north-western frontier.

Following their reciprocal exchange of status and symbolic power, the Manchus worked alongside the Dalai Lama to centralize power within Tibetan Buddhism, eliminating or otherwise suborning the Dalai Lama's rivals and reconstituting him as a focal point for loyalty among all who claimed allegiance to Tibetan Buddhism.[192] Critically, however, this allegiance was one that was mediated and legitimated by the Qing emperor. Whereas previously the Dalai Lama had sought to exert his authority in an unmediated fashion, the Manchus forged a Faustian pact with the Dalai Lama, underwriting his power, but at the cost of securing his enduring subordination and dependence on the Manchu emperor as his sole protector and patron.

The centralization of religious authority constituted a critical Manchu intervention, not only in the religious practices of Tibetan Buddhists, but in the geopolitics of the northwest. It won the Manchus a spiritually powerful client, and mitigated the risk of Qing enemies attempting to mobilize Tibetan Buddhism as a resource for resistance. Beyond this

---

[189] Elverskog, *Our Great Qing*, p. 104.
[190] N. Chia, 'The Lifanyuan and the inner Asian rituals of the early Qing (1644–1795)', *Late Imperial China*, 14(1) (1993), 71. See also Farquhar, 'Emperor as Bodhisattva', 19.
[191] Woodside, 'The Ch'ien-lung reign', p. 236.   [192] Elverskog, *Our Great Qing*, p. 105.

reform, the Manchus also worked alongside the Dalai Lama to rationalize systems of Tibetan Buddhist belief, articulating a more clearly codified orthodoxy (the Gelukpa sect) that would form the chief framework for Mongol spiritual belief.[193] Along the Mongol frontier in the late seventeenth and early eighteenth centuries, the Manchus thus worked with Tibetan Buddhist religious elites and local Mongol rulers to make Tibetan Buddhism more 'legible' and susceptible to appropriation within the Qing imperial repertoire. To take one particularly horrific example of this process in action, in one instance a Mongol ruler rounded up all shamans in his banner and burned them alive on a wooden pyre, simultaneously affirming his commitment to ideological orthodoxy, while eliminating a competing source of heterodox authority within his ranks.[194] This coercive rationalization of belief – alongside the centralization of religious hierarchy – was additionally necessary to make Tibetan Buddhism more easily capable of being incorporated into the Qing iconography of rule, with the Manchu emperor being repositioned as *cakravartin* (universal ruler), to be owed unquestioned allegiance by the Mongol leadership.[195]

Alongside the centralization of religious hierarchy and the rationalization of Tibetan Buddhist religious belief, the Manchus finally had to systematically negotiate the foregrounding of Tibetan Buddhism as a focal point of Mongol collective identity. On this point, Elverskog is explicit in emphasizing that this process was not one of unilateral top-down imposition, but emerged from a complex serious of interactions between Manchu suzerains and local Mongolian elites.[196] Mongols did not simply submit to new narratives of identity foisted on them by Manchu administrators. Instead, the incorporation of the Mongols entailed an internalization of a new form of collective identity more coherent and more fixed than what had come previously. This process was protracted, iterative and interactive. It also harnessed and rechannelled indigenous processes of ideological reformation – not least a revival of Mongol religious activity exemplified in the translation of the Tibetan Buddhist canon into Mongolian – that predated Qing intervention by several decades.[197] But its result was to progressively concretize a form of Mongol identity that equated being Mongol with being Buddhist, and being Buddhist with owing supreme allegiance to the Manchu emperor as both *cakravartin* (universal ruler) and *Manjusri* (personification of

---

[193] Ibid., p. 118.   [194] Ibid., p. 119.
[195] T. D. DuBois, *Religion and the Making of Modern East Asia* (Cambridge: Cambridge University Press, 2011), pp. 103–4.
[196] Elverskog, *Our Great Qing*, pp. 120–1.
[197] Farquhar, 'Emperor as Bodhisattva', 16–17.

Buddha's intellect). At the culmination of this process, 'being Mongol and being Buddhist became inherently incorporated in a Buddhist Qing identity. The three had become intertwined: being Mongol and being Buddhist also entailed being Qing'.[198]

The institutional innovation of the Lifan Yuan frontier governance system, together with the sculpting of a reformulated Mongol collective identity more amenable to Qing rule, were pivotal to the consolidation of Manchu control over the northwest. Additional practices, including marital alliances between the Qing court and local elites, reciprocal gift exchange and the joint participation of Mongol nobles and the Qing emperor in ritual annual hunts, further solidified the affective bonds tethering the Mongols to the Qing imperial project. Indeed, over time, rituals such as Mongol pilgrimages to the Qing court and participation in imperial hunts recast the relationship between Beijing and Inner Asia from a foreign policy problem, to one of imperial administration.[199] Critically, whereas earlier Sinic dynasties had always engaged Inner Asia defensively, through the hierarchical prism of a civilized/barbarian dichotomy, the Manchus took advantage of their shared Inner Asian heritage to systematically cultivate a shared sense of mutual affinity and identity with the Mongols and other Inner Asian imperial constituencies.[200] The resulting model of segregated incorporation helped the Manchus to close the steppe frontier by permanently melding East Asia's Sinic sedentary core with its steppe Inner Asian frontier, synthesizing the strengths of the former's incomparable agricultural wealth with the latter's niche resources in cavalry-based irregular warfare.

Notwithstanding the magnitude of the Manchus' achievements, maintaining a diversity regime of segregated incorporation was not without serious challenges. Like all empires grounded in a model of heterogeneous contracting, the Manchus had to take great care to ensure that legitimation strategies mobilized to integrate one imperial constituency did not risk endangering the allegiance of others. To take one example, though the Manchus surreptitiously encouraged Tibetan Buddhists (both Mongols and others) to identify the emperor as *Manjusri*, they were careful not to explicitly embrace this identity in contexts where it might offend the religious sensibilities of others (e.g., Han Chinese Confucians).[201] More fundamentally, even the most dextrous mobilization and manipulation of cultural diversity had its limits as a means of pacifying and securing the empire. On the Inner Asian steppe in particular, the proliferation of local warlords, combined with a vast open frontier

---

[198] Elverskog, *Our Great Qing*, p. 100.
[199] Chia, 'The Lifanyuan and inner Asian rituals of the early Qing', 60.   [200] *Ibid.*, p. 63.
[201] Farquhar, 'Emperor as Bodhisattva', 26.

that seemingly favoured raiders over rulers, left the Qing vulnerable to attack. Though their strategy of extending their diversity regime of segregated incorporation was successful in winning the allegiance of some Mongols, it failed to quash all challengers. Before concluding this portion of my inquiry, then, we must briefly consider the Manchus' elimination of their last steppe competitor.

Explaining the Success of the Pax Manjurica, III: The Elimination of the Zunghars and the Closing of the Eurasian Steppe Frontier

The Zunghar confederacy was the last nomadic polity to seriously threaten the Qing Empire, and their destruction marked the Manchus' final consolidation of hegemony throughout eastern Eurasia.[202] A Western Mongolian people whose polity centered around what is now Xinjiang, the Zunghars – like the Manchus – had been a deeply fragmented kaleidoscope of feuding lineages before the seventeenth century. But at roughly the same time that Hong Taiji began cultivating a Manchu polity, the Zunghar patriarchs also launched their own state-building project.[203] The parallels between the Manchu and Zunghar state-building projects were remarkable, and this very symmetry likely fed into the Manchus' hostility to the Zunghar khanate.

Like Hong Taiji, the Zunghar patriarch Batur Hongtaiji (r. 1635–53) sought to centralize control over tribal chiefs, while exploiting trade with neighbouring sedentary polities to build up the patronage resources necessary to consolidate his power.[204] Batur and his successors recognized the need to shift from an exclusively pastoral economy, towards greater reliance on agriculture, commerce and natural resource exploitation (principally mining salt and precious metals) if the Zunghars were to survive.[205] Successive Zunghar leaders furthermore tried to manipulate trade relations with Russia and China, to secure access to the guns, silver and specialist craftsmen (e.g., gunsmiths and ironsmiths) needed to modernize their military base away from an almost exclusive reliance on irregular light cavalry.[206] As the Zunghar state matured, Zunghar rulers undertook further 'self-strengthening' measures, including the establishment of walled cities to attract and protect merchants and the development of a rudimentary tax system.[207]

Though it never achieved Qing China's level of bureaucratic sophistication or centralization, the Zunghar khanate by the late seventeenth century constituted a formidable local power. Under Galdan, one of its

---

[202] Perdue, 'Military mobilization', 757.   [203] Perdue, China Marches West, p. 105.
[204] Ibid., p. 105.   [205] Ibid., p. 303.   [206] Ibid., p. 304.   [207] Ibid., p. 307.

most powerful chieftains (r. 1671–97), the Zunghars 'claimed control over the vast reaches of present-day Xinjiang, Inner and Outer Mongolia, and parts of present-day Qinghai, Tibet and Kazakhstan'.[208] Like the Manchu patriarch Nurhaci, Galdan was a skilled alliance builder, being tied to a welter of Mongolian, Turkish and Tibetan allies through webs of personal, tribal and ethnic loyalties.[209] The larger (if remote) danger that a pan-Buddhist, pan-Mongol confederation of Mongolian (Oirat) peoples might emerge under Zhungarian leadership, encompassing Tibet, Qinghai, Zungharia and northern Mongolia, must have therefore given the Manchus further pause.[210] Galdan's imperial ambitions and apparent contempt for the Manchus, purportedly revealed in his rhetorical question 'Are we to become the slaves of those who were once at our command?'[211] further sharpened the Zunghars' perceived threat to the Qing Empire. As Chinese dynasties had historically most often been threatened by nomadic powers from the northwest, the Manchus were determined to bring the Zunghars to heel.[212]

The Manchus' destruction of Zungharia played out over decades (1690–1760), marked by periods of uneasy peace as well as war. During this time, the Manchus marshalled many expedients to manage the Zunghars, ranging from punitive expeditions through to attempts to appease the Zunghars through their incorporation into the tributary trade system.[213] Any attempt to recount the Manchus' elimination of Zungharia must therefore run the risk of simplification and teleology. With this caution in mind, the Manchus' strategy for subduing Zungharia can be simplified to encompass the following elements: isolation and enclosure, long-range conquest, wedging and extermination.

The territorial containment of the Zunghars, and their isolation from potential sanctuaries and external allies, was critical to their eventual defeat. In his preparations to strike at Galdan, the Kangxi emperor moved early to block the Zunghars' escape options, by signing China's first ever border treaty with Russia. The 1689 Treaty of Nerchinsk was motivated by multiple factors. These included the need to routinize and stabilize relations between Moscow and Beijing as two vast expanding agrarian empires, as well as the two sovereigns' desire to fix and routinize the movements of the mobile nomadic populations that traversed their frontiers. For present purposes, however, the treaty was most important

---

[208] Perdue, 'Military mobilization', 758.   [209] Ibid.
[210] J. A. Millward, *Beyond the Pass: Economy, ethnicity, and empire in Qing Central Asia, 1759–1864* (Stanford: Stanford University Press, 1998), p. 28.
[211] Narangoa and Cribb, *Historical Atlas of Northeast Asia*, p. 54.
[212] Perdue, 'Military mobilization', 757.
[213] Di Cosmo, 'Qing colonial administration in inner Asia', pp. 292–3.

for enclosing the Zunghars between the Russian and Qing empires, preventing them from either forging an alliance or establishing cross-border sanctuaries in the Tsar's territory. Using Russian fur-traders' access to the Qing Empire's market as a lever of influence, Manchu negotiators induced the Russians to withhold aid from the Zunghars, and to assist in the forced repatriation of any 'rebels' who fled into Russian territory.[214] Assisted by Jesuit cartographers, the Manchus meanwhile also demarcated the previously fluid frontier between the two empires with unprecedented precision, enfolding the as-yet-unconquered Zunghar khanate firmly within Qing borders.[215]

Alongside efforts to sandwich the Zunghars between the borders of the Romanov and Qing empires, the Manchus also committed to overcoming the logistical barriers that had formerly stopped sedentary societies from 'solving' the military threat posed by steppe polities. Recall that all pre-ceding rulers of China – whether Sinic or barbarian conquest dynasties – faced supposedly insuperable security problems emanating from the open frontier of the Asian steppe. The huge scale of the steppe had formerly enabled pastoralist raiders to strike at will against wealthy and vulnerable sedentary empires, and then to retreat into the interior – beyond the reach of retribution – when necessary.[216] The steppe's semi-arid character moreover meant that pre-industrial armies – which depended either on agricultural supplies transported from faraway depots or from foraging local resources to sustain themselves – inevitably faltered in their pursuit of steppe raiders.[217] As their lines of communication and supply became overextended, sedentary armies were forced to either abandon the hunt, or risk the threat of slow starvation with the onset of winter.[218]

The magnitude of the Zunghar threat – which threatened the Manchus along a 'vast crescent-shaped front' and jeopardized stable relations not only with Russia but also the Mongol and Tibetan peoples still tenuously under Qing control – provoked a proportionately massive response.[219] To overcome the logistical constraints that had thwarted all previous dynas-ties, the Qianlong emperor tapped into China's vast agricultural wealth and formidable bureaucracy to perfect an empire-wide system of

---

[214] P. C. Perdue, 'Boundaries and trade in the early modern world: Negotiations at Nerchinsk and Beijing', *Eighteenth-Century Studies* 43(3) (2010), 345. As Russian state caravans mediated the fur trade and provided a crucial source of revenue to the Russian treasury, the fur trade was a key Russian state interest, and access to the Chinese market thus an especially potent source of leverage for the Manchus. See P. C. Perdue, 'Boundaries, maps, and movement: Chinese, Russian, and Mongolian empires in early modern Central Eurasia', *International History Review* 20(2) (1998), 271.
[215] Perdue, 'Boundaries, maps, and movement', 285–6.
[216] Perdue, 'Military mobilization', 776.   [217] Ibid.   [218] Ibid.
[219] Millward, *Beyond the Pass*, p. 245.

granaries.[220] Though motivated in part by famine relief concerns (and more pointedly by a desire to pre-empt the threat of internal rebellion provoked by peasant hardship), the extension of the granary system into the empire's northwest transformed the logistics of steppe military campaigns. In particular, the empire's development of a network of grain magazines extending towards the frontier helped Qing armies to sustain themselves on the steppe for years on end, thereby transcending the ninety-day limit for punitive campaigns that had previously constrained retaliation against the Zunghars.[221] Far from an isolated measure, this logistical innovation coincided with concerted efforts to commercially develop the northwest, with a view to enabling the Manchu armies to draw off agricultural surplus to reliably supply their troops, but without inflicting unnecessary popular hardship on the local peasantry.[222] As the need to expand cultivation to support frontier conquest grew, the Manchus moreover sponsored extensive military colonization, as well as the forced mobilization of transported convict settlers, to further develop the agricultural base necessary to sustain their anti-Zunghar campaigns.[223]

The Qing logistical revolution was far from cheap, and efforts to yield a so-called forward defence dividend by moving the Qing defence perimeter from Shaanxi-Gansu to the far-northwest never paid off economically.[224] But together with the diplomatic and cartographic enclosure of the Zunghars, the Qing logistical revolution helped the Manchus overcome a loss of strength gradient that had until that time foiled rulers' efforts to permanently unite China and Inner Asia. Vital though these innovations were, however, they were effective only when deployed in concert with Qing cultural diplomacy. The Manchus masterfully monopolized the forms of cultural and symbolic capital necessary to isolate the Zunghars from potential Mongol allies, paving the way for their destruction. We have already seen the great lengths the Manchus went to harness the spiritual and charismatic power of Tibetan Buddhism, as part of their efforts to sculpt Mongol identities in ways conducive to entrenching Qing domination. But the Manchus also appropriated Tibetan Buddhism to pre-empt the risk of the Zunghars emerging as alternative patrons and protectors for the Mongols.

At the height of their power, 'using religion as a rallying point, the Zunghars threatened to unite the peoples and lands of Tibet, Kokonor, Zungharia and Mongolia into a pan-Buddhist front against the Qing empire'.[225] This danger was especially grave under the rule of Galdan

[220] Perdue, 'Military mobilization', 777.   [221] Ibid., p. 779.   [222] Ibid., pp. 777–9.
[223] Perdue, *China Marches West*, p. 342.   [224] Millward, *Beyond the Pass*, pp. 245–6.
[225] J. A. Millward, 'Qing inner Asian empire and the return of the Torghuts' in R. W. Dunnell, M. C. Elliott, P. Foret and J. A. Millward (eds.), *New Qing Imperial*

(r. 1671–97), who had spent time as a Gelukpa Tibetan monk before his rise to political power, and who at one point enjoyed the diplomatic backing of the fifth Dalai Lama in his struggles against other western Mongol factions.[226] The Manchus' vigorous efforts to monopolize the spiritual and symbolic capital of Tibetan Buddhism – culminating in their 'Lamaist-Caesaro-papist' pact with the Dalai Lama – were driven in large part by their attempt to pre-empt the Zunghar challenge. Religious patronage of Tibetan Buddhism thus served a dual function for the Manchu: it both enhanced their authority and affinity with many of the most important Mongol lineages, while also driving a wedge between the latter and the Zunghars.[227]

In the zero-sum competition between the Manchus and the Zunghars for allies on Eurasia's inner frontier, religious and cultural patronage proved vital weapons for the Manchus in isolating their steppe enemies, preparatory to their eradication. This was evident not only with respect to Tibetan Buddhism, but can also be seen in the Manchus' appropriation, monopolization and reconceptualization of a second key source of symbolic and cultural capital on the steppe, namely the cult of Genghis Khan.[228] Historically, Mongol peoples had universally venerated Genghis Khan. Throughout the Eurasian steppe, war-like aristocratic lineages laid claim to his legacy as a means of both legitimating lineage-based forms of political authority, and also to licence campaigns of conquest. Indeed, as we have seen in previous chapters, claiming a genealogical connection (fictive or not) with Genghis Khan and his successors was key to the legitimating formulas of both the Mughals and the Manchus. It acquired even greater significance for the latter as they sought to wrest the allegiances of remaining Mongol lineages away from the Zunghars, and towards the Qing Empire.

The idea that supreme political authority derived from divinity, and was indeed mediated by Genghis Khan as 'Holy Lord' and exemplar of the all-conquering universal monarch, was alongside Tibetan Buddhism the most potent source of legitimation among the Mongols.[229] In marginalizing the Zunghars, the Manchus undeniably benefited from the fact that Zunghar leaders such as Galdan could not lay claim to descent from Genghis Khan, and so

History: The making of inner Asian empire at Qing Chengde (London: Routledge, 2004), pp. 91–105.

[226] Ibid., p. 99.

[227] J. Waley-Cohen, 'Religion, war, and empire-building in eighteenth-century China', *International History Review*, 20(2) (1998), 341–2.

[228] Elverskog, *Our Great Qing*, p. 89.   [229] Ibid., p. 96.

were forced to rely on more exclusively Buddhist legitimating codes to sustain their power.[230] But the Manchus eventually went further than claiming their own kinship tie to Genghis Khan. Instead, from the Kangxi emperor onwards, Manchu propagandists increasingly identified the Qing emperor ever more closely with Genghis Khan himself. Though this began by asserting that the emperor derived his authority from divine grace as personified by Genghis Khan, during the eighteenth century the Manchus increasingly asserted that the Qing emperor *was* Genghis Khan, the 'Holy Lord', and that Mongol nobles ultimately owed their local power to His divine grace.[231]

In appropriating, monopolizing and reconceptualizing both Tibetan Buddhism and the Mongol cult of Genghis Khan, the Manchus eventually enticed and ensnared the remaining Mongol tribes as dependent allies, while crippling the legitimation efforts of the rival Zunghar confederacy. This cultural statecraft was of course hardly enough by itself to defeat the Zunghars. But together with the Zunghars' diplomatic and cartographic enclosure and the Qing logistics revolution, it did play a decisive role in sabotaging the Zunghars' emergence as a rival pole of power. This mammoth, decades-long effort was, however, not enough to pound the Zunghars into total submission. Instead, following a final rebellion by Zunghar chieftains in the late 1750s, the Qianlong emperor ordered an extermination campaign to eliminate what was left of the Zunghar polity, an estimated population of at least 600,000. The resulting violence, which killed or dispersed 80 per cent of the Zunghars, has been described as 'arguably the eighteenth century genocide par excellence'.[232] With the Zunghars' extermination in 1759, the Manchus arrived at a horrific Final Solution to the 'steppe problem' that had bedevilled all preceding imperial dynasties. From this point onwards, the age of 'free-range and free-lance powers from Central Eurasia' was over.[233] This left the Manchus free to enjoy their hegemony as Asia's undisputed hegemon, at a time when the Mughals had long since succumbed to internal decay – and when a new challenger, in the form of the English East India Company, was only just beginning to stir.

---

[230] P. C. Perdue, 'The Qing Empire in Eurasian time and space: Lessons from the Galdan campaigns' in L. A. Struve (ed.), *The Qing Formation in World-Historical Time* (Cambridge, MA: Harvard University Press, 2004), p. `70.

[231] Elverskog, *Our Great Qing*, p. 79.

[232] Levene, 'Empires, native peoples, and genocide', p. 188.

[233] J. A. Millward, 'The Qing formation, the Mongol legacy and the "end of history" in early modern Central Eurasia' in L. A. Struve (ed.), *The Qing Formation in World-Historical Time* (Cambridge, MA: Harvard University Press, 2004), p. 115.

Map 5.2 The Qing Empire and its expansion
Source: https://creativecommons.org/licenses/by/4.0/deed.en.

Conclusion

This chapter has sought to explain the great divergence in the Mughal and Manchu empires' trajectories over the eighteenth century. Despite having both enjoyed regional hegemony in the late seventeenth century, the Mughal Empire unravelled from the early 1700s, even as the Manchus radically expanded their own dominion. This divergence stemmed largely from differences in the two regimes' aptitude in accommodating cultural diversity over the course of large-scale territorial expansion. Both the Mughal and Manchu empires arose out of frontier warlords' superior capacity in building multicultural conquest coalitions. They endured thereafter because rulers successfully kept conquest coalitions bound to the centre through customized legitimation scripts and integrative institutions, which acculturated elites into a common imperial service culture.

The Mughal and Manchu empires managed the challenges of cultural diversity very differently, respectively favouring models of syncretic versus segregated incorporation. Different models of imperial suzerainty (galactic versus fractal, distinguished by variations in the mix of direct versus indirect rule) also differentiated the two empires, as did their approaches to maritime frontier governance. Despite these differences, both empires confronted the same challenge of conciliating and incorporating local collaborators as they tried to extend their rule into new hinterlands. The Deccan would have been hard enough for the Mughals to conquer already, given the region's cultural and geographical distinctiveness from Indo-Persian northern India. But Aurangzeb's abandonment of syncretism for sectarianism made this task virtually impossible, dooming the empire to costly and interminable pacification campaigns in the south. Beyond the Deccan, the consolidation of Sikhdom moreover dramatized local elites' ability to differentiate and distance themselves from the centre, and eventually carve out more compact successor states as the empire imploded.

Conversely, the Manchus' system of segregated incorporation proved easier to extend into new hinterlands. And the Manchu leadership proved more dextrous and more flexible in their outreach efforts towards potential collaborators in newly conquered territories. The Qing Dynasty never shied away from forcible cultural assimilation where necessary (e.g., the campaigns in the southwest). Nor did they refrain from genocidal violence where they perceived no viable alternative to securing their power from steppe rivals. But the Manchus' doubling of their empire mostly depended on their ability to curate subject communities into governable imperial constituencies, and bind these communities into Qing-centric networks through specialized frontier institutions such as the Lifan Yuan.

By the mid-eighteenth century, the political landscapes of South and East Asia looked profoundly different. In South Asia, the Mughal Empire had been gutted from within and devastated from without. Persian and Afghan attacks had left Delhi's treasuries empty. Moreover, while the Mughal emperor remained the region's titular suzerain – and the aura of Mughal authority remained a potent source of symbolic capital – real power had ebbed to regional polities. These included the Maratha confederacy and the Sikhs in the west; Hyderabad and Mysore in the south; Awadh in the centre; and Bengal (now independent in all but name) in the east. Clinging to the subcontinent's littoral, European company-states such as the French and English East India companies were meanwhile also gradually emerging as significant power brokers in their own right. By the 1750s, South Asia was commercially dynamic but politically fragmented. From a unipolar order centred on Mughal hegemony in the 1700s, it had devolved decades later into a regional order marked by 'immature anarchy'.[234] A multipolar distribution of material power – reminiscent of a protean state system – undeniably prevailed. But the rudiments of an international society – in the form of agreed rules and norms that would have given this pluralism a chance of permanence – were absent. This lethally competitive Hobbesian hothouse would provide the matrix out of which the British Raj would soon evolve.

The Manchus by contrast not only preserved unipolar dominance in East Asia, but also extended its breadth geographically through near-continuous wars of conquest. They meanwhile comprehensively either subdued or eliminated both state and non-state challengers to their hegemony. From the Zheng confederacy in the southeast, to the Zunghar confederacy in the northwest, the Manchus tore apart non-state rivals, eliminating the model of marchland mercantilism that had formerly flourished intermittently on China's sea and steppe frontiers. Appropriating Confucian models of tributary diplomacy and associated cultural capital, they browbeat neighbouring Confucian monarchies into submission, while employing diplomacy and carefully regulated trading privileges to contain Romanov Russia, their most powerful (and potentially threatening) non-Confucian state neighbour. The importation of modern western cartographic techniques finally allowed the Manchus to more carefully delimit both their steppe and maritime frontiers, prefiguring a hardening of imperial borders from the late eighteenth century.

The Manchus thus emerged at the end of the eighteenth century ruling over a bigger, tougher, wealthier and more diverse empire than ever before. Unipolar East Asia moreover seemed to vindicate the Manchu model of power through universal conquest, and peace through segregated incorporation. It is against this backdrop that we should read the Manchus' apparent intransigence and conservatism when they later faced Western attempts at diplomacy and trade. Far from being hidebound by 'timeless' traditions predisposing them to introversion and insularity, the Manchus had proved highly violent – and highly successful – extraverts and innovators throughout the eighteenth century. Their self-confidence furthermore rested not on fealty to an adopted Confucian inheritance, but on their own unmatched achievements in expanding their territory, unifying steppe and sown, incorporating local collaborators and crushing upstart outsiders seeking to mix trade and politics on the empire's frontiers. The impact of this legacy on later Western attempts to pry open the Qing Empire to trade and diplomacy will be examined in Chapter 7. But before we consider this clash of empires, we must first examine the rise of the EIC in India – a subject that forms the focus of Chapter 6.

---

[234] On the concept of immature anarchy, see Buzan, *People, States and Fear*, pp. 96–101.

6   The East India Company and the Rise of British India, 1740–1820

[A]s faithful adherents to His Majesty [the Mughal Emperor], as protectors of the people of God, and as defenders of their own possessions
which they owe to the Royal *farmans*, the English have been compelled
to draw their swords in support of His Majesty's dominions, in their own
protection, and in the cause of humanity.[1]

This chapter examines the English East India Company's (EIC's) improb-
able rise to dominance in South Asia from the mid-eighteenth century
through to 1820. Chartered in 1600 to mediate England's trade with Asia,
for its first century, the EIC operated at the sufferance of local rulers.[2] From
the early eighteenth century, however, the Mughal Empire's decline sparked
a surge in competitive state-building throughout South Asia. From 1740,
the globalization of Anglo-French rivalries dragged the EIC into this
competition.[3] This hastened the EIC's militarization and metamorphosis
into a territorial power, until it defeated all comers (both European and
indigenous) to establish hegemony throughout India.

In examining the rise of the British Raj, we confront a similar puzzle to
that of explaining the emergence of the Mughal and Manchu empires.
Like their Asian counterparts, the EIC's agents were vastly outnumbered
outsiders, who originally lacked the capacity and desire to dominate the
pre-existing empires with which they traded. Established as a trading
concern, the EIC's shareholders remained hyper-sensitive to the danger
of their profits being corroded through territorial expansion. Indeed, they
were at first loathe even to finance the fortifications needed to secure the
EIC's factories in India and beyond.[4] The great costs and high wastage

---

[1] EIC's letter to the Mughal emperor, cited in K. S. Datla, 'The origins of indirect rule in
India: Hyderabad and the British imperial order', *Law and History Review*, 33(2)
(2015), 341.
[2] See generally G. van Meersbergen, 'The diplomatic repertories of the East India companies in Mughal South Asia, 1608–1717', *Historical Journal*, 62(4) (2019), 875–98.
[3] P. J. Marshall, 'British expansion in India in the eighteenth century: A historical revision',
History, 60(198) (1975), 34.
[4] B. Watson, 'Fortifications and the 'idea' of force in early English East India Company
relations with India', *Past and Present*, 88 (1980), 71–2.

associated with sending European soldiers to Asia further counselled against conquest.[5] As commercially motivated foreigners, the EIC lacked the will, the military capacity and the local legitimacy necessary to pursue an empire-building project in Asia. And yet, barely a century after Aurangzeb's death in 1707, the EIC had eclipsed the Mughals and all others as India's pre-eminent power. How did this happen?

Building on this book's central argument, I argue that the EIC built its empire through customization. Company officials refashioned indigenous material and normative resources to transform the EIC into a uniquely competitive conquest machine, first building and then binding a multicultural coalition into an emerging company-ruled Indian Empire. As the Mughal Empire's decline threatened the security of EIC interests, ambitious and unscrupulous company employees seized the opportunity to re-invent the EIC as a territorial power. Though political intrigue was at least as important as war-fighting in bringing about the 'Company Raj', my focus here lies in detailing the construction of the company armies that spearheaded the EIC's conquests. Demographically insignificant relative to the local population, the EIC nevertheless benefited from the matchless Indian military labour market. Possessing as few as 1,000 soldiers as late as the 1750s, by 1820 the company's armies numbered 300,000.[6] The vast majority were Indians, attracted to the EIC by the more attractive employment conditions (ranging from more reliable pay through to more generous pensions) the company offered relative to its rivals.[7] The EIC's superior credit-worthiness initially helped it to attract and retain soldiers, while its synthesis of Western and indigenous military advantages enabled the creation over time of a uniquely competitive 'hybrid military machine'.[8] Beyond material incentives, the EIC also triumphed because it proved especially adept at harnessing and reformulating indigenous religious and ethnic identities to win and keep its soldiers' allegiance.[9] This curation of indigenous identities was critical to tying the expanding Company Raj to its armed forces, underwriting the hierarchies on which the empire was built.

This chapter proceeds in six sections. The first sets the scene by charting the onset of competitive state-building as Persian, Afghan, European and local actors scrambled for power following the Mughal

---

[5] P. D. Curtin, *Death by Migration: Europe's encounter with the tropical world in the nineteenth century* (Cambridge: Cambridge University Press, 1989), p. 4.

[6] P. Lawson, *The East India Company: A history* (New York: Longman, 1993), p. 148.

[7] See generally G. J. Bryant, 'Indigenous mercenaries in the service of European imperialists: The case of the sepoys in the early British Indian army, 1750–1800', *War in History*, 7 (1) (2000), 2–28.

[8] K. Roy, 'The hybrid military establishment of the East India Company in South Asia: 1750–1849', *Journal of Global History*, 6(2) (2011), 218.

[9] See, for example, Alavi, 'The makings of company power'.

Empire's decline. The second section provides a précis of the phases of the company's expansion, before critically engaging existing explanations for the same. The third to fifth sections advance my substantive explanation for the rise of the Company Raj. The discussion conforms broadly to the template of emergence, institutionalization, legitimization and consolidation established earlier in my analysis of the rise of the Mughals and the Manchus. This is to underscore the critically important parallels in Mughal, Manchu and British experiences of empire formation. The final section sums up this chapter's findings and teases out its broader implications. Here, I revisit and elaborate on the key parallels linking British colonial expansion with its Mughal and Manchu precedents and counterparts. I do so both to accent the highly derivative character of Western imperialism in Asia stressed throughout this book, but also to better isolate those aspects of Western expansion that were genuinely distinctive. Here I also foreshadow the tensions that nearly destroyed the British Empire as it encroached more deeply into South and East Asia in the mid-nineteenth century, and which I explore in detail in Chapter 7.

The Mughal Collapse and Competitive State-Building during the Eighteenth Century Interregnum

Since its arrival in South Asia in the early seventeenth century, the EIC had thrived under Mughal protection. But after Aurangzeb's death, the Mughal Empire started to unravel. Later generations of EIC officials would characterize post-Aurangzeb India as entering a period of violent chaos, which only the EIC's ascendancy arrested.[10] But this was untrue. Certainly, Aurangzeb's death heralded a grave weakening of Mughal power, and a transformation of political authority throughout India. But this transformation did not involve a general breakdown of governmental power. Instead, the eighteenth century saw widespread decentralization, as ambitious Mughal governors (*nawabs*) repatriated less revenue to Delhi, instead diverting it to finance their own proto-states.[11] Starved of revenue, the empire became more vulnerable to external predation. Successive attacks by Persians and Afghans from the 1730s then further dramatized its weakness.[12] This prompted a further withdrawal of money and support, accelerating the empire's decline.[13]

---

[10] This traditional position is outlined and critiqued in B. Stein, 'Eighteenth century India: Another view', *Studies in History*, 5(1) (1989), 1–26.

[11] Sana, 'Was there an agrarian crisis in Mughal north India?', 20.

[12] Axworthy, *The Sword of Persia*, p. 213. See also Bayly, *Rulers, Townsmen and Bazaars*, p. 15.

[13] On the 'relocation' of economic growth away from a supra-local state and towards areas 'nurtured by the local elite', see N. Hatekar, 'Farmers and markets in the pre-colonial

The decentralization of power was hardly unique to Mughal India in the eighteenth century. Instead, it reflected a more general phenomenon throughout Eurasia and the Americas – from which only Qing China and Romanov Russia were truly exempt – in which an earlier period of commercialization nourished the rise of local states that increasingly slipped the leash of imperial authority.[14] Crucially, the Mughal Empire's slow-motion implosion did not prompt economic decline. The Indian subcontinent did not experience a catastrophic contraction of production and long-distance trade of the kind witnessed, for example, following the Western Roman Empire's collapse.[15] Even as they aggrandized power, local strongmen still sought to sustain the commerce necessary to finance their state-building ambitions.[16] The vast credit networks that had knitted the subcontinent together at the empire's height remained intact.[17] Surprisingly also, the empire's loss of real political power did not translate into a commensurate loss of prestige. Instead, state-builders continued to pledge nominal fealty to the emperor, and sought to harness the symbols of Mughal authority even while undermining the empire's substantive capacities for rule.[18]

Eighteenth-century India thus witnessed a paradoxical combination of change and continuity. Despite the breakdown of Mughal power, India remained commercially dynamic. The continuing potency of the Mughals' symbolic authority meanwhile provided the subcontinent's elites with a common idiom of political legitimacy, even as the empire's real power waned.[19]

Offsetting these continuities, eighteenth-century India did see a hugely increased militarization of society as power devolved to local state-builders. This was clearest in the transformation of the Indian military labour market. Historically, northern India was already 'bristling' with armed peasants well before the eighteenth century.[20] But in the Mughal

---

Deccan: The plausibility of economic growth in a traditional society', *Past and Present*, 178(1) (2003), 122. See also Bayly, *Rulers, Townsmen and Bazaars*, p. 15.

[14] See generally C. A. Bayly, *Imperial Meridian: The British Empire and the world, 1780–1830* (London: Routledge, 1989).

[15] On the rejection of the eighteenth century as the 'Dark Ages' for India in favour of one identifying it as a period of (admittedly regionally uneven) prosperity, see S. Alavi, 'Introduction' in S. Alavi (ed.), *The Eighteenth Century in India* (Oxford: Oxford University Press, 2002), p. 37.

[16] Bayly, *Rulers, Townsmen and Bazaars*, pp. 11–12.

[17] C. A. Bayly, *Indian Society and the Making of the British Empire* (Cambridge: Cambridge University Press, 1990), pp. 36–8.

[18] Bayly, *Rulers, Townsmen and Bazaars*, p. 13.

[19] Asher and Talbot, *India Before Europe*, p. 288.

[20] J. F. Richards, 'Warriors and the state in early modern India', *Journal of the Economic and Social History of the Orient*, 47(3) (2004), 397.

era, armed peasants had typically formed a supplementary levy for the empire, even while keeping their primary vocation as farmers.[21] Conversely, the rise of militarized local states accelerated the growth of the professionalized peasant soldier as a distinct class of social actor.[22] The institution of the armed peasantry not only increased in scale, but also changed its nature. Henceforth, ambitious warlords could draw from a huge pool of increasingly professional peasant soldiers, more numerous and more effective than their part-time predecessors.[23] This development amplified centrifugal pressures, which only intensified once Europeans introduced modern drill and discipline to Indian armies from mid-century. Mughal decline and local state-building significantly increased the EIC's insecurity. This was especially so given the tiny military resources then at the company's disposal. The cost-conscious Board of Directors back in London insisted on keeping the EIC's overheads to a minimum.[24] Consequently, the EIC had as few as two thousand troops defending its sprawling interests across the entire Indian subcontinent as late as the mid-eighteenth century.[25] Deteriorating political stability on the subcontinent nevertheless brought to the fore a basic tension between the EIC's imperatives of profit and security. This tension worsened from the 1740s, as European rivalries intruded on the subcontinent.[26] Specifically, the increasingly global rivalry between France and Britain posed a grave threat to the EIC's interests throughout Asia. For whereas the company could buy off rapacious local rulers, the French East India Company sought nothing less than the EIC's expulsion from India, and so posed an existential threat.[27]

The French Company's introduction of new techniques of administration and military mobilization made it especially dangerous to the EIC. Unsuccessful in its trading activities, the French Company resorted to tax-farming of the territories under its control to supplement its income.[28] Anxious to enhance its own security while maximizing its offensive capabilities against the EIC, the French Company also introduced the practice of recruiting Indian peasant soldiers and equipping them with Western weapons, drill and discipline.[29] These innovations would

---

[21] Alavi, *The Sepoys and the Company*, p. 12.   [22] Ibid.   [23] Ibid.

[24] P. B. Buchan, 'The East India Company 1749–1800: The evolution of a territorial strategy and the changing role of the directors', *Business and Economic History*, 23(1) (1994), 52.

[25] Lawson, *The East India Company*, p. 83.

[26] Marshall, 'British Expansion in India in the eighteenth century', 34.   [27] Ibid.

[28] D. Baugh, *The Global Seven Years War, 1754–1783: Britain and France in a great power contest* (London: Routledge, 2014), pp. 68–71.

[29] K. Roy, 'The armed expansion of the English East India Company: 1740s–1849' in D. P. Marston and C. S. Sundaram (eds.), *A Military History of India and South Asia:*

eventually push the EIC to emulate and improve on these techniques, forging the hybrid military machine that would ultimately propel the EIC to universal dominance.

The Phases of Company Expansion and Existing Explanations for the Rise of the Raj

The British conquest of India can be roughly divided up into four phases, encompassing its initial emergence as a territorial power (1750s–1784); its destruction of peer competitors and establishment of subcontinental paramountcy (1784–1818); its post-war consolidation and institutionalization (1818–39); and its final thrust into the northwest, beginning with the disaster of the First Afghan War (1839–42) and culminating in the conquest of Punjab in 1849.

The mid-eighteenth century saw the EIC transition from a trading-focused maritime company-state to a territorial power driven as much by conquest as by commerce. This was a largely an unplanned and improvised reaction to India's transforming strategic circumstances. The spread of Anglo-French rivalry to India proved especially catalytic. Whereas before the British and French had agreed to isolate conflicts in Europe from spreading to the subcontinent, this restraint broke down during the war of the Austrian Succession (1740–8).[30] In 1746, Joseph Dupleix, governor of the French Company's main settlement at Pondicherry, mobilized a new army of several thousand native infantry (*sepoys*) to seize Madras from the EIC.[31] Dupleix's capture of Madras formed part of a larger strategy to carve out a great empire for the French Company throughout southern India. Though he failed in this endeavour, Dupleix's actions were immensely consequential. For the fall of Madras (though temporary) dramatized the EIC's vulnerability, while demonstrating the utility of deploying Western-trained Indian troops in battle. Henceforth, Europeans and Indians alike slowly began to recognize the value of developing armed forces that combined Western techniques of drill and discipline with India's immense existing reserves of professional peasant soldiers.[32] This in turn helped propel the EIC's transformation into a large-scale conquest enterprise.

From the East India Company to the nuclear age (Bloomington: Indiana University Press, 2008), p. 5.

[30] J. A. Lynn, 'Heart of the sepoy: The adoption and adaption of European military practice in South Asia, 1740–1805' in E. O. Goldman and L. C. Eliason (eds.), *The Diffusion of Military Technology and Ideas* (Stanford: Stanford University Press, 2003), p. 45.

[31] Baugh, *The Global Seven Years War*, p. 66.

[32] This is not to suggest that this recognition came quickly or easily for the Europeans, who initially bemoaned what they saw as the sepoys' lack of discipline and unit cohesion under fire. See Bryant, 'Indigenous mercenaries', 21.

The capture of Madras prompted the EIC to begin raising sepoy armies of its own, beginning with a 3,000-troop cohort deployed in the Battle of Cuddalore in 1748.[33] By the 1750s, both the EIC and the French Company maintained armies of about 10,000 sepoys each,[34] and Indian-manned armies thereafter became a permanent feature of the two increasingly militarized company-states. First forged to defend against French expansion, the sepoy armies of the EIC's Madras Presidency were soon deployed with great effect further north, providing a critical asset enabling the EIC's seizure of the Mughal Empire's richest province – Bengal.

By the 1750s, Bengal remained a nominal feudatory of the distant and powerless Mughal emperor. But the *nawab* (governor), Siraj al-Daula, was by this time the province's de facto ruler.[35] Facing fierce external predation from Maratha raids, al-Daula was compelled to continue his predecessors' costly work of centralizing his state and modernizing his military. This brought him into collision with the EIC, which had long enjoyed trading privileges and immunities from taxation under the Mughal emperor's authority, and resented the governor's moves to curtail the company's liberties as part of his efforts at fiscal self-strengthening. The governor meanwhile bridled at the EIC's efforts to extend its privileges to include its local commercial allies, rightly fearing that this would corrode his fiscal base at a time of worsening insecurity.[36] The company's continuing expansion and fortification of its settlements in Calcutta moreover posed a real threat to Bengal's security from within. In time, the governor deemed this threat so serious that he expelled the company from its Calcutta stronghold – sparking an intervention that removed him from power, and eventually installed the company in his place.[37]

The company's takeover of Bengal from 1757 saw company officials stage a coup in collusion with Bengali conspirators to overthrow the al-Daula, and install a more accommodating ruler following the EIC's military victory at the Battle of Plassey. Over the next decade, once al-Daula's successor proved less pliant than the company and its local allies had hoped, the EIC again resorted to regime change to secure a favourable political dispensation.[38] Following the Battle of Buxar (1764), the Treaty of Allahabad confirmed the company's political supremacy in Bengal, the EIC winning from the Mughal emperor the *diwani* – the all-important right to collect tax revenue and maintain civil

---

[33] Lynn, 'heart of the sepoy', p. 46.   [34] Ibid.   [35] Bryant, 'Indigenous mercenaries', 4.

[36] G. J. Bryant, *The Emergence of British Power in India, 1600–1784: A grand strategic interpretation* (Suffolk: Boydell & Brewer, 2013), p. 171.

[37] P. J. Marshall, *Bengal: The British bridgehead, Eastern India 1740–1828* (Cambridge: Cambridge University Press, 1988), p. 76.

[38] Ibid., p. 85.

administration throughout the province.[39] Thereafter, the EIC ruled Bengal under the emperor's nominal authority, while hoarding the vast majority of the province's revenues. This wealth was never enough to cover the costs of territorial administration.[40] The EIC's misrule more-over exacerbated a massive famine in Bengal in 1769–73, which killed up to a third of the province's population, threatened the company with bankruptcy and prompted tighter surveillance over the EIC's activities from the British state.[41] These new restrictions notwithstanding, Bengal's wealth would prove 'the Atlas sustaining British interests in Asia', the province supplying the bulk of the military and fiscal resources on which the company's later conquests in India would be founded.[42]

The passage of Pitt's India Act in 1784 further shortened the company's leash, and included crucial provisions forbidding the EIC's agents from undertaking any further wars of conquest.[43] Governors-general thereafter sought for a time to defend the EIC through adherence to classic balance of power strategies in India, forswearing any goals more ambitious than the company's traditional pursuits of profit and security.[44] The revolutionary and Napoleonic wars, however, revived the Anglo-French antagonism with renewed intensity, their hostility fur-ther compounded with more renewed (if often fitful) efforts at collabor-ation between France and the EIC's powerful Indian rivals, most notably the southern Indian state of Mysore.[45]

Reflecting this intensifying rivalry and insecurity, the tenure of gov-ernor-general Richard Wellesley (1798–1805) marked a shift in the EICs grand strategy, from balance of power to the pursuit of hegemony. Wellesley's tenure saw the crushing of Mysore as an independent polity; the expulsion of French influence and the consolidation of exclusive EIC patronage over key Indian client states such as Hyderabad; and the decisive defeat of the last remaining indigenous threat to British suprem-acy, with the EIC's victory in the Second Anglo-Maratha War (1803–5) and occupation of Delhi.[46] Wellesley's vaulting ambition, pro-consular pretensions and appetite for expensive conquests eventually prompted his

[39] Ibid., p. 89.
[40] P. J. Marshall, *The Making and Unmaking of Empires: Britain, India and America c. 1750–1783* (Oxford: Oxford University Press, 2005), p. 256.
[41] N. B. Dirks, *The Scandal of Empire: India and the creation of imperial Britain* (Cambridge, MA: Harvard University Press, 2006), p. 54.
[42] Marshall, *The Making and Unmaking of Empires*, p. 257.
[43] Lawson, *The East India Company*, p. 124.
[44] Bryant, *The Emergence of British Power in India*, p. 223.
[45] K. Yazdani, 'Foreign relations and semi-modernization during the reigns of Haidar Ali and Tipu Sultan', *British Journal of Middle Eastern Studies*, 45(3) (2018), 399–403.
[46] J. Keay, *India: A history* (London: Grove Press, 2011), p. 410.

recall to London.[47] But his time in office signified a tectonic shift in company policy, which his successors were largely compelled to follow. Thereafter, successive governors-general eschewed balance for paramountcy, and prosecuted further campaigns either to forcibly annex new territories and bring neighbours to heel (as in the Anglo-Ghurkha War), or to stamp out the last embers of Maratha resistance by forcibly demilitarizing the remnants of its armies (as in the Third Anglo-Maratha War).[48]

During third phase of the company's imperial expansion, from 1818 through to 1839, company officials were largely preoccupied with digesting the EIC's huge conquests, and consolidating and further institutionalizing their system of suzerain over-rule. This period saw the company perfect its system of indirect rule, through which it subordinated Indian feudatories to EIC suzerainty, guaranteeing them domestic autonomy in exchange for recognition of the EIC's supremacy and monopoly over feudatories' foreign relations. 'Subsidiary alliances' transferred the financial burden for support of garrisoned EIC troops to the 'princely states' themselves, while a company resident ensured that client rulers governed in conformity with EIC standards of 'civilized' administration.[49] Beyond the subcontinent itself, the company meanwhile extended its tentacular influence west into the trucial states of the Persian Gulf, and east, where it established the Straits Settlements in Southeast Asia as part of its broader commercial and diplomatic thrust towards the Qing Empire.[50]

The fourth phase of the EIC's expansion saw the company extend its influence deep into the northwest, as it sought to consolidate control over the invasion routes through which conquerors (including the Mughals) had traditionally come to seize India. Motivated in part by anxieties about Russian designs over the Raj, this phase opened with the company's inglorious defeat in the First Afghan War, arguably imperial Britain's worst defeat in Asia prior to the fall of Singapore in 1942. It nevertheless also saw the company eliminate and absorb Punjab, the last powerful local Indian state. In so doing, the company not only strengthened its north-western defences against external threats. It also secured control over a potent and modern Sikh army – which would, in time, play a disproportionate role in securing Britain from the near loss of its Indian empire during the Sepoy 'Mutiny' of 1857.[51]

---

[47] Ibid.   [48] Ibid., p. 411.   [49] Ibid., p. 383.
[50] R. Travers, 'Imperial revolutions and global repercussions: South Asia and the world, c. 1750–1850' in D. Armitage and S. Subrahmanyam (eds.), *The Age of Revolution in Global Context, c. 1760–1840* (London: Palgrave Macmillan, 2010), pp. 158–9.
[51] Keay, *India: A history*, p. 439.

This survey of the company's conquest of India has been necessarily brief. But the improbability of the EIC's ascendancy should already be clear. Chartered for trade and profit, neither the EIC's management, its shareholders nor its agents in India aspired to large-scale territorial rule, let alone subcontinental dominance. The company's militarization was driven by deteriorating security conditions flowing from Mughal entropy, local state-building and the pressures of French expansion. The 'Bengal revolution' that transformed the EIC from a network of littoral enclaves into a large-scale territorial power moreover owed much to local agency and intrigue (Bengali as well as British), and occurred despite fierce opposition to expansion from London. Both the British state and the EIC's directors subsequently strongly opposed the company's further expansion, which moreover occurred in the face of fierce (and very nearly successful) opposition from sophisticated, militarily powerful and aggressively modernizing Indian polities. The great cultural distance separating Britons from locals, coupled with the super-abundance of credit, weapons and mercenaries throughout India freely available to local state-builders, further counselled against the company's conquest of India. So, how did it happen?

In contrast to the rise of the Mughal and Qing empires, the British conquest of India has received a great deal of attention from Western historians, historical sociologists and political scientists. Explanations based on supposed Western military superiority, the conjunctural outcomes of capitalism's uneven and combined development, and expansion patterns conditioned by local configurations of social ties are among the most prominent accounts of the EIC's Indian expansion, and so form the focus of critical scrutiny below. My purpose here is to specify the grounds of my disagreement with existing accounts, so as to clarify by contrast my own argument.

Appeals to the EIC's military superiority constitute one of the most prominent and earliest explanations for the rise of the Raj. The idea that European expansion was made possible by an early modern Western military revolution – centred around the triumvirate of broadside-firing capital ships, artillery and modern fortresses – has long been a staple of accounts of European colonial conquest.[52] The undeniable centrality of violence to British expansion moreover lends military-centric explanations an undeniable plausibility at first glance. Nevertheless, even a brief acquaintance with the historical record of the EIC's takeover of India soon discredits such accounts. This is particularly so for efforts to locate the EIC's triumphs in the realm of military-technical innovation. For at the time of the British conquest of India, the technological

---

[52] The classic statement of this thesis remains Parker, *The Military Revolution*.

differences separating Western from Indian armed forces were negligible.[53] Certainly, the West had historically pioneered important military technologies. But innovations such as gunpowder weaponry had by the time of the EIC's conquest long since rapidly spread to Indian polities, via both Western and Ottoman sources.[54] This was evident not only on land, but also at sea, where Mysore had gone so far as to build a navy and attempt to develop Western-style chartered companies to offset Europeans' traditional maritime supremacy.[55] Indians had moreover not simply imitated Europeans, but also innovated military technologies themselves that Europeans later appropriated following their conquest of India. To take one example, Mysorean rockets sufficiently impressed EIC officers in the Anglo-Mysore wars that they later reverse engineered them, eventually producing Congreve rockets, which the British used to great effect following Mysore's destruction in wars in Europe as well as Asia.[56]

It is true that Europeans helped introduce modern methods of drill and discipline into Indian-based armies from the 1740s, and that this marked a critical inflection point in the subcontinent's military evolution.[57] But these and other innovations also spread rapidly if unevenly from the French and English East India companies to local state-builders, mitigating any comparative advantage Westerners might otherwise have wrung from them.[58] The presence of European and European-trained officers on the Indian military labour market further hastened the spread of modern infantry tactics, making any European attempt to monopolize such techniques extremely challenging.[59] In many instances local conditions in any case still favoured 'hit and run' styles of warfare centred on irregular light cavalry, rather than infantry-

---

[53] Peers, 'Revolution, evolution, or devolution', p. 92.

[54] Ibid., p. 95. See also generally I. A. Khan, *Gunpowder and Firearms: Warfare in medieval India* (New Delhi: Oxford University Press, 2004).

[55] See I. A. Khan, 'The regulations of Tipu Sultan for his state trading enterprise' in I. Habib (ed.), *Confronting Colonialism: Resistance and modernisation under Haidar Ali and Tipu Sultan* (London: Anthem Press, 2002), pp. 148–60. See also R. Kumar, 'The Mysore navy under Haidar Ali and Tipu Sultan' in I. Habib (ed.), *Confronting Colonialism: Resistance and modernisation under Haidar Ali and Tipu Sultan* (London: Anthem Press, 2002), pp. 175–81.

[56] See generally L. Cooper, 'Asian sources of British imperial power: The role of the Mysorean rocket in the Opium War' in A. Anievas and K. Matin (eds.), *Historical Sociology and World History: Uneven and combined development over the longue durée* (London: Rowman & Littlefield, 2016), pp. 111–26.

[57] Roy, 'The armed expansion of the English East India Company', p. 5.

[58] Peers, 'Revolution, evolution, or devolution', p. 91.

[59] Roy, 'Military synthesis in South Asia', 664. Roy notes that the EIC identified preventing the spread of European military knowledge to Indian polities as a priority, and unsuccessfully employed a range of legal and financial expedients to prevent this leakage.

centred warfare based on pitched battles.[60] This further undermines Western military superiority as a presumed explanation for the rise of the Raj.

The most compelling evidence against the thesis of Western military superiority, however, lies in the incredibly near-run character of the EIC's victories against its Indian rivals. It took no less than four wars for the EIC to subdue and conquer Mysore, for example, the first two of which the EIC lost convincingly. The Duke of Wellington would likewise much later aver that the Battle of Assaye, in the Second Anglo-Maratha War, was the most hard-fought in his career – quite some claim, given the Duke of Wellington's later victory over Napoleon's armies at Waterloo.[61] By contrast, the EIC's subordination of other powerful Indian polities – from the Bengal revolution to the submission of Hyderabad – was achieved as much through subversion as through military violence.[62] This suggests the need to look beyond a fictitious Western military superiority for the sources of the EIC's success.

Marxist approaches to the conquest of India – especially those focusing on the theory of Uneven and Combined Development (UCD) – adopt a more holistic approach to those seeking the origins of the West's rise in factors entirely endogenous to it. As we have seen in Chapter 5, UCD theorists attribute the Mughal Empire's fall to an agrarian-fiscal crisis, arising from the intersection of the Maratha insurgency with the frailties of the Mughal revenue system, and crystallizing in enervating large-scale peasant rebellions against Mughal rule.[63] They thus correctly stress the Mughal Empire's decline as a critical antecedent to the rise of the Raj, even if they mis-specify its root causes. Alongside these local factors, UCD theorists also rightly recognize the importance of an increasingly globalized Anglo-French antagonism in propelling the EIC towards militarization and large-scale territorial conquest. The UCD schema then finally foregrounds the conjuncture between the crisis of Asian tributary empires, and the precocious violence of European maritime expansionists, to account for the emergence of British India.[64]

Notwithstanding its Marxist lineage, then, the UCD approach explicitly privileges 'geopolitical combination' as its primary causal mechanism explaining the EIC's conquest of India.[65] UCD theorists undoubtedly provide a rich account of the sociological origins of Europeans' supposed 'comparative advantage in the means of violence'.[66] But like more conventional variants of the military superiority

---

[60] Peers, 'Revolution, evolution, or devolution', p. 94.   [61] Keay, *India: A history*, p. 410.
[62] Lawson, *The East India Company*, p. 92.
[63] Anievas and Nisancioglu, 'How did the West usurp the rest?', 58–62.   [64] Ibid., p. 65.
[65] Ibid.   [66] Ibid., p. 64.

thesis, UCD theorists assert the unqualified supremacy of Western arms over Indian competitors, as well as stressing its *proximate sufficiency* in explaining the rise of the Raj. Thus, for example, writing of the Battle of Plassey that heralded the EIC's conquest of Bengal, Anievas and Nisancioglu observe that '[in] the end, this superiority in the means of violence would prove crucial in the fall of the Mughal Empire to the British'.[67]

Despite its sophisticated general attempt to seek the conjunctural causes of the EIC's rise in the intersection of local and global forces, the UCD account in its details thus remains vulnerable to the same criticisms I have levelled at more parsimonious variants of the military superiority thesis. Anievas and Nisancioglu note in passing the critical importance of local intermediaries and collaborators – especially financiers and merchant groups – in facilitating the EIC's rise to hegemony.[68] But they leave unaddressed the fundamental processes through which the EIC enlisted these collaborators into the company's nascent imperial project. In particular, UCD accounts remain silent on the puzzle of precisely how the EIC harnessed 'eastern resource portfolios'[69] to construct its multi-ethnic (and overwhelmingly Indian) conquest coalition that enabled its takeover of India. The foundations of the EIC's divide and conquer strategy – critical especially from Richard Wellesley's rule onwards in suborning polities like Awadh and Hyderabad without violence – are likewise omitted from sustained consideration. Given their materialist foundations and coercion-centric explanation for British India's rise, finally, UCD accounts offer little insight into the means through which the EIC later legitimized its dominance to indigenous imperial constituencies, and so stabilized its new empire.

The final explanation of British India's conquest relevant to this discussion is the relational institutionalist account Paul MacDonald offers in his account of the social foundations of colonial era 'peripheral conquest'.[70] Discounting endogenous explanations for the Western ascendancy, MacDonald instead appeals to differences in the density and configuration of social ties within local societies to explain why the British found it so much easier to suborn some Indian polities (e.g., Awadh, Hyderabad) than others (e.g., Sindhia).[71] For MacDonald's argument, as for mine, the EIC's success as a conquest enterprise depended on the cooperation of indigenous collaborators, and the local resources (material, organizational and cultural) they could offer the

---

[67] Ibid.   [68] Ibid., p. 65.
[69] Hobson, *The Eastern Origins of Western Civilization*, p. 21.
[70] MacDonald, *Networks of Domination.*   [71] Ibid., p. 81.

EIC.[72] MacDonald thus argues that some local societies – marked by a high density of ties between indigenous elites and a low density of ties linking them to the EIC – proved far more difficult for the company to envelope than others, where an inverse configuration (low indigenous intra-elite density of ties, high density of ties to the EIC) prevailed.[73] This is because divide and conquer strategies presupposed the existence of elite fragmentation and disunity within target polities that the EIC could exploit, as well as strong social ties linking the EIC to the indigenous allies and collaborators it needed to facilitate successful conquest.

As noted, MacDonald's emphasis on the importance of local collaborators reflects my own stress on the centrality of building and binding multicultural conquest coalitions as a prerequisite for early modern empire-building. MacDonald's broader thesis – that configurations of social ties in target societies are critical determinants of conquerors' success or failure – is likewise compatible with the argument I advance here. *Indeed, our accounts of the EIC's conquest of India do not vary in essence so much as emphasis.* Though MacDonald notes in passing that the British 'used the iconography of the previous [Mughal] system to lower the social costs of collaboration',[74] I argue that the EIC's manipulation of local forms of symbolic and cultural capital was critical in easing the path of colonial conquest. This reflects a more fundamental difference in our respective explanatory foci. MacDonald dedicates his main focus to examining the social foundations of divide and rule. By contrast, this book's argument foregrounds define and rule as the central prerogative of early modern imperial statecraft. The curation of indigenous imperial constituencies was key both to building the military means of conquest in the first place, and then to stabilizing and consolidating the empires that emerged from this process. To illustrate these claims, I now turn to a consideration first of the processes through which the EIC built its Bengal-based 'hybrid' military machine,[75] before then examining how the EIC further refined local forms of cultural affiliation to extend its power into neighbouring polities, and then to consolidate its dominance over local populations once it had won regional paramountcy.

Building the EIC's Hybrid Military Machine

In understanding the EIC's transformation into a militarily potent territorial power, we must again note one of the key obstacles it had to

---

[72] Ibid.   [73] Ibid.   [74] Ibid., p. 88.
[75] On the hybridity of the EIC's military, see generally Roy, 'The hybrid military establishment of the East India Company in South Asia'.

overcome, namely the numerical insignificance of Britons in India. Vastly outnumbered relative to locals, the EIC was forced to fashion its armies overwhelmingly from indigenous human resources. The EIC's military capabilities were as a result genuinely hybrid in character, promiscuously combining European and Indian techniques, technologies and resources. In the competitive hothouse of Indian geopolitics, the EIC was moreover far from the only polity strenuously engaging in military modernization. Local rivals such as Mysore and the Maratha Confederacy rapidly assimilated European military technologies and techniques, as well as being centres of innovation in their own right.[76] The EIC's militarization was lastly also largely defensive and improvised in character, especially in its early stages. The EIC's cost-conscious directors bitterly opposed the company's expansion, rightly fearful of the damaging impact it would have for the company's profitability.[77] From the passage of Pitt's India Act in 1784, the company was moreover legislatively prohibited from engaging in wars of expansion, providing a formal (if ultimately ineffective) brake on its burgeoning imperial tendencies.[78]

These caveats aside, the growth in the company's military power from the mid-eighteenth century to the early nineteenth century was truly prodigious. Before the onset of intense Anglo-French rivalry on the subcontinent in the 1740s, the company's combined forces amounted to scarcely more than 1,000 men under arms, with even the senior Presidency (Calcutta) possessing a mere 500 troops tasked largely with guard duties.[79] By contrast, by 1805, the Bengal army had metastasized into one of the world's most powerful modern armies, numbering 64,000 troops – part of a combined total of 154,500 EIC soldiers spread across the subcontinent.[80] Thereafter, the company's armies continued to grow, totalling more than 300,000 by 1820, following the end of the Third Anglo-Maratha War (1817–19).[81]

The EIC's militarization was a critical precondition for its later colonial dominance. In explaining this evolution below, I first consider initial advantages the company possessed following its de facto takeover of Bengal in 1765, which undeniably helped account for its success. But my main focus is on two interrelated processes that together drove the

---

[76] See, for example, generally G. J. Bryant, 'Asymmetric warfare: The British experience in eighteenth century India', *Journal of Military History*, 68(2) (2004), pp. 431–69; and I. Habib (ed.), *Confronting Colonialism: Resistance and modernisation under Haidar Ali and Tipu Sultan* (London: Anthem Press, 2002).
[77] Lawson, *The East India Company*, p. 91.   [78] Ibid., p. 124.   [79] Ibid., p. 66.
[80] R. Callahan, 'The company's army, 1757–1798' in P. Tuck (ed.), *The East India Company, 1600–1858*, 6 vols., V: *Warfare, expansion, and resistance* (London: Routledge, 1998), p. 24.
[81] Lawson, *The East India Company*, p. 148.

EIC's military development. The first was the company's creeping establishment of monopsonistic control over the Indian military labour market,
as it leveraged its greater financial capabilities to position itself as Indian
mercenaries' employer of choice. The second was company officials'
curation of forms of cultural affiliation among Indian military elites, to
win their durable identification with the EIC's emerging imperial structure. In its early phases of expansion, the company confronted the same
challenges as other nascent empires considered in this book, in that it
needed to first build a multicultural conquest coalition, and then find
ways of binding its indigenous allies to emergent structures of imperial
rule. Undeniably, the techniques the company fostered to achieve these
outcomes were unique to it, and their ultimate success depended as much
on the frailties of its competitors as on the company's own intrinsic
strengths. But there remain sufficient similarities in the company's strategies with other empires to warrant fruitful comparisons, which I tease
out in the chapter's conclusion.

The EIC's transition from trading corporation to territorial empire
began in earnest following the Mughal emperor's award of rights of tax
collection (the *diwani*) and civil administration within Bengal to the company in 1765. Even before then, the company had already won dominance
along the Indian seaboard, possessing significant armed settlements in
Madras and Bombay in addition to Calcutta. To this initial advantage,
the Bengal revolution gave the company access to India's richest and most
fertile deltaic zone.[82] Bengal and the other territories encompassing the
Gangetic flood plains were naturally more productive agriculturally, and so
could yield more taxes, than other regions.[83] In winning control over
Bengal – as much through subversion as through force of arms – the EIC
had thus positioned itself well for the post-imperial melee that followed
Mughal decline. Other contenders for power may have dominated a larger
proportion of India's landmass, the Marathas exerting control over perhaps
75 per cent of the subcontinent at the height of their power.[84] But through
its administration of Bengal and its creeping subordination of neighbouring
Awadh (India's second most fertile region after Bengal), the EIC early on
managed to secure control of India's most formidable revenue base. This
ensured that the Bengal Presidency would become 'the financial and
military dynamo behind the rise of British power in India'.[85]

The Bengal land revenues were critically important for the emerging
EIC empire in two senses. Most immediately, while the land revenues

[82] Roy, 'Rethinking the origins', 1130.   [83] Ibid., p. 1131.
[84] Cooper, *The Anglo-Maratha Campaigns*, p. 8.
[85] Callahan, 'The company's army', p. 22.

themselves were never enough to fund the EIC's military enterprises, they did provide the company with sufficient collateral to be able to raise the necessary war credit from local capital markets.[86] The EIC carried very high debt-to-revenue ratios over the course of its expansion, rising from 120 per cent in 1793 to 300 per cent in 1809, and raised ninety per cent of its war finances from Indian bankers, rather than the British money market back in London.[87] The Bengal land revenues thus provided the EIC with a sound basis for borrowing and later servicing the huge debts necessary to make large-scale conquest possible. They also further cemented the EIC's symbiotic relationship with indigenous financial concerns, thereby deepening the social foundations of the company-state.[88]

Second, the very imperative of maximizing revenue yields from the Bengali economy prompted the EIC to modernize the province's system of public finance administration, and especially its revenue collection arrangements. Under Indian administrations, the landlord class (*zamindars*) had rarely suffered the threat of asset confiscation, even when they had failed to meet their assigned revenue demands.[89] By contrast, the EIC instituted a new property regime, which simultaneously provided more reliably enforceable security of tenure for landlords, but made this security conditional on their fulfilment of their revenue collection responsibilities.[90] Failure to meet these revenue requirements would lead to asset forfeiture and the company's sale of estates to the highest bidder. Pursuit of this policy enabled the EIC to 'separate the good from the bad zamindar' through the mechanism of the market rather than outright (and costly) coercion, maximizing revenue extraction.[91] The break-up of large estates that the policy triggered also had the virtuous side-effect of diluting the military and nobility element of the landlord class, while bringing in larger numbers of new zamindars as company clients.[92] In this way, fiscal modernization not only strengthened the EIC's public finances, but again helped to foster another indigenous constituency whose interests were now aligned with that of the company.

Having secured a firm fiscal footing, the EIC then built its armies by tapping into the vast Indian North Indian military labour market, eventually converting this institution exclusively to serve the company's ends. This process of conversion was protracted and complex, but can be compressed into three phases. In the first phase, the EIC positioned itself as Indian mercenaries' employer of choice, due to its greater reliability as

---

[86] Roy, 'Rethinking the origins', 1138.   [87] Ibid., pp. 1138–9.
[88] Lawson, *The East India Company*, p. 92.   [89] Roy, 'Rethinking the origins', 1150.
[90] Ibid., p. 1151.   [91] Ibid.   [92] Ibid.

a paymaster and willingness to provide benefits to soldiers and their families beyond any that rival Indian polities could offer. In the second phase, the company then began selectively integrating entire sectors of the north Indian mercenary market more permanently into the EIC's military establishment. The process of institutional conversion concluded following the Third Anglo-Maratha War, with the company's final violent eradication of the remnants of the Indian military labour market in a series of post-conquest 'pacification' campaigns. As we are interested here in the company's initial construction of its conquest machine, I confine my analysis to the first two phases of the conversion process.

The EIC's emergence as a militarized conquest state depended critically on its proximity to (and ability to readily access) the northern Indian military labour market.[93] Wedded to the profession of arms by ties of tradition and kinship as well as by financial necessity, India's professionalized peasant soldiers owed allegiance to clan and locality rather than country or emperor.[94] Indian military recruiters – themselves members of the communities they represented – generally sought employment for their charges with financial considerations foremost in mind.[95] Because of its greater fiscal capacity – built off its Bengal land revenues and the extensive financial relationships these revenues had facilitated with Indian creditors – the company was able to fund its wars through deficit financing in a way that its indigenous rivals could not. This earned the company a reputation as a more reliable paymaster than its adversaries.[96] Consequently, the company could sustain its soldiers continuously as a modern standing army in peacetime and in war, rather than having to cobble together motley coalitions anew from the market at the start of each campaign.[97] Over time, continuous service within the company armies cultivated a stronger *esprit de corps* among its troops, enhancing their combat effectiveness.[98] As the company expanded, it could moreover afford to pre-emptively buy up more scarce military specialists (gunnery-men, European and Eurasian infantry officers), denying these resources to its enemies and so widening the gap between the company's military capabilities and those of its adversaries.[99]

---

[93] Callahan, 'The company's army', p. 22.
[94] Bryant, 'Indigenous mercenaries', 8; Richards, 'Warriors and the state in early modern India', 395–6.
[95] Bryant, 'Indigenous mercenaries', 26.   [96] Ibid., p. 15.
[97] Peers, 'Revolution, evolution, or devolution', p. 101.
[98] D. M. Peers, '"The habitual nobility of being": British officers and the social construction of the Bengal army in the early nineteenth century', *Modern Asian Studies*, 25(3) (1991), 551.
[99] Occasionally, the use of this financial muscle was even more surgically targeted, as, for example, in the EIC's successful bribing of European officers to defect from the Maratha

The Company's superior creditworthiness thus laid the basis for a symbiotic commercial relationship with India's mercenaries in addition to its financial elites. Crucially, the company's relationship with India's military class was not confined to the recruitment of north Indian infantrymen, but extended also to the irregular cavalry the EIC needed to enhance its operational range, and enable pursuit of adversaries that chose not to confront the company's forces in pitched battle.[100] The EIC's financial reliability also assisted it in establishing monopsonistic control over key secondary markets, including for the mounts Indian cavalrymen needed to pursue their vocation.[101] Over time, the company made major inroads as well into the market for bullocks and other beasts of burden necessary to sustain its armies' growing lines of communication and supply.[102] Similarly, the company's financial clout enabled its agents to recruit networks of spies across India, giving it the 'real-time' intelligence necessary to pre-empt the diplomacy and military manoeuvres of its enemies.[103]

The company's fiscal strength helped it to position itself as a preferred commercial partner within India's market for force. But the real key to its success lay in its ability in the second phase of institutional conversion to permanently integrate sections of this market into its military establishment. To a degree, this was gradually accomplished through the sheer durability of the EIC's economic ties with Indian military entrepreneurs, which were further consolidated as the company picked off competing Indian polities (and potential alternative employers for Indian mercenaries) one by one. But alongside market incentives, the EIC also deployed ideational inducements to strengthen its soldiers' affective attachments to the company, and so solidify the EIC apparatus as a multi-ethnic (if Briton-led and dominated) conquest coalition. The conversion of the military labour market to company ends, and the curation of Indian subjectivities in conformity with the company's nascent imperial vision, were thus inextricably entwined processes. Two examples – drawn from the company's recruitment of high-caste peasant infantrymen in Awadh, Bihar and Banaras, and its recruitment of irregular light cavalry in the Ceded and Conquered Provinces – suffice to illustrate this larger phenomenon.

As the Calcutta Presidency expanded its armies, it drew most of its infantrymen from high-caste Hindu peasant-soldiers based in the

---

armies immediately before the Battle of Assaye in the Second Anglo-Maratha war – effectively guaranteeing victory for the company. See P. Barua, 'Military developments in India, 1750–1850', *Journal of Military History*, 58(4) (1994), 608.
[100] Roy, 'Military synthesis in South Asia', 686.
[101] See generally Alavi, 'The makings of company power'.
[102] Roy, 'Military synthesis in South Asia', 687.   [103] Ibid., pp. 688–9.

neighbouring regions of Awadh, Bihar and Banaras. The rationale behind this selection was at first entirely pragmatic. Bengal's location positioned it centrally within the north Indian military labour market, while the disbanding of local Indian polities' armies released large numbers of up-country Rajputs and Brahmins for service just as the EIC was expanding its Bengal army.[104] Over time, however, company officials developed a positive preference for recruiting high-caste peasant soldiers wherever possible, and began to manage the Bengal army in ways that radically strengthened – and later partially reconstituted – their soldiers' caste-based corporate identity. The company thus scrupulously accommodated the dietary and ritual requirements of its Hindu soldiers, and encouraged them to celebrate key religious festivals such as Holi and Ramlila.[105] It also extended privileges to its peasant soldiers that elevated them above the Brahmin priestly class that had traditionally dominated them, for example, exempting sepoys from paying pilgrim dues when entering Hindu temples.[106] Such policies cumulatively entrenched a new 'military religious tradition' that marked out the sepoys as an elite partially separate from India's traditional society, and powerfully indebted to the company for their exalted status.[107]

The company's motives for curating a separate high caste identity for its sepoy armies were admittedly diverse. Company officers saw in the Indian high-caste peasant a counterpart to the 'sturdy independent peasantry' of Britain, and assumed from this analogy that high-caste peasants likewise possessed the same physical and character virtues deemed necessary to pursue the warrior vocation.[108] An 'analogical sociology',[109] by which colonial governance was grounded in the search for homologous hierarchies between Britain and its colonies, thus undeniably informed company recruitment strategies. At a more pragmatic level, restricting military recruitment to the high-caste peasantry – a small fragment of India's population – also had the important benefit of preventing the emergence of a cross-class 'armed nation' equivalent to the Sikh kingdom, which had by this time already emerged as one of the most formidable post-Mughal polities.[110]

Beyond these conscious motives, however, the company's solicitous accommodation of the sepoys' religious preferences also had profound

---

[104] Peers, 'The habitual nobility of being', 550.
[105] G. Rand and K. A. Wagner, 'Recruiting the "martial races": Identities and military service in colonial India', *Patterns of Prejudice*, 46(3–4) (2012), 237–8. See also Alavi, *The Sepoys and the Company*, pp. 81–2.
[106] Alavi, *The Sepoys and the Company*, p. 86.
[107] Rand and Wagner, 'Recruiting the "martial races"', 238.
[108] Peers, 'The habitual nobility of being', 550.   [109] Cannadine, *Ornamentalism*, p. 43.
[110] Alavi, *The Sepoys and the Company*, p. 45.

political consequences, which company officials could only dimly antici-
pate. Specifically, it helped to create a powerful new indigenous constituency for empire, contributing also to an entrenchment of caste hierarchy
as a key foundation for imperial rule. Drawing from Eric Hobsbawm's
notion of 'invented tradition', Seema Alavi catalogues an exhaustive set of
practices through which the company 'reinvented' high-caste identity in
the regimental context.[111] The incorporation of regimental standards as
an object of veneration in the morning ritual of *puja*, and European
officers' participation in holy festivals to the pointed exclusion of traditional Hindu religious authorities, are just two instances of the new
fusion of religious and military identities the company's policies
promoted.[112] Far from merely reproducing extant hierarchies, these
practices importantly modified and reconfigured them in ways that
broadened the company's indigenous social base. Thus in Bihar, a 'high
recruiting zone' for the company, the Bhumihar Brahmins became a key
source of company sepoys.[113] The popularity of company service
stemmed partly from its potential to relieve the Bhumihars from their
tenuous and contested caste status within the region. This is because the
Bhumihars' ancestors had taken to agriculture, and the resulting stigma
had seen all other Brahmins deny them high-caste status recognition.[114]
Military service within the company conversely promised to reaffirm and
even restore the Bhumihar Brahmins' high-caste status, enabling them to
reposition themselves favourably within indigenous social hierarchies.[115]

The curation of a high caste identity in the Bengal army marked one of
the most conspicuous examples of company officials' mobilization and
modification of indigenous ideational resources to help build their conquest coalition. But, as the company was dragged further north and west in
its conflicts with the Marathas, its military needs diversified. In particular,
the Marathas' strengths in cavalry warfare compelled the EIC to develop
an equivalent capability to offset this advantage.[116] This again entailed
tapping into Indian resource portfolios, and adapting the company's
legitimation strategies to most effectively draw indigenous allies into the
EIC's military establishment. In the Conquered and Ceded Provinces,
especially in the areas surrounding Delhi, the company did so by drawing
judiciously on Mughal practices and conceptions of legitimacy to entice
Rohilla and Afghan troopers into the EIC's service.[117] Eurasian officers,
who enjoyed bicultural competence owing to their mixed heritage and
previous employment in both European and Indian polities' service,

---

[111] Ibid., p. 75.   [112] Ibid., pp. 80–3.   [113] Ibid., p. 51.   [114] Ibid.   [115] Ibid.
[116] Alavi, 'The makings of company power', 439.
[117] Alavi, *The Sepoys and the Company*, pp. 232–3.

proved crucial as brokers in mediating this process.[118] Alavi thus notes that James Skinner, a key Eurasian company intermediary, resurrected the Mughal tradition of the durbar as a means of inducting leading cavalrymen into the company's service.[119] Similarly, Skinner also blended Mughal uniforms and cavalry warfare traditions with Western drill and discipline, further underscoring the hybrid foundations of the company's evolving military establishment.[120]

Not merely an expedient to assist recruitment, Skinner's innovations help to 'construct a new idiom of legitimacy for the Company', which won the allegiance of both cavalrymen from established noble traditions, as well as warriors from mobile pastoralist populations, that had previously been marginalized from the political life of preceding Indian polities.[121] The cultural capital attached to established Mughal conceptions of rank, courtliness and martial valour thus attracted two constituencies to the company. It drew in nobles that were already familiar with the expectations, privileges and roles associated with Mughal military service, and which successor Indian states had imitated and thus preserved in northern India following the Mughal Empire's decline.[122] But it also attracted formerly stigmatized pastoralist and semi-pastoralist communities, for whom service in the company offered a chance of status enhancement and upward mobility they had previously been denied.[123] Coupled with generous material incentives, the company's co-optation and partial reinvention of Mughal cultural resources thus helped recruit and acculturate new constituencies to the EIC's service. These constituencies brought with them military skills and assets that proved indispensable to settling and 'pacifying' the company empire's sparsely populated provinces in India's north and west, and to thus consolidating the EIC's hold over the subcontinent.

The preceding examples provide only two illustrations of a much broader set of processes by which the company converted the institution of the Indian military market to serve its own ends, using both its financial strength and its 'soft power' cultural statecraft to do so. Undeniably, the schematic presentation of evidence here invites the danger of crediting company officials with more foresight and strategic acumen than they generally possessed. To be clear, the company's expansion was largely chaotic, episodic and reactive. Consequently, we must acknowledge that the imperial agglomeration that emerged from the company's wars was much more a product of incremental improvisation than considered institutional design. Likewise, a more comprehensive account of the

---

[118] Alavi, 'The makings of company power', 440.   [119] Ibid.   [120] Ibid.
[121] Ibid., p. 454.   [122] Ibid.   [123] Ibid.

Company Raj would afford greater attention to the manifold internal weaknesses and divisions of Indian polities, which enabled them to be either defeated or otherwise suborned.

These qualifiers aside, my key claim remains that the company's expansion necessitated the sustained curation of indigenous forms of cultural affiliation to build a viable conquest coalition. This evolution has important parallels with the Mughal and Qing processes of empire formation previously considered, which I take up at the end of this chapter. Before doing so, however, we must first consider how the EIC organized cultural diversity to permanently bind its conquest coalition to the company, thereby stabilizing and legitimizing its dominion for the longer term.

The Consolidation and Legitimization of the Company Raj

Historical interrogations of the Raj today often focus on the undeniably critical role that racial and civilizational hierarchies played in underpinning British domination in South Asia.[124] This emphasis is hardly misplaced, especially for the post-1857 era of Crown rule following the Indian Mutiny. But there is a danger in projecting ideas of 'scientific racism' and late colonial 'civilizing missions' back to the conquest and immediate post-conquest eras of the late eighteenth and early nineteenth centuries. Such anachronisms run the risk of overstating the initial cultural estrangement between British rulers and Indian subjects. This consequently makes it harder to account for how the company was able to win over local collaborators and consolidate its rule in India in the first place.

Undeniably, the EIC lacked the ready-made cultural familiarity with locals that had aided the Mughals in consolidating power in northern India. But at least in the empire's early stages, the company creatively misperceived cultural and sociological parallels between British and Indian society, in ways that paradoxically helped it to engage with indigenous collaborators and thereby legitimize its power. This was evident first in its appropriation of Mughal symbols and practices to stabilize the company's de facto paramountcy under a patina of local legitimacy. The company's systematic curation of religious forms of affiliation among its subjects – especially Hinduism – then later provided a more comprehensive and systematically institutionalized basis for company supremacy. Consistent with this book's larger argument and the experiences of the other empires I have considered, the company reconfigured indigenous

---

[124] For a fascinating recent exploration of this theme, see J. Mohan, 'The glory of ancient India stems from her Aryan blood: French anthropologists "construct" the racial history of India for the world', *Modern Asian Studies*, 50(5) (2016), 1576–618.

identities as it sought to bind its diverse coalition of collaborators to emerging structures of imperial rule. Whereas the Mughal order at its height had rested on a model of *syncretic incorporation*, and the Manchu order on one of *segregated incorporation*, the Company Raj alternatively organized cultural diversity around a system of *ecumenical incorporation*. After briefly considering its mobilization of Mughal symbols and practices to aid the company's rise, the remainder of this section anatomizes the character and workings of this system.

As I established in Chapter 4, the EIC originally established itself in the Mughal Empire through ingratiation, involving the company's meek conformity with Mughal norms of court ceremonial and political incorporation. In its first incarnation as an armed merchant diaspora, the company had had no choice but to familiarize itself with Mughal conceptions of legitimacy, and to inveigle itself into the Mughal order as a vassal to the emperor.[125] Later, following the empire's decline, the EIC established itself as a territorial power in Bengal as a nominal servant of the Emperor. Through its acceptance of the *diwani* and this office's obligations of revenue collection and civil administration, the company derived its local legitimacy from acting in the emperor's name.[126] Far from merely a convenient fiction, the EIC did, in fact, pay a substantial yearly tribute to the imperial treasury (something that the preceding *nawab* administrations had long since ceased doing), even if it kept the lion's share of Bengal's wealth for itself.[127] Thereafter, the company continued to ritually enact its submission to the Mughal emperor down to 1843, and only formally foreswore allegiance to the emperor following the 1857 Mutiny and the ensuing transition from EIC to Crown rule.[128]

The EIC thus retained the illusion of subordination to the Mughal emperor for decades after the Mughals' practical authority had evaporated, and indeed for a long time after the company had itself displaced the Mughals as India's paramount power. The rationale for doing so was strategic rather than sentimental. For the company determined that retaining this fictional allegiance was essential to avoid 'exciting the possible alarm and opposition of the Indian rulers and people by openly proclaiming British sovereignty or its [the EIC's] revocation of Mughal sovereignty'.[129] This prudence is testament to the degree to which

---

[125] See generally Barbour, 'Power and distant display'.

[126] Stern, *The Company-State*, p. 208.

[127] S. Meurer, 'Approaches to state-building in eighteenth century Bengal' in A. Fluchter and S. Richter (eds.), *Structures on the Move: Technologies of governance in transcultural encounter* (Heidelberg: Springer, 2012), p. 222.

[128] M. H. Fisher, 'The imperial coronation of 1819: Awadh, the British and the Mughals', *Modern Asian Studies*, 19(2) (1985), 240.

[129] Ibid.

company officials acknowledged the potent symbolic capital that still resided in the Mughal imperial office. But this recognition is even more evident in the parallel policies company agents meanwhile simultaneously pursued in appropriating Mughal practices and symbols for themselves, while surreptitiously chipping away at the bonds of loyalty that nominally linked the Mughal emperor to his remaining Indian vassals.

The appropriation of Mughal practices and symbols was evident in the company's enticement of collaborators in both Bengal and in the Ceded and Conquered Provinces. In Bengal, the EIC assiduously groomed local *zamindars* to help the company gain access to Bengal's land revenues, and also to fast-track recruitment of soldiers into the company's high-caste peasant army. In direct imitation of Mughal practice, the EIC drew *zamindar* allies into its embrace by providing them with a *khilat* symbolizing their incorporation into the Company Raj.[130] Long-established practices of ritual gift exchange, symbolizing vassals' bodily incorporation into the household of the suzerain power, were thus re-tooled by the company from Mughal precedents to strengthen its ties with indigenous elites. Similarly, as we have already seen, James Skinner explicitly drew upon Mughal iconography to attract irregular Muslim cavalry to the company's service in the Ceded and Conquered Provinces, and reinvented the Mughal court tradition of the durbar to provide a ritualized focal point for intermediaries' integration and public submission to the EIC.[131]

In appropriating Mughal practices and symbols, the company sought to fill the bonds linking it to local intermediaries with affective content, so as to naturalize their collaboration. At the same time, the EIC also consciously undermined the residual bonds of solidarity linking Indian polities to the Mughal emperor. To take one example, in 1819, the EIC successfully pushed the *nawab* of Awadh – a *de jure* subordinate of the Mughal emperor but a *de facto* tributary of the company – to renounce his allegiance to the emperor and declare himself king of an independent Shi'ite state.[132] The goal of this policy was to weaken the emperor's remaining symbolic authority, and to foreclose the possibility of the emperor becoming a figurehead for opposition to the EIC's creeping hegemony. Reluctant themselves to alienate local opinion by renouncing the company's submission to the emperor, the EIC instead aimed 'to try to fragment it [the Mughal Empire] without making the Company appear overtly treasonous.'[133] Accordingly, the company sponsored Awadh's *nawab* as a sovereign monarch, and helped stage-manage a coronation that blended Mughal and European royal rituals, the latter culminating in

---

[130] Alavi, *The Sepoys and the Company*, p. 63.   [131] Ibid., p. 247.
[132] Fisher, 'The imperial coronation of 1819', 251.   [133] Ibid., p. 250.

the *nawab*'s acceptance of a European-style crown.[134] In promoting Awadh's secession from the Mughal Empire, then, the EIC weakened the emperor's grip on Indian rulers' sentiments and loyalties, without overtly challenging his authority and so risking concerted resistance to the company's rise.

The foregoing examples of the EIC's cultural statecraft attest to the continuing attraction Mughal practices and symbols held for indigenous elites, and the great store the company agents placed in appropriating and manipulating these practices and symbols to consolidate the company's power and build a more enduring basis for collaboration with local intermediaries. But they also disclose a deeper truth. In both its conquest and immediate post-conquest phases, the EIC cultivated a distinctly mestizo character. This was evident in both its public self-representation and in its institutional character. When the EIC seized power in Bengal, it nominally did so as a loyal servant of the Mughal emperor, and tenaciously clung to this camouflage throughout the era of the Company Raj. Administratively, the company also perpetuated many of the practices of its Indian predecessors, for example, keeping Persian as the official language of company rule in Bengal down to 1837.[135] Retention of Persian provided an important point of continuity between pre-colonial and colonial administrations, aiding the company in the task of conciliating and integrating local elites.[136] But the company's preference for Persian also reflected the fact that many British officers and administrators came to develop a genuine appreciation for Persian language and poetry and Mughal culture, some even going so far as to adopt Persian *noms de plume* in their literary pursuits.[137]

The cultural gulf separating rulers from ruled in the early Company Raj was thus narrower and less unbridgeable than it would be after 1857. High-ranking company officials possessed greater cultural familiarity (and in some cases, affinity) with their Indian subjects than their late-Victorian and Edwardian successors. They initially sought to rule in an 'Indian idiom', legitimizing their empire by mobilizing the full panoply of Indian ceremonial traditions and practices, and then blending them with their Western counterparts.[138] E. M. Collingham notes that in fashioning a form of ceremonial appropriate to legitimize their rule, the British 'borrowed from the rituals of their own country (mace bearers and state carriages) as well as from the Mughals (elephants, stick bearers, spearmen and peacock plumes)'.[139] Beyond state ceremonial, this

---

[134] Ibid., pp. 260–1.
[135] T. Rahman, 'Decline of Persian in British India', *South Asia*, 22(1) (1999), 50.
[136] Ibid., p. 48.   [137] Ibid., p. 49.   [138] Collingham, *Imperial Bodies*, p. 14.
[139] Ibid., p. 16.

hybridization also extended even to the bodily practices of the early British administrators (the *nabobs*) themselves, with early company rulers favouring Indian habits of diet, dress, deportment, hygiene (including for the British, the then novel use of shampoo) and leisure.[140]

Cultural hybridization in the Company Raj thus stemmed from a self-conscious strategy of imperial legitimation, as well as reflecting the proclivities and embodied experiences of at least a portion of the EIC elite. At first, the company's efforts to indigenize its authority were improvised and haphazard, reflecting the idiosyncrasies of the company's agents and the varying legitimation requirements they faced in the empire's diverse localities. As the EIC consolidated its rule, however, the need became more pressing to settle on a more comprehensive strategy for legitimizing and institutionalizing the Company Raj. The management of religious difference – through a model of imperial rule I characterize as *ecumenical incorporation* – would prove central to this enterprise.

Like the other empires I have considered, the Company Raj ruled through difference. By this, I mean that it curated, organized and in the process reconfigured indigenous identities, and then legitimized its dominance through a governance model grounded in the management of cultural diversity. From the outset of its rule, the company privileged communal identities – organized around the central and antagonistic binary of Hindu/Muslim – as the foundation of its diversity regime. In their early vision of empire, the EIC's upper echelons conceived their governing mandate as explicitly restorative in purpose. Company officials imagined India as Hindu in its essence, a great and ancient civilization laid low by the 'despotic' rule of successive Muslim invaders culminating in the Mughals.[141] Comparing their role in India to that of the ancient Romans in Greece, the British legitimized their power on the need to revive a classical civilization that was only momentarily moribund.[142] Indian *qua* Hindu civilization could be redeemed. But this would require British intercession. And they could redeem India only by governing 'Hindus' and 'Muslims' as discrete categories of people. They would be subject to their own separate bodies of law, and bound to the Company Raj through customized compacts that reflected and reinforced communal identity as the subcontinent's defining fault line.

The Company Raj's diversity regime crystallized around a host of practices. The most important took hold in the realms of education, law and company patronage of religious institutions, encompassing respectively the Raj's epistemic, judicial and pastoral foundations.

---

[140] Ibid., p. 17.   [141] Ibid., p. 15.   [142] Ibid.

At the epistemic level, Warren Hastings (Bengal's first governor-general) determined from the EIC's first days as a territorial ruler that its Indian subjects could be best ruled through indigenous intermediaries and institutions.[143] The imperative of collaboration yielded a need for the EIC to discover and codify the systems of knowledge underpinning Indian legal arrangements.[144] Accordingly, one of Hastings' first initiatives was to establish institutions to study the languages and laws of India's Islamic and Hindu communities.

The Calcutta Madrassa (established 1780) and the Sanskrit College at Banaras (established 1791) eventually emerged as the chief institutions through which the company sought to clarify and institutionalize Islamic and Hindu legal codes, and train separate cadres of Muslim and Hindu legal specialists to interpret and administer these bodies of law.[145] Concurrently, the EIC meanwhile sponsored other institutions to train EIC officials in Indian classical and vernacular languages, as well as Indian literature and science. The purposes driving this huge educational undertaking were diverse. Certainly, the attempt to 'recover' India's supposedly timeless wisdom gelled with the academic passions of many early EIC administrators, as well as serving a broader project of locating Indian and Western civilizations 'on an evaluative scale of progress and decay'.[146] Company officials moreover sought to cultivate the legitimacy of colonial rule by patronizing Indian actors and institutions deemed to embody Indian traditions.[147] But the most compelling reason driving the company's educational initiatives was more prosaic. Strengthening Britons' knowledge of Indian languages and laws enhanced the EIC's ability to govern through indigenous intermediaries, while minimizing its vulnerability to subterfuge from these very same collaborators.[148] And stabilizing Indian languages and laws provided the company with a more cohesive linguistic and legal infrastructure – grounded in the appearance of indigenous provenance and legitimacy – through which to rule.

Consistent with this imperative, administrators from Hastings onwards resolved to rule as much as possible through Indian rather than British law. The EIC conceived the former as being naturally bifurcated along Hindu ('Gentoo') and Islamic lines. Invoking the spirit of Justinian, the emperor renowned for his codification of the laws of the Roman Empire, company officials dedicated themselves to distilling and reinstituting the essence of India's 'ancient constitution'.[149] This entailed the systematic translation and study of legal texts, and the elimination of accretions and customs that had supposedly corrupted Hindu and Muslim legal

---

[143] Cohn, *Colonialism and Its Forms of Knowledge*, p. 26.   [144] Ibid.   [145] Ibid., pp. 47–8.
[146] Ibid., p. 46.   [147] Ibid.   [148] Ibid., p. 144.   [149] Ibid., p. 146.

traditions over time.[150] Concurrent with this process of codification, the EIC meanwhile established a hybrid judicial system, composed of 'a complex intertwining of Muslim, Hindu and British authority in a patchwork legal order'.[151] Thus in Bengal, Indian subjects remained subject to the pre-existing Muslim system of criminal law, which continued to be administered in the lower courts entirely by Mughal officials.[152] But separate Hindu and Muslim legal codes, administered with the help and advice of dedicated Indian experts (*pandits* and *maulvis*), governed Indian civil disputes.[153] British subjects meanwhile fell under the jurisdiction of English-led courts.[154]

The company's plural legal order – in which different courts claimed jurisdiction over different classes of persons – was by no means strange for Britons familiar with the heteronomy that had long shaped Western legal traditions. Indeed, Lauren Benton notes that Hastings' reordering of Bengal drew in part from his misunderstanding that Hindu law was somehow analogous to canon law in medieval Christendom.[155] This is by itself unsurprising. The search for local analogues to Western traditions was common enough for European colonialists, as they sought to better understand and so control indigenous intermediaries. Nevertheless, the EIC's attempt to build its legal order on local foundations had dramatically reconstitutive effects on Indian society, not least because it reified and ossified the Hindu/Muslim binary as India's defining divide. This was evident not merely in the educational and legal domains, but finally also in the direct superintendence over Indian religious governance that the company eventually also assumed.

The curation of a distinct and nominally unitary 'Hindu' religious identity arguably constitutes the Company Raj's most important historical legacy. Recounting the rise of a 'Hindu Raj' under company rule, historian Robert Frykenberg observes that the EIC's establishment of a modern all-Indian Hindu identity encompassed both institutional and ideological dimensions.[156] At the institutional level, the Company Raj progressively assumed supervision over temples and charitable endowments, eventually establishing 'a huge informational, institutional, and intellectual infrastructure for an officially supported reification of religion'.[157] Orientalists scholars, working in conjunction with Indian collaborators, meanwhile collected, integrated, reconstructed and

---

[150] Ibid., p. 144.   [151] Benton, 'Colonial law and cultural difference', 570.
[152] Ibid., p. 567.   [153] Ibid.   [154] Ibid., p. 566.   [155] Ibid., p. 567.
[156] R. E. Frykenberg, 'Constructions of Hinduism at the nexus of history and religion', *Journal of Interdisciplinary History*, 23(3) (1993), 535.
[157] Ibid., p. 537.

publicized a unitary 'establishment Hinduism', conceived as a '*single* and *ancient* religion' synonymous with India itself.[158]

Historically, the very word 'Hindu' had originated from Persian rather than Sanskrit, denoting the people living in the vicinity of the Indus river rather than any cohesive all-India religious tradition.[159] Its use as a self-referential identifier among Indians moreover only developed in the fifteenth and sixteenth centuries.[160] And even then Indians used it only as a marker to distinguish 'indigenous' Indians from 'foreigners', rather than to signify a unified community of believers subscribing to a common faith.[161] By contrast, the term 'Hinduism' dates from the early nineteenth century, acquiring broad currency among Indians as well as Westerners only from this time.[162] This timing is far from coincidental, for the emergence of a coherent common denominator Hinduism was critically important in consolidating EIC rule. Thus, Frykenberg notes: 'In a continent so highly pluralistic, such a Hinduism helped to reinforce the construction of any single huge overarching political order.'[163]

The construction of a form of all-India 'syndicated Hinduism'[164] was by no means an exclusively British enterprise, foisted on passive or resistant locals. On the contrary, local intermediaries – notably the lettered Brahmin castes – were fundamentally implicated in the production of modern Hinduism. In particular, Brahmin scribal elites were pivotal in the 'textualization' of Hinduism, locating its spiritual core in certain Sanskrit texts and Brahminical styles of devotion, at the expense of more fluid and locally idiosyncratic beliefs and forms of worship.[165] In this sense, then, it is perhaps better to speak of a co-curation of modern Hinduism, stemming from the company's need to make India legible and governable, and Brahmin elites' dovetailing desires to consolidate their religious authority and social status within the emerging colonial hierarchy.[166]

Hinduism was thus never an exclusively British creation. Instead, it emerged through a complex interweaving of Western and indigenous agency.[167] This crucial caveat aside, we have seen that the construction of the Hindu as a distinctive collective identity suffused company

---

[158] Ibid., p. 539.
[159] R. King, 'Orientalism and the modern myth of "Hinduism"', *Numen*, 46(2) (1999), 162.
[160] Ibid.   [161] Ibid.   [162] Ibid. See also Truschke, *Aurangzeb*, p. 17.
[163] Frykenberg, 'Constructions of Hinduism', 540.   [164] Ibid., p. 549.
[165] King, 'Orientalism and the modern myth of "Hinduism"', 166–7. Interestingly, King notes that this text-centric conception of Hinduism resonated with British administrators and informed their thinking in part because of its affinity with Protestantism's central emphasis on text as the locus of religious worship.
[166] Ibid.   [167] Frykenberg, 'Construction of Hinduism', 533.

practices ranging from military recruitment through to education, administration and jurisprudence. This reification (and partial reconfiguration) of religious identity was also to a degree apparent in the company's treatment of its Muslim subjects. In contrast to those Indians that came to identify as Hindus, self-consciously Islamic conceptions of legitimacy and community had long held sway among South Asian Muslims. In particular, the subordination of Islamic subjects to sharia law had been a key source of legitimacy for the Mughal emperors, even if in practice it had only been applied primarily to the gentry and urban merchant elites.[168]

The advent of company rule, however, saw the emergence of an 'Anglo-Muhammadan' jurisprudence that elevated Islam as being exclusively determinative of South Asian Muslims' identity, and sought to obliterate all differences (geographical as well as doctrinal) that had formerly distinguished the subcontinent's diverse Islamic communities.[169] In parallel with the company's textualization of Hinduism, company officials embraced a scriptural literalism that mistook the Koran as a 'fixed body of immutable rules beyond the realm of interpretation and judicial discretion', and sought to inflexibly apply it in administering justice to the EIC's Muslim subjects.[170] This practice took no account of long-established traditions through which Islamic judges and lawyers had flexibly reconciled Koranic precepts with local customs. Equally importantly, it eventually had the effect of reformulating South Asian Islamic identities along more exclusive lines. Anglo-Muhammadan law under the EIC compelled litigants to present themselves as Muslim or Hindu.[171] It also explicitly identified being Muslim with conformity to a highly conservative form of sharia, which had previously held sway only among a portion of the Mughal gentry and urban elite.[172] Both tendencies cemented the estrangement between Hindu and Muslim on which British rule was increasingly based – an estrangement that would also paradoxically much later drive the Raj's destruction.

Conclusion

This chapter has examined the EIC's rise to dominance in South Asia, with a view to situating its ascendancy in comparison to its Mughal and Manchu counterparts. In revisiting this chapter's findings and drawing out their implications, I first foreground the common empire-building challenges and congruent responses the EIC shared with its Asian comparators. I then consider the distinctive disadvantages and advantages that shaped the EIC's ascent relative to its Asian counterparts, and that left

---

[168] Anderson, 'Islamic law and the colonial encounter', pp. 170–1. [169] Ibid., p. 172. [170] Ibid., p. 176. [171] Ibid., p. 181. [172] Ibid.

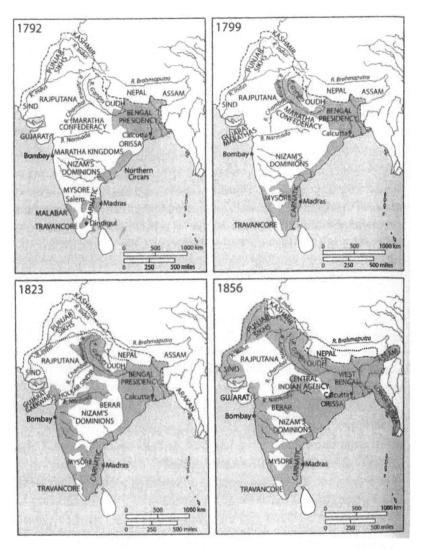

Map 6.1 The British Raj and its expansion
Source: Andrew Phillips and J. C. Sharman, *Outsourcing Empire: How Company-States Made the Modern World* (Princeton University Press, 2020), p. 140.

their indelible imprint on the Company Raj. I conclude by foreshadowing the Company Raj's deep contradictions in its post-conquest consolidation phase after 1820. In their violent resolution, these contradictions forced a transformation of imperial hierarchies, not only in British-dominated South Asia, but also ultimately in Qing-dominated East Asia as well.

The EIC's takeover of South Asia seems especially unlikely, given the obvious differences distinguishing it from either the Mughals or the Manchus. Both the Mughal and Qing empires emerged out of long-established steppe traditions of universal empire. Babur and his successors revered the legacies of Genghis Khan and Tamerlane, and their successors invoked genealogical links (both real and imagined) to these conquerors in legitimating the Mughal imperial project.[173] Likewise, veneration of Genghis Khan played an equally prominent role in legitimating the Qing imperial enterprise, especially in cementing the Manchus' hold over the steppe.[174] Undeniably, neither Babur nor Nurhaci, the respective founders of the Mughal and the Manchu empires, could have either desired or envisaged the vast sedentary empires their exploits eventually spawned. Mughal and Manchu warlords marched a crooked path to conquest, marked by chaotic improvisation and opportunism more than the calculated pursuit of a well-considered grand strategy. But unlike the EIC, the Mughals and the Manchus operated in a mental universe that conceived conquest as glorious and legitimate, rather than a costly distraction from the business of trade.

This contrast between the EIC and its Asian counterparts is essential, and I explore its implications below. But it should not distract us from less obvious but equally important similarities in the origins of the Mughal, Manchu and British empires, as well as the common challenges each confronted.

Turning to origins, these empires all evolved from the military and commercial activities of marginal actors located at the geographical and cultural fringes of Asia's existing centres of wealth and power. Whether originating on the steppe or the sea, these actors leveraged niche military advantages (respectively in cavalry and blue water naval warfare) to insinuate their way into Indian and Chinese courts and ports. Trading and raiding from Asia's terrestrial and littoral frontiers, Inner Asian warlords and European company-states could use the threat of limited coercion to extort commercial privileges from host societies. But they could also respectively temporarily retreat into the vastness of the Eurasian interior, or regroup to other coastal enclaves along their littoral trading networks, if they met concerted opposition.

---

[173] See generally Balabanlilar, *Imperial Identity in the Mughal Empire*.
[174] Elverskog, *Our Great Qing*, p. 79.

More important than coercion, however, was the connective role these marginal actors played as armed commercial intermediaries along Eurasian long-distance trading networks. The economic dynamism that marked the early modern Eurasian Transformation greatly enhanced urban elites' appetites for exotic luxuries, in both Europe and Asia. In their different ways, Mughal, Manchu and European imperialists all benefited from this commercial expansion, which they tapped to build the war chests that later enabled military expansion. This connection between trade and conquest was evident even for the Mughals, who primarily benefited from the unique combination of resources that came from their early occupation of the thriving commercial entrepot of Kabul. Kabul gave Babur access to a taxable peasantry, pasturage on which to raise warhorses, Indian bills of credit and gunpowder weaponry via the long-distance trade between Afghanistan and the Ottoman Empire.[175] Ensconced in Kabul at the intersection of key overland trading routes, Babur was able to cobble together out of these elements the precise combination of tax revenues, warhorses, freebooters, credit and guns necessary to enable conquest of the proverbially rich and populous territories of the Indo-Gangetic plain.[176]

The connection between trade, war and empire-building was even more intimate and direct for the Manchus and the EIC. Recall that Nurhaci built his initial ascent among the Jurchen on what was essentially a highly militarized commercial monopoly, based on control over the trade in hinterland luxury commodities with the Ming Dynasty. Ginseng especially furnished the profits that filled Nurhaci's war chest, and that financed his successors' later conquest of China.[177] The EIC likewise tried to build its fortune on drugs, specifically by arbitraging profits through monopolizing the East-West long-distance trade in fine spices. Though the Dutch soon evicted its agents from the Spice Islands, the desire to secure monopolistic control over the drug trade (first in spices, then later in tea and opium) remained key to the EIC's financial fortunes for the first two centuries of its operation, and its ostensible *raison d'être* throughout most of this period.[178]

Despite their differences, then, the nuclei of the Mughal, Manchu and British empires developed out of a particular form of frontier capitalized coercion that took hold during the Eurasian Transformation. The advantages of a frontier location, possession of niche military capabilities, and

---

[175] Gommans, *Mughal Warfare*, pp. 24–5.   [176] Ibid.

[177] Rawski, *Early Modern China and Northeast Asia*, p. 79.

[178] On tea as a crucial imperial commodity, see generally Rappaport, *A Thirst for Empire*. On opium's critical role for the EIC and the British imperial presence in Asia more generally, see Trocki, *Opium, Empire and the Global Political Economy*.

the arbitrage and brokerage opportunities afforded by the Eurasia-wide growth in long-distance trade (especially in luxury commodities) together helped nourish a new form of polity.[179] This type of polity resembled in some ways the 'shadow empires' that had recurrently formed along the Eurasian steppe frontier since antiquity.[180] Entrepreneurial warlords had a long history of siphoning wealth from neighbouring sedentary societies, harnessing the profits from this trading and raiding to temporarily unify clans and lineages into larger confederacies.[181] But the early modern period saw a diversification in the form and sources of these shadow empires, with European thalassocracies emerging on Eurasia's maritime frontier to complement a revival of steppe pastoral confederacies. Critically, these new frontier empires acquired a far greater degree of institutional durability and sophistication than their ancient and medieval predecessors, to the extent that they permanently transformed the political organization of the South and East Asian populations over which they ruled.

Beyond parallels in its origins with its Asian comparators, the Company Raj confronted similar challenges as it made the transition to full-fledged territorial empire. Like the Mughals and Manchus before them, company officials were compelled by dint of their small numbers to organize culturally diverse coalitions for conquest. Later, they also had to contrive a durable system of government that bound these imperial constituencies to the centre in common subjection, while minimizing opportunities for subversive collaboration between them. Following Mughal precedents, the EIC exploited India's bottomless market for mercenaries to build the company's armies, only to later establish monopsonistic control over this market, so converting an Indian institution to the company's ends. The company moreover mimicked its Asian counterparts in curating the ethnic and religious identities of its imperial constituencies, to better bind them into emerging structures of imperial rule. In appropriating and repurposing the symbolic capital of the Mughal Empire, finally, the EIC followed Asian precedents yet again. Just as the Mughals themselves had hijacked India's Persephone high culture for their own ends, so too did the EIC win over local allies – and so undercut Mughal authority – by weaving Mughal rituals of incorporation into the Company Raj's own

---

[179] Though outside the scope of this study, tsarist Russia's expansion into Siberia – via the mediation of the Stroganov family and on the basis of profits extracted from the booming early modern fur trade – also fits with this general model. See Y. Slezkine, *Arctic Mirrors: Russia and the small peoples of the north* (Ithaca: Cornell University Press, 1994), pp. 12–13.

[180] On the concept of 'shadow empires', see generally Barfield, 'The shadow empires'.

[181] Ibid.

nascent legitimating codes. This use of cultural appropriation as a strategy of imperial statecraft finds analogues too in the Manchus' mobilization of diverse forms of symbolic capital – from the Sinic Mandate of Heaven through to Tibetan Buddhism – to secure their rule.

The final noteworthy parallel between the three empires under review is that all stabilized imperial hierarchies through the construction of distinctive diversity regimes.

The Mughals at their height institutionalized a rule through difference via a diversity regime of syncretic incorporation, most famously manifest in the religious eclecticism of Akbar's court. Akbar's imperial vision self-consciously strove to legitimize Mughal power through an attempt at spiritual synthesis. Akbar himself sought to both embody and reconcile India's diverse faiths in his person, and to formulate a belief system that honoured these faiths while distilling the common transcendent truths underlying them.[182]

The Manchus by contrast entrenched a diversity regime based on segregated incorporation, and which grew over time to institutionalize ethnic rather than religious difference as its dominant organizing principle. To repeat an earlier observation, Manchus controlled cultural diversity by incarnating it.[183] They separately represented themselves as the embodiments of universal authority to each of their key imperial constituencies. But they remained careful to code-switch between identities depending on their audience, mindful of the fact that legitimating codes sacred to one constituency could risk dangerously alienating others.[184]

Like the Mughals and the Manchus, the EIC also ruled through difference. It followed Asian precedents in curating indigenous collective identities, customizing its appeals to different imperial constituencies, and entrenching both within a coherent and over time increasingly institutionalized diversity regime. It moreover did so for much the same reasons as the Mughals and Manchus. As frontier parvenu conquerors, the EIC had to build diverse conquest coalitions to establish its empire, and later had to also find ways to bind these coalitions to the emerging Company Raj.

Certainly, the EIC enjoyed some unique institutional advantages that aided its victories. Not least of these was its superior creditworthiness, built in large part from its efficient management of the Bengal land revenues.[185] The EIC's greater institutional coherence – as a chartered

[182] Khan, 'Tracing sources of principles of Mughal governance', 51.
[183] Crossley, *A Translucent Mirror*, p. 221.
[184] Farquhar, 'Emperor as Bodhisattva', p. 26.
[185] Callahan, 'The company's army', p. 22. See also generally Roy, 'Rethinking the origins'.

corporation rather than a personalistic dynasty – moreover rendered it less susceptible to fragmentation through subversion or intrigue than its Indian opponents.[186]

Offsetting these advantages, the Company Raj also confronted meaningful and unique disadvantages as a conquest regime. Unlike the traditions of universal steppe empire that fed Mughal and Manchu expansion, the EIC's commercial motives and chartered character delayed, constrained and initially inhibited its transition to a conquest empire. Far from whetting their appetite for territory, the EIC's takeover of Bengal antagonized the company's cost-conscious directors, and prompted parliamentary intervention to (unsuccessfully) proscribe further territorial expansion.[187] Certainly, the pressures of war with neighbouring Indian polities rapidly weakened the practical force of this prohibition. But territorial conquest under successive governor-generals re-emerged mainly as a costly by-product of defending the company's existing territorial assets – and thus the EIC's financial viability – rather than being an end in and of itself. Indeed, it was only from Richard Wellesley's tenure, under the shadow of the Napoleonic Wars, that the EIC began to pursue a project of paramountcy.[188] And even then, this was only after efforts to contrive a balance of power in India had failed, leaving only retrenchment or hegemony as viable long-term options for the company.

Unlike the consensus for conquest among Mughal and Manchu elites, the EIC's transition to empire was marked by ambivalence – and in some cases outright opposition – both from within the company, and among British political and commercial metropolitan elites.[189] This ambivalence reflected and reinforced the greater cultural distance between the EIC and Indians, relative to that which had distinguished the Mughals and the Manchus from their own newly conquered subjects. EIC officials could not hope to replicate the cultural syncretism of the Mughals in their interaction with their Indian subjects. This was not least because the EIC derived its local legitimacy at least in part from its status as a nominal vassal to the Mughal emperor. Nor could EIC officials have easily replicated the Manchu model of segregated incorporation, given Britons' unfamiliarity and cultural distance from their Indian subjects.

The EIC in the decades immediately after Bengal's conquest had an undeniably mestizo character. It derived its authority and status from the Mughal emperor – to whom the company nominally swore allegiance – and retained Persian as its language of administration as it assumed greater powers of governance. Key company administrators maintained

---

[186] Keay, *India: A history*, p. 385.   [187] Lawson, *The East India Company*, p. 124.
[188] Ibid., p. 135.   [189] Ibid., p. 124.

an active interest and immersion in the Mughals' Persephone high culture, reflected in their literary, culinary and aesthetic appetites.[190] The company's armies were manned by high-caste Indian sepoys, and Indian commercial elites (*banians*) supplied it with the bulk of its war credit.[191] Indian *maulvis* and *pandits* dispensed civil justice within the company's jurisdiction, while Mughal officials retained their authority over criminal justice in the country courts under company rule.[192] As the company's influence extended from its coastal city-colonies into the hinterland, it finally repurposed key Mughal rituals and practices, such as the *durbar* and the granting of the *khilat* to company feudatories, to incorporate Indian allies into its expanding imperium.[193]

For all of this undeniable hybridity, however, Britons remained undeniably alien and culturally distinct 'strangers' from their Indian subjects.[194] This strangeness precluded them from adopting a diversity regime that resembled either the Mughal model of syncretic incorporation or the Manchu model of segregated incorporation. Company officials did not hope to conjure a higher spiritual synthesis from reconciling India's diverse belief systems. Nor, however, did they aspire to separately embody the diverse traditions of their imperial constituencies, through discrete and separate performances of these audiences' collective identities. Instead, as the Company Raj took shape from Warren Hastings' rule onwards, it settled uneasily and tentatively on a diversity regime grounded in ecumenical incorporation.

Under this model, the company's right to rule was temporary, and contingent on its ability to resurrect Indian 'civilization' through a revival of its 'ancient constitution', and the reconstruction of the distinct and separate Hindu and Muslim legal codes that held this order together.[195] As strangers and formal feudatories to the Mughal emperor, the EIC could neither embody nor reconcile India's different traditions. But it could stand above the fray, and help secure a higher order that recognized the potency of India's discrete religious *qua* legal traditions, and entrenched them as separate but mutually reinforcing foundations of a company-sponsored civic order.

This early vision of ecumenical incorporation was perhaps best exemplified in a statue of Warren Hastings, which resides to this day in the

---

[190] Rahman, 'Decline of Persian in British India', 49.
[191] Roy, 'Rethinking the origins', 1139.
[192] Benton, 'Colonial law and cultural difference', 566.
[193] Alavi, 'The makings of company power', 440.
[194] J. E. Wilson, *The Domination of Strangers: Modern governance in Eastern India, 1780–1835* (London: Palgrave Macmillan, 2008).
[195] Cohn, *Colonialism and Its Forms of Knowledge*, p. 146.

gardens of the Victoria Memorial in Kolkata. Hastings stands resplendent in the toga of a Roman senator, reflecting British conceptions of themselves as Romans to India's Greeks, and of Hastings in particular as a latter-day Justinian, reclaiming civilization through a project of legal codification.[196] Hastings towers above a Brahmin pandit with a palm-leaf manuscript, and a Muslim maulavi studying a Persian manuscript.[197] As the supreme representative of company authority in India, Hastings' right to rule derives from his status as a law-giver. Crucially, this right is grounded in a framework of legal pluralism rather than monism. And this system of legal pluralism is self-consciously ecumenical rather than secular. For it privileges religious identity as the fountainhead of Indian laws. And it presupposes a Hindu/Muslim binary as India's essential and eternal cultural fault line, around which the company's system of rule must be organized.

By the end of the Third Anglo-Maratha War, then, the company had consolidated near-total rule over the subcontinent, with only Sikh-dominated Punjab standing as the last meaningful obstacle to complete company hegemony in India. The Company Raj's ecumenical vision of empire had moreover appeared – temporarily at least – to stabilize its hold on power. Yet, despite defeating a host of powerful European and indigenous adversaries, the EIC's dominance remained fragile and open to contestation. As the direct threat of military competition from peer competitors receded, company officials were forced to confront two self-generated tensions that threatened their rule.

First, though territorial rule had diluted its originally mercantile purpose, it had not eradicated it entirely. The quest for East-West trading monopolies continued to motivate company officials, even as successive renewals of its charter stripped the EIC of most of its remaining commercial privileges. Indeed, as the company forfeited many of the mercantile prerogatives that had initially defined it, those few that it retained grew correspondingly more important. In particular, by the 1820s, the company's interest in expanding its opium trade with the Qing Empire was growing more intense. As Britain's thirst for Chinese tea continued to grow, Indian opium stood as one of the only tradeable commodities that Britain could exchange for it.[198] Equally, taxes collected from opium production were by this time meaningfully contributing to company revenues, helping to offset the crushing costs of administering and defending the Company Raj.[199] These considerations together helped

---

[196] Ibid., p. 30.   [197] Ibid.   [198] Lawson, *The East India Company*, p. 157.
[199] D. R. Headrick, *The Tools of Empire: Technology and European imperialism in the nineteenth century* (Oxford: Oxford University Press, 1981), p. 45.

spur the company towards eastern commercial expansion – propelling it towards an inevitable confrontation with the Qing Empire.

Alongside economic pressures for eastward expansion, by the 1820s an incipient transformation of British world views was meanwhile also beginning to unsettle the Company Raj. New actors had begun to challenge the established Orientalist vision of empire that had formerly underpinned company rule. As we have seen, this vision cast the EIC's imperial vision as essentially conservative and restorative, dedicated to resurrecting Indian civilization through the recovery of its indigenous religious *qua* legal traditions. In stark contrast, a new generation of officials, merchants and missionaries dreamed of 'liberating' Indians from hidebound tradition, assimilating them instead to a single – and avowedly anglicized – civilizational standard.[200]

Economic pressures for eastwards expansion, and anglicizing pressures to transform the imperial purpose of the Company Raj, thus together threatened established imperial hierarchies in East and South Asia in the decades following the EIC's rise to Indian hegemony. The first would put the British on a collision course with the Qing Empire, culminating in war, millenarian rebellion and an eventual coalescence of a hybrid Anglo-Qing hierarchy in East Asia. The second would meanwhile catalyse in the Indian Mutiny, a crisis so severe that it ended the Company Raj and dissolved the last threadbare fiction of Mughal suzerainty. Paradoxically, however, the transfer from company to Crown rule would also spark a revival of many of the most conservative and traditionalizing elements of the Company Raj in its early post-conquest phase. Crown officials doubled down on the early imperial model of ecumenical incorporation, substantially abandoning the assimilationist project of anglicization that had so very nearly cost Britain its Indian Empire. Following their mid-century near-death experiences, then, both the Qing Empire and British India would re-emerge seemingly revitalized, as the twin pillars of an authoritarian and avowedly conservative pan-Asian international order, grounded in a common colonial pattern of rule through difference. The mid-century crises of Qing and EIC imperialism, the post-crisis reconstruction of these empires and the consequences of their revival for international order in Asia, form the subjects of Chapter 7.

---

[200] Metcalf, *Ideologies of the Raj*, p. 34.

7　Crises of Empire and the Reconstitution of International Orders in South and East Asia, 1820–1880

This chapter considers the causes, course and outcomes of the parallel crises that convulsed the British Raj and the Qing Dynasty in the mid-nineteenth century, and radically reconstituted international orders in both South and East Asia. This book has so far focused mainly on explaining imperial international orders' emergence and consolidation. I have conversely paid only secondary attention to issues of order maintenance, renovation and resilience. These questions form this chapter's focus.

Traditional accounts of international order in nineteenth-century Asia typically privilege the relentless expansion of a European-dominated international society, and the defensive modernization of Asian societies this expansion helped spur.[1] But my account of international orders' evolution has conversely stressed Western imperialism's derivative character, which is sharply illuminated when considered alongside its Asian predecessors and counterparts. For the EIC, as for the Mughals and the Manchus, the construction and preservation of diverse conquest coalitions, and the pre-emption of potential counter-coalitions, formed the primary imperatives of imperial statecraft. Diversity regimes likewise stood as keystone institutions in the Raj, as they did in the Mughal and Manchu empires. Finally, as Chapter 6 demonstrated, the diversity regime of the British Raj was nominally restorative rather than transformative in character. At least from the perspective of the company's Orientalist scholar-administrators, the warrant for British rule stemmed from the restorationist goal of restoring Hindu civilization to its pre-Islamic conquest glory. And the company would preserve order by ruling through a model of ecumenical incorporation that promised justice for the EIC's Hindu and Muslim subjects through the administration of laws

---

[1] Within International Relations, classic texts in this vein include H. Bull and A. Watson (eds.), *The Expansion of International Society* (Oxford: Clarendon Press, 1984); and Gong, *The Standard of 'Civilization'*.

that supposedly reflected their separate and distinct religious *qua* legal traditions.

Both the British Raj and the Qing Empire – Asia's two resident super-powers in the early-mid nineteenth century – were thus fundamentally conservative in their constitutions. Whether favouring a model of ecumenical or segregated incorporation, both orders rested on the idea that their empires faithfully reflected and preserved the diverse and discrete cultural identities of their respective imperial constituencies. At least down to 1820, a combination of geographic distance and Manchu strength moreover largely insulated British-dominated South Asia and Qing-dominated East Asia from one another. But after 1820, British commercial (and later, military) encroachment into East Asia became more persistent, insistent and sustained than before. Likewise, within South Asia, the Orientalism of the early Company Raj came under increasing challenge from a muscular form of transformational liberalism. This alternative vision of empire repudiated the Orientalist ideas underpinning the Raj's existing diversity regime. Rather than seeking to restore Hindu civilization to its former glory, or passively govern Hindus and Muslims through their own separate laws, Anglicist modernizers instead identified civilization exclusively with the West.[2] With this new chauvinism came a determination to govern India (and later, other Asian polities) through strategies of assimilation rather than incorporation – abandoning the model of rule that had so recently secured the EIC's dominance over the subcontinent.

The Anglicists' Sisyphean effort to coercively civilize Asian polities ultimately nearly wrecked both the British Raj and the Qing Sinosphere. Within British India itself, the Anglicists' civilizational chauvinism undermined the empire's legitimating ideology and prevailing diversity regime, as well as corroding the credibility of the alliances with local collaborators on which company rule rested. As the spirit of 'reform' increasingly informed colonial governance, the Raj lost much of the hybrid character that had previously tied it to indigenous allies. To cite one example, the abandonment of Persian for English as the empire's language of administration attenuated the empire's connections to large parts of India's scribal elites. This alienated the Raj from a crucial constituency, and also further weakened the company's ability to maintain the convenient (if increasingly threadbare) fiction that it ruled in the Mughal emperor's name.[3] The resulting estrangement between the Raj and its indigenous allies – and the broader strains that Indian reform brought with it – eventually

[2] Metcalf, *Ideologies of the Raj*, p. 34.
[3] Rahman, 'Decline of Persian in British India', 51.

culminated in the Indian Mutiny and the near-destruction of British power in the subcontinent. After this near-death experience, the British reverted to a profoundly conservative form of governing, which radically reinforced the model of ecumenical incorporation that had first sustained the Company Raj in its early decades.[4] The British thereafter remained shackled to an imperial ideology and corresponding diversity regime that saw the preservation of peace and the conservation of cultural difference among its Indian subjects as being inextricably interlinked. This pro-foundly conservative vision – which denied the unity of India as anything other than a 'mere geographic expression'[5] – set the template for British rule down to its extinction in 1947.

British civilizational chauvinism had equally transformative effects in Qing-dominated East Asia. While the Manchus had repulsed company overtures before 1820, from this time on a combination of material and ideational pressures steadily intensified the British threat to the Qing Empire. At the material level, British demand for Chinese tea and the EIC's burgeoning supplies of Indian opium generated intense commercial pressures to forcibly open the Qing Empire to trade with the West.[6] Beyond these economic motives, the ideological impulse to transform East Asia through the introduction of 'commerce and Christianity' reinforced the company's expansionist tendencies.[7] The Opium Wars (1839–42 and 1856–60), and China's subsequent forced integration into a European-dominated international society, mark the most conspicuous outcomes of this encounter between the British Raj and the Qing Empire. But they must be read in conjunction with the cataclysmic upheaval of the concurrent Taiping Rebellion, which stemmed in part from British encroachment, and played an equally decisive role in so weakening the Manchus as to compel their accommodation with the West. The mid-century crisis of the Qing Empire also yielded a conservative transformation of the Manchu order comparable to the Raj's post-1857 reinvention. With the direct assistance of the British (through their 'Cooperative Policy'), the Manchus doubled down on their earlier model of segregated incorporation within the empire, while making only superficial adjustments to their relations with Western barbarians on their maritime frontiers.[8] Like the British Raj, the Manchus

---

[4] Cannadine, *Ornamentalism*, p. 45.   [5] Darwin, *Unfinished Empire*, p. 212.
[6] Lawson, *The East India Company*, p. 157.
[7] On the significance of 'commerce and Christianity' as an ideological lodestar of nine-teenth-century British imperialism, see generally A. Porter, '"Commerce and Christianity": The rise and fall of a nineteenth-century missionary slogan', *Historical Journal*, 28(3) (1985), 597–621.
[8] On China's conservative restoration at this time, see generally M. C. Wright, *The Last Stand of Chinese Conservatism: The T'ung-Chih Restoration, 1862–1874* (Stanford: Stanford University Press, 1962).

continued to opt for a model of governance grounded in the conservation of difference among culturally irreconcilable imperial constituencies. Internationally, meanwhile, East Asia did not suddenly lurch from Sinocentric suzerainty to Westphalian sovereign anarchy. Instead, a hybrid order prevailed down to the 1890s, in which the Manchus selectively integrated the practices of Western diplomacy into their repertoire of 'barbarian management' techniques, while otherwise continuing to use existing Confucian and steppe strategies to preserve order within and beyond the empire.[9]

This chapter proceeds in five sections. I begin with a comparative panoramic overview of the British Raj and the Qing Empire in c. 1820. Here I pay particular attention to their broad structural similarities. I stress especially the critical importance of define and rule strategies in preserving British and Manchu dominance, and the accompanying centrality of incorporative diversity regimes to the constitution of both empires. The second section then outlines the commercial and ideational pressures that propelled an attempted transformation of the company's mode of rule in India, as well as stoking British commercial and military expansion into Qing-dominated East Asia after 1820. I then explore the corrosive impact of transformational liberalism on both the British Raj and the Qing Empire in the third and fourth sections, detailing the profound crises of imperial governance that nearly destroyed both empires in the mid-nineteenth century. The final section rounds out the chapter with a comparative examination of international orders in South and East Asia following the reconstitution of the Raj and the Qing Empire after 1860. Here I argue that the mid-century crises of empire described here put paid to British attempts to coercively civilize Asian polities for a generation, and locked in conservative models of diversity management that sustained the Raj and the Qing Dynasty down to their destruction in the twentieth century.

The Company Raj and the Qing Empire in c. 1820

By c. 1820, the British Raj and the Qing Empire respectively dominated South and East Asia. At first glance, these empires were radically different. The British Raj had only recently consolidated. The company's victory in the third Anglo-Maratha War (1817–18) had affirmed its *de facto* dominion over the subcontinent. But the Sikh kingdom to the

---

[9] On the hybridity of late Qing diplomacy, see generally K.-H. Kim, *The Last Phase of the East Asian World Order: Korea, Japan, and the Chinese Empire, 1860–1882* (Berkeley: University of California Press, 1979).

empire's northwest remained for now a potent brake against further expansion.[10] Additionally, the company had yet to slough off the disguise of its *de jure* submission to the Mughal emperor, who would remain British India's titular suzerain down to the Indian Mutiny of 1857–9. By contrast, the Qing Empire had thoroughly matured by c. 1820. Having doubled in size during wars of conquest during the eighteenth century, the empire by the early nineteenth century had reached its maximum territorial expanse. In contrast to the EIC, the Qing emperor also ruled as the empire's undisputed supreme ruler in his own right, his quasi-divine status affirmed through the empire's diverse multitude of religious traditions.[11] Likewise, the Qing had by this time also perfected their systems of imperial administration and regional diplomacy. The imperial bureaucracy – governed by meritocratic appointment through the examination system – remained the world's most sophisticated system of direct rule, reputedly profoundly influencing the Indian Civil Service (ICS) in its resort to recruitment through competitive examination.[12] And while the British were still improvising their system of indirect rule over neighbouring client states in the 1820s, Qing practices of colonial over-rule via the Lifan Yuan had by this time fully consolidated.

Notwithstanding these important differences, we can attribute many of the contrasts between the British Raj and the Qing Empire to their different stages in the imperial life cycle. That is, many of the key contrasts between the two empires owed more to the fact that the British Raj was only recently formed and still inchoate, whereas the Manchus had by this time had nearly two centuries to entrench their rule. More fundamentally, these differences obscure profound similarities in both empires' constitutions, as well as common vulnerabilities that the crises of the mid-nineteenth century would soon cruelly expose.

At the most basic level, the British Raj and the Qing Empire were minority conquest regimes, where frontier barbarians had secured system-wide dominance through their mobilization of diverse conquest coalitions drawn from indigenous majorities. Owing to their structurally similar origins, both empires relied on inter-linked strategies of define and rule and divide and rule to maintain themselves in power. Imperial rule rested on the curation, preservation and institutionalization of cultural difference among various imperial constituencies, and the prevention of cross-sectoral mobilization between them. As we have seen, these strategies of define and rule and divide and rule eventually crystallized in

---

[10] Keay, *India: A history*, p. 416.
[11] See generally Crossley, *A Translucent Mirror*; and Elverskog, *Our Great Qing*.
[12] S.-Y. Teng, 'Chinese influence on the Western examination system: Introduction', *Harvard Journal of Asiatic Studies*, 7(4) (1943), 292–5.

diversity regimes, which formed the institutional bedrock of both imperial systems. A comparison of British and Qing diversity regimes suffices to illuminate their key parallels and points of divergence, as well as fore-shadowing the comparable vulnerabilities both faced by the early-mid nineteenth century.

At the core of the Orientalist vision informing the early Company Raj was the conviction that the British imperial mission in India was a temporary expedient, aimed at resuscitating an 'authentic' Hindu civil-ization temporarily laid low by Muslim conquest and ensuing centuries of despotism.[13] In contrast to either the Mughals or the Manchus, British dominance was from the outset marked by profound ambivalence. This is in part because system-wide rule in India was so contrary to the declared commercial goals of the company. But it also reflected company officials' keen awareness of the profound challenges of legitimating their domin-ance as foreign interlopers, and the necessity of cloaking British power as much as possible in the camouflage of indigenous idioms of rule.[14] Accordingly, the British ruled as nominal servants of the Mughal emperor; justified their early dominion in India in restorationist terms; and adopted a model of rule that purported to reflect, protect and pre-serve the innate religious *qua* cultural differences of their Indian subjects.

Like the other empires considered in this study, the British favoured strategies of define and rule and divide and rule to preserve their domin-ance. In the case of the British Raj, these strategies crystallized in a diversity regime I have characterized as one of ecumenical incorpor-ation. Early company dominance in India was ecumenical rather than secular or sacerdotal in character. The EIC did not seek to sideline religion in its claims on public power. But nor did it try to legitimize company rule by claiming sacred legitimacy for itself. Instead, the EIC positioned itself as far as possible as a neutral arbiter between the empire's faith communities, as well as a patron of the empire's religious establish-ments and their accompanying systems of law.[15] The early Company Raj's ethos was moreover incorporative rather than assimilative. Rather than seeking to efface cultural difference through assimilation to a single civilizational standard, company officials instead aimed to recognize and entrench cultural diversity as the foundation of their power. This conser-vative orientation was for example reflected in the company's deep

---

[13] Cohn, *Colonialism and Its Forms of Knowledge*, p. 146.
[14] See for example Fisher, 'The imperial coronation of 1819', 250.
[15] See generally Anderson, 'Islamic law and the colonial encounter'. On the centrality of religious patronage as a foundation of the Company Raj, see also P. van der Veer, *Imperial Encounters: Religion and modernity in India and Britain* (Princeton: Princeton University Press, 2001), pp. 20–1.

hostility to the introduction of British Christian missionaries to India, for
fear that their interference would inflame local religious sensitivities and
so jeopardize company rule.[16]

Finally, the British Raj realized its diversity regime in practice through
a combination of authoritative and coercive institutions, which
I canvassed in detail in Chapter 6. Recapitulating briefly, the EIC
anchored its rule first in a judicial order grounded in legal pluralism.
Recalling the Roman emperor Justinian, company officials legitimized
their power through a self-conception that foregrounded the EIC's status
as a 'law-giver'.[17] Through this lens, company rule offered an antidote to
the 'anarchy' that had supposedly accompanied the Mughal Empire's
decline. Working with indigenous judges and legal experts, the company
built a governance system that aimed to provide a restored foundation for
justice, grounded in civil and criminal codes supposedly recovered from
local traditions. 'Anglo-Hindu' and 'Anglo-Muhammedan' legal systems
between them supplied the broad institutional framework for company
rule in its crucial early decades.[18] These legal codes progressively
entrenched in practice and ingrained into everyday life distinct and eventually more polarized Hindu and Islamic religious identities, consistent
with British define and rule and divide and rule strategies.

Alongside the authoritative institution of colonial legal pluralism,
a massive apparatus of coercion buttressed the Company Raj. Like legal
pluralism, the EIC's military machine was built overwhelmingly from
indigenous ingredients. Improvised and regionally diverse they might
have been, but the company's early experiments mobilizing Indian military labour soon powerfully reinforced the diversity regime underpinning
the EIC's rule. As we have seen, the Bengal army – the original bedrock of
company military power – consisted primarily of high-caste peasant
infantry. In all aspects of regimental life, as well as in the military colonies
they granted to retired *sepoys* for settlement, the company scrupulously
adhered to the requirements of caste identity.[19] This marked out their

---

[16] The exclusion of missionaries from proselytizing in India ended with the renewal of the
company's charter in 1813. See Lawson, *The East India Company*, p. 150. Due to intense
lobbying from Britain's powerful evangelical constituency, the imperial government was
moreover eventually forced to abandon direct patronage of local religious establishments
by the late nineteenth century, opening up a crucial public space for local elites to take
over. See van der Veer, *Imperial Encounters*, p. 21.

[17] Metcalf, *Ideologies of the Raj*, p. 13.

[18] Anderson, 'Islamic law and the colonial encounter'; Benton, 'Colonial law and cultural
difference'.

[19] See generally Alavi, *The Sepoys and the Company*. On the special importance of retired
sepoy colonies in extending the company's power into the hinterland, see S. Alavi, 'The
company army and rural society: The invalid Thanah 1780–1830', *Modern Asian Studies*,
27(1) (1993), 147–78.

soldiers as a separate and privileged imperial constituency, while at the same time solidifying caste *qua* religious identities as a foundational fault line of the new imperial order. Beyond Bengal, especially in the Ceded and Conquered territories around Delhi, the Raj alternatively re-purposed locally potent military traditions stressing fealty to Islam and the Mughal emperor to attract irregular cavalry into the company's service.[20] These improvised expedients steadily accreted over time to form one of the world's largest and most formidable military establishments – and one that once again embodied a regime of ecumenical incorporation, where the management of communal difference formed a primary warrant for imperial rule.

Like the British Raj, the Qing Empire also rested on principles of define and rule and divide and rule. The Qing vision of empire nevertheless lacked the ambivalence of the Company Raj. The Manchus from the outset insisted on the unqualified legitimacy of their right to rule. Like the British in their mobilization of Mughal idioms of legitimacy, the Manchus harnessed the legitimating formulas of conquered societies to shore up their power, most notably in laying claim to the Heavenly Mandate.[21] But in contrast to the company's fictitious presentation of itself as a mere servant of the Mughal emperor, the Manchus unapologetically asserted their aspirations to unmediated supreme power. Undeniably, superficial parallels united the two empires' legitimating ideologies. In each of the discrete idioms (e.g., Chinese, Manchu, Mongolian, Tibetan) in which it legitimized itself, the Qing Empire tied the legitimacy of Manchu rule to the emperor's capacity to restore the political and cosmic harmony previously lost under the ailing Ming Dynasty.[22] Themes of restoration, masking the genuinely revolutionary changes wrought through parvenu conquerors' overthrow of the pre-existing ruling order, thus played out in both the Qing Empire and the Company Raj. But company Orientalism conceived the EIC's redemptive mission as temporary, the EIC's governing mandate theoretically limited to the time necessary to restore authentic Indian (read: Hindu) civilization to its former glory. The Manchus conversely conceived their mandate as essential to preserve political *qua* cosmic order, and eternal in its temporal remit. Far earlier than the British in India, the Manchus furthermore buttressed their imperial vision with a highly developed sense of ethnic superiority based on the Manchus' supposedly matchless martial prowess.[23]

[20] Alavi, 'The makings of company power', 454.
[21] Wang, 'Claiming centrality in the Chinese world', 104.
[22] Leibold, *Reconfiguring Chinese Nationalism*, p. 28.
[23] See generally Elliott, *The Manchu Way*; and Waley-Cohen, *The Culture of War in China*.

These differences aside, the Manchus also consolidated their power on the basis of define and rule and divide and rule strategies, which coalesced in the form of a distinctive diversity regime not entirely unlike that of the Company Raj. In the Company Raj, Orientalists early on conceptualized their empire's diversity in ways that foregrounded communal *qua* religious divisions, and settled on a diversity regime defined by the imperative of ecumenical incorporation. Conversely, as we have seen in previous chapters, the Qing Empire accorded at least equal significance to ethno-linguistic divisions as it did religious fault lines when mapping the empire's cultural topography. The Qing ethos of 'imperial simultaneity'[24] – in which the emperor simultaneously and separately incarnated different constituencies' ideas of legitimate rulership – also distinguished the Manchu order from the Raj. The Manchu order was also segregated rather than ecumenical. Rather than positioning themselves as neutral arbiters of different constituencies as per the company, the Manchus instead siloed their interactions with subject populations, to mitigate against the risk that legitimating idioms resonant with one constituency might dangerously alienate others.[25]

Both the Company Raj and the Qing Empire nevertheless embraced diversity regimes that stressed themes of incorporation over assimilation. Cultural difference – be it religious or ethno-linguistic – was managed in ways that preserved and reified the heterogeneity of conquered populations, and thus upheld imperial systems of minority rule. Like the Company Raj, the Qing Empire also realized its diversity regime in practice through a combination of authoritative and coercive institutions. Legal pluralism featured in the Qing as well as British empires, though without ever enjoying the same ideological prominence for the Manchus as for the would-be Justinians of the Company Raj. By contrast, emperor-centric sacerdotal rituals and religious patronage figured far more conspicuously in the Manchus' ruling repertoires and authoritative institutions, forming a key practice-based means of performing and sustaining imperial authority. Again, the Manchus customized these rituals and forms of patronage for each of their main imperial constituencies, consistent with a diversity regime grounded in the principle of segregated incorporation.[26] On the coercion side of the ledger, the banner system of military organization meanwhile privileged and entrenched forms of 'ethnic' identity, and provided the institutional lynchpin around which the Manchus managed, organized and mobilized the multicultural military coalition necessary to sustain themselves in power.[27]

---

[24] Crossley, *A Translucent Mirror*, p. 12.   [25] Ibid.
[26] Leibold, *Reconfiguring Chinese Nationalism*, p. 28.   [27] Elliott, *The Manchu Way*.

Despite very real differences in their ideological content and institutional structures, my main point here is to stress underlying commonalities between the early Company Raj and the mature Qing Empire. Above all, these were both *profoundly conservative* empires that predicated their legitimacy and their methods of rule on the systematic reification of cultural difference among their imperial constituencies. Incorporation and the preservation of difference, rather than its transcendence through assimilation to a common civilizational standard, formed the basis of minority rule in both systems. This ethos suffused the entire business of empire. It could for example be seen in these empires' legitimating idioms and rituals, systems of justice and administration, and practices of military mobilization and organization.

The Company Raj and the Qing Empire both rested on minority conquerors' use of interlinked strategies of define and rule and divide and rule to govern vast and hugely diverse imperial spaces. By c. 1820, these strategies, and the diversity regimes that consolidated with their maturation, sustained two enormous, authoritarian, overwhelmingly agrarian empires that dominated their respective regions. Notwithstanding their divergent origins, both empires depended critically on their alliances with local collaborators to sustain conquest elites in power. Both were moreover profoundly conservative in their respective imperial visions, and practices of diversity management and colonial rule. Because of these structural similarities, both were finally extremely vulnerable to the disruptive impact of radical ideologies that directly challenged these empires' conservative foundations. It is precisely this danger that would materialize from the 1820s, as transformational liberalism emerged to eventually pose as an existential threat to both the Company Raj and the Qing Empire. I now turn to a consideration of this threat in general terms, before then proceeding to an examination of the interlocking crises of imperial order that it unleashed in both empires in the third and fourth sections.

Transformational Liberalism and the Challenge to the *Ancien Régime* in the Company Raj and the Qing Empire

The mid-nineteenth century saw a crisis of empires in Asia that permanently transformed the constitution of both the British Raj and the Qing Empire. In British India, the mutiny of portions of the company's military establishment nearly threw off British rule, and hastened the extinction of the Mughal imperial office and the formal transfer of suzerainty to the British Crown. Likewise, the Qing Empire faced a devastating conjunction of external predation and internal rebellion in the 1850s, in the

Second Opium War and the Taiping Rebellion. The dynamics of these imperial crises, and their neglected interconnections, form the subject of the remainder of this chapter. Before sketching out these crises, however, I first consider the common constellation of ideological and material forces that undermined the British and Qing imperial orders in the lead up to the upheavals of the 1850s.

In the early decades of the nineteenth century, as the British reflected on the speed and magnitude of their system-wide conquest of South Asia, the fragile Orientalist consensus that had undergirded company expansion began to fray. Select company officials continued to admire aspects of Indian culture, and conceive the company's mission in India in restorationist terms. But after 1820, these Orientalist views increasingly gave way to a very different vision of empire that aimed to revise the ideological foundations of the Company Raj, and recast the purpose of British power in both South and also East Asia. A volatile admixture of liberalism and evangelical Christianity, I characterize this intellectual movement as *transformational liberalism.*[28] This portrayal admittedly downplays the often fierce religious zeal that motivated British reformers in Asia. But it gestures towards the intellectual genealogy of the reform movement (the radical liberalism of the late eighteenth and early nineteenth centuries), as well as foregrounding its genuinely transformative ambitions. A comprehensive analysis of transformational liberalism lies outside the scope of this inquiry. For present purposes, it is enough to note its core ideas and vision for the British Empire in Asia; its broad policy prescriptions; its foremost sponsors; and the larger structural forces that made it such a potentially potent force for corrosion to both the British Raj and the Qing Empire.

Transformational liberalism entailed first and foremost a vision of British imperial purpose in Asia that departed radically from what company officials had improvised during the EIC's initial frenzy of territorial conquest. At the most basic level, this vision conceived Britons' task in Asia as transformative rather than restorative, and grounded in an assimilative rather than an incorporative ethos. Simplifying dramatically, liberal reformers started from the proposition that Anglo-Saxon 'civilization' marked the apogee of human progress, and that Britons possessed an indefeasible duty to spread the benefits of this civilization to humanity, through a combination of conquest, commerce, education and religious proselytization.[29] Through liberal eyes, the legitimacy of Britain's

---

[28] For an excellent general account of liberal, utilitarian and evangelical ideas and their impact on British India, see E. Stokes, *The English Utilitarians and India* (Oxford: Clarendon Press, 1959).

[29] Metcalf, *Ideologies of the Raj*, p. 34.

conquest of India and other colonies was not self-evidently legitimate. The 'barren and precarious hegemony of the sword'[30] could not suffice as the warrant for British dominion in Asia. Nor for that matter could liberals abide Orientalists' justification of empire, as a necessary expedient to revive a temporarily moribund Indian civilization. Instead, they conceived the British imperial mission as an antidote to a tyrannical constellation of Oriental Despotism, Protectionism, and Idolatry that had previously stifled the moral and material progress of those peoples newly subject to British rule.[31] Through this lens, British power could never be rendered legitimate through the management of the empire's cultural diversity, no matter how deftly this fundamentally conservative task was accomplished. Rather, liberal reformers envisaged an India transformed through the introduction and continued spread of British language, habits, manners, commerce, religion and practices of government.[32] In particular, reformers aimed to transform the sensibilities and orientation of a sufficient portion of India's political and commercial elites, such that they would form a loyal anglicized (read: civilized) indigenous buttress for colonial rule.[33]

At the outset of company rule, EIC officials based their power and authority on define and rule and divide and rule strategies. These strategies assumed that India's cultural diversity was ineradicable, and that the best company officials could do was manage this diversity in ways that ensured a minimum of public order, while keeping onside the indigenous allies needed to sustain the empire. To the extent that the company had any positive imperial vision, it lay in the Orientalists' mission to restore Indian civilization to its former glories. By contrast, liberal reformers saw Britain's imperial mission as redemptive rather than restorative. Cast in its most abstract terms, liberals envisaged that a trinity of 'Responsible Government', 'Free Trade' and 'Protestant Piety' would unleash India's creative energies, and cast off the torpor of Oriental Despotism, Protectionism and Idolatry that had formerly condemned Indians to misery.[34]

The transformational liberalism that gained momentum after c. 1820 was not merely an abstract ideological critique of the EIC's rule in India. Rather, it entailed a clear series of policy prescriptions, which challenged the very foundations of the Company Raj, and eventually of the British presence in Asia more generally. Most fundamentally, liberal reformers sought to coercively 'open' both the Company Raj and other Asian

---

[30] Stokes, *The English Utilitarians and India*, p. 283.   [31] Ibid., p. 34.
[32] Metcalf, *Ideologies of the Raj*, p. 34.   [33] Ibid.
[34] Stokes, *The English Utilitarians and India*, p. 34.

polities to the supposedly beneficent influences of British commerce and Christianity. In relation to British India itself, reformers railed against the residual commercial monopolies the company kept following the 1813 renewal of its charter. Mobilizing long-standing critiques of the company's privileges alongside newly ascendant critiques of protectionism, liberals argued for the existence of a moral imperative to open India up fully to trade with Britain.[35] Advocates of this position held that doing so would mutually enrich Britons and Indians, and cleaved to the more general liberal conviction that expanded ties of commerce would corrode parochial prejudices, and contribute to humanity's common advance.[36] Similar sentiments accompanied liberals' advocacy for expanded trade with the Qing Empire, a view that only strengthened following the Manchus' forcible rebuff to EIC trading entreaties in 1793 and again in 1816.[37]

Beyond arguing for an end to both monopoly and restrictions (both British and indigenous) on trade, many reformist liberals also agitated for India's opening to Christian missionary activity. Company officials had previously successfully resisted Christian pressures to be allowed to proselytize in India. This resistance sprang from pragmatism rather than ideology. In its first incarnation, the company's *raison d'être* had been commercial rather than evangelical. Accordingly, for most of its history, the EIC remained largely indifferent to Indians' religious convictions, confining itself in matters of religion to overseeing the spiritual welfare of the EIC's European employees.[38] Following its metamorphosis into a territorial power, the company moreover assumed significant de facto responsibilities for patronizing the empire's Hindu and Muslim religious establishments.[39] This further jaundiced the company against missionary activity, given the risks that proselytization would antagonize Hindu and Muslim collaborators, and so jeopardize the Company Raj's stability.[40] Conversely, liberal reformers condemned as idolatry the Company Raj's patronage of indigenous religious establishments, and proposed instead the duty to proselytize as an integral component of Britain's 'civilizing mission' in Asia.[41]

Finally, at the most general level, liberal reformers after c. 1820 showed a contempt for indigenous hierarchies of all kinds in Asia, be they

---

[35] Metcalf, *Ideologies of the Raj*, p. 29.
[36] B. Stanley, '"Commerce and Christianity": Providence theory, the missionary movement, and the imperialism of free trade, 1842–1860', *Historical Journal*, 26(1) (1983), 75.
[37] Ibid.   [38] Stern, *The Company-State*, p. 109.
[39] Van der Veer, *Imperial Encounters*, p. 21.
[40] Lawson, *The East India Company*, p. 150.
[41] Van der Veer, *Imperial Encounters*, p. 21.

economic, religious or political. Though liberal proposals for reform varied, they reflected a common tendency to disparage indigenous hierarchies as sclerotic impediments to progress and the civilization of Asian polities. Thus, within the Company Raj, reformers lobbied among other things for the strengthening of private property rights through the abolition of traditional systems of land tenure; the sidelining of indigenous religious leaders and the elimination of supposedly barbaric practices sanctioned by these leaders; and the territorial annexation of Princely States where the ruler had died without producing a male heir.[42] Beyond South Asia, these proposals were initially less sweeping, and confined to expanding Britain's commercial penetration of East Asia.[43] But the same impatience with local hierarchies abounded, alongside a faith in the transformative effects of commerce and Christianity, provided indigenous barriers to British expansion could be overcome.

Transformational liberalism was by no means monolithic. Nor was it ever universally hegemonic. Rather, its internal heterogeneity reflected the diverse range of sponsors that spearheaded the reform movement. Most notably, Eric Stokes has written of a powerful merchant-missionary alliance as the decisive coalition pushing for a transformation of Britain's imperial mission from the 1820s.[44] Reformers during this era conceived a natural affinity between free trade and Protestant Christianity, with both being seen as essential vehicles for the civilization of Asian peoples.[45] Beyond this merchant-missionary alliance, reformist ideals also found a constituency among a section of the company elite, who sought to slough off the EIC's earlier conservatism and instead embrace the ambitious goal of progressively civilizing India through Anglicization.[46]

The ambitious – even hubristic – vision of reform that drove sections of the British imperial elite after c. 1820 marked a profound departure from the company's earlier willingness to conciliate and bind indigenous collaborators to the colonial state through customization. Likewise, whereas company agents had previously been merely occasional supplicants to the Qing court, the new imperial vision called for more sustained and aggressive efforts to open the Qing Empire up to Western commerce and Christianity.[47] Transformational liberalism therefore implied a two-fold expansion of the Western presence in Asia.

---

[42] Metcalf, *Ideologies of the Raj*, p. 27.   [43] Stanley, 'Commerce and Christianity', 75.
[44] Stokes, *The English Utilitarians and India*, pp. 39–40.
[45] Ibid. See also Stanley, 'Commerce and Christianity', 75.
[46] Lawson, *The East India Company*, p. 152.
[47] Stanley, 'Commerce and Christianity', 75.

Within the Company Raj, the push for reform warranted a reconfiguration of the company's authority claims over its Indian subjects. The mission to 'civilize' India at least theoretically licensed more radical interventions into Indian society than before, to cultivate new imperial constituencies, and to bring the company's governance system into closer conformity with liberal civilizing prescriptions. On the former front, liberals pushed for education reforms to create an anglicized Indian elite to help administer the empire. This elite would remain subordinate to the exclusively British Indian Civil Service (ICS), but be socialized as imperial loyalists fully inculcated with the supposed virtues of British civilization.[48] Crucially, the move to cultivate this new loyalist constituency coincided with efforts to modernize the empire's governance, most notably by replacing Persian with English as the company's official language of administration.[49] This latter decision solidified an emerging nexus between anglicization and upward mobility for Indian elites, as well as marginalizing many of the Persephone administrators that had previously been so critical in the day-to-day running of the Company Raj.[50]

In addition to cultivating a new anglicized elite, liberal reformers also sponsored efforts to revise traditional systems of land tenure, as well as either pushing client rulers in the Princely States to adopt more civilized forms of rule, or alternatively proposing even the outright annexation of these polities into British India.[51] As we will see below, both projects were only partially attempted, and were at best temporarily successful. They moreover fostered estrangement among key indigenous intermediaries. Aggravating this problem, reformers meanwhile simultaneously pushed the Company Raj to withdraw from its direct patronage of Indian religious establishments. In particular, charges of 'idolatry' forced the company to step back from its prior financial and institutional support for Hindu religious elites.[52] This reconfiguration of its authority claims made the Company Raj both more intrusive and less enmeshed within existing indigenous power networks – prefiguring the EIC's near-fatal crisis of legitimacy during the Indian Mutiny.[53]

Beyond the Raj, the liberal impulse for reform also helped drive an eastern expansion of the company, into both Southeast Asia and the Qing Empire. By 1824, an Anglo-Dutch treaty had carved up much of maritime Southeast Asia between these two colonial powers. Henceforth, an

---

[48] Lawson, *The East India Company*, p. 152.
[49] Rahman, 'Decline of Persian in British India', 49.   [50] Ibid.
[51] C. Keen, *Princely India and the British: Political development and the operation of empire* (London: I. B. Tauris, 2012), pp. 10–12.
[52] Van der Veer, *Imperial Encounters*, p. 21.   [53] Metcalf, *Ideologies of the Raj*, p. 37.

Anglo-Dutch political condominium – underwritten by British naval power – helped protect the Dutch East Indies as a de facto security client of the company.[54] British settlement of what would become known as the Straits Settlements meanwhile won the EIC control over the Sea Lines of Communication (SLOCs) linking the Indian and Pacific oceans, as well as providing a secure territorial springboard from which to expand commercially into the Qing Empire.[55]

For transformational liberals, the Qing Empire represented a final frontier, promising unlimited opportunities for proselytization and profit. The evangelical Christian impulse to expand into China would prove both durable and far-reaching in its effects, and helped sow the seeds for a millenarian uprising that nearly toppled the Manchus in the 1850s. Of more immediate impact, however, was the commercial drive to open China's markets to Western commerce. The belief that free trade would advance humanity's moral and material progress was quite literally an article of faith for the merchant-missionary alliance underwriting transformational liberalism.[56] But shifts in the political economy of the Company Raj from the 1800s gave this impulse far greater practical force than it would have otherwise possessed.

Britain's growing trade deficit with the Qing Empire, and the rising importance of opium as a revenue source for the Company Raj, together proved especially potent in propelling the EIC's eastern expansion from the 1820s. From the late eighteenth century, Britain's burgeoning demand for Chinese tea had aggravated and hugely expanded a perennial trade deficit with China.[57] In the meantime, as parliament stripped the company of its other commercial monopolies, opium cultivation and export developed as an increasingly lucrative revenue source for the EIC.[58] From the early 1800s, as the practical boundaries between the British imperial state and the EIC were meanwhile blurring, these structural trends began to intersect. That is, the sale of opium to consumers within the Qing Empire emerged as potential means of both reducing Britain's trade deficit with China, while also enhancing the fiscal strength of a Company Raj that was otherwise being denuded of its trading privileges in Asia.[59] These practical imperatives reinforced the expansionary impulses that already defined transformational liberalism – further fuelling a confrontation between the Company Raj and the Qing Empire.

---

[54] A. Webster, *Gentleman Capitalists: British imperialism in Southeast Asia, 1770–1890* (London: I. B. Tauris, 1998), pp. 85–6.
[55] Ibid.   [56] Stokes, *The English Utilitarians and India*, pp. 39–40.
[57] Lawson, *The East India Company*, p. 157.   [58] Headrick, *The Tools of Empire*, p. 44.
[59] Ibid., p. 45.

With its embrace of an aggressively assimilationist civilizing mission, transformational liberalism proved profoundly antagonistic to the diversity regime underwriting the Company Raj. 'Rather than reconciling government to the nature and traditions of Indian society ... the foundation of British rule was to be *a policy of assimilation*, where Indian society would be reshaped along the lines of British society.'[60] Seeking cultural transformation over conservation, reformists roundly rejected the model of ecumenical incorporation that had formerly sustained British define and rule and divide and rule strategies for maintaining company dominance.

By contrast, the confrontation between the liberal civilizing mission and the diversity regime underpinning Qing rule was both less immediate and less comprehensive. Liberals did not seek the overthrow of Manchu dominance. And the Qing diversity regime of segregated incorporation was for free trade advocates a matter of indifference, if not total ignorance. Nevertheless, even the more limited liberal demands on the Qing Empire marked an assault on its systems of legitimation, and sparked inevitable resistance. Liberal pressures to open the Qing Empire up to greater trade and diplomatic exchange directly challenged an imperial order predicated on the emperor's status as a semi-divine ruler.[61] The discrete legitimating codes that enabled the Manchus to engage different imperial constituencies jointly stressed the emperor's semi-sacred character – a conception that precluded the empire's engagement with Western polities on equal terms.[62] Likewise, liberal demands for openness cut against the practices of tributary diplomacy, which the Manchus had appropriated from their Ming predecessors, and maintained as an effective means of insulating the empire's volatile maritime frontier from destabilizing outside influences.

In different ways, then, transformational liberalism profoundly jeopardized the minority conquest regimes then dominating South and East Asia. Regardless of their status as supposedly distinct Western versus Eastern empires, both the Company Raj and the Manchu Empire rested on define and rule and divide and rule strategies anchored in the reification and conservation of cultural difference among diverse imperial constituencies. Accordingly, the transformative and assimilationist ambitions of the liberal civilizing mission were anathema to both imperial orders.

---

[60] Mantena, *Alibis of Empire*, p. 28, emphasis added.
[61] For an excellent recent account of the clash between competing British and Qing belief systems, and the resulting diplomatic complications, see D. E. Banks, 'Fields of practice: Symbolic binding and the Qing defense of Sinocentric diplomacy', *International Studies Quarterly*, 63(3) (2019), 546–57.
[62] Ibid., pp. 551–2.

The crises of legitimacy that liberalism eventually sparked in both empires will now be considered, alongside an examination of the conservative reconstructions of order that these crises eventually inspired.

Imperial Crises I: The Indian Mutiny and the Reconstruction of International Order in South Asia

The Indian Mutiny of 1857–9 constituted the gravest crisis of British power in India prior to decolonization and triggered permanent and profound changes in the way the British organized imperial authority – and by extension international order – in South Asia. The mutiny is relevant here as a manifestation of deeper failures of British define and rule strategies. These failures arose from widespread Indian opposition to an imposed liberal civilizing mission that clashed with the regime of ecumenical incorporation on which the Company Raj rested. Below I consider some of the more disruptive British reforms that nourished Indian opposition; the course of the 'Mutiny' itself; and the transformations in the British model of imperial rule that followed the empire's near-terminal crisis.

The mid-century crisis of British rule in India stemmed first from a shift in its vision of empire – away from Orientalist restoration, and towards liberal transformation. This about-turn was most visible in the company's approach towards educating their Indian collaborators. In the early decades of conquest and consolidation, the company remained content to delegate lower-level tasks of administration and adjudication to indigenous elites. These collaborators – often holdovers from the Mughal Empire and its successor polities – served as vital cultural as well as political brokers between the company and local Indian communities.[63] They moreover retained many of the practices and forms of cultural affiliation – most notably an attachment to Persian as both a language of administration and a vibrant literary heritage – that had for generations helped define South Asia's lettered elites.[64]

In its first incarnation, moreover, the Company Raj had not simply stopped at co-opting the Persianate administrative class. Rather, the company proved an active and powerful patron of the study of both Persian, as well as Arabic and Sanskrit.[65] It also spent huge sums founding educational institutions – most notably the Calcutta Madrassa and Benares College – that aimed to codify Islamic and Hindu bodies of law,

---

[63] Metcalf, *Ideologies of the Raj*, p. 22.
[64] Rahman, 'Decline of Persian in British India', 52.
[65] Cohn, *Colonialism and Its Forms of Knowledge*, pp. 24–5.

and train indigenous scholars and jurists in their content and application.[66] Company elites saw this patronage as practically worthwhile, because it helped prepare for service indigenous elites who were cheaper to employ than their European counterparts, as well as more familiar with the particular needs and challenges of the diverse communities the Raj now ruled. Alongside considerations of cost and administrative efficiency, the company also deemed cultural and religious patronage politically expedient, as a means of conciliating indigenous lettered elites to British rule, and so nurturing a local 'empire of opinion' conducive to company supremacy.[67] Besides these instrumental considerations, finally, Orientalists embraced the continued patronage of local languages as an integral component of their imperial mission to 'rejuvenate' Indian civilization.[68]

From the 1820s, however, liberals increasingly contested the company's language and education policies, as well as the broader Orientalist vision underwriting them. Anglicizers advocated that the company abandon its earlier mission of rejuvenating India's classical cultures, for policies that introduced Indians comprehensively to the language, customs, practices and values of a supposedly superior British civilization. Encapsulated most notoriously in Thomas Babington Macaulay's 1835 Minute on Indian Education, anglicizers pushed for the termination of company patronage of Asian languages; the replacement of Persian by English as the empire's language of administration; and the education of Indian elites exclusively in English, with a modern Western curriculum replacing an earlier focus on the study of Asian languages, laws, religion and culture.[69]

In making their case for change, anglicizers deliberately overdrew the contrast between the Orientalist model and their own. Existing company policies had not aimed to hermetically insulate Indian elites from Western knowledge. Rather, company officials had long seen the value of introducing their Indian collaborators to Western education, particularly in the natural sciences. But they had sought to do so through a gradual process of 'engraftment' that conveyed such knowledge through instruction in local languages, and did not presuppose a vast and unbridgeable divide between Western and Indian epistemes.[70] By contrast, anglicizers

---

[66] Ibid., p. 47.
[67] Bayly, *Indian Society and the Making of the British Empire*, p. 114. See also Mantena, *Alibis of Empire*, p. 24.
[68] Collingham, *Imperial Bodies*, p. 15.
[69] Rahman, 'Decline of Persian in British India', 50–1.
[70] S. Evans, 'Macaulay's minute revisited: Colonial language policy in nineteenth-century India', *Journal of Multilingual and Multicultural Development*, 23(4) (2002), 262–3.

condemned the company's Orientalist policies as patronizing 'error' to the detriment of Indian progress, and proposed a revolutionary overhaul of the company's educational institutions to produce a new class of anglicized Indians, 'who may be interpreters between us and the millions whom we govern – a class of persons Indian in blood and colour, but English in tastes, in opinions, in morals and in intellect'.[71]

Fiercely opposed by the company's Orientalist faction and their local allies, the anglicizers' proposed revolution in Indian education was only partially successful. Though anglicizers managed to replace Persian with English as the Company Raj's administrative language after 1837, they failed in their push for the company to end all large-scale subsidies for the study of Asian languages and culture.[72] Nevertheless, from the 1830s, the Anglicist model of civilizing Indian elites through assimilation to Western civilization was undeniably ascendant. Henceforth, a succession of governors-general abandoned the company's earlier conservative emphasis on ecumenical incorporation, instead preferring to perpetuate British power through reference to an assimilationist vision of liberal transformation.[73] The societal reach of this vision was in practice limited to a small section of India's lettered elites. Moreover, while portions of this constituency were alienated by anglicization, others embraced what they saw as a pathway of upward professional and social mobility.[74] These caveats aside, the Anglicists' qualified triumph over the Orientalists marked a significant departure from the Company Raj's earlier model of administration and legitimation, one that weakened their social ties with important local intermediaries on which imperial rule had previously rested.

The company's partial embrace of anglicization, and the relative decline of the Orientalists, together marked a highly disruptive reconceptualization of the empire's legitimating vision. Alongside these changes in the empire's constitution, liberal reformers further sowed the seeds of Indian dissent by unilaterally revising the terms of the company's engagement with Indian client rulers in the Raj's penumbra of indirectly ruled states. In the company's early conquest and consolidation phase, the empire had selectively and strategically preserved the privileges of a plethora of client rulers in territories adjacent to the Raj.[75] As the EIC

---

[71] T. Macaulay, 'Minute by the Honourable T. B. Macaulay, dated the 2nd February 1835' in H. Sharp (ed.), Selections from Educational Records, 1781–1839, Pt. I (Delhi: National Archives of India, 1965 [1920]), pp. 107–17, https://bit.ly/3cigZsy (accessed 20 April 2018).
[72] Evans, 'Macaulay's minute revisited', 274–5.   [73] Mantena, Alibis of Empire, p. 28.
[74] Bayly, Indian Society and the Making of the British Empire, p. 122.
[75] Keen, Princely India and the British, p. 8.

tightened its grip on the subcontinent, it progressively monopolized these polities' foreign relations, and secured greater control over their public finances.[76] But this insidious corrosion of the Princely States' de facto sovereignty coincided with the Company Raj's scrupulous recognition of its clients' *de jure* authority.

By contrast, from the 1830s, liberal reformers again began to undermine the credibility of the bargains underwriting the Raj's relations with its local intermediaries. In the case of the Princely States, the Raj's interference in matters of local succession marked the most conspicuous expression of this new imperial high-handedness. Previously, British Residents – the colonial agents that from the late eighteenth century formed the power behind the throne in the Princely States – were more willing to let indigenous tradition guide matters of succession, provided the company's vital interests were upheld in the process. But with the advent of reform, this more measured and flexible approach gave way to a new insistence on standardizing rules of succession, with the option of liquidating Princely sovereignty through territorial annexation when these conditions were not met.[77] Most contentiously, the Raj articulated a so-called doctrine of lapse. This doctrine determined that where client rulers died without male issue, their dynasty's claims on local sovereignty ceased. This in turn licensed the Raj to directly annex the Princely State and absorb it into the empire's directly ruled territories. Previously, dynasties could perpetuate themselves by adopting an heir.[78] But under the new dispensation, failure to produce a male heir virtually ensured the extinction of a dynastic line, and with it the very survival of their kingdom.[79]

Not content with interfering in the succession of arrangements of their client states, by the 1850s the drive for reform extended even to the EIC's relations with the Mughal emperor himself, who at that time still remained the Raj's titular suzerain. Thus in 1852, the EIC agreed to support the heir apparent to the Mughal throne over his fraternal rivals. But the company tied this support to a number of humiliating preconditions. These included a downgrading of the son's title (from emperor to 'king's son'), the transfer of the imperial palace (the Red Fort) to the company, and submission to a new form of ceremonial marking a relationship of equality between the Mughals and the governor-general of the EIC.[80] In 1856, when the heir apparent unexpectedly predeceased his octogenarian father, Emperor Bahadur Shah II, the EIC went further, refusing outright to recognize his preferred successor. Instead, the EIC determined at this time that the Mughal line would be

[76] Ibid.   [77] Ibid., p. 28.   [78] Ibid.   [79] Ibid.   [80] Ibid., p. 29.

extinguished upon the elderly emperor's death.[81] With this plan to retire the fiction of Mughal suzerainty, the EIC effectively cast off the camouflage that had previously legitimated its de facto dominance to many of its most powerful intermediaries. Unsurprisingly, this move again estranged Indian collaborators, further corroding the political foundations of local support for the Company Raj.

The company's policies of anglicization (in the educational sphere) and its creeping dispossession of indigenous dynasties alienated two core constituencies critical to the Company's Raj's survival. Anglicization – and with it the toppling of Persian as the empire's *lingua franca* – marginalized many of the Persephone clerks and jurists that had until then been the mainstay of the Raj's administration. Dynastic dispossession through the doctrine of lapse meanwhile endangered power-holders that still held significant landed wealth and traditional authority, despite their decline under the company's predatory patronage. And the humiliation (and pending extinction) of the Mughal Dynasty inadvertently imperilled the EIC by removing a figurehead and focal point for Indian loyalties that had previously masked the reality of company rule.

Most important and infamous, however, was the reform movement's corrosive impact on the most indispensable instrument of company rule – the Bengal Army. On the eve of the mutiny, the Bengal Army was the main coercive foundation of British power in Asia. The largest modern army east of Suez, the Bengal Army numbered 139,807 'natives', led by 26,089 European officers.[82] The biggest of the three Presidency armies (the others being the Madras and Bombay armies), the Bengal Army had recently seen action in the First Afghan War (1839–42), the conflict against Scindia (1843), the two Anglo-Sikh Wars (1845–6 and 1848–9), and the Second Burma War (1852).[83] Already wearied by near-continuous fighting along the Raj's bloody and expanding frontiers, the Bengal Army was also especially prone to disaffection in the wake of the company's new enthusiasm for annexation. This was because many of the army's recruits hailed from Awadh, a once powerful kingdom that the company had controversially annexed in accordance with the doctrine of lapse, following the death of its last indigenous ruler in 1856.[84] Additionally, the company's more rigorous taxation regime for Awadh threatened the interests of the small landholders, the class from whom much of the Bengal Army was drawn.[85]

Finally, beyond these material considerations, the company's push for reform also sat uneasily with the sepoys' religious sensibilities. As we have

---

[81] Ibid., p. 30.   [82] I. Habib, 'The coming of 1857', *Social Scientist*, 26(1–4) (1998), 6.
[83] Ibid.   [84] Bayly, *Indian Society and the Making of the British Empire*, p. 180.   [85] Ibid.

seen, the EIC had previously deliberately cultivated a high caste Hindu peasant infantry as the foundation of its Bengal Army.[86] Across each of its Presidency armies, the company had also made extensive use of Muslim troops, particularly in light cavalry. In both instances, the EIC had long sought to entrench a sense of *esprit de corps* among its soldiers by stressing an affinity between the warrior vocation, service to the company, and religious devotion.[87] Paradoxically, by trying to infuse military service with religious significance, the company thus left itself highly vulnerable to religiously inspired challenges to its rule.

By the eve of the mutiny, the combination of a more overbearing EIC administration, alongside the at times literally evangelical aspirations of some of its more zealous officials, together deeply unsettled the foundations of the Company Raj. Notoriously, the spark for the Bengal Army's rebellion lay in rumours that the cartridges for the army's new Enfield rifles were sealed with a combination of pig and cow fat, necessitating that Muslim and Hindu soldiers violate dietary restrictions when tearing open the cartridges with their teeth.[88] But this catalyst arose from a larger context in which the company had moved away from an earlier template of rule, emphasizing ecumenical incorporation, and towards one that stressed coercive assimilation in accordance with the tenets of a centralized, authoritarian vision of empire grounded in transformational liberalism. It was this shift that fatally jeopardized the system of collaboration underwriting company rule. And it was this shift that the British abruptly reversed, in favour of an extensively renovated version of the older regime of ecumenical incorporation, once they had suppressed the rebellion.

The course of the 'Mutiny' has been chronicled extensively elsewhere. Here it is enough to note the rebellion's scale and significance, as a prelude to exploring its implications for the imperial order's post-1857 character and constitution. Beginning on 10 May 1857 in Meerut, north of Delhi, the rebellion rapidly spread throughout northern India, as rebels captured key cities, most notably Delhi and Lucknow. An estimated 70,000 soldiers joined the rebellion, while another 30,000 deserted – profoundly weakening the key instrument of coercion on which the EIC's power rested.[89] Moreover, though the rebellion did not reach beyond Hindustan, it soon extended from the Bengal Army itself to draw in a host of other social actors. These ranged from pensioned-off client rulers and their retinues, determined to reclaim power, to peasants seeking relief from the company's exacting and inflexible taxation regime.[90]

---

[86] Alavi, *The Sepoys and the Company*, p. 45.   [87] Ibid.
[88] Darwin, *Unfinished Empire*, p. 248.   [89] Ibid., p. 250.   [90] Ibid., pp. 250–1.

Evidence of a prior conspiracy to overthrow the British remains scant. But the speed of the rebellion's spread, and the broad coalition it encompassed, both attest to the underlying fragility of company rule. The rebels' justifications for violence likewise illuminate the EIC's self-inflicted legitimation crisis with its turn towards transformational liberalism. Following their capture of Delhi, the rebels conscripted the Mughal emperor as their figurehead, and framed the rebellion as a legitimist movement to restore the emperor and expel the English usurpers. In mobilizing support, the rebels also turned to key figures in the *ulama*, who obligingly cast the conflict in religious terms, as a fight to expel the fanatical Protestant Christian 'Franks'.[91] Notwithstanding the sectarian character of this appeal, the rebellion reflected deeper anxieties about the company's supposedly evangelizing impulses that Hindus and Muslims shared. The rebellion's restorationist and religious impulses thus both reflected popular hostility to the company's turn from ecumenical incorporation to liberal assimilation. This hostility ran deep, and could be defused following the rebellion's suppression only through a radical overhaul of the Raj's entire system of rule.

British power faltered but did not fall with the rebellion. The rebellion's failure to spread beyond Hindustan gave the British the opportunity first to mount a rearguard action, and then to mobilize additional reinforcements from Britain to eventually recapture key cities such as Delhi, Lucknow and Cawnpore, effectively killing the rebels' aspirations to establish a rival regime to the Company Raj.[92] Sporadic resistance continued for two years, the viceroy only declaring a 'state of peace' in July 1859. The human cost of the conflict was catastrophic, claiming the lives of at least 100,000 Indians, as well as 2,000 British soldiers killed in action and another 9,000 lost through disease.[93] Notoriously, rebel massacres of European civilians prompted British forces to pursue indiscriminate retaliation and civilian victimization in their reconquest of India. These memories of rebel terror and British counter-terror marked a defining trauma for late Victorian Britain, and haunted post-conflict efforts to secure political reconciliation between British rulers and Indian subjects.[94]

Beyond these immediate consequences, the rebellion compelled the victorious British to reconstitute their empire on new institutional, ideological and military foundations. At an institutional level, the

[91] Ibid., p. 247.   [92] Ibid., p. 255.   [93] Ibid., p. 256.
[94] See generally C. Herbert, *War of No Pity: The Indian Mutiny and Victorian trauma* (Princeton: Princeton University Press, 2008).

biggest and most important changes came at the empire's apex. Following his capture, the Mughal emperor Bahadur Shah II was put on trial in the Red Fort for his alleged complicity in the rebellion, and eventually exiled to Burma, where he died shortly afterwards.[95] The emperor's trial and exile symbolically confirmed an evaporation of Mughal power that had long been practically evident. Concurrent with the Mughal monarchy's extinction, the British also confirmed the transfer of power from company to Crown following the rebellion's suppression. Finally, in 1876, Queen Victoria assumed the title of Empress of India, completing the transition to formal British suzerainty over the subcontinent.[96]

Profoundly important though they were by themselves, the larger significance of these institutional changes lay in the ideological volteface they also represented. Following the Indian mutiny, British appetites for transformational liberalism waned, being succeeded by a programmatic and self-consciously conservative vision of the empire. The project of anglicizing India along liberal lines had always had its critics, especially among Britain's conservative establishment. With the near-collapse of British rule in India, conservatives seized on the revolt as evidence of the company's culpability in advancing a liberal civilizing mission, which they decried as both subversive of British authority, and disrespectful of Indian customs and tradition.[97] In its place, conservatives argued for an alternative conception of empire, grounded in reverence for indigenous Indian hierarchies, and in the British Crown's commitment to the defence of the systems of custom and prescriptive right attached to these hierarchies.

The outlines of this new vision of empire were clear as early as the Queen's Proclamation of 1858. An 'ideological supplement'[98] to the Government of India Act, the proclamation centred around Victoria's commitment to uphold 'the ancient rights, usages and customs' of India from the colonial state's encroachment.[99] The proclamation explicitly extended guarantees to India's princes against the threat of territorial annexation, as well as confirming their right to ensure princely succession

---

[95] W. Dalrymple, *The Last Mughal: The fall of a dynasty, Delhi, 1857* (New York: Vintage Books, 2008), p. 8.
[96] Cannadine, *Ornamentalism*, p. 45.
[97] M. Stubbings, 'British conservatism and the Indian Revolt: The annexation of Awadh and the consequences of liberal empire, 1856–1858', *Journal of British Studies*, 55(4) (2016), 733.
[98] Ibid., p. 742.
[99] Proclamation by the Queen in Council to the Princes, Chiefs and People of India (published by the Governor-General at Allahabad, 1 November 1858). Available at: www .csas.ed.ac.uk/mutiny/confpapers/Queen'sProclamation.pdf (accessed 7 September 2018).

through adoption if required.[100] More generally, Victoria committed the colonial government to 'respect the rights, dignity and honour of native princes as our own',[101] affirming the central place of princely and aristocratic collaborators within the renovated British imperial order. Sensitive to what they believed were the religious sentiments driving the revolt, the British also committed themselves to honouring the empire's faith traditions, and refraining from any further attempts at Christian proselytization.[102]

In its essence, the post-1857 Raj reverted to significantly renovated incorporative diversity regime of the kind that had characterized the Company Raj in early first decades. Recalling that collaboration remains the foundation for successful imperial rule, the British in the aftermath of the revolt scrambled to revive the alliances on which their power rested. During this time, the British remained hostage to key imperatives of imperial statecraft, notably the necessity to build and bind multicultural conquest coalitions, while blocking the formation of anti-imperial countercoalitions. And as an alien conquest dynasty, the British faced the additional challenges of needing to curate imperial constituencies consonant with these needs, through interrelated practices of define and divide and rule. The renovated empire reflected these demands, in its treatment of religion, its reconstitution of the Raj's military machine and in its renewed partnership with Indian aristocrats.

Religion marked the sphere in which the British reversion to an incorporative rather than an assimilative diversity regime was starkest. As noted, the most important post-1857 initiative in this sphere was negative, in the new British reluctance to foist Christianity on local populations. Instead, the British re-dedicated themselves to a mode of rule that foregrounded communal divisions as the key cleavage in Indian society. Consistent with this outlook, they renewed their commitment to governing through distinct Anglo-Hindu and Anglo-Muslim systems of law.[103] The British likewise resumed their earlier posture as protectors of India's faith traditions, as well as indispensable guarantors of inter-communal harmony.[104]

Beyond these instances of simple reversion, however, the expanding bureaucratic reach of the colonial state further entrenched supposedly innate categories of religious identity far deeper into the Indian population than before. The inclusion of caste in successive colonial censuses

---

[100] Cannadine, *Ornamentalism*, p. 44.
[101] Proclamation by the Queen in Council (accessed 7 September 2018).
[102] Stubbings, 'British conservatism and the Indian Revolt', 747.
[103] Anderson, 'Islamic law and the colonial encounter', pp. 181–5.
[104] Metcalf, *Ideologies of the Raj*, p. 48.

thus codified and 'froze' a category of identity that had formerly been far more flexible.[105] This institutionalization in turn restructured 'relations of public worship, physical mobility, marriage and inheritance' to an unprecedented degree.[106] Similarly, the inclusion of Muslim and Hindu as categorical identifiers in the colonial census consolidated these identities as opposed and antagonistic.[107] These moves were undeniably consistent with imperial imperatives of define and divide and rule. They also perpetuated a conception of Indian society – as both intrinsically devout and hopelessly religiously polarized – that would define the British Raj down to its dissolution.

Whereas the Raj's curation of religious identities had some continuities with the early Company Raj, no such continuity characterized the post-1857 reorganization of the empire's military system. Here, the mutiny of the Bengal Army put paid to any possibility of simply resurrecting historical precedents. Instead, in the decades following the Crown's takeover of British India, the empire's armies were transformed through resort to selective ethnic military mobilization. Specifically, the Indian military became increasingly composed of so-called martial races. Minority groups supposedly innately suited to the warrior vocation, communities such as the Ghurkhas, Pathans, Sikhs and Rajputs eventually came to comprise three quarters of the Indian Army by 1914, despite collectively constituting a tiny minority of the total Indian population.[108] Crucially – and consistent with the book's larger argument – these groups often did not comprise pre-existing collectivities, but were rather curated into existence through the intervention of the British colonial state. Thus, for example, the British contrived the ethnonym 'Ghurkha', and then deliberately tried to cultivate a shared sense of *esprit de race* by sponsoring an idiosyncratic 'hill Hinduism' that distinguished the Ghurkhas from other Hindus.[109] Likewise, the British distinguished the elite Ghurkha units through the use of distinctive uniforms and headgear.[110] These aimed at affirming their separateness and innate suitability for armed service. Simultaneously, however, such markers of distinction implicitly also warranting the pre-emptive exclusion of the majority of Indians from

[105] Frykenberg, 'Constructions of Hinduism', 539.
[106] Cannadine, *Ornamentalism*, p. 42.
[107] Frykenberg, 'Constructions of Hinduism', 539. See also M. Birnbaum, 'Recognizing diversity: Establishing religious difference in Pakistan and Israel' in A. Phillips and C. Reus-Smit (eds.), *Culture and Order in World Politics* (Cambridge: Cambridge University Press, 2020), pp. 259–60.
[108] Rand and Wagner, 'Recruiting the "martial races"', 234.
[109] K. Roy, 'The construction of regiments in the Indian army: 1859–1913', *War in History* 8(2) (2001), 134.
[110] Ibid., pp. 134–5.

military recruitment, on the presumption that their 'non-martial' ethnic character automatically rendered their enlistment futile.[111] In this way, the British were able to sustain a vast military establishment staffed with reliable collaborators, while at the same justifying the enforced demilitarization of the vast majority of their Indian subjects.

The British state's renewed post-revolt reconciliation with India's princes and aristocrats finally marked an intermediate renovation their existing imperial template. In its early decades of expansion, the company had repeatedly found diplomatic advantage in propping up India's princes, while surreptitiously subverting their existing ties of fealty to the Mughal emperor.[112] The idea of mobilizing client rulers and the indigenous aristocracy to buttress British power was thus far from new, notwithstanding the high-handed treatment of these clients at the peak of the liberal reformist era. But following the post-revolt restoration of British power, aristocratic clients were courted far more assiduously, and integrated much more systematically into the imperial hierarchy, than had previously been the case.

Most critically, the abolition of company rule and the fiction of Mughal suzerainty together opened up an unmediated relationship between the British Crown and Indian feudatories for the first time. Following Victoria's assumption of the title Empress of India in 1876, the British monarch sat at the pinnacle of a meticulously gradated hierarchy of status that directly integrated Indian rulers into a wider imperial system, based on ties of vertical association and reciprocal obligations between Crown and clients.[113] Once again, the process of mobilizing these client rulers was importantly (re)constitutive, rather than simply entailing the conscription of pre-existing and already fully formed constituencies. Thus, at the 1877 Imperial Assemblage in Delhi publicly celebrating the empress's ascension, ninety of India's leading princes were presented with silk banners emblazoned with their coats of arms. Significantly, these banners were shield-shaped in the European style, with crests again following European forms of heraldry.[114] The banners moreover depicted lineage histories, including their earlier associations to Mughal rule, and their later connections to the British.[115] In presenting these banners, the British conceptualized the Indian princes as English knights, now

---

[111] Notably, this excessive dependence on a relatively small number of indigenous allied constituencies introduced its own vulnerabilities to the apparatus of British rule; selective ethnic military mobilization constrained imperial power as much as it enabled it. See Omissi, 'Martial races', 22.

[112] Fisher, 'The imperial coronation of 1819', 250.

[113] Stubbings, 'British conservatism and the Indian Revolt', 734.

[114] Cohn, 'Representing authority in Victorian India', p. 191.   [115] Ibid.

perpetually tied to the empress through ties of feudal loyalty.[116] Critically, in codifying new ritual idioms of power through a synthesis of indigenous and European iconographies, the British sought to refashion elite indigenous subjectivities, to allow their clients to slot more snugly into a pan-imperial aristocratic hierarchy.

The post-1857 retreat from transformational liberalism and Christian proselytization; the revolutionary transformation of the Indian military around the construction of martial races; the reconfiguration of British ties to Indian aristocratic clients – these together marked a comprehensive overhaul of the entire apparatus of British power in South Asia. From the near-death trauma of the Indian Revolt, the British succeeded in preserving their imperium. But this had come at the cost of jettisoning an alternative, assimilationist model of liberal empire that contradicted the company's diversity regime and so almost fatally weakened ties with indigenous collaborators. It moreover necessitated a return to an incorporative diversity regime that had important parallels with that which had first sustained the ascendant Company Raj. In its second incarnation, however, Britain's Indian Empire was far more deliberately and systematically conservative than before. '[O]nce the target of reformers, India had now become the hope of reactionaries.'[117] British rule in India would henceforth be based on the perpetuation of communal division, and on intensified cooperation with martial minorities, landlords and aristocratic feudatories. In time, the British would moreover extend their alliances with conservative client rulers throughout the Indian Ocean littoral, eventually dominating Eurasia's southern littoral in collaboration with indigenous autocrats.[118] In East Asia, too, initial British efforts to impose transformational liberalism would similarly yield a revived conservative international order, again following a near-terminal crisis. It is to a consideration of this crisis and the reconstituted order that it produced that we now turn.

Imperial Crises II: The Late Qing Cataclysm and the Reconstruction of International Order in East Asia

The Qing Empire in the mid-nineteenth century experienced a multi-dimensional cataclysm that permanently changed its constitution, as well as the broader international order the Manchus dominated. Within IR, accounts of this period privilege the Opium Wars (1839–42 and

---

[116] Ibid.
[117] H. G. Hutchins, *The Illusion of Permanence: British imperialism in India* (Princeton: Princeton University Press, 1967), xi, cited in Cannadine, *Ornamentalism*, p. 45.
[118] Bose, *A Hundred Horizons*, pp. 25–6.

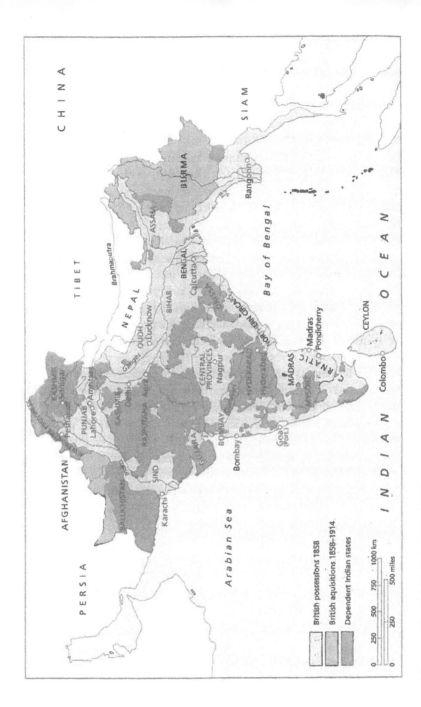

Map 7.1 The British Raj, 1858–1947
Source: Andrew Phillips and J. C. Sharman, *International Order in Diversity: War, Trade and Rule in the Indian Ocean* (Cambridge University Press, 2015), p. 194.

1856–60) and the Qing Empire's subsequent conscription into a Western-dominated international society.[119] Preoccupied with China's 'century of humiliation' (1839–1943), generations of Chinese nationalists have reinforced this bias.[120] But existing accounts – at least within IR – generally under-specify the imperial legitimation crisis within the Qing Empire that Western encroachment helped spark, but did not exclusively determine. They also overlook the fundamentally conservative ideological and institutional consequences of this crisis. Most significantly for this inquiry, they do not consider the late Qing crisis comparatively, as one instance of a broader reconfiguration of Eurasian empires that cumulatively reshaped world politics at this time.

Far from being reducible to Western encroachment alone, the late Qing crisis encompassed a combination of external pressure and internal rebellion. From the 1840s, British commercial expansion did destabilize portions of the Qing Empire's southern maritime periphery. But at least at first, the Manchus adapted existing practices of 'barbarian management' to contain this intrusion. Rather than directly challenging the empire's legitimacy, British infiltration into the Qing maritime frontier was more significant for its indirect effects, primarily in its introduction of new ideological influences that helped inspire the Taiping rebellion (1851–64), the deadliest and most damaging revolt against Qing rule.

In my previous work, I have stressed the intersection of Western encroachment and the Taiping rebellion as catalysts for the East Asian international order's transformation.[121] This assessment holds true over the long term. But it obscures the Qing Empire's surprising adaptiveness and resilience in the medium term. It also fails to locate the Taiping rebellion alongside contemporaneous revolts in the empire's ethnically mixed borderlands in the southwest and the northwest, or to fully articulate the impact these revolts jointly exercised on the empire's constitution. Like the British Raj, the Qing Empire escaped oblivion, its rulers reconstituting it following a near-terminal crisis. This involved a recalibration of the empire's existing diversity regime, as well as a refinement of its diplomatic practices and frontier management strategies.

Western encroachment forced the Qing Empire to adapt existing institutions (treaty ports) and develop new ones (the Zongli Yamen) to

---

[119] See for example S. Suzuki, *Civilization and Empire: China and Japan's encounter with European international society* (London: Routledge, 2009), pp. 57–8.

[120] On the significance of the 'century of humiliation' to modern Chinese nationalism, see generally Z. Wang, *Never Forget National Humiliation: Historical memory in Chinese politics and foreign relations* (New York: Columbia University Press, 2012).

[121] A. Phillips, *War, Religion and Empire: The transformation of international orders* (Cambridge: Cambridge University Press, 2011), chapter 7.

manage this new challenge. But the Qing continued to administer relations with their East Asian Confucian tributaries through the Board of Rites down to the Sino-Japanese war (1894–5).[122] Likewise, the Lifan Yuan administered relations with the Manchus' Central Asian dependencies (and Tibet) down to its abolition in 1912.[123] This ambidextrous model of diplomacy roughly mirrored the Qing diversity regime of segregated incorporation, which persisted – albeit with significant modifications – after the mid-century crisis had passed. Finally, after 1860 the Qing Empire persisted in part through a new partnership with Britain. Chastened by the Indian Revolt, disabused of transformational liberalism, and anxious to avoid further Asian territorial expansion, Britain's 'Cooperative Policy' explicitly aimed to preserve the Qing Empire and facilitate its reconstruction.[124] The result of this collaboration was a hybrid international order that synthesized Western, Qing and Confucian practices, and persisted almost down to the empire's final dissolution in 1911.

As with my examination of the British Raj, the following analysis sketches the contours and course of the Qing imperial crisis, before exploring its long-term constitutional effects.

Turning first to the contours and course of the Qing crisis, let us begin with the First Opium War (1839–42). The First Opium War is the traditional point of departure for studies examining China's forced entry into European international society.[125] Without denying its importance, this interpretation of the First Opium War is problematic for two reasons. First, framing the conflict as the opening act in China's forced 'opening' to the West fails to locate it within the context of a broader crisis of legitimation that was largely internal the Qing Empire. Second, the traditional narrative overstates Western agency and ambitions in imposing a preferred order on the Manchus. The concessions Britain won from the Manchus were modest, and the institutional arrangements governing the post-war settlement were mainly of Manchu rather than Western design. The subversive ideological influences the British introduced into the empire nevertheless helped influence the mid-century rebellions, which together with renewed foreign aggression did force more fundamental changes to Qing imperial administration and diplomacy after 1860.

---

[122] See generally Kim, *The Last Phase of the East Asian World Order*.
[123] Wang, 'From masterly brokers to compliant protégées', p. 1664.
[124] I. C. Y. Hsu, 'Late Ch'ing foreign relations, 1866–1905' in J. K. Fairbank and K.-C. Liu (eds), *The Cambridge History of China*, 15 vols., XI: *Late Ch'ing, 1800–1911*, Pt. II (Cambridge: Cambridge University Press, 1978), p. 73.
[125] Suzuki, *Civilization and Empire*, pp. 57–8.

The First Opium War formed part of a larger process of British commercial and military expansion in Asia. It was also simultaneously an expression of ideological proselytization under the banner of transformational liberalism. The conflict marked a culmination of British efforts dating back to the 1790s to open the Qing Empire to greater trade and diplomatic exchange. Throughout the eighteenth century, rising British demand for Chinese tea and porcelain had aggravated its trade deficit with China. For Britain, the sale of Indian opium to Chinese consumers offered an expedient way to remedy this deficit.[126] As the EIC held a monopoly on the refinement and distribution of Indian opium, the trade in Indian opium also offered an invaluable means of shoring up the Company Raj's fiscal strength.[127] Beyond these material considerations, rising philosophical support for free trade provided ideological reinforcement to expand Britain's commercial reach into the Qing Empire.[128] These pressures merely intensified after 1833, when the abolition of the EIC's monopoly on the China trade strengthened a powerful constituency of private traders long impatient to win greater access to the Chinese market.[129]

Determined though the British were to expand trade with the Qing Empire, the Manchus proved equally resolute in resisting these pressures. Successive British missions to the empire had foundered on British refusal to conform to the ceremonial strictures of Qing tributary diplomacy.[130] Given that the Qing Empire was largely economically self-sufficient, the Manchus also had little material incentive to accommodate British demands. Indeed, as Chinese opium consumption grew from the late eighteenth century, the accompanying social and economic disruption fortified the Manchus' resolve to resist Western encroachment. Besides its negative impact on public health, the Manchu court decried the opium trade's larger economic effects.[131] In particular, the Manchus resented the drain on silver that the trade brought with it, believing that the outflow of specie was destabilizing the empire's monetary system and so fuelling political and social instability.[132] The endemic corruption among government officials charged with regulating Western commerce in Canton provided further grounds for forcibly suppressing the opium trade.[133] These considerations together motivated the Manchus to prosecute their anti-opium campaigns with renewed zeal from 1839 – and it was

[126] Lawson, *The East India Company*, p. 157.
[127] Headrick, *The Tools of Empire*, p. 45.
[128] Stokes, *The English Utilitarians and India*, p. 39.
[129] Lawson, *The East India Company*, p. 157.   [130] Banks, 'Fields of practice', 552–4.
[131] Fairbank, 'The canton trade and the Opium War', pp. 178–9.   [132] Ibid.   [133] Ibid.

this reassertion of imperial authority that drew the Qing Empire into war with Britain.

Though initially controversial in Britain (opium was banned in Britain and many parliamentarians denounced British participation in what they saw as an unjust conflict), Lord Melbourne's ministry ultimately fully committed to war with the Qing Empire. The reasons for doing so were diverse, but converged on a determination to expand trade with the Qing Empire, and to establish institutional safeguards to protect the lives, liberty and property of British merchants mediating this trade.[134] After three desultory years of fighting, the British succeeded in wresting the territorial concession of Hong Kong, and in winning British merchants' rights to residency in five designated treaty ports in southern China.[135] Most importantly, the post-war settlement paved the way for the later development a more formal system of commercial extraterritoriality. This system would ultimately grant British residents immunity from Qing jurisdiction, making them subject instead to British laws administered by British courts.[136]

The 'unequal treaty' system – conferring unilateral rights of commercial extraterritoriality on Western residents in the Qing Empire – eventually formed the mainstay of European informal imperialism in Northeast Asia. Nevertheless, we must not overstate the short-term consequences of the First Opium War. For the Western intrusion was at first highly localized, confined to a few tiny toeholds on the Qing Empire's southern maritime periphery. Though Britain won rights of residency in four other ports besides Canton (privileges which were soon extended to other foreigners), the vast majority of the Qing Empire remained off limits to Westerners.[137] Likewise, though the Treaty of Nanjing guaranteed the British consul regular access to Qing imperial officials, this did not amount to formal diplomatic recognition between the British and Qing empires. With the exception of Hong Kong, the Qing Empire moreover remained territorially intact after the conflict.

Besides the modest character of British demands and Qing concessions, the initial arrangements governing the Western presence were also hardly novel. As a minority conquest dynasty, the Manchus had long presided over an imperial order based on 'ethnic legal pluralism', where different legal codes governed the empire's discrete imperial

---

[134] Ibid., pp. 194–5.   [135] Ibid., p. 212.

[136] J. K. Fairbank, 'The creation of the treaty system' in J. K. Fairbank (ed.), *The Cambridge History of China*, 15 vols., X: *Late Ch'ing, 1800–1911*, Pt. I (Cambridge: Cambridge University Press, 1978), p. 217.

[137] Ibid., p. 221.

constituencies.[138] Accordingly, the Manchu system of segregated incorporation could potentially be extended to pacify and integrate the new Western barbarians without radically changing its character. Indeed, by the Treaty of Nanjing, a precedent for this arrangement already existed, in extraterritorial privileges and rights of residence the Manchus had granted to traders from the Central Asian khanate of Kokand in 1836.[139] Far from being a radically new innovation, then, the treaty port system that began to solidify from the First Opium War was hybrid in character, in that it bore the imprint of Qing ethnic legal pluralism as much it reflected Western ideas of positive international law.

Most fundamentally, the First Opium War did not dramatically change either the Manchus' model of imperial administration, or their diplomatic and frontier management practices. The embryonic treaty port system codified and expanded Western commercial privileges, and slightly broadened the geographic footprint of Western trading operations. But the Qing system of segregated incorporation over diverse imperial constituencies remained firmly in place. Likewise, the limited Western intrusion had no impact on the Qing Empire's management of frontier relations either in Central Asia, where the Lifan Yuan remained in operation, or in Confucian East Asia, where the Board of Rites continued to administer tributary diplomacy with its dependent satellites there. Most tellingly, the Manchus had yet to establish a modern foreign ministry through which to engage the Western powers in regular diplomacy. Instead, the expanded trading concessions granted to Britain, France, the United States and later other powers were doled out on a bilateral and improvised basis, without any expectation that they would cumulatively accrete into an entirely new system of diplomatic practice.[140]

Despite its retrospective significance then, the initial Western intrusion was more a sideshow than a seismic shift for the Qing Empire. But this caveat should not diminish its profound indirect impact. For the expanded Western presence introduced subversive ideas into an already volatile local context in southern China. These ideas eventually helped inspire the Taiping rebellion, the most destructive of a cluster of rebellions that cumulatively reduced the empire's population from approximately 410 million in 1850, down to 350 million by 1873.[141] It was the

---

[138] P. K. Cassel, *Grounds of Judgment: Extraterritoriality and imperial power in nineteenth-century China and Japan* (Oxford: Oxford University Press, 2012), p. 17.
[139] P. K. Cassel, 'Excavating extraterritoriality: The "judicial sub-prefect" as a prototype for the mixed court in Shanghai', *Late Imperial China*, 24(2) (2003), 156.
[140] Fairbank, 'The creation of the treaty system', pp. 226–7.
[141] Figures cited in Fairbank and Goldman, *China: A New History*, p. 216.

devastation these rebellions wrought, alongside renewed Western predation in the Second Opium War (1856–60) that necessitated far-reaching renovations to the Qing Empire. Consequently, I will now sketch this intersection of domestic crisis and foreign aggression, before teasing out its long-term structural effects.

The Taiping rebellion was not only the most destructive revolt of late Qing rule, but also history's largest ever civil war. Raging from 1851 to 1864 in the middle and lower Yangtze river valley – the empire's most fertile territory – the conflict claimed an estimated twenty million lives, and almost toppled the Qing Dynasty. Led by Hong Xiuquan, a failed candidate for the imperial bureaucracy who imagined himself as God's second son and the younger brother to Jesus Christ, the Taiping ('Heavenly Kingdom') rebels aimed to overthrow the Manchus and establish a Christian theocracy in its place.[142] The Taiping rebels' theology was idiosyncratic at best. It indiscriminately mixed elements of evangelical Christianity with indigenous millenarian themes, alongside anti-Manchu nativism, and a proto-communist programme advocating the abolition of private property and conventional social ranks.[143] Given its fanatical anti-Confucianism and hostility to traditional hierarchies, the Taiping movement unsurprisingly first found purchase at the empire's social margins. In particular, many of its earliest adherents were Hakkas (literally 'guests').[144] A Sinicized but linguistically distinct minority recently settled in Guangxi province, the Hakkas lacked the lineage structures and more established patterns of settlement characteristic of other Guangxi residents.[145] Frequently landless and victims to violent persecution from their neighbours, many Hakkas found in the Taiping message and organization (the God Worshipping Society) a powerful vehicle for voicing their grievances, and pursuing a more just social order.[146]

At their peak, the Taiping rebels conquered and administered vast swathes of the Qing Empire, following their capture of Nanjing (China's traditional southern imperial capital) in 1853. As significant as the material destruction the rebellion inflicted was, it was also notable for the comprehensiveness of the ideological challenge it presented. This multidimensional challenge comprised an attack on Manchu dominance; on the Confucian order supporting the Manchus throughout China

[142] Ibid., p. 207.
[143] P. A. Kuhn, 'The Taiping Rebellion' in J. K. Fairbank (ed.), *The Cambridge History of China*, 15 vols., X: *Late Ch'ing, 1800–1911*, Pt. I (Cambridge: Cambridge University Press, 1978), p. 217.
[144] Fairbank and Goldman, *China: A New History*, p. 206.
[145] J. D. Spence, *God's Chinese Son: The Taiping heavenly kingdom of Hong Xiuquan* (New York: W. W. Norton, 1996), p. 25.
[146] Fairbank and Goldman, *China: A New History*, p. 206.

proper; and on the broader model of segregated incorporation sustaining the Qing Empire.

Throughout the rebellion, the Taiping rebels fostered anti-Qing xenophobia, decrying the Manchus as existentially unfit to rule.[147] Such sentiments carried an undeniable popular resonance, particularly in southern maritime China, where clandestine criminal networks (the Triads) had long harboured Ming restorationist sentiment.[148] That said, Taiping xenophobia was opportunistic rather than programmatic. In contrast to the Indian Revolt, for example, the expulsion of 'foreign' rulers was for the Taiping rebels a supplementary justification for revolt, rather than the primary driver of rebellion.[149] Equally, while the Mughal Emperor was a rallying point for the Indian rebels, who also recruited segments of the traditional Indian elites to their cause, the Taiping revolutionaries denounced the entire Confucian social order as anathema to God's will.[150] The Confucian conception of the emperor as the pivot linking the sacred and the mundane worlds came in for special criticism. But wherever Taiping rule extended, the revolutionaries sought to eradicate or expel the Confucian scholar-gentry, and to establish a nominally classless theocratic utopia free of traditional economic and social distinctions.[151]

The final dimension of the Taiping challenge was its rejection of the Qing model of segregated incorporation, in favour of a unitary and indeed proto-totalitarian universal alternative. Recall that the Qing Empire ostentatiously encompassed diverse faiths. Indeed, it depended on the emperor's ability to harness spiritual authority from different religious traditions to shore up his control over key intermediaries. In stark contrast, the Taiping revolutionaries were fanatically opposed to all religions apart from their own, and aimed to impose a uniform model of theocratic rule throughout the Heavenly Kingdom.[152] Certainly, the revolutionary government was chaotic and ill-formed in practice. But in theory it aimed to convert all imperial subjects to the Taiping faith, and to unite them in common subjection to Hong Xiuquan, who as God's second son would then help usher in God's kingdom on earth.[153] The sectarian character of

---

[147] T. H. Reilly, *The Taiping Heavenly Kingdom: Rebellion and the blasphemy of empire* (Seattle: University of Washington Press, 2004), p. 99.

[148] F. Michael, *The Taiping Rebellion: History and documents*, 3 vols., I: *History* (Seattle: University of Washington Press, 1966), p. 16.

[149] Reilly, *The Taiping Heavenly Kingdom*, p. 99.   [150] Ibid.

[151] Ibid. See also generally P. A. Kuhn, 'Origins of the Taiping vision: Cross-cultural dimensions of a Chinese rebellion', *Comparative Studies in Society and History*, 19(3) (1977), 350–66.

[152] Reilly, *The Taiping Heavenly Kingdom*, p. 99.   [153] Ibid., p. 104.

this vision radically challenged Qing methods of rule via segregated incorporation, further threatening the imperial order.

The uncompromising nature of the Taiping challenge eventually proved its undoing, uniting a broad coalition of enemies that brought about its defeat and disappearance following the Manchus' recapture of Nanjing in 1864. But while the Taiping rebellion was the Qing Empire's most destructive upheaval, it is crucial to note several other key revolts that also besieged the Manchus at this time. With tax revenues and soldiers diverted to defeating the Heavenly Kingdom and pacifying the empire's Sinic core, the Manchus lost their grip on the empire's ethnically mixed borderlands in the southwest and the northwest. Thus, in Guizhou, the Qing had to fend off the so-called Miao rebellion (1854–73), a multi-ethnic revolt supposedly led by disaffected Miao 'barbarians', and which some estimates suggest claimed the lives of 4.9 million out of a total of 7 million imperial subjects.[154] In the neighbouring province of Yunnan, the Panthay rebellion (1856–73) similarly saw the Hui Muslim minority help spearhead an anti-Manchu uprising. This rebellion culminated in the establishment of a multi-ethnic but nominally Muslim sultanate that survived for over fifteen years, and even unsuccessfully sought diplomatic recognition from Britain before victorious Qing forces finally extinguished it.[155] Meanwhile, in the northwest, a Muslim revolt (1864–77) likewise saw Qing forces temporarily expelled from Xinjiang. Following the Manchus' expulsion, Uzbek warlord Yakub Beg forged a centralized, precociously modern and self-consciously Islamic state that swore fealty to the Ottoman Empire, and received extensive diplomatic and military support from Istanbul before the Manchus' eventual reconquest of the territory.[156]

The rebellions sketched above do not exhaust the internal challenges the Manchus faced at this time. Besides the Taiping rebellion and the borderland revolts, large-scale peasant uprisings, violent subversion by secret societies and opportunistic banditry rounded out the threat landscape. The complexities of these challenges notwithstanding, the gargantuan magnitude and protracted nature of the threat they collectively posed to Qing power is beyond dispute.

---

[154] R. D. Jenks, *Insurgency and Social Disorder in Guizhou: The 'Miao' Rebellion, 1854–1873* (Honolulu: University of Hawaii Press, 1994), p. 25. Note that Jenks himself disputes the veracity of this casualty estimate, but nevertheless concedes that the long-running rebellion massively depopulated the province.

[155] D. G. Atwill, *The Chinese Sultanate: Islam, ethnicity and the Panthay Rebellion in Southwest China, 1856–1873* (Stanford: Stanford University Press, 2005).

[156] H.-D. Kim, *Holy War in China: The Muslim rebellion and state in Chinese Central Asia, 1864–1877* (Stanford: Stanford University Press, 2004), pp. 183–4.

For the better part of three decades, the Manchus struggled to suppress internal rivals, and prevent their multicultural empire from splitting into pieces. Beset by domestic challenges, the Manchus' weakness invited renewed foreign aggression mid-way through this crisis. Thus, in October 1856, the governor of Hong Kong, John Bowring, ordered the shelling of Canton in retaliation for alleged Qing transgressions of the Treaty of Nanjing. The immediate trigger for British hostility was the Qing Empire's seizure of the British ship *Arrow*, and the internment of its Chinese sailors, on suspicion of piracy.[157] Though British protests swiftly prompted Qing efforts at reconciliation, Bowring used the incident as a pretext to extort greater commercial and eventually diplomatic concessions from the Qing Empire.[158]

Much more so than its predecessor, the Second Opium War (1856–60) constituted a deep and sustained assault on the Qing Empire. Though it began on the empire's southern periphery, it ended with an alliance of Anglo-French forces besieging the imperial capital, and with the famed Summer Palace in ruins. British (and later also French) aims were moreover far more ambitious, and far more damaging to Qing prestige, than before. Previously, the British had sought a modest expansion of commercial concessions. But war aims in the second conflict included a dramatic broadening of trading privileges; the legalization of the opium trade; the opening of the Qing Empire to Christian evangelization; and the establishment of permanent diplomatic relations – on the basis of sovereign equality – between the empire and Western states.[159] This last demand in particular openly contradicted the emperor's universalistic pretensions – and thus violated the entire system of legitimation underpinning the Qing imperial project.[160]

The point from the preceding survey is to highlight the genuinely existential character of the crisis that afflicted the Qing Empire during the mid-nineteenth century. What began as piecemeal foreign aggression on the empire's maritime frontier swiftly escalated into a system-wide breakdown of order. The Taiping rebellion combined Western ideological influences with folk millenarianism and anti-Manchu nativism. The ensuing rise of the Heavenly Kingdom threatened the Manchus' control over the Sinic core of their empire more seriously than had any preceding upheaval in the history of the Qing Dynasty. Borderland revolts in the northwest and southwest – including the temporary secession of key territories – meanwhile jeopardized the empire's territorial integrity. Renewed Western aggression during the Second Opium War then

---

[157] Fairbank, 'The creation of the treaty system', p. 246.   [158] Ibid.   [159] Ibid., p. 252.
[160] Ibid., p. 250.

inflicted fresh indignities, forcing the empire to accept permanent foreign legations in the imperial capital, and to diplomatically engage with Western states on equal terms.

Transformations in Qing strategies of imperial administration and diplomatic practice testify to the gravity of this mid-century crisis. Turning first to imperial administration, the Manchus' post-crisis model of governance reflected a paradoxical combination of continuity and change. At the macro level, the Manchus broadly remained faithful to an established diversity regime based on principles of segregated incorporation. The near-simultaneous outbreak of multiple rebellions in both the Sinic core and the multicultural borderlands alerted the Manchus to the fragility of their grip on power. At the same time, however, the defeat of these rebellions and the reconquest of lost territories seemed to vindicate Manchu strategies of define and divide and rule. With rare, transient and opportunistic exceptions, rebellious constituencies had failed to coordinate their efforts or join forces. This collective action failure enabled the Manchus to sequentially suppress a cluster of disparate uprisings, rather than having to simultaneously confront a united front of anti-Qing resistance. The Manchus' siloed model of imperial governance meant that they faced localized legitimation crises among discrete imperial constituencies. The firewalls separating these constituencies remained largely intact during the mid-century crisis, and were pivotal to the empire's survival. This resilience counselled against radically revising the Qing mode of rule via segregated incorporation once the crisis had passed.

These broad observations aside, the vast scale of the Qing crisis spurred important adjustments to imperial administration. Thus, within the empire's Sinic core, the Taiping challenge significantly strengthened the Confucian character of Qing rule. In the face of a shared revolutionary threat, the Manchus and the scholar-gentry drew closer together, with the Manchus doubling down on their reliance on Confucianism as a legitimating resource.[161] This renewed embrace of Confucianism was an expedient short-term measure. But it came with a significant diffusion of power downwards to provincial (and overwhelmingly Han Chinese) strongmen. Loyalist generals such as Zeng Guofan played critical roles in mobilizing and leading provincial armies to suppress the Taiping revolution, and so were critical allies in assuring the Qing Dynasty's survival.[162] But reliance on these regional strongmen partially but permanently shifted the balance of power between Manchus and Han. This was so even after the provincial armies were demobilized, and despite the

---

[161] Fairbank and Goodman, *China: A New History*, p. 213.   [162] Ibid., p. 212.

Manchus' surprisingly successful post-conflict efforts to re-establish their control over the means of coercion.[163]

Following the mid-century rebellions, then, the Qing Dynasty became even more Confucian than before, at least within the core eighteen provinces in which the majority of the empire's population lived. The corresponding recalibration of relations between the Manchus and the Han moreover made the former even more dependent on the scholar-gentry's collaboration than before. By contrast, imperial governance changed more visibly in the empire's borderlands. Certainly, the Manchus never entirely abandoned segregated incorporation as their preferred model of rule. But in trying to shore up the empire from renewed centrifugal pressures, the Manchus relied on expedients that adulterated and in some cases entirely contradicted this model. Administrative centralization thus increasingly replaced indirect rule in many frontier territories from the 1870s onwards, in bureaucratic aspiration if not in everyday reality.[164] Similarly, in strengthening their hold over restive provinces in the southwest and northwest, the Manchus began subjecting locals to coercive Sinicization, while also sponsoring large-scale Han Chinese settlement in these regions. To take but one example, in 1884 Xinjiang was formally incorporated as a province of the Qing Empire.[165] Thereafter, the Manchus ruled through a governor and a Chinese-style model of civil administration, while indigenous intermediaries were meanwhile subject to far more direct control than before.[166]

More conspicuous than these administrative reforms, the Qing Dynasty also sponsored large-scale Han colonization to more directly entrench their rule in Xinjiang and other peripheral parts of the empire. Historian James Millward goes so far as to argue that the ensuing 'Hanization' of the empire was the 'price' the Manchus paid to retain power and maximize their external security.[167] Thus, 'Han colonization and implementation of Chinese-style administration of frontier regions, from Xinjiang, Mongolia, and Manchuria and Taiwan, became standard dynastic policy as foreign pressures mounted in the latter part of the nineteenth century.'[168] Writing in a similar vein, Eric Setzekorn observes:

Post-1877 Qing administration in these areas had little of the pragmatic variety of structure or methods utilized by the early Qing state, and relied instead on traditional Han forms of government based around county and provincial

---

[163] E. A. McCord, 'Militia and local militarization in late Qing and early Republican China: The case of Hunan', *Modern China*, 14(2) (1988), 161–2.
[164] Millward, *Beyond the Pass*, p. 250.   [165] Ibid.   [166] Ibid.   [167] Ibid., p. 251.
[168] Ibid., p. 250.

administrative structures. The homogenization of Qing government was buttressed by the large-scale settlement of Han from East China and government sponsorship of Confucian norms.[169]

To reiterate, the post-rebellion era did not see an abandonment of the Manchus' preferred model of segregated incorporation, which had proved its worth in preventing a coalescence of the mid-century rebellions that would otherwise have surely ended Qing rule. But in their quest to re-centralize power, the Manchus *did* embrace expedients – from administrative rationalization to state-sponsored Han settler colonialism – that introduced significant strains into their empire. Coercive Hanization sat uneasily with the Manchu ethos of imperial simultaneity, and threatened in the longer term to undermine the delicate diversity regime that sustained the Qing Dynasty. In the immediate term, however, this volatile mix proved sufficiently stable to fend off serious internal challenges, at least down to the 1890s.

The volatile combination of continuity and change characterizing Qing imperial administration found its analogue in the Manchus' post-crisis approach to diplomacy. The most conspicuous change to Qing diplomacy was the establishment of a modern foreign office (the Zongli Yamen) for managing Western foreign relations after 1860. The subsequent translation of a text on Western international law in 1864, the granting of an imperial audience to foreign diplomats without the kowtow in 1873, and the establishment of Qing diplomatic missions abroad after 1876 likewise signified important milestones in the empire's apparent assimilation of Western diplomatic norms, and its incorporation into a Western-dominated international society.[170] Overlaying these arrangements, the consolidation of an extremely obtrusive set of hybrid governance arrangements in the treaty ports marked a further departure from traditional Qing practice. Following the Second Opium War, treaty powers enjoyed consular jurisdiction over nationals residing in the treaty ports.[171] Additionally, they enjoyed administrative control over concession areas in treaty ports, as well as the right to station troops there and to also deploy warships in Qing waters.[172] The post-war settlement also granted access rights to foreign shipping in Qing coastal waters along the empire's riverine waterways, as well as limiting the Qing Empire's rights to impose tariffs on foreign goods.[173]

Despite these meaningful changes, however, Qing diplomacy remained profoundly ambidextrous down to the late nineteenth century. In their

---

[169] E. Setzekorn, 'Chinese imperialism, ethnic cleansing, and military history, 1850–1877', *Journal of Chinese Military History*, 4(1) (2015), 84.
[170] Hsu, 'Late Ch'ing foreign relations', p. 70.
[171] Fairbank, 'The creation of the treaty system', pp. 259–60.   [172] Ibid.   [173] Ibid.

dealings with Western states, the Manchus submitted to Western diplomacy and the strictures of positivist international law. Indeed, in time, Qing diplomats proved adept at harnessing these new ideas and practices to balance and to a certain extent constrain Western and later Japanese territorial ambitions.[174] But they did so while simultaneously maintaining the pre-existing system of tributary diplomacy – mediated via the Board of Rites – when dealing with their Asian neighbours. Thus, John Fairbank notes: 'Between 1860 and 1894 tribute was presented from Korea in twenty five years, from Liu-ch'iu [the Ryukyu Islands] in eight years, from Annam (Vietnam) in five years, from Nepal four times and from Burma once.'[175] Despite efforts at administrative centralization, meanwhile, the Manchus preserved the Lifan Yuan down to the monarchy's abolition in 1912. This institution blurred the boundaries between frontier management and diplomacy in Qing-dominated Central Asia, and its survival underscored the continuity in the Manchus' attempts to manage their foreign relations after the mid-century crisis had passed.

The post-crisis persistence of the Board of Rites and the Lifan Yuan alongside the newly created Zongli Yamen illustrates a larger point – that the Qing Dynasty continued to silo its diplomacy into discrete and diverse institutions long after the empire's supposed assimilation into Western international society. At least before the humiliations of the Sino-Japanese War (1894–5), the 'scramble for concessions' (1898) and the anti-Boxer intervention (1901), the Manchus largely succeeded in limiting Western encroachment and preserving the empire's territorial integrity. They moreover did so through a repertoire of diplomatic techniques that structurally mirrored the regime of segregated incorporation that upheld the empire domestically.

Having survived the traumas of the mid-century rebellions and foreign aggression, the Manchus after 1860 stood at the hub of a diverse web of diplomatic relationships, each mediated via customized institutional arrangements. The Lifan Yuan enabled the Manchus to preserve their primacy through much of Central Asia, in that it upheld an earlier system of indirect rule over local clients even as Beijing began the painstaking process of overlaying these arrangements with an embryonic system of provincial bureaucratic administration. With the empire's continental frontier largely secure, the Board of Rites meanwhile perpetuated the fiction of Qing suzerainty in maritime East Asia. Though ultimately this did not prevent key Confucian tributaries (Annam and Korea) from being

[174] Mark Mancall, *China at the Center: 300 Years of Foreign Policy* (New York: The Free Press, 1984), pp. 138–41.
[175] Fairbank, 'The creation of the treaty system', p. 260.

detached from the Qing orbit, it did slow the process and give the
Manchus additional time to pursue 'self-strengthening' initiatives.
Notwithstanding the indignities of the 'unequal treaties', the Manchus'
assimilation of Western diplomatic practice finally gave them a means of
simultaneously appeasing and containing a new and formidable military
threat.[176]

Institutional overlay and elaboration – rather than the obliteration of
existing arrangements for Western alternatives – thus best characterize
the Manchus' post-crisis management of their foreign relations. This
pattern was in part a tribute to Manchu pragmatism and dexterity. But
it relied on a supportive international context – and more specifically
upon the patronage of the strongest 'barbarian' power, Great Britain.
As instigator of the two opium wars and a one-time evangelist of transformational liberalism, Britain had done more than any other foreign
actor in the pre-1860 period to destabilize the Qing Empire. The post-
1860 period nevertheless saw an about-face in British foreign policy, with
Britain committing to preserving the Qing Empire's political stability and
advancing the British Empire's commercial goals through peaceful
means.[177] The reasons for this policy reversal were both strategic as well
as ideological. Strategically, perceptions of imperial overstretch cau-
tioned against territorial expansion in East Asia.[178] The spectre of
Russian power – and the need to focus British energies first and foremost
on protecting India from a Russian advance – proved particularly constraining in this regard.[179]

Aside from these strategic considerations, the chastening trauma of the
Indian Revolt constituted a sharp rebuke to liberal ambitions in Asia. As we
have seen, conservatives seized on the revolt as evidence of liberal chauvinism and over-reach, and successfully agitated for British India's conservative reconstruction. Faced with the prospect of the Qing Empire's collapse
after 1860, Britain pivoted from confrontation to conciliation. The
Cooperative Policy would emerge as the East Asia counterpart to conservative reconstruction in British India. Intellectually, this entailed repudi-
ation of the very possibility that Britain's subcontinental conquests would
be repeated in the Qing Empire. Practically, the Cooperative Policy manifested itself in diplomatic support for the Qing Empire's territorial integrity,
military support against the Qing Empire's internal enemies and institutional support for the modernization of the Qing imperial state.[180]

Beginning with diplomatic and military considerations, British diplomacy even prior to the end of the Second Opium War aimed for the Qing

---

[176] Ibid.   [177] Hsu, 'Late Ch'ing foreign relations', p. 71.   [178] Ibid.   [179] Ibid., p. 90.
[180] Ibid., p. 73.

Empire's opening and the monarchy's preservation, rather than territorial conquest. An early parley with representatives of the Taiping Heavenly Kingdom quickly confirmed for Britain the desirability of maintaining the Manchus in power, as an eminently more predictable regime.[181] Accordingly, Britain refrained from further attempts to engage the Taiping revolutionaries, and committed to the Manchu cause once the Second Opium War was concluded on terms favourable to Britain.[182] Likewise, the British thereafter generally withheld support from separatist regimes (e.g., Yunnan's Dali Sultanate) seeking diplomatic recognition, to forestall the Qing Empire's territorial disintegration.[183] Beyond diplomatic support, Britain also extended considerable military aid to the Manchus to suppress domestic insurgencies. Most famously, the Ever Victorious Army – a force composed of Western-trained Chinese soldiers led by Western officers – played a key role in many of the later battles to defeat the Taiping rebellion.[184]

More fundamental and long-lasting than diplomatic and military assistance, however, was Britain's integral role in trying to help modernize the Qing central state. This was most evident in Britain's establishment and operation of the Imperial Maritime Customs Service, charged with collecting customs revenues on behalf of the Qing Empire. Much like Britain's earlier securing of the *Diwani* in Bengal, this was an innovation that emerged against the backdrop of local political turmoil and robust proconsular British activism.[185] In contrast to the Bengal experience, however, management of the Qing Customs Service did not foreshadow territorial aggrandizement, or the fiscal hollowing out of an existing empire from within. Rather than simply serving as parasitic tax farmers, the British sponsored far-reaching administrative rationalization that ultimately dramatically raised the Qing state's fiscal-extractive capacity.[186] This in turn

---

[181] Spence, *God's Chinese Son*, p. 195.   [182] Hsu, 'Late Ch'ing foreign relations', p. 71.
[183] Interestingly, however, in the case of the Dali Sultanate, the Government of India proved significantly more sympathetic to aspects of the Panthay cause than the Foreign Office, the latter eventually successfully prevailing over the former in the interests of preserving Anglo-Chinese relations. See B. L. Evans, 'The Panthay Mission of 1872 and Its legacies', *Journal of Southeast Asian Studies*, 16(1) (1985), 117–28.
[184] See generally R. J. Smith, *Mercenaries and Mandarins: The ever-victorious army in nineteenth century China* (New York: KTO Press, 1978).
[185] For further background on the origins of the Imperial Maritime Customs Service, see H. van de Ven, *Breaking with the Past: The maritime customs service and the global origins of modernity in China* (New York: Columbia University Press, 2014), chapter 1.
[186] R. S. Horowitz, 'International law and state transformation in China, Siam, and the Ottoman Empire during the nineteenth century', *Journal of World History*, 15(4) (2004), 471.

permitted the Manchus to finance a far-reaching (if ultimately unsuccess-ful) military modernization.[187]

The broad point to be taken from this analysis is the Qing Empire's remarkable resilience in the face of near-overwhelming domestic turmoil and foreign aggression, and the empire's ability to renovate existing institutions, incorporate foreign practices and establish alliances of con-venience with erstwhile barbarian enemies to ensure the empire's sur-vival. Against immense odds, the empire survived the mid-century crises, and refounded itself on ostensibly conservative foundations. The Taiping challenge in particular strengthened the Manchus' ideological commit-ment to Confucianism and partnership with the scholar-gentry, even as it left them even more dependent on the latter's collaboration than before. Unsuccessful borderland rebellions meanwhile reaffirmed the wisdom of an imperial order built on segregated incorporation, even if the restored order significantly adulterated and undermined this system through selective coercive Hanization. The ambidexterity of Qing diplomacy likewise marked a historical continuation of sorts, albeit with the import-ant selective integration of Western diplomacy into the Manchus' reper-toire of barbarian management techniques. Finally, the partial integration of British as co-administrators of the empire echoed earlier patterns of co-optation – even as it underscored the increasing cultural and institutional hybridity of the resuscitated Qing imperial enterprise.

Conclusion

This chapter has examined the mid-century crises of the British and Qing empires in South and East Asia, and their subsequent reinvention. The core theme I have stressed is these empires' astonishing resilience in the face of near-terminal legitimation crises, and empire-builders' dexterity in adapting their legitimating ideologies and diversity regimes to reconnect with indigenous collaborators.

The analysis began with a consideration of an increasingly expansionist British Empire in Asia. This expansionist disposition was territorial, commercial and ideological. Transformational liberals repudiated the Orientalist template for ruling India, instead championing a range of policies aimed at civilizing India through Westernization. These policies eventually extended to the marginalization of local scribal, religious, aristocratic and military collaborators, undermining the political founda-tions of the company's rule. Concurrently, in the same spirit of reform,

[187] Ibid.

transformational liberals pushed for the Qing Empire's commercial opening – eventually bringing the two empires into conflict. British civilizational chauvinism ultimately proved fatally subversive of the Company Raj. The Indian Revolt shook the Raj to its foundations, and catalysed widespread conservative pushback against a now discredited liberal programme. The dissolution of the Mughal monarchy and the displacement of company by Crown ostensibly read as markers of modernization. But these changes came alongside a sustained British effort to reconcile with local aristocratic and religious intermediaries, in deference to (and in defence of) supposedly timeless indigenous hierarchies. The reinvention of the Indian military on the foundation of martial races meanwhile fortified the coercive backstop to British suzerainty.

British encroachment on the Qing Empire proved similarly destabilizing, and likewise fed into crises that compelled this empire's extensive renovation as well. While British aggression during the First Opium War (1839–42) amounted to little more than nibbling at the Qing Empire's maritime edges, it did help to facilitate the entry of ideological influences that later decisively shaped the Taiping rebellion. The destructiveness of this abortive social revolution gravely weakened the Qing Empire during an era of increasing foreign (mainly Western) pressure. At the same time, borderland rebellions threatened to break apart the vast multi-ethnic mosaic that the Manchus had united through conquest in the preceding two centuries. These calamities cumulatively forced a significant recalibration of the Qing imperial project. An ostensible rededication to a strategy of segregated incorporation coincided with administrative Sinicization in the empire's outer territories. Extensive state-sponsored Han settler colonialism further fortified the Manchus' centripetal designs. Following the Second Opium War (1856–60), finally, a conservative Anglo-Qing partnership then sought to preserve the empire's territorial integrity and promote its administrative and military modernization. An increasingly ambidextrous form of Manchu diplomacy, grounded in the simultaneous operation of the Lifan Yuan, the Board of Rites and the Foreign Office, meanwhile stabilized Qing foreign relations along their neuralgic continental and maritime frontiers.

The British Raj and the Qing Empire were of course distinct in many ways. But we can see important parallels between them following their mid-century reinvention. Both remained minority conquest regimes, and so beholden to the imperatives that came with this status. Both still relied on strategies of define and divide and rule, to legitimate their power and to curate the imperial constituencies whose collaboration they needed to administer and enforce their rule. Both fashioned their legitimating ideologies in large part through techniques of customization that aimed to discretely engage collaborators while preventing the emergence of more inclusive (and potentially subversive) forms of collective identity among subject populations. Britons and Manchus also each relied extensively on processes of institutional overlay and conversion to mobilize the local resources necessary to assert and maintain power. Finally, in the wake of their mid-century crises, both empires explicitly stressed the conservative character of their rule, to shore up their connections to key collaborators.

Besides these key parallels, however, the British and Qing empires also saw important divergences in their post-crisis evolution. For the British, the Indian Revolt significantly slowed efforts to coercively modernize India. Beneath the appearance of administrative rationalization with the shift from company to Crown rule, the need to conciliate local power-holders gave new life to traditional hierarchies. Client rulers in the Princely States thus had their privileges confirmed, while Calcutta eschewed territorial annexation and moderated its earlier pressures for political, legal and administrative reform.[188] Meanwhile, efforts to create an anglicized Indian elite did not completely halt. But the conservative turn in post-1857 colonial policy revived an earlier focus on expanding Indian education in vernacular languages.[189] The reconstruction of the Indian military around minority martial races meanwhile further reinforced regional particularism.[190] And in the wake of the Indian Revolt, the colonial government proved far more deferential to local religious sentiment.[191] The entrenchment of exclusive religious categories in successive colonial censuses, and renewed colonial sponsorship of religious education, together further consolidated communal division as the focal fault line of the British Raj.[192]

The Qing Empire also preserved fundamental aspects of its pre-crisis constitution. Most importantly, segregated incorporation, based primarily on ethnic rather than religious forms of collective identity, remained the empire's default form of divide and rule. But the combined stresses of internal rebellion and persistent external pressure did force important modifications to the Qing way of empire. The imposition of Chinese-style bureaucratic administration on the empire's outer territories – and with it the steady dilution of earlier forms of indirect rule there – contrasted sharply with Britain's treatment of the Princely States. Likewise, the creeping Hanization of these territories through state-sponsored Han settler colonialism has no analogue in British India. Qing efforts at administrative and military self-strengthening – efforts often pursued

[188] Cannadine, *Ornamentalism*, p. 44.   [189] Evans, 'Macaulay's minute revisited', 276–8.
[190] Omissi, 'Martial races', 22.
[191] Anderson, 'Islamic law and the colonial encounter', pp. 181–5.
[192] Frykenberg, 'Constructions of Hinduism', 539.

with British help – meanwhile exerted centripetal effects on the Qing Empire not seen in British India. In extending Chinese-style direct rule to the outer territories and expanding the Han Chinese territorial footprint, the Manchus lastly began to inadvertently compromise the firewalls that had previously separated subject populations, undermining their hold on power over the longer term.

Significant as the British and Qing reconfigurations of empire were for South and East Asia individually, what also stands out from this period is the steady integration of a pan-Asian maritime international order over this period. Up to as late as 1820, South and East Asia were dominated by empires – one adolescent, the other mature – that remained largely insulated from one another. But after this time, a combination of British commercial, territorial and ideological expansion, roughly synchronous crises of company and Qing imperialism, and conservative reconstitutions of empire yielded a radically different international system in maritime Asia. From 1860 down to the late nineteenth century, revived minority conquest regimes in South and East Asia interacted with far more sustained frequency, and in a far more institutionalized manner, than before.

Throughout the Indian Ocean littoral, Britain not only claimed suzerainty in South Asia, but also over a far-flung necklace of satrapies, Crown colonies, Princely States and client rulers allied in varying degrees of subordination to Calcutta. In East Asia, meanwhile, an Anglo-Qing condominium meanwhile saw the rise of new semi-sovereign arrangements. There, ancient Chinese customs of commercial extraterritoriality were codified and radically expanded via the framework of Western positive international law, eventually congealing in the form of the treaty port system. Britain's far-flung network of dependencies in the Indian Ocean, and the hybrid hierarchy of the East Asian treaty port system, thus together laid the foundations for maritime Asia's emergence as an integrated commercial and strategic regional super-complex after 1860. This order – itself built on the twin foundations of the revived British and Qing conquest regimes – would falter only as these empires later hastened towards destruction in the twentieth century.

Conclusion

From the sixteenth century down to c. 1900, the international relations of Asia were largely defined by conquest from the periphery, as 'barbarian' conquerors from Eurasia's steppe, forest and ocean frontiers forged vast polyglot empires in South and East Asia. Unlike the fleeting achievements of late medieval conquerors such as Genghis Khan and Tamerlane, the legacies of Mughal, Manchu and British empire-builders have endured. In absorbing South Asia's diverse communities within universal empires, Mughal and British conquerors achieved a level of political unity not seen there since the days of Ashoka, laying the foundations for the modern mega-state of India. The Manchus meanwhile doubled the size of the empire they had seized from the Ming Dynasty, eventually bequeathing a polity roughly matching the territorial boundaries of the modern People's Republic of China (PRC).

Not simply agents of unity, Eurasia's triumphant barbarians also entrenched patterns of division that decisively shaped South and East Asia's twentieth-century transitions from empire to sovereign anarchy. Recall that the Mughal, Manchu and British empires originated from strategies of define and conquer and define and rule. Vastly outnumbered, minority rulers depended on indigenous soldiers, creditors and administrators to make imperial conquest possible. Minority rule subsequently depended on diversity regimes that curated and sustained patterns of cultural difference binding local intermediaries to the imperial centre, while pre-emptively blocking the emergence of anti-imperial coalitions.

The eventual collapse of British India and the Qing Empire testifies to the long-term limits of these strategies. From the foundation of the Congress Party, Indian intellectuals localized Western discourses of individual liberty and constitutionalism to challenge British hegemony.[1] Likewise, anti-Manchu agitators drew freely on originally Western

---

[1] See generally C. A. Bayly, *Recovering Liberties: Indian thought in the age of liberalism and empire* (Cambridge: Cambridge University Press, 2012).

discourses of nationalism to topple the Qing Dynasty.[2] Critically, however, these revolutionaries often inadvertently reinforced the axes of cultural differentiation inscribed in imperial diversity regimes, even while fighting to overthrow alien rule. Thus, in South Asia, the Indian independence movement fractured along communal fault lines. The empire's partition in 1947 then further entrenched the patterns of religious polarization on which British rule had rested. Likewise, anti-Manchu dissidents exploited reified categories of ethnic difference first institutionalized by the Manchus when mobilizing against the dynasty. Subsequent republican and communist governments in China moreover both drew on Qing precedents to manage cultural diversity following the dynasty's demise.[3]

Early modern barbarian conquests in South and East Asia thus left paradoxical legacies of unity and division. India and China's contemporary dominance in their respective regions owes much to the centripetal impact of Mughal, Manchu and British empire-building. But the most volatile cultural conflicts in both countries also owe their origins to barbarian strategies of define and conquer and define and divide and rule. Contemporary government propagandists in India and China have been especially strident in asserting national unity as a historical inevitability, while downplaying or ignoring the role of barbarian conquerors played in forging that unity. Indian and Chinese nationalists have also cast national unity as a natural reflection of India and China's status as latter-day expressions of ancient Indic and Sinic civilizations.[4] This idea of unity as an organic outgrowth of 'manifest [civilizational] heritage' has undeniable political potency.[5] Nevertheless, not only is this claim historically inaccurate. More fundamentally, it also obscures transitions from pluralism to (post)-imperial unity that are critically important both for IR scholars, and for students of the historical sociology of empires. These transitions from pluralism to imperial hierarchy – and the incongruous prominence of liminal conquerors in driving these transitions – have been

[2] See, for example, J. Spence, *The Search for Modern China* (New York: W. W. Norton, 1999), p. 258.

[3] See generally J. A. Millward, 'Qing and twentieth-century Chinese diversity regimes' in A. Phillips and C. Reus-Smit (eds.), *Culture and Order in World Politics* (Cambridge: Cambridge University Press, 2020), pp. 71–92.

[4] For India, see, for example, the discussion in L. T. Flaten, *Hindu Nationalism, History and Identity in India: Narrating a Hindu past under the BJP* (London: Routledge, 2016). For the resurgence of China as a supposed civilizational state, see W. Zhang, *The China Wave: Rise of a civilizational state* (Hackensack: World Century, 2012).

[5] The phrase 'manifest heritage' – a direct allusion to the American idea of manifest destiny – is drawn from Millward, 'Qing and twentieth-century Chinese diversity regimes', p. 72.

this book's central focus. Accordingly, the Conclusion first summarizes the book's argument, before teasing out its larger implications.

Recapping the Argument

At its core, this book has sought to understand how hierarchies emerge and endure. I have confined my focus to a specific type of hierarchy – empire – and to a particular time and place – early modern Eurasia. The inquiry's temporal scope (c. 1500–1900) is warranted given the revolutionary impact successive projects of universal conquest had in transforming the world's most populous regions, South and East Asia, during this time. And the inquiry's geographic focus enabled a detailed comparison of 'Western' (British) and 'Eastern' (Mughal and Manchu) minority conquest regimes that historical studies of empire rarely explore.

The book began with the claim that late medieval and early modern Eurasia witnessed an interlocking series of transformations, which cumulatively made new forms of empire-building possible after c. 1500. Militarily, innovations in cavalry warfare and blue water naval warfare granted steppe and sea 'nomads' much greater capacities to harass and even conquer Eurasia's wealthiest and most populous sedentary societies. Economically, the growth of long-distance trade in luxury commodities meanwhile offered immensely lucrative arbitrage opportunities for frontier traders and raiders. This expanded commerce generated huge reserves of liquid wealth that could potentially be channelled into empire-building projects. Concurrently, the extreme violence and trauma that had accompanied the first late medieval barbarian conquests spurred critical cultural innovations throughout Eurasia. Within the Persephone and Sinic worlds, external predation prompted lettered elites to innovate far-reaching civilizing projects. These projects – which articulated a far clearer and more systematic distinction between barbarians and civilized peoples than before – aimed to pacify warrior elites by acculturating them to sedentary standards of civility. Paradoxically, however, these civilizing projects also proved flexible enough for barbarians to appropriate for their own ends. This further empowered the latter to formulate the legitimating ideologies necessary to eventually co-opt the local allies needed for universal conquest.

The Eurasian Transformation revolutionized the distribution of military capabilities, commercial opportunities and cultural resources along Eurasia's land and sea frontiers. This made it far easier for cashed-up barbarians to overwhelm sedentary power centres, and cement control over large and diverse empires over the longer term. Given their low numbers and cultural marginality, however, barbarians were nevertheless dependent on indigenous allies for both conquest and colonial adminis-tration. Mughals, Manchus and Britons each confronted the same gen-eric empire-building imperatives. To conquer on a subcontinental scale, each found it necessary to build multi-conquest coalitions and to then bind them to nascent imperial hierarchies. Each also then found it neces-sary to secure their rule by pre-emptively blocking the rise of potential countervailing coalitions among their colonial subjects.

Mughal, Manchu and British imperialists each addressed these chal-lenges through a strategy I have dubbed conquest by customization. In the conquest phase, this entailed innovating define and conquer practices that aimed to curate indigenous identities supportive of conquest and alien rule. It also involved converting and repurposing indigenous mater-ial, ideational and institutional resources to serve imperial ends. In the consolidation phase, conquest dynasties then cemented their rule through articulating a legitimating ideology drawn from a combination of indigenous and introduced cultural resources. Beyond these ideo-logical innovations, finally, each of the empires considered ultimately rested on diversity regimes. These regimes gave concrete institutional form to the bespoke bargains barbarian conquerors struck with various imperial constituencies, while also ordering and conserving cultural dif-ference in ways conducive to the perpetuation of alien rule.

While shaped by common imperatives, the Mughal and Manchu empires and the British Raj were far from identical. First wave conquerors in each case enjoyed their own unique military and institutional niche advantages, which decisively shaped their pathways to domination. Likewise, once they had secured their empires, imperial elites in each instance justified their rule through resort to radically distinctive legitim-ating ideologies. Most fundamentally, though the imperative of define and rule remained universal, the diversity regimes each empire pioneered varied significantly. Mughal religious syncretism, Manchu ethnic segre-gation and the communal ecumenicism of the Company Raj each repre-sented distinctive solutions to the challenges of managing cultural diversity in ways supportive of imperial rule. These differences were profoundly consequential. But they nevertheless represented instances of *bounded variation*. From Delhi and Calcutta through to Beijing, empire-builders generally tried to incorporate cultural heterogeneity rather than trying to obliterate it or assimilate it to a common civilizational standard. This was in keeping with their pervasive dependence on indi-genous collaborators as the foundation of colonial rule. Conversely, on those rare occasions when empire-builders *did* opt for assimilative strat-egies of diversity management (e.g., the Mughal Empire under Aurangzeb, the EIC during the era of transformational liberalism), this generally foreshadowed widespread violence and far-reaching crises of imperial authority.

Ultimately, the Mughal, Manchu and British empires each fell by the wayside. The Mughals faltered through internal weakening, before the EIC first subverted then replaced them. The Manchus were meanwhile the first of the world's great empires to succumb to the twentieth-century globalization of nationalism, with British India following suit in 1947. In hindsight, these empires' demise carries with it a sense of inevitability. Nevertheless, the final portion of this inquiry wrote against this teleology of inevitable decline, by foregrounding the British and Qing empires' extraordinary resilience during the crises both suffered during the mid-nineteenth century.

The Indian Revolt and the late Qing cataclysm triggered far-reaching renovations in the British and Manchu empires. The Indian Revolt compelled the British to renounce transformational liberalism, and to reconstitute the Raj on unabashedly conservative foundations. Ostensibly, this renovation resembled a throwback to the ecumenical incorporation of the Company Raj. But post-revolt British India rested on a far more systematic commitment to preserving Indian 'tradition' than before. This commitment was practically grounded in a revived compact with indigenous aristocratic intermediaries, and in a solemn commitment to refrain from either infringing on Indians' religious traditions or abridging elites' customary privileges.[6]

The revived Qing Empire similarly adapted to its own mid-century crisis in part through doubling down on its earlier strategy of segregated incorporation. In particular, the Taiping rebellion dramatically strengthened the Manchus' alliance with their Han Confucian intermediaries in the Empire's Sinic core. Beneath this appearance of continuity, however, the empire survived not least because of its willingness (albeit reluctant) to strategically accommodate Western interlopers after the Second Opium War, principally through an informal entente with Britain. This alignment enabled the Manchus to selectively employ barbarian diplomatic practices to shore up its maritime periphery, while also drawing on Western barbarian expertise and personnel to partially modernize the Qing state. Along its multi-ethnic terrestrial periphery, meanwhile, the Qing Empire tightened its grip on restive provinces through selective Sinification, from the extension of Chinese-style civil administration to the frontiers, to sponsorship of large-scale Han settler colonialism in the northwest and the southwest.[7]

---

[6] Cannadine, *Ornamentalism*, p. 44.
[7] Millward, *Beyond the Pass*, p. 250; Setzekorn, 'Chinese imperialism, ethnic cleansing, and military history', 84.

Ultimately, these reforms did not save either the British Raj or the Qing Empire from extinction. Indeed, in doubling down on divide and rule practices, the mid-century reforms in some ways aggravated the internal fault lines that eventually destroyed both empires. The point stands, however, that empire-builders in both cases showed surprising agility in adapting their legitimation strategies and diversity regimes to new circumstances. Recognition of this agility forces us to revise existing conceptions of Asia's absorption into a Western-dominated international society in the mid-late nineteenth century. Western transformational liberalism was undoubtedly devastatingly disruptive. But it proved equally subversive to both Western and Eastern empires. Moreover, liberal over-reach eventually catalyzed far-reaching conservative renovations in both South and East Asia. These reforms failed to permanently inoculate either the Raj or the Qing Empire from destruction. But they did give both of them a new lease of life, ensuring their preservation (albeit in radically revised forms) into the twentieth century.

Explaining Universal Conquest and the Rise of International Hierarchies

In keeping with this book's focus on hierarchy, I have sought to theorize a distinctive pathway through which hierarchies emerge out of multi-actor international systems. More directly, this book has sought to better understand *one* pathway towards universal conquest. International Relations scholarship has traditionally fixated disproportionately on the operation of the balance of power within sovereign state systems.[8] This focus has privileged the preservation of plural international systems, rather than their subsumption within empires. But the topic of conquest has not been entirely neglected. Victoria Tin-bor Hui's pioneering analysis of Warring States China decisively demonstrated how endogenous self-strengthening – primarily involving innovations in military mobilization and fiscal extraction – can equip formerly marginal states with the material capabilities necessary to undertake universal conquest.[9] Paul MacDonald's work has meanwhile illuminated how configurations of social ties within indigenous societies influence the availability of local collaborators, thus determining the feasibility of colonial conquest.[10]

---

[8] See, for example, L. Dehio, *The Precarious Balance: Four centuries of European power struggle* (New York: Alfred A. Knopf, 1962). However, for an excellent attempt to extend the geographical range of balance-of-power theory beyond its traditional Eurocentric focus and qualify its presumed universality, see S. J. Kaufman, R. Little and W. C. Wohlforth (eds.), *The Balance of Power in World History* (Basingstoke: Palgrave Macmillan, 2007).
[9] Hui, *War and State Formation.*   [10] MacDonald, *Networks of Domination.*

Beyond IR, finally, historians have meanwhile long stressed the importance of overwhelming military-technological supremacy, the devastation
to indigenous societies from introduced pandemics, or some combination
of the two in enabling European expansion throughout the New World.[11]

This book has not attempted to offer a general theory of universal
conquest. Instead, I have tried to explain how universal conquest was
possible in historically unlikely circumstances. At first glance, the conquerors this book studies present as highly implausible empire-builders.
While all enjoyed niche military advantages, these were insufficient by
themselves to enable the conquest of wealthier and more populous societies. Just as importantly, none of these advantages were so distinctive as
to prevent their imitation or import into the societies barbarians eventually conquered. The demographic insignificance and cultural marginality
of barbarian conquerors should have further inhibited their advance.

Instead, the unique conjunction of the Eurasian Transformation
empowered traders and raiders to exploit the brokerage opportunities of
the early modern frontier to assemble vast new empires. Niche military
advantages – combined with the ability to withdraw beyond the reach
of sedentary societies' retribution when necessary – provided liminal
predators with the coercive power necessary to harass Eurasia's main
sedentary power centres. The growth of long-distance trade in luxury
commodities – along Eurasia's steppe and sea corridors – then provided
these actors with the arbitrage opportunities from which war chests could
be built and allies (eventually) bought. And the ideological self-defence
mechanisms sedentary societies developed to tame warrior elites (in the
form of civilizing projects) eventually proved susceptible to appropriation
and repurposing to forge the identity bridges connecting barbarian
invaders with indigenous collaborators.

The Eurasian Transformation facilitated the distinct model of expansion –
conquest through customization – analysed in this book. Given the world-
historical importance of early modern empire-building in the Old World,
teasing out the logic of conquest by customization is intrinsically valuable.
This is because at a minimum it suggests an alternative model of imperial
expansion, radically different from better canvassed alternatives in the New
World. The latter typically involved the subjugation of indigenous populations, either through physical annihilation or coercive cultural assimilation.
Conversely, Old World expansion after the Eurasian Transformation
instead foregrounded indigenous collaboration – secured through the

---

[11] D. R. Headrick, *Power Over Peoples: Technology, environments, and Western imperialism,
1400 to the present* (Princeton: Princeton University Press, 2012); W. H. McNeill, *Plagues
and Peoples* (New York: Bantam Doubleday, 1998).

management and manipulation of cultural diversity – as central to colonial conquest and rule.

Beyond its historical significance, this study carries more general lessons for understanding the dynamics of conquest. For the barbarian conquests of early modern South and East Asia flourished in structural circumstances that, while distinctive, were far from unique. Considered at the most abstract level, this wave of conquest emerged from a dramatic growth in interaction capacity, evidenced in the accelerating spread of military innovation and commercial exchange across Eurasia from the late medieval period. This surge in interaction capacity generated new nuclei of power at the steppe, forest and maritime edges of the Old World. There, brokers took advantage of their location at the interstices of diverse military, commercial and cultural networks of interaction to cobble together new forms of proto-polity, beyond the effective grasp of sedentary rulers. The existence of lightly governed (and in many cases, truly stateless) enclaves on these frontiers further aided this process of insurgent polity formation. On land, the vastness of the Eurasian steppe permitted entrepreneurial warlords to operate beyond the effective fighting range of sedentary armies. Conversely, on the Eurasian littoral, customs of commercial extraterritoriality often enabled intruders to assemble proto-polities within the very heart of sedentary power centres, establishing toeholds from which large-scale territorial expansion could later take place.

In both instances, ungoverned or lightly governed spaces provided liminal predators with the freedom necessary to trade, hoard capital, hone niche military innovations and begin forming the alliances necessary to pursue universal conquest. Meanwhile, the identity topography of sedentary power centres provided a further point of entry for would-be conquerors. In particular, the cosmopolitan character of Persephone and Sinic civilizing projects left them open to appropriation by outsiders, who could harness them first for purposes of ingratiation and ideological outreach to allies, and then later as components of composite imperial legitimating ideologies once barbarian rule was secure.

Surging interaction capacity in late medieval and early modern Eurasia made a new form of polity-building possible. This distinctive form of frontier 'capitalized coercion' derived from the brokerage opportunities that emerged along Eurasia's terrestrial and maritime frontiers at this time.[12] The existence of ungoverned or lightly governed enclaves along

---

[12] On capitalized coercion as a distinctive trajectory in European state formation, see Tilly, *Coercion, Capital and European States*, pp. 151–60. My advocacy of frontier capitalized coercion as a trajectory of Eurasian empires extends upon but necessarily modifies Tilly's

these frontiers gave barbarians the freedom to initiate processes of proto-polity formation unmolested. And the ideological defences sedentary elites had meanwhile crafted to tame barbarians and indigenous warrior elites paradoxically further nourished liminal predators, by providing them with cosmopolitan systems of meaning and collective identification that they later could adopt and repurpose to legitimize alien rule.

The model of polity-building and universal conquest I have explored in this book has broader implications and extensions beyond the cases I have considered. The Ottoman Empire presents as a similar case of universal conquest from the frontier, and one that is potentially amenable to comprehension through the framework I have advanced in this book. Like the barbarian dynasties considered in the preceding chapters, the Ottomans also began as frontier predators operating at the edges of a core sedentary power centre (in this case, Byzantium).[13] Beyond this positional similarity, the Ottomans also pursued similar strategies of define and conquer and define and rule as they expanded. Rather than conquering through strategies of coercive homogenization (either in the Turkic or Islamic register), the Ottomans anticipated later early modern barbarian waves of expansion in their pragmatic adoption of incorporative diversity management strategies, along the lines of the define and conquer model detailed in this study.[14]

This symmetry between Ottoman expansion and the later Mughal, Manchu and British conquests is suggestive in two senses. First, it reinforces the observation that empires – not sovereign state systems – predominated across Eurasia during the centuries spanning the late medieval and early modern eras. Reading world history through a Eurocentric lens, one can easily mistake this period as being defined by the steady breakdown of universalisms (evidenced in the failure of papal and imperial visions of universal monarchy), followed by the rise of an irreducibly plural Westphalian sovereign state system. But once we broaden our historical horizons beyond Western Europe, it is clear that logics of domination and universal conquest – rather than balancing and sovereign anarchy – predominated in the Old World at this time.

Second, the apparent symmetry between the Ottomans and the later cases this book examines suggests a general pattern of peripheral conquest dominating throughout this epoch. Besides the Ottomans, the

concept of capitalized coercion to reflect the distinct system characteristics of the Old World following the changes wrought by the Eurasian Transformation.
[13] Barkey, *Empire of Difference*, p. 1.
[14] For an outstanding analysis of the Ottoman Empire's diversity regime, see A. Zarakol, 'The Ottomans and diversity', in A. Phillips and C. Reus-Smit (eds.), *Culture and Order in World Politics* (Cambridge: Cambridge University Press, 2020), pp. 49–70.

Russian Empire from the fifteenth century stands as a similar case of conquest from the margins that also eventually saw the 'roll up' of political diversity within the framework of a universal empire.[15] Certainly, the Russian case is distinctive, in that the Russians more often employed coercive homogenization – through religious proselytization and forced Russification – as key tools within their empire-building repertoire.[16] Equally, Russian expansion into Siberia is also distinguishable from the other cases, in that Siberia's low population density limited Russian scope for expanding principally via the co-optation of powerful indigenous intermediaries. These caveats aside, the Russian case also saw formerly marginal actors follow paths of conquest similar to the cases considered. In particular, Russian reliance on the profits earned from the long-distance trade in luxury commodities (e.g., sable) proved critical in fuelling their territorial expansion.[17] Likewise, the Russian court's skilful construction of multi-ethnic conquest coalitions, and its subsequent maintenance of incorporative imperial rights regimes once its empire had been won, invite obvious parallels with the Mughal, Manchu and East India Company cases.[18]

The larger point is that there is important scope for extending this study's model of conquest through customization to a range of other key case studies in Eurasian comparative political development. More ambitiously still, a comparative study along these lines opens up exciting possibilities for radically rethinking international systems' historical development from the late medieval period onwards. To extend an observation flagged earlier, IR scholars are used to thinking of the international system's development principally as the story of the Westphalian state system's emergence and later worldwide spread. This Eurocentric outlook relegates universal conquest to antiquity, or alternatively to exclusively European colonial expansion.

By contrast, this book's findings suggest a compelling need to even the ledger both analytically – through a greater emphasis on conquest and hierarchy over the emergence of sovereign anarchy – and geographically, through a focus on the comparative evolution of Western and non-Western empires. A bird's-eye view of the world political map in c. 1400 reveals a far larger multitude of independent polities than what

---

[15] On system roll up, see again Nedal and Nexon, 'Anarchy and Authority', 170.
[16] This trend seems particularly pronounced from the 1860s, to a certain extent overturning an earlier more incorporative approach to the management of cultural diversity within the empire. See, for example, U. Hofmeister, 'Civilization and Russification in Tsarist Central Asia, 1860–1917', *Journal of World History*, 27(3) (2016), 411–42.
[17] Slezkine, *Arctic Mirrors*, pp. 12–13. See also generally E. Monahan, *The Merchants of Siberia: Trade in early modern Eurasia* (Ithaca: Cornell University Press, 2016).
[18] See generally Burbank, 'An imperial rights regime'.

we would see in c. 1900. In the interval between these two time periods, conquerors rolled up a wide range of plural international systems into universal empires. This system roll up occurred not merely in South and East Asia, but also on the Russian steppe and throughout Southwest Asia. In three of these four instances, moreover, frontier barbarians spearheaded these conquests, prevailing over and eventually absorbing some of the world's most powerful sedentary societies. Before decolonization and the twentieth-century profusion of independent sovereignties, the world had first witnessed a tectonic and centuries-long political reordering in the other direction. Throughout the early modern period, conquest, political consolidation and the growth of gargantuan multicultural empires were the rule, not the exception. Only Western Europe escaped this trend – and even then, only narrowly, with Napoleon's defeat and the post-1815 spread of nationalism likely saving Western European polities from subsumption within a revived continental empire.[19]

Following from the above, my argument here is that IR scholars' models for understanding international systems' comparative development stand to be significantly enriched through a more sustained consideration of trajectories of early modern Old World conquest. Instances of universal conquest are more common, more recent and (at least from a Western European standpoint) geographically far closer than mainstream IR scholarship has traditionally assumed. Recognizing this reality – and acknowledging that non-Europeans were historically at least as (and until the nineteenth century *more than*) successful as conquerors as Europeans forces us beyond conventional Westphalia-centric conceptions of the modern international system's development.[20] At the same time, recognizing universal conquest as a historically common phenomenon has the added advantage of productively provincializing West(phalian) Europe. This is because it compels us towards more systematic consideration of exactly *why* Western Europe escaped the Eurasia-wide trend towards system roll up and universal conquest – and thus to considering what exactly was exceptional about Western European development in the centuries leading up to its fleeting worldwide ascendancy.

Rethinking the Rise of the West through the Lens of Eurasian History

In addition to providing a general account of imperial hierarchies' emergence throughout early modern Eurasia, this book has also critically

---

[19] On this point, see Hui, 'Toward a dynamic theory of international politics', 198–200.
[20] See generally Sharman, *Empires of the Weak*.

engaged one of the social sciences' most enduring puzzles – the 'rise of the West' to world dominance. Chapter 1 critically canvassed a broad range of accounts, grouped under the heads of Western exceptionalism, global entanglements and frontier encounters.

My analysis finds very little support for Western exceptionalism as a satisfactory account of the rise of the West, and least in Asia. Western military dominance was either too limited (confined to blue water naval warfare) or came too late to account for the EIC's geopolitical ascendancy from the mid-eighteenth century. Certainly, Western naval military innovation allowed Europeans to eke out an existence as maritime frontier predators. But such marginal military advantages as the West did possess did not translate into large-scale territorial dominance or control – a goal Europeans in any case did not generally seek in Asia before the mid-late eighteenth century.[21]

Moving beyond a purely military focus, the institution of company-states *did* provide Westerners with a powerful mechanism for engaging in long-distance commerce and (eventually) conquest, one that did prove superior to both European sovereign state competitors (Portugal) and Asia's resident unarmed trading diasporas in managing the challenges of trade, war and diplomacy in maritime Asia.[22] That said, we should not overstate the self-contained import of this advantage. For company-states flourished in large part because of the congruence between their heteronomous character and existing indigenous Asian traditions of commercial extraterritoriality.[23] Most notably, where traditions of commercial extraterritoriality were expansive – as in South Asia – company-states could establish the city-colonies that would much later form the springboards for large-scale territorial conquest. Conversely, Westerners were far more constrained in northeast Asia, where traditions of commercial extraterritoriality were far more restrictive, and neither sovereign states nor company-states could take hold in any but the most limited ways before the mid-late nineteenth century. The interaction between Western institutional innovations and local environmental conditions mattered as much as the supposedly inherent properties of the institutions themselves – radically qualifying if not completely repudiating Western exceptionalism.

One of this book's core insights is that Western expansion in Asia came about as much through insinuation and incorporation as it did via

---

[21] Z. Biedermann, *(Dis)Connected Empires: Imperial Portugal, Sri Lankan diplomacy, and the making of a Habsburg conquest in Asia* (Oxford: Oxford University Press, 2019), chapter 1.
[22] Stern, *The Company-State.* See also Phillips and Sharman, *Outsourcing Empire.*
[23] I explore this correspondence in greater detail in Phillips, 'Asian incorporation', pp. 199–220.

imposition. This argument not only runs counter to claims of Western exceptionalism, but also suggests affinities with approaches (notably Global Historical Sociology and theorists of Uneven and Combined Development) that privilege themes of global entanglement when comprehending Western expansion into Asia. Both global historical sociologists and UCD theorists rightly capture the interplay between Western intrusion and conducive local social and political circumstances in enabling the rise of the West. In privileging global relations of primitive accumulation and unequal exchange, they also correctly highlight the importance of mobilizing indigenous resource portfolios as being critical to Western expansion.

These virtues aside, as we have seen, global historical sociologists and UCD theorists generally leave the dynamics of indigenous cooperation significantly under-specified. This omission is problematic in the first instance because it risks inadvertently repeating a key weakness of Western exceptionalism – namely its stress on external imposition over insinuation and local collusion as key drivers of the 'rise' of the West. Additionally, however, this omission also obscures the hybrid character of the imperial international orders that emerged in South and East Asia following the Western ascendancy. The EIC's dependency on local collaborators profoundly shaped the character, purpose, mode and means of imperial conquest and governance in India, in ways that significantly constrained the strength of the Raj in both its company and Crown incarnations. Western power in Qing-dominated northeast Asia was even more restricted. Even following the Opium Wars and the Qing Empire's forced opening to the West, Westerners depended fundamentally on Qing collaboration to advance their interests. Whether dominating through paramountcy in South Asia, or via a Western-Qing synarchy in much of Northeast Asia, Western power was straitjacketed by the entangling alliances it struck with local collaborators. These dependencies are insufficiently captured through explicitly globalist forms of theorizing, which overstate the trajectory, form and magnitude of Western dominance in Asia.

Finally, I also considered a category of explanations (which I characterized as falling under the rubric of frontier encounters) that paid far closer attention to the local interactions between Western intruders and indigenous actors in trying to account for the Western ascendancy. Both network-relational and postcolonial accounts of the dynamics of imperial emergence offered key insights explaining the rise of the West, from which I have drawn appreciatively in this book. Echoing Paul MacDonald,[24] this book reaffirms the importance of conducive

---

[24] MacDonald, *Networks of Domination*.

configurations of social ties as a key prerequisite for imperial expansion. Similarly, my argument clearly echoes postcolonialists' stress on the importance of define and divide and rule strategies for establishing and maintaining empires.[25] These intellectual debts notwithstanding, this study deliberately and systematically sought to explore the parallels and interrelationships between Western and Asian early modern empire-building. Reiterating my earlier critique, there was nothing exceptional about the West that pre-ordained the East-West power flip. And this lack of exceptionalism extended to both would-be imperialists' dependence on local allies and favourable configurations of social ties, as well as to their generic reliance on define and conquer and define and divide and rule strategies.

With these observations in mind, a key upshot of my analysis is that scholars should focus less on trying to explain the rise of the West *per se*. Rather, in making sense of early modern international relations, we might more productively seek to explain how Western and Asian empire-builders *jointly* carved out larger and more enduring imperial international systems from the sixteenth century onwards, and how these imperial projects intersected and interacted with one another. Certainly, Western conquest was distinctive, in that Western polities eventually proved more capable of knitting together transcontinental structures of unequal exchange (both ideational as well as material) and primitive accumulation. But the Western ascendancy – both within Asia and globally – would not have been possible without the prior success of Mughal and Qing empire-builders.

The *Pax Mughalica* and the *Pax Manchurica* together established the political stability in which trade and commerce could flourish in South and East Asia. The resulting prosperity drew in armed Western traders, who then insinuated themselves as vassals into both empires. Later, as the power of both empires ebbed, Westerners mimicked the styles of empire-building that the Mughals and Manchus had earlier mastered. The ensuing interactions led to a formal transfer of empire from the Mughals to the (British) Crown after 1857, and the establishment of synarchic governance arrangements in the Qing Empire in partnership with a revived Manchu monarchy after 1860. The resulting hybrid international orders – one based on imperial paramountcy, the other on synarchy – then formed the basis for a pan-Asian international order that spanned maritime Asia down to the early twentieth century, and formed the chrysalis out of which a later order of Asian nation-states subsequently developed.

[25] See, for example, Cohn, *Colonialism and its Forms of Knowledge*; Said, *Orientalism*.

Rethinking Modernity and the Historical Evolution of the Global International System

Beyond accounting for the rise of imperial hierarchies in early modern Asia and critically engaging the question of the Western ascendancy, this book finally has larger implications for how we theorize about modernity and the evolution of the global international system. In centring my narrative around empires' rise in Asia and in adopting an explicitly comparative focus, I have departed from traditionally Eurocentric approaches to the evolution of the modern international system. This is because conventional narratives typically take the Peace of Westphalia as 'ground zero' for the modern international system's origins, and track modernity's progress through the subsequent global spread of the sovereign state system.[26]

By contrast, this study starts from the supposition that Westphalia was an outlier in early modern Eurasia. From the sixteenth century, plural international systems were more often rolled up into imperial hierarchies, rather than being either the precursors to local sovereign state systems or extensions of an expanding Westphalian order. Before the international system reconfigured as a universal sovereign state monoculture in the mid-twentieth century, Asia, in particular, saw the envelopment of political and cultural diversity within a succession of vast subcontinental empires. Early modern globalization helped catalyse the growth of gargantuan barbarian imperial enterprises, which between them laid the foundations for modern-day China and India, the world's two most populous states. As Asian powers resume their historical primacy in the twenty-first century, these processes of imperial aggregation should warrant at least as much attention as Europe's idiosyncratic Westphalian *Sonderweg*.

More directly and positively, this book highlights the need for greater recognition of the genuinely polycentric foundations of the modern international system. The idea of a diffusion of modernity from a Westphalian ground zero unintentionally privileges the West as modernity's vanguard agents, and retrojects a later and fleeting period of Western dominance back into to the early modern period. Conversely, this book has shown multiple 'epicentres' of early modernity. South Asia's encompassment within the Mughal Empire, and the unprecedented success of the Qing imperial enterprise, both proved foundational for these regions' integration into genuinely global systems of military, economic, cultural and diplomatic exchange. Far from being indispensable catalysts for these

---

[26] See, for example, Bull and Watson (eds.), *The Expansion of International Society*. For an excellent critique of this narrative, see T. Kayaoglu, 'Westphalian eurocentrism in international relations theory', *International Studies Review*, 12(2) (2010), 193–217.

developments, Western interlopers were at least initially peripheral bene-ficiaries of South and East Asian imperial consolidation. South and East Asians early on set the terms of Western incorporation. Only later, as the Mughal Empire faltered, did the EIC belatedly take up the imperial mantle, and then largely through imitation and adaptation of Mughal practices of conquest and rule. Meanwhile, the Qing Empire's residual power placed definite upper limits on Western ambitions in littoral East Asia, and forced a compromise system of synarchy that channelled forces of diplomatic, political and economic modernization in the region down to the late 1890s.

Acknowledging the modern international system's polycentric origins is not by itself an original claim. Early modern historians have long noted the diverse actors that helped inaugurate a genuinely 'global' age from the fifteenth century onwards.[27] Nevertheless, from an IR perspective, this intervention is valuable in creating room for a more genuinely expansive and inclusive conception of the modern international system's long-term historical evolution. This move is consistent with the push in the discip-line towards a more genuinely Global International Relations.[28] But it also suggests the need to revisit key puzzles within IR. In particular, the traditional focus on the balance of power as a mechanism for regulating inter-polity rivalries can be fruitfully re-engaged with a knowledge of its evident and persistent failures in early modern South and East Asia. When we limit our geographic focus to developments west of the Oder-Neisse, we are in danger of coming away with an exaggerated sense of the reliability of the balance of power as a safeguard against universal con-quest. Conversely, once we expand our field of vision to encompass international systems beyond Europe, the recurrent failures of balance of power mechanisms to prevent conquest become more immediately apparent. Seen through this lens, the modern international system's recent (post-1500) historical development has been shaped at least as much by the success of projects of universal conquest as by their failure. Accordingly, a more sustained engagement with the Mughal, Qing and other cases (e.g., Romanov Russia, Ottoman expansion into the Middle East) is warranted, both to understand the circumstances of the modern world's creation, but also to provide a more historically informed basis for

---

[27] See, for example, J. H. Bentley, S. Subrahmanyam and M. E. Wiesner-Hanks (eds.), *The Cambridge World History*, 7 vols., VI: *The Construction of a Global World, 1400–1800 CE*, Pt. I (Cambridge: Cambridge University Press, 2015); J. H. Bentley, S. Subrahmanyam and M. E. Wiesner-Hanks (eds.), *The Cambridge World History*, 7 vols., VI: *The Construction of a Global World, 1400–1800 CE*, Pt. II (Cambridge: Cambridge University Press, 2015).

[28] A. Acharya, 'Global international relations (IR) and regional worlds: A new agenda for international studies', *International Studies Quarterly*, 58(4) (2014), pp. 647–59.

theorizing about when balance of power mechanisms will succeed or fail in preventing bids for universal hegemony.

Similarly, the topic of cultural diversity and its relationship to international order has recently emerged as a productive line of inquiry for scholars interested in understanding international systems' constitution and evolution.[29] Within this vein, the lessons of early modern 'barbarian' conquests in Asia are of immediate relevance. For Mughal, Manchu and British empire-builders, who to varying degree faced stigmatization as 'outsiders', the organization and management of cultural diversity was critically important for empires' creation and maintenance. This inquiry has broadened the geographic remit of studies on cultural diversity and international order to encompass South Asia. More fundamentally, however, I have sought to demonstrate how questions of diversity management were critically important for imperial orders' creation as well as their maintenance. Large-scale conquest in the early modern period demanded the mass mobilization of indigenous military manpower – something that barbarians could only accomplish through sophisticated cultural statecraft. Equally, once empire-builders had settled on a particular diversity regime (whether syncretic, segregated or ecumenical in form), they subsequently became deeply constrained in their methods of rule. In the British case in particular, efforts to depart from the prevailing diversity regime in the early nineteenth century proved disastrous, and forced a rapid retrenchment of liberal transformationalist ambitions. Acknowledging these constraints is key, in demonstrating the constraining as well as constitutive effects of diversity regimes for international orders, and the consequences of these constraints for shaping international orders' subsequent evolution in Asia.

Lastly, this book highlights and provides historical depth to the regional variations in international order that have long distinguished South from East Asia. In South Asia, as we have seen, the Mughals provided over a loose suzerain order governed by a diversity regime that stressed the integrative power of syncretic incorporation, and in which the Mughals furthermore claimed to exert no meaningful claims to political authority in the maritime domain. Conversely, the Manchus inherited from their Ming predecessors a precociously bureaucratized imperial state, as well as a vigilant attitude towards the regulation of maritime space. To these institutional and ideational legacies, the Manchus then added a diversity regime centred on segregated ethnic incorporation. This regime proved highly adaptive in enabling the Manchus to vastly increase the size of their

---

[29] See, for example, Reus-Smit, *On Cultural Diversity*; and Phillips and Reus-Smit, *Culture and Order in World Politics*.

empire, but reinforced a tendency to exert maximum control where possible over traders and raiders on the empires' steppe and maritime frontiers.

The results of this variation in South and East Asian international orders were of immense consequence. Today, IR scholars increasingly trace the global international system's origins to the so-called global transformation dating from approximately 1860 onwards.[30] Without detracting from the global transformation's importance, a key finding of this study is that the global transformation was itself mediated and refracted through regionally diverse international orders that had their origins in early modernity. Thus, the Mughal model of empire proved supremely effective in incorporating South Asia's immense heterogeneity. But it also eventually proved equally permeable and susceptible to Western infiltration, subversion and appropriation. Conversely, the Qing imperial state proved bigger, tougher and less immediately susceptible to Western infiltration. The resulting delay in onset of full-scale Western predation helped ensure that China was not subject to formal Western colonialism in the same way as India – fundamentally conditioning South and East Asia's subsequent trajectories.

As we enter into an incipient age of Asian Great Power supremacy, it is critical that we comprehend the relatively recent origins of 'India' and 'China' in the barbarian conquests of the early modern era. Despite their ancient civilizational lineages, India and China in their current geopolitical incarnations are creatures of recent provenance and barbarian authorship. The variations in conquerors' approaches to diversity management moreover continue to cast a long shadow on the internal dynamics of both of these megastates. In investigating the origins, course and evolution of barbarian universal conquest in South and East Asia, I hope here to have made a modest contribution to understanding two countries, India and China, that between them will be decisive in shaping international order in the coming decades.

---

[30] Buzan and Lawson, *The Global Transformation.*

References

Abu-Lughod, J., *Before European Hegemony: The world-system AD 1250–1350* (Oxford: Oxford University Press, 1991).

Acharya, A., 'Global international relations (IR) and regional worlds: A new agenda for international studies', *International Studies Quarterly*, 58(4) (2014), pp. 647–59.

The End of American World Order (London: Polity, 2014).

Adas, M., 'Imperialism and colonialism in comparative perspective', *International History Review*, 20(2) (1998), 371–88.

Ahmed, A., 'The role of ulema in Indo-Muslim history', *Studia Islamica*, 31 (1970), 1–13.

Ahram, A. I. and King, C., 'The warlord as arbitrageur', *Theory and Society*, 41(2) (2012), 169–86.

Alam, M., 'The pursuit of Persian: Language in Mughal politics', *Modern Asian Studies*, 32(2) (1998), 317–49.

Alavi, S., 'The makings of company power: James Skinner in the ceded and conquered provinces, 1802–1840', *Indian Economic and Social Review*, 30 (4) (1993), 437–66.

'The company army and rural society: The invalid Thanah 1780–1830', *Modern Asian Studies*, 27(1) (1993), 147–78.

The Sepoys and the Company: Tradition and transition in Northern India, 1770–1830 (Delhi: Oxford University Press, 1995).

'Introduction' in S. Alavi (ed.), *The Eighteenth Century in India* (Oxford: Oxford University Press, 2002), pp. 1–56.

Allen, D. W., *The Institutional Revolution: Measurement and the economic emergence of the modern world* (Chicago: University of Chicago Press, 2011).

Anderson, M. R., 'Islamic law and the colonial encounter in British India' in D. Arnold and P. Robb (eds.), *Institutions and Ideologies: A SOAS South Asia reader* (London: Routledge Curzon, 1993), pp. 165–85.

Andrade, T., 'The rise and fall of Dutch Taiwan, 1624–1662: Cooperative colonization and the statist model of European expansion', *Journal of World History*, 17(4) (2006), 429–50.

How Taiwan Became Chinese: Dutch, Spanish and Han colonization in the seventeenth century (New York: Columbia University Press, 2008).

'Beyond guns, germs, and steel: European expansion and maritime Asia, 1400–1750', *Journal of Early Modern History*, 14(1–2) (2010), 165–86.

The Lost Colony: The untold story of China's first great victory over the West (Princeton: Princeton University Press, 2011).

'Was the European sailing ship a key technology for European expansion? Evidence from East Asia', *International Journal of Maritime History*, 23(2) (2011), 17–40.

The Gunpowder Age: China, military innovation and the rise of the West in world history (Princeton: Princeton University Press, 2017).

Andrade, T. and Hang, X. , 'Introduction: The East Asian maritime realm in global history, 1500–1700' in T. Andrade and X. Hang (eds.), *Sea Rovers, Silver, and Samurai: Maritime East Asia in global history, 1550–1700* (Honolulu: University of Hawaii Press, 2016), pp. 1–27.

Anievas, A. and Nişancıoğlu, K., *How the West Came to Rule: The geopolitical origins of capitalism* (London: Pluto Press, 2015).

'How did the West usurp the rest? Origins of the great divergence over the *longue durée*', *Comparative Studies in Society and History*, 59(1) (2017), 34–67.

Arjomand, S. A., 'The salience of political ethic in the spread of Persianate Islam', *Journal of Persianate Studies*, 1(1) (2008), 5–29.

'Unity of the Persianate world under Turko-Mongolian domination and divergent development of imperial autocracies in the sixteenth century', *Journal of Persianate Studies*, 9(1) (2016), 1–18.

'Persianate Islam and Its regional spread' in P. Michel, A. Possamai and B. S. Turner (eds.), *Religions, Nations, and Transnationalism in Multiple Modernities* (London: Palgrave Macmillan, 2017), pp. 67–84.

Asher, C. B. and Talbot, C., *India Before Europe* (Cambridge: Cambridge University Press, 2008).

Atwill, D. G., *The Chinese Sultanate: Islam, ethnicity and the Panthay Rebellion in Southwest China, 1856–1873* (Stanford: Stanford University Press, 2005).

Aust, M., '*Rossia Siberica*: Russian-Siberian history compared to medieval conquest and modern colonialism', *Review (Fernand Braudel Center)*, 27(3) (2004), 181–205.

Axworthy, M., *The Sword of Persia: Nader Shah, from tribal warrior to conquering tyrant* (London: I. B. Tauris, 2009).

Baker, A., 'Divided sovereignty: Empire and nation in the making of modern Britain', *International Politics*, 46(6) (2009), 691–711.

Balabanlilar, L., 'Lords of the auspicious conjunction: Turco-Mongol imperial identity on the sub-continent', *Journal of World History*, 18(1) (2007), 1–39.

Imperial Identity in the Mughal Empire: Memory and dynastic politics in early modern South and Central Asia (London: I. B. Tauris, 2012).

Banks, D. E., 'Fields of practice: Symbolic binding and the Qing defense of Sinocentric diplomacy', *International Studies Quarterly*, 63(3) (2019), 546–57.

Barbour, R., 'Power and distant display: Early English "ambassadors" in Moghul India', *Huntington Library Quarterly*, 61(3–4) (1998), 343–68.

Barfield, T. J., 'The shadow empires: Imperial state formation along the Chinese-nomad frontier' in S. E. Alcock, T. N. D'Altroy, K. D. Morrison and Carla M. Sinopoli (eds.), *Empires: Perspectives from archaeology and history* (Cambridge: Cambridge University Press, 2001), pp. 10–41.

'Steppe empires, China, and the silk route: Nomads as a force in international trade and politics' in A. M. Khazanov and A. Wink (eds.), *Nomads in the Sedentary World* (London: Routledge, 2001), pp. 234–49.

Barkey, K., *Empire of Difference: The Ottomans in comparative perspective* (Cambridge: Cambridge University Press, 2008).

'Political legitimacy and Islam in the Ottoman Empire: Lessons learned', *Philosophy and Social Criticism*, 40(4–5) (2014), 469–77.

Barua, P., 'Military Developments in India, 1750–1850', *Journal of Military History*, 58(4) (1994), 599–616.

Baugh, D., *The Global Seven Years War, 1754–1783: Britain and France in a great power contest* (London: Routledge, 2014).

Bayly, C. A., *Rulers, Townsmen and Bazaars: North Indian society in the age of British expansion, 1770–1870* (Oxford: Oxford University Press, 1983).

'The pre-history of "communalism"? Religious conflict in India, 1700–1860', *Modern Asian Studies*, 19(2) (1985), 177–203.

Imperial Meridian: The British Empire and the world, 1780–1830 (London: Routledge, 1989).

Indian Society and the Making of the British Empire (Cambridge: Cambridge University Press, 1990).

'The first age of global imperialism, c. 1760–1830', *Journal of Imperial and Commonwealth History*, 26(2) (1998), 28–47.

Empire of Information: Intelligence gathering and social communication in India, 1780–1870 (Cambridge: Cambridge University Press, 1999).

'"Archaic" and "modern" globalization in the Eurasian and African arena, c. 1750–1850' in A. G. Hopkins (ed.), *Globalization in World History* (New York: W. W. Norton, 2002), pp. 47–73.

'Distorted development: The Ottoman Empire and British India, circa 1780–1916', *Comparative Studies of South Asia, Africa and the Middle East*, 27(2) (2007), 332–44.

Recovering Liberties: Indian thought in the age of liberalism and empire (Cambridge: Cambridge University Press, 2012).

Bell, C., *The End of the Vasco da Gama Era* (Sydney: The Lowy Institute, 2007).

Bentley, J. H., 'Hemispheric integration, 500–1500 CE', *Journal of World History*, 9(2) (1998), 237–54.

'Sea and ocean basins as frameworks of historical analysis', *Geographical Review*, 89(2) (1999), 215–24.

Bentley, J. H., Subrahmanyam, S. and Wiesner-Hanks, M. E. (eds.), *The Cambridge World History*, 7 vols., VI: *The Construction of a Global World, 1400–1800 CE*, Pt I (Cambridge: Cambridge University Press, 2015).

Subrahmanyam, S. and Wiesner-Hanks, M. E. (eds), *The Cambridge World History*, 7 vols., VI: *The Construction of a Global World, 1400–1800 CE*, Pt II (Cambridge: Cambridge University Press, 2015).

Benton, L., 'Colonial law and cultural difference: Jurisdictional politics and the formation of the colonial state', *Comparative Studies in Society and History*, 41(3) (1999), 563–88.

Law and Colonial Cultures: Legal regimes in world history, 1400–1900 (Cambridge: Cambridge University Press, 2002).

'Legal spaces of empire: Piracy and the origins of ocean regionalism', *Comparative Studies in Society and History*, 47(4) (2005), 700–24.

Benton, L. and Clulow, A., 'Empires and protection: Making interpolity law in the early modern world', *Journal of Global History*, 12(1) (2017), 74–92.

Clulow, A., 'Webs of protection and interpolity zones in the early modern world' in L. Benton, A. Clulow and B. Attwood (eds.), *Protection and Empire: A global history* (Cambridge, Cambridge University Press, 2017), pp. 49–71.

Berkel, M., van, 'The people of the pen: Self-perceptions of status and role in the administration of empires and polities' in M. van Berkel and J. Duindam (eds.), *Prince, Pen, and Sword: Eurasian perspectives* (Leiden: Brill, 2018), pp. 384–451.

Berkel, M., van and Duindam, J. (eds.), *Prince, Pen, and Sword: Eurasian perspectives* (Leiden: Brill, 2018).

Biedermann, Z., 'Portuguese diplomacy in Asia in the sixteenth century: A preliminary overview', *Itinerario*, 29(2) (2005), 13–37.

'The matrioshka principle and how it was overcome: Portuguese and Habsburg imperial attitudes in Sri Lanka and the responses of the rulers of Kotte (1506–1598)', *Journal of Early Modern History*, 13(4) (2009), 265–310.

(Dis)Connected Empires: Imperial Portugal, Sri Lankan diplomacy, and the making of a Habsburg conquest in Asia (Oxford: Oxford University Press, 2019).

Birnbaum, M., 'Recognizing diversity: Establishing religious difference in Pakistan and Israel' in A. Phillips and C. Reus-Smit (eds.), *Culture and Order in World Politics* (Cambridge: Cambridge University Press, 2020), pp. 250–70.

Blake, S. P., 'Courtly culture under Babur and the early Mughals', *Journal of Asian History*, 20(2) (1986), 193–214.

Bose, S., *A Hundred Horizons: The Indian Ocean in the age of global empire* (Cambridge, MA: Harvard University Press, 2009).

Brack, J., 'Theologies of auspicious kingship: The Islamization of Chinggisid sacral kingship in the Islamic world', *Comparative Studies in Society and History*, 60(4) (2018), 1143–71.

Brown, K. B., 'Did Aurangzeb ban music? Questions for the historiography of his reign', *Modern Asian Studies*, 41(1) (2007), 77–120.

Bryant, G. J., 'Indigenous mercenaries in the service of European imperialists: The case of the sepoys in the early British Indian army, 1750–1800', *War in History*, 7(1) (2000), 2–28.

'Asymmetric warfare: The British experience in eighteenth century India', *Journal of Military History*, 68(2) (2004), 431–69.

The Emergence of British Power in India, 1600–1784: A grand strategic interpretation (Suffolk: Boydell & Brewer, 2013).

Buchan, P. B., 'The East India Company 1749–1800: The evolution of a territorial strategy and the changing role of the directors', *Business and Economic History*, 23(1) (1994), 52–61.

Bull, H. and Watson, A. (eds.), *The Expansion of International Society* (Oxford: Clarendon Press, 1984).

Burbank, J., 'An imperial rights regime: Law and citizenship in the Russian Empire', *Kritika: Explorations in Russian and Eurasian History*, 7(3) (2006), 397–431.

Burbank, J. and Cooper, F., *Empires in World History: Power and the politics of difference* (Princeton: Princeton University Press, 2010).

Buzan, B., *People, States and Fear: The national security problem in international relations* (London: Harvester Wheatsheaf, 1983).

'Culture and international society', *International Affairs*, 86(1) (2010), 1–25.

Buzan, B. and Lawson, G. , *The Global Transformation: History, modernity and the making of international relations* (Cambridge: Cambridge University Press, 2015).

Callahan, R., 'The company's army, 1757–1798' in P. Tuck (ed.), *The East India Company, 1600–1858*, 6 vols., V: *Warfare, expansion, and resistance* (London: Routledge, 1998), pp. 21–31.

Canfield, R. L. (ed.), *Turko-Persia in Historical Perspective* (Cambridge: Cambridge University Press, 2002).

Cannadine, D., *Ornamentalism: How the British saw their empire* (Oxford: Oxford University Press, 2002).

Cassel, P. K., 'Excavating extraterritoriality: The "judicial sub-prefect" as a prototype for the mixed court in Shanghai', *Late Imperial China*, 24(2) (2003), 156–82.

Grounds of Judgement: Extraterritoriality and imperial power in nineteenth-century China and Japan (Oxford: Oxford University Press, 2012).

Chandra, S., 'Jizya and the state in India during the 17th century', *Economic and Social History of the Orient*, 12(3) (1969), 322–40.

Chang, M. G., *A Court on Horseback: Imperial touring and the construction of Qing rule, 1680–1785* (Cambridge, MA: Harvard University Press, 2007).

Chaudhuri, K. N., 'The economic and monetary problem of European trade with Asia during the seventeenth and eighteenth centuries', *Journal of European Economic History*, 4(2) (1975), 323–58.

The Trading World of Asia and the East India Company, 1660–1760 (Cambridge: Cambridge University Press, 1978).

Trade and Civilization in the Indian Ocean: An economic history from the rise of Islam to 1750 (Cambridge: Cambridge University Press, 1985).

Chen, F. T.-S. 'The Confucian view of world order' in M. W. Janis and C. Evans (eds.), *Religion and International Law* (Leiden: Martinus Nijhoff Publishers, 2004), pp. 27–49.

Chia, N., 'The Lifanyuan and the inner Asian rituals of the early Qing (1644–1795)', *Late Imperial China*, 14(1) (1993), 60–92.

Chin-Keong, N., 'Information and knowledge: Qing China's perceptions of the maritime world in the eighteenth century' in A. Schottenhammer (ed.), *The East Asian Maritime World 1400–1800: Its fabrics of power and dynamics of exchanges* (Wiesbaden: Harrassowitz Verlag, 2007), pp. 87–98.

Chow, K.-W., *The Rise of Confucian Ritualism in Late Imperial China: Ethics, classics, and lineage discourse* (Stanford: Stanford University Press, 1994).

Cipolla, C. M., *Guns, Sails and Empires: Technological innovation and the early phases of European expansion* (New York: Minerva Press, 1965).

Clark, I., *The Hierarchy of States: Reform and resistance in the international order* (Cambridge: Cambridge University Press, 1989).

Clulow, A., 'European maritime violence and territorial states in early modern Asia, 1600–1650', *Itinerario*, 33(3) (2009), 72–94.

Cohn, B. S., 'Representing authority in Victorian India' in E. Hobsbawm and T. Ranger (eds.), *The Invention of Tradition* (Cambridge: Cambridge University Press, 1983), pp. 165–210.

Colonialism and its Forms of Knowledge: The British in India (Princeton: Princeton University Press, 1996).

Collingham, E. M., *Imperial Bodies: The physical experience of the Raj, c.1800–1947* (London: Polity, 2001).

Cooley, A. and Spruyt, H., *Contracting States: Sovereignty transfers in international relations* (Princeton: Princeton University Press, 2009).

Cooper, R. G. S., *The Anglo-Maratha Campaigns and the Contest for India: The struggle for control of the South Asian military economy* (Cambridge: Cambridge University Press, 2003).

Cooper, L., 'Asian sources of British imperial power: The role of the Mysorean rocket in the Opium War' in A. Anievas and K. Matin (eds.), *Historical Sociology and World History: Uneven and combined development over the longue durée* (London: Rowman & Littlefield, 2016), pp. 111–26.

Cosmo, N., di, 'Qing colonial administration in inner Asia', *International History Review*, 20(2) (1998), 287–309.

'State formation and periodization in inner Asian history', *Journal of World History*, 10(1) (1999), 1–40.

'Did guns matter? Firearms and the Qing formation' in L. A. Struve (ed.), *The Qing Formation in World-Historical Time* (Cambridge, MA: Harvard University Press, 2004), pp. 121–66.

'The Manchu conquest in world-historical perspective: A note on trade and silver', *Journal of Central Eurasian Studies*, 1 (2009), 43–60.

'From alliance to tutelage: A historical analysis of Manchu-Mongol relations before the Qing conquest', *Frontiers of History in China*, 7(2) (2012), 175–97.

Cranmer-Byng, J. L. and Wills, J. E. Jr, 'Trade and diplomacy with maritime Europe, 1644–c. 1800' in J. E. Wills Jr (ed.), *China and Maritime Europe, 1500–1800: Trade, settlement, diplomacy, and missions* (Cambridge: Cambridge University Press, 2010), pp. 183–254.

Crossley, P. K., *A Translucent Mirror: History and identity in Qing imperial ideology* (Berkeley: University of California Press, 1999).

'Making Mongols' in P. K. Crossley, H. F. Sui and D. S. Sutton (eds.), *Empire at the Margins: Culture, ethnicity, and frontier in early modern China* (Berkeley: University of California Press, 2006), pp. 58–82.

Curtin, P. D., *Cross-Cultural Trade in World History* (Cambridge, Cambridge University Press, 1984).

Death by Migration: Europe's encounter with the tropical world in the nineteenth century (Cambridge: Cambridge University Press, 1989).

The World and the West: The European challenge and the overseas response in the age of empire (Cambridge: Cambridge University Press, 2012).

Dale, S. F., *The Muslim Empires of the Ottomans, Safavids, and Mughals* (Cambridge: Cambridge University Press, 2010).

Dalrymple, W., *The Last Mughal: The fall of a dynasty, Delhi, 1857* (New York: Vintage Books, 2008).

Darwin, J., *After Tamerlane: The rise and fall of global empires, 1400–2000* (London: Bloomsbury Press, 2008).

Unfinished Empire: The global expansion of Britain (New York: Bloomsbury Press, 2012).

Datla, K. S., 'The origins of indirect rule in India: Hyderabad and the British imperial order', *Law and History Review*, 33(2) (2015), 321–50.

Dehio, L., *The Precarious Balance: Four centuries of European power struggle* (New York: Alfred A. Knopf, 1962).

Deudney, D. H., 'Regrounding realism: Anarchy, security, and changing material contexts', *Security Studies*, 10(1) (2000), 1–42.

Bounding Power: Republican security theory from the polis to the global village (Princeton: Princeton University Press, 2008).

Dirks, N. B., *The Scandal of Empire: India and the creation of imperial Britain* (Cambridge, MA: Harvard University Press, 2006).

Disney, A. R., *A History of Portugal and the Portuguese Empire: From beginnings to 1807*, 2 vols., II: *The Portuguese Empire* (Cambridge: Cambridge University Press, 2009).

Dolan, S. P. and Heirbaut, D., '"A patchwork of accommodations": Reflections on European legal hybridity and jurisdictional complexity' in S. P. Dolan and D. Heirbaut (eds.), *The Laws' Many Bodies, c.1600–1900* (Berlin: Duncker & Humblot, 2015), pp. 9–34.

Doyle, M. W., *Empires* (Ithaca: Cornell University Press, 1986).

D'Souza, R., 'Crisis before the fall: Some speculations on the decline of the Ottomans, Safavids and Mughals', *Social Scientist*, 30(9–10) (2002), 3–30.

DuBois, T. D. *Religion and the Making of Modern East Asia* (Cambridge: Cambridge University Press, 2011).

Duindam, J., 'Rulers and elites in global history: Introductory observations' in M. van Berkel and J. Duindam (eds.), *Prince, Pen, and Sword: Eurasian perspectives* (Leiden: Brill, 2018), pp. 1–31.

Dunne, T., 'Society and hierarchy in international relations', *International Relations* 17(3) (2003), 303–20.

Dunne, T. and Reus-Smit, C. (eds.), *The Globalization of International Society* (Oxford: Oxford University Press, 2017).

Eaton, R. M., *The Rise of Islam and the Bengal Frontier, 1204–1760* (Berkeley: University of California Press, 1993).

'The Persianate cosmopolis (900–1900) and the Sanskrit cosmopolis (400–1400)' in A. Amanat and A. Ashraf (eds.), *The Persianate World: Rethinking a shared sphere* (Leiden: Brill, 2018), pp. 63–83.

Elias, N., *The Civilizing Process: Sociogenetic and psychogenetic explanations* (London: Blackwell Publishing, 2000).

Elliott, M. C., 'Manchu widows and ethnicity in Qing China', *Comparative Studies in Society and History*, 41(1) (1999), 33–71.

The Manchu Way: The Eight Banners and ethnic identity in late Imperial China (Stanford: Stanford University Press, 2001).

'Ethnicity in the Qing Eight Banners' in P. K. Crossley, H. F. Sui and D. S. Sutton (eds.), *Empire at the Margins: Culture, ethnicity and frontier in early modern China* (Berkeley: University of California Press, 2006), pp. 27–57.

Elliott, M. C. and Chia, N. , 'The Qing hunt at Mulan' in R. W. Dunnell, M. C. Elliott, P. Foret and J. A. Millward (eds.), *New Qing Imperial History: The making of inner Asian empire at Qing Chengde* (London: Routledge, 2004), pp. 66–83.

Elverskog, J., *Our Great Qing: The Mongols, Buddhism and the state in late Imperial China* (Honolulu: University of Hawaii Press, 2006).

Erikson, E., *Between Monopoly and Free Trade: The English East India Company, 1600–1757* (Princeton: Princeton University Press, 2014).

Evans, B. L., 'The Panthay Mission of 1872 and its legacies', *Journal of Southeast Asian Studies*, 16(1) (1985), 117–28.

Evans, S., 'Macaulay's minute revisited: Colonial language policy in nineteenth-century India', *Journal of Multilingual and Multicultural Development*, 23(4) (2002), 260–81.

Fairbank, J. K., 'Synarchy under the treaties' in J. K. Fairbank (ed.), *Chinese Thought and Institutions* (Chicago: Chicago University Press, 1957), pp. 204–31.

'The canton trade and the Opium War' in J. K. Fairbank (ed.), *The Cambridge History of China*, 15 vols., X: *Late Ch'ing, 1800–1911*, Pt I (Cambridge: Cambridge University Press, 1978), pp. 163–212.

'The creation of the treaty system' in J. K. Fairbank (ed.), *The Cambridge History of China*, 15 vols., X: *Late Ch'ing, 1800–1911*, Pt I (Cambridge: Cambridge University Press, 1978), pp. 213–63.

Fairbank, J. K. and Goldman, M. , *China: A new history* (Cambridge, MA: Belknap Press, 2006).

Farquhar, D. M., 'Mongolian versus Chinese elements in the early Manchu state', *Ch'ing-shih wen-t'i*, 2(6) (1971), 11–23.

'Emperor as Bodhisattva in the governance of the Ch'ing Empire', *Harvard Journal of Asiatic Studies*, 38(1) (1978), 5–34.

Faruqi, M. D., 'At empire's end: The Nizam, Hyderabad, and eighteenth-century India', *Modern Asian Studies*, 43(1) (2009), 5–43.

The Princes of the Mughal Empire, 1504–1719 (Cambridge: Cambridge University Press, 2012).

Fenech, L. E., 'The Khalsa and the Rahit' in P. Singh and L. E. Fenech (eds.), *The Oxford Handbook of Sikh Studies* (Oxford: Oxford University Press, 2014), pp. 240–9.

Fernando-Armesto, F., *Before Columbus: Exploration and colonization from the Mediterranean to the Atlantic, 1229–1492* (Philadelphia: University of Pennsylvania Press, 1987).

Pathfinders: A global history of exploration (New York: W. W. Norton, 2007).

Fisch, J., 'Law as a means and as an end: Some remarks on the function of European and non-European law in the process of European expansion' in

W. J. Mommsen and J. A. de Moor (eds.), *European Expansion and Law: The encounter of European and indigenous law in 19th- and 20th-century Asia and Africa* (Oxford: Berg, 1992), pp. 15–38.

Fisher, M. H., 'The imperial coronation of 1819: Awadh, the British and the Mughals', *Modern Asian Studies*, 19(2) (1985), 239–77.

A Short History of the Mughal Empire (London: I. B. Taurus, 2016).

Flaten, L. T., *Hindu Nationalism, History and Identity in India: Narrating a Hindu past under the BJP* (London: Routledge, 2016).

Flores, J., 'The sea world of the *Mutasaddi*: A profile of port officials from Mughal Gujarat (c.1600–1650)', *Journal of the Royal Asiatic Society*, 21(1) (2011), 55–71.

Flynn, D. O. and Giráldez, A., 'Born with a "silver spoon": The origin of world trade in 1571', *Journal of World History*, 6(2) (1995), 201–21.

Foltz, R., *Religions of the Silk Road: Premodern patterns of globalization* (New York: Palgrave Macmillan, 2010).

Frank, A. G., *ReOrient: Global economy in the Asian age* (Berkeley: University of California Press, 1998).

Frykenberg, R. E., 'Constructions of Hinduism at the nexus of history and religion', *Journal of Interdisciplinary History*, 23(3) (1993), 523–50.

Fukuyama, F., *The Origins of Political Order: From prehuman times to the French Revolution* (New York: Farrar, Straus and Giroux, 2012).

Garza, A., de la,*The Mughal Empire at War: Babur, Akbar and the Indian Military Revolution, 1500–1605* (London: Routledge, 2016).

Gavin, R. and Wagner, K. A., 'Recruiting the "martial races": Identities and military service in colonial India', *Patterns of Prejudice*, 46(3–4) (2012), 232–54.

Gebhardt, J., 'Negotiating barriers: Cross-cultural communication and the Portuguese mercantile community in Macau, 1550–1640', *Itinerario*, 38(2) (2014), 27–50.

Geyer, M. and Bright, C., 'World history in a global age', *American Historical Review*, 100(4) (1995), 1034–60.

Giersch, C. P., *Asian Borderlands: The transformation of Qing China's Yunnan frontier* (Cambridge, MA: Harvard University Press, 2006).

Gilpin, R., *War and Change in World Politics* (Cambridge: Cambridge University Press, 1981).

Glosny, M. A. and Nexon D. H., 'The outsider advantage: Why liminal actors rise to system-wide domination', unpublished manuscript presented at the Weatherhead Center for International Affairs, Harvard University, 2018.

Go, J., 'Global fields and imperial forms: Field theory and the British and American empires', *Sociological Theory*, 26(3) (2008), 201–29.

Goddard, S. E., 'When right makes might: How Prussia overturned the European balance of power', *International Security*, 33(3) (2008–9), 110–42.

Goh, E., *The Struggle for Order: Hegemony, hierarchy, and transition in post-Cold War East Asia* (Oxford: Oxford University Press, 2013).

Goldstone, J. A., 'Efflorescences and economic growth in world history: Rethinking the "rise of the West" and the industrial revolution', *Journal of World History*, 13(2) (2002), 323–89.

Gommans, J., 'The Eurasian frontier after the first millennium AD: Reflections along the fringe of time and space', *Medieval History Journal*, 1(1) (1998), 125–43.

'The silent frontier of South Asia, c. AD 1100–1800', *Journal of World History*, 9 (1) (1998), 1–23.

Mughal Warfare: Indian frontiers and highroads to empire, 1500–1700 (London: Routledge, 2002).

'Warhorse and gunpowder in India c. 1000–1850' in J. Black (ed.), *War in the Early Modern World* (London: Routledge, 2004), pp. 105–27.

'Warhorse and post-nomadic empire in Asia, c. 1000–1800', *Journal of Global History*, 2(1) (2007), 1–21.

Gommans, J. and Kolff, D. H. A. , 'Introduction' in J. Gommans and D. H. A. Kolff (eds.), *Warfare and Weaponry in South Asia 1000–1800* (Oxford: Oxford University Press, 2001), pp. 1–42.

Gong, G. W., *The Standard of 'Civilization' in International Society* (Oxford: Oxford University Press, 1984).

Gordon, S., *The Marathas, 1600–1818* (Cambridge: Cambridge University Press, 1993).

Grewal, J. S., *The Sikhs of the Punjab* (Cambridge: Cambridge University Press, 1991).

Gungwu, W., 'The Chinese urge to civilize: Reflections on change', *Journal of Asian History*, 18(1) (1984), 1–34.

Guy, R. K., 'Who were the Manchus? A review essay', *Journal of Asian Studies*, 61 (1) (2002), 151–64.

Habib, I., *The Agrarian System of Mughal India, 1556–1707* (Oxford: Oxford University Press, 1963).

'The coming of 1857', *Social Scientist*, 26(1–4) (1998), 6–15.

(ed.), *Confronting Colonialism: Resistance and modernisation under Haidar Ali and Tipu Sultan* (London: Anthem Press, 2002).

Hang, X., *Conflict and Commerce in Maritime Asia: The Zheng family and the shaping of the modern world, c.1620–1720* (Cambridge: Cambridge University Press, 2015).

'The shogun's Chinese partners: The alliance between Tokugawa Japan and the Zheng family in seventeenth-century maritime East Asia', *Journal of Asian Studies*, 75(1) (2016), 111–36.

Hasan, F., 'Conflict and cooperation in Anglo-Mughal trade relations during the reign of Aurangzeb', *Journal of the Economic and Social History of the Orient*, 34 (4) (1991), 351–60.

State and Locality in Mughal India: Power relations in Western India, c.1572–1730 (Cambridge: Cambridge University Press, 2004).

Hatekar, N., 'Farmers and markets in the pre-colonial Deccan: The plausibility of economic growth in a traditional society', *Past and Present*, 178(1) (2003), 116–47.

Headrick, D. R., *The Tools of Empire: Technology and European imperialism in the nineteenth century* (Oxford: Oxford University Press, 1981).

Power Over Peoples: Technology, environments, and Western imperialism, 1400 to the present (Princeton: Princeton University Press, 2012).

Helleiner, E., *Forgotten Foundations of Bretton Woods: International development and the making of the postwar order* (Ithaca: Cornell University Press, 2014).

Henley, D., 'Conflict, justice, and the stranger-king indigenous roots of colonial rule in Indonesia and elsewhere', *Modern Asian Studies*, 38(1) (2004), 85–144.

Herbert, C., *War of No Pity: The Indian Mutiny and Victorian trauma* (Princeton: Princeton University Press, 2008).

Herman, J., 'Collaboration and resistance on the southwest frontier: Early eighteenth-century Qing expansion on two fronts', *Late Imperial China*, 35 (1) (2014), 77–112.

Ho, D. D., 'The burning shore: Fujian and the coastal depopulation, 1661–1683' in T. Andrade and X. Hang (eds.), *Sea Rovers, Silver, and Samurai: Maritime East Asia in global history, 1550–1700* (Honolulu: University of Hawaii Press, 2016), pp. 260–89.

Ho, P.-T., 'In defence of Sinicization: A rebuttal of Evelyn Rawski's "reenvisioning the Qing"', *Journal of Asian Studies*, 57(1) (1998), 123–55.

Hobsbawm, E., *The Age of Empire, 1875–1914* (London: Vintage, 1989).

Hobson, J. M., *The Eastern Origins of Western Civilization* (Cambridge: Cambridge University Press, 2004).

'The twin self-delusions of IR: Why "hierarchy" and not "anarchy" is the core concept of IR', *Millennium: Journal of International Studies*, 42(3) (2014), 557–75.

Hobson, J. M. and Sharman, J. C. , 'The enduring place of hierarchy in world politics: Tracing the social logics of hierarchy and political change', *European Journal of International Relations*, 11(1) (2005), 63–98.

Hofmeister, U., 'Civilization and Russification in Tsarist Central Asia, 1860–1917', *Journal of World History*, 27(3) (2016), 411–42.

Holt, M. P., *The French Wars of Religion, 1562–1629* (Cambridge: Cambridge University Press, 2005).

Horowitz, R. S., 'International law and state transformation in China, Siam, and the Ottoman Empire during the nineteenth century', *Journal of World History*, 15(4) (2004), 445–86.

Horsman, R., *Race and Manifest Destiny: The origins of American Anglo-Saxonism* (Cambridge, MA: Harvard University Press, 1981).

Hsu, I. C. Y., 'Late Ch'ing foreign relations, 1866–1905' in J. K. Fairbank and K.-C. Liu (eds.), *The Cambridge History of China*, 15 vols., XI: *Late Ch'ing, 1800–1911*, Pt II (Cambridge: Cambridge University Press, 1978), pp. 70–141.

Hui, V. T.-B., 'Toward a dynamic theory of international politics: Insights from comparing ancient China and early modern Europe', *International Organization*, 58(1) (2004), 175–205.

War and State Formation in Ancient China and Early Modern Europe (Cambridge: Cambridge University Press, 2005).

Hutchins, H. G., *The Illusion of Permanence: British imperialism in India* (Princeton: Princeton University Press, 1967).

Irwin, D. A., 'Mercantilism as strategic trade policy: The Anglo-Dutch rivalry for the East India trade', *Journal of Political Economy*, 99(6) (1991), 1296–314.

Jackson, P. T. and Nexon, D. H., 'Relations before states: Substance, process and the study of world politics', *European Journal of International Relations*, 5(3) (1999), 291–332.

Jacques, M., *When China Rules the World: The end of the Western world and the birth of a new global order* (London: Penguin, 2012).

Jenks, R. D., *Insurgency and Social Disorder in Guizhou: The 'Miao' Rebellion, 1854–1873* (Honolulu: University of Hawaii Press, 1994).

Jha, M. K., 'South Asia, 1400–1800: The Mughal Empire and the Turco-Persianate tradition in the Indian subcontinent' in J. Fairey and B. P. Farrell (eds.), *Empire in Asia: A new global history*, 2 vols., I: *From Chinggisid to Qing* (London: Bloomsbury Academic, 2018), pp. 141–70.

Jones, E., *The European Miracle: Environments, economies and geopolitics in the history of Europe and Asia* (Cambridge: Cambridge University Press, 2003).

Kang, D. C., 'Hierarchy in Asian international relations: 1300–1900', *Asian Security*, 1(1) (2005), 53–79.

'Hierarchy and legitimacy in international systems: The tribute system in early modern East Asia', *Security Studies*, 19(4) (2010), 591–622.

Kaufman, S. J., Little, R. and Wohlforth, W. C. (eds.), *The Balance of Power in World History* (Basingstoke: Palgrave Macmillan, 2007).

Kayaoglu, T., *Legal Imperialism: Sovereignty and extraterritoriality in Japan, the Ottoman Empire, and China* (Cambridge: Cambridge University Press, 2010).

'Westphalian eurocentrism in international relations theory', *International Studies Review*, 12(2) (2010), 193–217.

Keay, J. *India: A history* (London: Grove Press, 2011).

Keen, C., *Princely India and the British: Political development and the operation of empire* (London: I. B. Tauris, 2012).

Keliher, M., 'The Manchu Transformation of Li: Ritual, politics, and law in the making of Qing China, 1631–1690'. PhD diss., Harvard University, 2015.

Kelly, R. E., 'A "Confucian long peace" in pre-Western East Asia?', *European Journal of International Relations*, 18(3) (2012), 407–30.

Khan, I. A., 'State in the Mughal India: Re-examining the myths of a counter-vision', *Social Scientist*, 29(1–2) (2001), 16–45.

'The regulations of Tipu Sultan for his state trading enterprise' in I. Habib (ed.), *Confronting Colonialism: Resistance and modernisation under Haidar Ali and Tipu Sultan* (London: Anthem Press, 2002), pp. 148–60.

Gunpowder and Firearms: Warfare in medieval India (New Delhi: Oxford University Press, 2004).

'Tracing sources of principles of Mughal governance: A critique of recent historiography', *Social Scientist*, 37(5–6) (2009), 45–54.

Kia, M., 'Moral refinement and manhood in Persian' in M. Pernau et al. (eds.), *Civilizing Emotions: Concepts in nineteenth century Asia and Europe* (Oxford: Oxford University Press, 2015), pp. 146–65.

Kim, H.-D., *Holy War in China: The Muslim rebellion and state in Chinese Central Asia, 1864–1877* (Stanford: Stanford University Press, 2004).

Kim, K.-H., *The Last Phase of the East Asian World Order: Korea, Japan, and the Chinese Empire, 1860–1882* (Berkeley: University of California Press, 1979).

King, R., 'Orientalism and the modern myth of "Hinduism"', *Numen*, 46(2) (1999), 146–85.

Kinra, R., 'Handling diversity with absolute civility: The global historical legacy of Mughal *Ṣulḥ-i-Kull*', *Medieval History Journal*, 16(2) (2013), 251–95.

Kivelson, V. A. and Suny, R. G., *Russia's Empires* (Oxford: Oxford University Press, 2017).

Kolff, D. H. A., 'The end of the *Ancien Régime:* Colonial war in India, 1798–1818' in J. A. de Moor and H. L. Wesseling (eds.), *Imperialism and War: Essays on colonial wars in Asia and Africa* (Leiden: E. J. Brill, 1989), pp. 22–49.

Naukar, Rajput, and Sepoy: The ethnohistory of the military labour market in Hindustan, 1450–1850 (Cambridge: Cambridge University Press, 1990).

Krasner, S. D., 'Organized hypocrisy in nineteenth-century East Asia', *International Relations of the Asia-Pacific*, 1(2) (2001), 173–97.

Kuhn, P. A., 'Origins of the Taiping vision: Cross-cultural dimensions of a Chinese rebellion', *Comparative Studies in Society and History*, 19(3) (1977), 350–66.

'The Taiping Rebellion' in J. K. Fairbank (ed.), *The Cambridge History of China*, 15 vols., X: *Late Ch'ing, 1800–1911*, Pt I (Cambridge: Cambridge University Press, 1978), pp. 264–317.

Kumar, R. 'The Mysore navy under Haidar Ali and Tipu Sultan' in I. Habib (ed.), *Confronting Colonialism: Resistance and modernisation under Haidar Ali and Tipu Sultan* (London: Anthem Press, 2002), pp. 175–81.

Kyriazis, N. and Metaxas, T., 'Path dependence, change and the emergence of the first joint-stock companies', *Business History*, 53(3) (2011), 363–74.

Lake, D. A., *Hierarchy in International Relations* (Ithaca: Cornell University Press, 2009).

Langlois, J. D. Jr, 'Chinese culturalism and the Yüan analogy: Seventeenth-century perspectives', *Harvard Journal of Asiatic Studies*, 40(2) (1980), 355–98.

Lapidus, I. M., 'Knowledge, virtue, and action: The classical Muslim conception of *adab* and the nature of religious fulfilment in Islam' in B. D. Medcalf (ed.), *Moral Conduct and Authority: The place of adab in South Asian Islam* (Los Angeles: University of California Press, 1984), pp. 38–61.

Lattimore, O., 'Inner Asian frontiers: Chinese and Russian margins of expansion', *Journal of Economic History*, 7(1) (1947), 24–52.

Laver, M. S., *The Sakoku Edicts and the Politics of Tokugawa Hegemony* (New York: Cambria Press, 2011).

Lawson, G., 'The global transformation: The nineteenth century and the making of modern international relations', *International Studies Quarterly*, 57(3) (2013), 620–34.

Lawson, P., *The East India Company: A history* (New York: Longman, 1993).

Lee, J.-Y., 'Diplomatic ritual as a power resource: The politics of asymmetry in early modern Chinese-Korean relations', *Journal of East Asian Studies*, 13(2) (2013), 309–36.

China's Hegemony: Four hundred years of East Asian domination (New York: Columbia University Press, 2016).

Leff, G., 'Heresy and the decline of the medieval church', *Past and Present*, 20(1) (1961), 36–51.

Lefèvre, C., 'In the name of the fathers: Mughal genealogical strategies from Babur to Shah Jahan', *Religions of South Asia*, 5(1–2) (2011), 409–42.

Leibold, J., *Reconfiguring Chinese Nationalism: How the Qing frontier and its indigenes became Chinese* (New York: Palgrave Macmillan, 2007).

Levene, M., 'Empires, native peoples, and genocide' in D. Moses (ed.), *Empire, Colony, Genocide: Conquest, occupation, and subaltern resistance in world history* (New York: Berghahn Books, 2008), pp. 183–204.

Li, G. R., 'State building before 1644' in W. J. Peterson (ed.), *The Cambridge History of China*, 15 vols., IX: *The Ch'ing Empire to 1800*, Pt I (Cambridge: Cambridge University Press, 2002), pp. 9–72.

Lieberman, V., 'Protected rimlands and exposed zones: Reconfiguring premodern Eurasia', *Comparative Studies in Society and History*, 50(3) (2008), 692–723.

Strange Parallels: Southeast Asia in global context, 2 vols., II: *Mainland Mirrors: Europe, Japan, China, South Asia, and the islands* (Cambridge: Cambridge University Press, 2009).

Little, R., *International Systems in World History: Remaking the study of international relations* (Oxford: Oxford University Press, 2000).

Lorge, P. A., *The Asian Military Revolution: From gunpowder to the bomb* (Cambridge: Cambridge University Press, 2008).

Lynn, J. A., 'Heart of the sepoy: The adoption and adaption of European military practice in South Asia, 1740–1805' in E. O. Goldman and L. C. Eliason (eds.), *The Diffusion of Military Technology and Ideas* (Stanford: Stanford University Press, 2003), pp. 33–62.

MacDonald, P., *Networks of Domination: The social foundations of peripheral conquest in international politics* (Oxford: Oxford University Press, 2014).

Macaulay, T., 'Minute by the Honourable T. B. Macaulay, dated the 2nd February 1835' in H. Sharp (ed.), *Selections from Educational Records, 1781–1839*, Pt I (Delhi: National Archives of India, 1965 [1920]), pp. 107–17. Available at: https://bit.ly/2NcqYHt (accessed 20 April 2018).

Mackay, J., 'Pirate nations: Maritime pirates as escape societies in late Imperial China', *Social Science History*, 37(4) (2013), 551–73.

'Legitimation strategies in international hierarchies', *International Studies Quarterly*, 63(3) (2019), 717–25.

Maier, C. S., *Leviathan 2.0: Inventing modern statehood* (Cambridge, MA: Harvard University Press, 2014).

Maloni, R., 'Europeans in seventeenth century Gujarat: Presence and response', *Social Scientist*, 36(3–4) (2008), 64–99.

Mamdani, M., *Citizen and Subject: Contemporary Africa and the legacy of late colonialism* (Princeton: Princeton University Press, 1996).

Define and Rule: Native as political identity (Cambridge, MA: Harvard University Press, 2012).

Mann, M., *The Sources of Social Power*, 4 vols., I: *A History of Power from the Beginning to AD 1760*, 2nd ed. (Cambridge: Cambridge University Press, 2012).

The Sources of Social Power, 4 vols., III: *Global Empires and Revolution, 1890–1945*, 2nd ed. (Cambridge: Cambridge University Press, 2012).

'Review article: The great divergence', *Millennium: Journal of International Studies*, 46(2) (2018), 241–8.

Mann, S., 'Women, families, and gender relations' in W. J. Peterson (ed.), *The Cambridge History of China*, 15 vols., IX: *The Ch'ing Empire to 1800*, Pt I (Cambridge: Cambridge University Press, 2002), pp. 428–72.

Mantena, K., *Alibis of Empire: Henry Maine and the ends of liberal imperialism* (Princeton: Princeton University Press, 2010).

Marshall, P. J., 'British expansion in India in the eighteenth century: A historical revision', *History*, 60(198) (1975), 28–43.

Bengal: The British bridgehead, Eastern India 1740–1828 (Cambridge: Cambridge University Press, 1988).

The Making and Unmaking of Empires: Britain, India and America c.1750–1783 (Oxford: Oxford University Press, 2005).

Mazower, M., *Hitler's Empire: How the Nazis ruled Europe* (New York: Penguin, 2008).

McCord, E. A., 'Militia and local militarization in late Qing and early Republican China: The case of Hunan', *Modern China*, 14(2) (1988), 156–87.

McNeill, W. H., *The Rise of the West: A history of the human community* (Chicago: University of Chicago Press, 1963).

The Pursuit of Power: Technology, armed force and society since AD 1000 (Chicago: Chicago University Press, 1982).

The Age of Gunpowder Empires, 1450–1800 (Washington, DC: American Historical Association, 1989).

Plagues and Peoples (New York: Bantam Doubleday, 1998).

Meersbergen, G. van, 'The diplomatic repertories of the East India companies in Mughal South Asia, 1608–1717', *Historical Journal*, 62(4) (2019), 875–98.

Melo, J. V., 'Seeking prestige and survival: Gift exchange practices between the Portuguese Estado da India and Asian rulers', *Journal of the Economic and Social History of the Orient*, 56(4–5) (2013), 672–95.

'In search of a shared language: The Goan diplomatic protocol', *Journal of Early Modern History*, 20(4) (2016), 390–407.

Meredith, R., *The Elephant and the Dragon: The rise of India and China and what it means for all of us* (New York: W. W. Norton, 2008).

Metcalf, T. R., *Ideologies of the Raj* (Cambridge: Cambridge University Press, 1997).

Meurer, S., 'Approaches to state-building in eighteenth-century Bengal' in A. Fluchter and S. Richter (eds.), *Structures on the Move: Technologies of governance in transcultural encounter* (Heidelberg: Springer, 2012), pp. 219–41.

Michael, F., *The Taiping Rebellion: History and documents*, 3 vols., I: *History* (Seattle: University of Washington Press, 1966).

Millward, J. A., *Beyond the Pass: Economy, ethnicity, and empire in Qing Central Asia, 1759–1864* (Stanford: Stanford University Press, 1998).

'Qing inner Asian empire and the return of the Torghuts' in R. W. Dunnell, M. C. Elliott, P. Foret and J. A. Millward (eds.), *New Qing Imperial History:*

The making of inner Asian empire at Qing Chengde (London: Routledge, 2004), pp. 91–105.

'The Qing formation, the Mongol legacy and the "end of history" in early modern Central Eurasia' in L. A. Struve (ed.), *The Qing Formation in World-Historical Time* (Cambridge, MA: Harvard University Press, 2004), pp. 92–120.

'Qing and twentieth-century Chinese diversity regimes' in A. Phillips and C. Reus-Smit (eds.), *Culture and Order in World Politics* (Cambridge: Cambridge University Press, 2020), pp. 71–92.

Mio, K., 'The Ch'ing Dynasty and the East Asian world', *Acta Asiatica*, 88 (2005), 87–109.

Mohan, J., 'The glory of ancient India stems from her Aryan blood: French anthropologists "construct" the racial history of India for the world', *Modern Asian Studies*, 50(5) (2016), 1576–618.

Moin, A. A., 'Islam and the Millennium: Sacred kingship and popular imagination in early modern India and Iran'. PhD diss., University of Michigan, 2010.

Moller, J., 'Why Europe avoided hegemony: A historical perspective on the balance of power', *International Studies Quarterly*, 58(4) (2014), 660–70.

Monahan, E., *The Merchants of Siberia: Trade in early modern Eurasia* (Ithaca: Cornell University Press, 2016).

Moosvi, S., 'The evolution of the "Manṣab" system under Akbar until 1596–7', *Journal of the Royal Asiatic Society of Great Britain and Ireland*, 2 (1981), 173–85.

Morgan, D., 'The decline and fall of the Mongol Empire', *Journal of the Royal Asiatic Society*, 19(4) (2009), 427–37.

Motyl, A. J., *Imperial Ends: The decay, collapse, and revival of empires* (New York: Columbia University Press, 2013).

Mulich, J., 'Transformation at the margins: Imperial expansion and systemic change in world politics', *Review of International Studies*, 44(4) (2019), 649–716.

Munkler, H., *Empires: The logic of world domination from Ancient Rome to the United States* (London: Polity Press, 2007).

Nadri, G. A., *Eighteenth-Century Gujarat: The dynamics of its political economy, 1750–1800* (Leiden: Brill, 2009).

Narangoa, L. and Cribb, R., *Historical Atlas of Northeast Asia 1590–2010: Korea, Manchuria, Mongolia, Eastern Siberia* (New York: Columbia University Press, 2014).

Nath, P., 'Through the lens of war: Akbar's sieges (1567–69) and Mughal empire-building in early modern north India', *South Asia: Journal of South Asian Studies*, 41(2) (2018), 245–58.

Climate of Conquest: War, environment, and empire in Mughal north India (Oxford: Oxford University Press, 2019).

Nedal, D. K. and Nexon, D. H., 'Anarchy and authority: International structure, the balance of power, and hierarchy', *Journal of Global Security Studies*, 4(2) (2019), 169–89.

Newbury, C., *Patrons, Clients, and Empire: Chieftaincy and over-rule in Asia, Africa, and the Pacific* (Oxford: Oxford University Press, 2003).

Nexon, D. H., *The Struggle for Power in Early Modern Europe: Religious conflict, dynastic empires, and international change* (Princeton: Princeton University Press, 2009).

Nexon, D. H. and Neumann, I. B., 'Hegemonic-order theory: A field-theoretic account', *European Journal of International Relations*, 24(3) (2018), 662–86.

Wright, T., 'What's at stake in the American empire debate', *American Political Science Review*, 101(2) (2007), 253–71.

Nichols, J., 'Forerunners to globalization: The Eurasian steppe and its periphery', *Studies in Slavic and General Linguistics*, 38 (2011), 177–95.

North, D. C., *Institutions, Institutional Change and Economic Performance* (Cambridge: Cambridge University Press, 1990).

Omissi, D., '"Martial races": Ethnicity and security in colonial India, 1858–1939', *War and Society*, 9(1) (1991), 1–27.

Onley, J., 'The Raj reconsidered: British India's informal empire and spheres of influence in Asia and Africa', *Asian Affairs*, 40(1) (2009), 44–62.

Osiander, A., *Before the State: Systemic political change in the West from the Greeks to the French Revolution* (Oxford: Oxford University Press, 2008).

Palat, R. A., 'Power pursuits: Interstate systems in Asia', *Asian Review of World Histories*, 1(2) (2013), 227–63.

Panikkar, K. M., *Asia and Western Dominance: A survey of the Vasco da Gama epoch of Asian history, 1498–1945* (London: George Allen & Unwin, 1953).

Park, S.-H., 'Changing definitions of sovereignty in nineteenth-century East Asia: Japan and Korea between China and the West', *Journal of East Asian Studies*, 13(2) (2013), 281–307.

Parker, G., *The Military Revolution: Military innovation and the rise of the West, 1500–1800* (Cambridge: Cambridge University Press, 1996).

Pearson, M. N., 'Shivaji and the decline of the Mughal Empire', *Journal of Asian Studies*, 35(2) (1976), 221–35.

'Merchants and states' in J. D. Tracy (ed.), *The Political Economy of Merchant Empires: State power and world trade, 1350–1750* (Cambridge: Cambridge University Press, 1991), pp. 41–116.

Peers, D. M., '"The habitual nobility of being": British officers and the social construction of the Bengal army in the early nineteenth century', *Modern Asian Studies*, 25(3) (1991), 545–69.

'Revolution, evolution, or devolution: The military and the making of colonial India' in W. E. Lee (ed.), *Empires and Indigenes: Intercultural alliance, imperial expansion, and warfare in the early modern world* (New York: New York University Press, 2011), pp. 81–107.

Peifer, D. C., 'Maritime commerce warfare: The coercive response of the weak?', *Naval War College Review*, 66(2) (2013), 83–109.

Perdue, P. C., 'Military mobilization in seventeenth and eighteenth-century China, Russia, and Mongolia', *Modern Asian Studies*, 30(4) (1996), 757–93.

'Boundaries, maps, and movement: Chinese, Russian, and Mongolian empires in early modern Central Eurasia', *International History Review*, 20(2) (1998), 263–86.

'The Qing Empire in Eurasian time and space: Lessons from the Galdan campaigns' in L. A. Struve (ed.), *The Qing Formation in World-Historical Time* (Cambridge, MA: Harvard University Press, 2004), pp. 57–91.

China Marches West: The Qing conquest of Central Eurasia (Cambridge, MA: Harvard University Press, 2005).

'Coercion and commerce on two Chinese frontiers' in N. di Cosmo (ed.), *Military Culture in Imperial China* (Cambridge, MA: Harvard University Press, 2009), pp. 317–38.

'Boundaries and trade in the early modern world: Negotiations at Nerchinsk and Beijing', *Eighteenth-Century Studies*, 43(3) (2010), 341–56.

'The tenacious tributary system', *Journal of Contemporary China*, 24(96) (2015), 1002–14.

Pettigrew, W. A., 'Corporate constitutionalism and the dialogue between the global and local in seventeenth-century English history', *Itinerario*, 39(3) (2015), 487–501.

Phillips, A., *War, Religion and Empire: The transformation of international orders* (Cambridge: Cambridge University Press, 2011).

'Civilizing missions and the rise of international hierarchies in early modern Asia', *Millennium: Journal of International Studies*, 42(3) (2014), 697–717.

'The global transformation, multiple early modernities, and international systems change', *International Theory*, 8(3) (2016), 481–91.

'Asian incorporation and the collusive dynamics of Western "expansion" in the early modern world' in J. Go and G. Lawson (eds.), *Global Historical Sociology* (Cambridge: Cambridge University Press, 2017), pp. 182–98.

'International systems' in T. Dunne and C. Reus-Smit (eds.), *The Globalization of International Society* (Oxford: Oxford University Press, 2017), pp. 43–62.

'Making empires: Hierarchy, conquest and customization' in A. Zarakol (ed.), *Hierarchies in World Politics* (Cambridge: Cambridge University Press, 2017), pp. 43–65.

Phillips, A. and Reus-Smit, C. (eds.), *Culture and Order in World Politics* (Cambridge: Cambridge University Press, 2020).

Phillips, A. and Sharman, J. C., *Outsourcing Empire: How company-states made the modern world* (Princeton: Princeton University Press, 2020).

Po, R. C., 'Mapping maritime power and control: A study of the late eighteenth century *Qisheng yanhai tu* (a coastal map of the seven provinces)', *Late Imperial China*, 37(2) (2016), 93–136.

The Blue Frontier: Maritime vision and power in the Qing Empire (Cambridge: Cambridge University Press, 2018).

Pollock, S., 'The vernacular millennium: Literary culture and polity, 1000–1500', *Daedalus*, 127(3) (1998), 41–74.

Pomeranz, K., *The Great Divergence: China, Europe, and the making of the modern world economy* (Princeton: Princeton University Press, 2000).

Porter, A., '"Commerce and Christianity": The rise and fall of a nineteenth-century missionary slogan', *Historical Journal*, 28(3) (1985), 597–621.

Prange, S. R., 'Scholars and the sea: A historiography of the Indian Ocean', *History Compass*, 6(5) (2008), 1382–93.

'A trade of no dishonor: Piracy, commerce, and community in the Western Indian Ocean, twelfth to sixteenth century', *American Historical Review*, 116 (5) (2011), 1269–93.

'The contested sea: Regimes of maritime violence in the pre-modern Indian Ocean', *Journal of Early Modern History*, 17(1) (2013), 9–33.

Pratt, M. L., *Imperial Eyes: Travel writing and transculturation* (London: Routledge, 2006).

Rahman, T., 'Decline of Persian in British India', *South Asia*, 22(1) (1999), 47–62.

Rappaport, E., *A Thirst for Empire: How tea shaped the modern world* (Princeton: Princeton University Press, 2017).

Rawski, E. S., 'The Qing Empire during the Qianlong reign' in R. W. Dunnell, M. C. Elliott, P. Foret and J. A. Millward (eds.), *New Qing Imperial History: The making of inner Asian empire at Qing Chengde* (London: Routledge, 2004), pp. 15–21.

Early Modern China and Northeast Asia: Cross-border perspectives (Cambridge: Cambridge University Press, 2015).

Reed, I. A., 'Chains of power and their representation', *Sociological Theory*, 35(2) (2017), 87–117.

Reilly, T. H., *The Taiping Heavenly Kingdom: Rebellion and the blasphemy of empire* (Seattle: University of Washington Press, 2004).

Reus-Smit, C., 'Struggles for individual rights and the expansion of the international system', *International Organization*, 65(2) (2011), 207–42.

Individual Rights and the Making of the International System (Cambridge: Cambridge University Press, 2013).

'Cultural diversity and international order', *International Organization*, 71(4) (2017), 851–85.

On Cultural Diversity: International theory in a world of difference (Cambridge: Cambridge University Press, 2018).

Richards, J. F., 'The imperial crisis in the Deccan', *Journal of Asian Studies*, 35(2) (1976), 237–56.

The New Cambridge History of India, V: *The Mughal Empire*, Pt I (Cambridge: Cambridge University Press, 1993).

'Warriors and the state in early modern India', *Journal of the Economic and Social History of the Orient*, 47(3) (2004), 390–400.

Ricklefs, M., *A History of Modern Indonesia since c.1300* (Berkeley: Stanford University Press, 1993).

Ringrose, D., *Europeans Abroad, 1450–1750* (London: Rowman & Littlefield, 2018).

Rosen, S., *Societies and Military Power: India and its armies* (Ithaca: Cornell University Press, 1996).

Roy, K., 'The construction of regiments in the Indian army: 1859–1913', *War in History*, 8(2) (2001), 127–48.

'Military synthesis in South Asia: Armies, warfare and Indian society, c.1740–1849', *Journal of Military History*, 69(3) (2005), 651–90.

'The armed expansion of the English East India Company: 1740s–1849' in D. P. Marston and C. S. Sundaram (eds.), *A Military History of India and*

South Asia: From the East India Company to the nuclear age (Bloomington: Indiana University Press, 2008), pp. 1–15.

'The hybrid military establishment of the East India Company in South Asia: 1750–1849', *Journal of Global History*, 6(2) (2011), 195–218.

'Horses, guns and governments: A comparative study of the military transition in the Manchu, Mughal, Ottoman and Safavid Empires, circa 1400 to circa 1750', *International Area Studies Review*, 15(2) (2012), 99–121.

Roy, T., *India in the World Economy: From antiquity to the present* (Cambridge: Cambridge University Press, 2012).

'Rethinking the origins of British India: State formation and military-fiscal undertakings in an eighteenth-century world region', *Modern Asian Studies*, 47(4) (2013), 1125–56.

Said, E., *Orientalism* (London: Routledge Kegan & Paul, 1978).

Sana, R. P., 'Was there an agrarian crisis in Mughal north India in the late-seventeenth and early-eighteenth centuries?', *Social Scientist*, 34(11–12) (2006), 18–32.

Sarkar, J. *A Short History of Aurangzib* (London: Orient Longman, 2009).

Schottenhammer, A., 'Characteristics of Qing China's maritime trade politics, *Shunzhi* through *Qianlong* reigns' in A. Schottenhammer (ed.), *Trading Networks in Early Modern East Asia* (Wiesbaden: Harrassowitz Verlag, 2010).

Setzekorn, E., 'Chinese imperialism, ethnic cleansing, and military history, 1850–1877', *Journal of Chinese Military History*, 4(1) (2015), 80–100.

Sgourev, S. V. and Lent, W. van, 'Balancing permission and prohibition: Private trade and adaptation at the VOC', *Social Forces*, 93(3) (2015), 933–55.

Shaffer, L., 'Southernization', *Journal of World History*, 5(1) (1994), 1–21.

Maritime Southeast Asia to 1500 (New York: M. E. Sharpe, 1996).

Sharman, J. C., *Empires of the Weak: The real story of European expansion and the creation of the new world order* (Princeton: Princeton University Press, 2019).

Sheikh, S., 'Aurangzeb as seen from Gujarat: Shi'i and millenarian challenges to Mughal sovereignty', *Journal of the Royal Asiatic Society*, 28(3) (2018), 557–81.

Shigeki, I., 'China's frontier society in the sixteenth and seventeenth centuries', *Acta Asiatica*, 88 (2005), 1–20.

Siddiqi, M., *The British Historical Context and Petitioning in India* (New Delhi: Aakar Books, 2005).

Siebenhüner, K., 'Approaching diplomatic and courtly gift-giving in Europe and Mughal India: Shared practices and cultural diversity', *Medieval History Journal*, 16(2) (2013), 525–46.

Singh, P., 'An overview of Sikh history' in P. Singh and L. E. Fenech (eds.), *Oxford Handbook of Sikh Studies* (Oxford: Oxford University Press, 2014), pp. 19–34.

Slezkine, Y., *Arctic Mirrors: Russia and the small peoples of the north* (Ithaca: Cornell University Press, 1994).

Smith, R. J., *Mercenaries and Mandarins: The Ever-Victorious Army in nineteenth century China* (New York: KTO Press, 1978).

Solomon, S., *Water: The epic struggle for wealth, power, and civilization* (New York: Harper Perennial, 2011).

Souza, G. B., *The Survival of Empire: Portuguese trade and society in China and the South China Sea 1630–1754* (Cambridge: Cambridge University Press, 2004).

Spence, J. D., *God's Chinese Son: The Taiping heavenly kingdom of Hong Xiuquan* (New York: W. W. Norton, 1996).

The Search for Modern China (New York: W. W. Norton, 1999).

Spruyt, H., *The Sovereign State and its Competitors* (Princeton: Princeton University Press, 1994).

Stanley, B., '"Commerce and Christianity": Providence theory, the missionary movement, and the imperialism of free trade, 1842–1860', *Historical Journal*, 26(1) (1983), 71–94.

Steensgaard, N., *Caravans, Carracks and Companies: The structural crisis in the European-Asia trade in the early 17th century* (Lund: Studenliterratur, 1973).

Stein, B., 'Eighteenth century India: Another view', *Studies in History*, 5(1) (1989), 1–26.

Steinberg, P. E., *The Social Construction of the Ocean* (Cambridge: Cambridge University Press, 2001).

Stern, P. J., *The Company-State: Corporate sovereignty and the early modern foundations of the British Empire in India* (Oxford: Oxford University Press, 2011).

'"Bundles of hyphens": Corporations as legal communities in the early modern British Empire' in L. Benton and R. J. Ross (eds.), *Legal Pluralism and Empires, 1500–1850* (New York: New York University Press, 2013), pp. 21–48.

Stokes, E., *The English Utilitarians and India* (Oxford: Clarendon Press, 1959).

Streusand, D. E., *The Formation of the Mughal Empire* (Delhi: Oxford University Press, 1991).

Islamic Gunpowder Empires: Ottomans, Safavids, and Mughals (London: Routledge, 2010).

Struve, L. A., 'Introduction' in L. A. Struve (ed.), *The Qing Formation in World-Historical Time* (Cambridge, MA: Harvard University Press, 2004), pp. 1–54.

Stubbings, M., 'British conservatism and the Indian Revolt: The annexation of Awadh and the consequences of liberal empire, 1856–1858', *Journal of British Studies*, 55(4) (2016), 728–49.

Subrahmanyam, S., 'A tale of three empires: Mughals, Ottomans, and Habsburgs in a comparative context', *Common Knowledge*, 12(1) (2006), 66–92.

Sun, L., 'The Economy of Empire Building: Wild ginseng, sable fur, and the multiple trade networks of the early Qing Dynasty, 1583–1644'. DPhil diss., University of Oxford, 2018.

Suzuki, S., *Civilization and Empire: China and Japan's encounter with European international society* (London: Routledge, 2009).

Suzuki, S., Zhang, Y. and Quirk, J. (eds.), *International Orders in the Early Modern World: Before the rise of the West* (London: Routledge, 2013).

Swope, K. M., 'Deceit, disguise, and dependence: China, Japan, and the future of the tributary system, 1592–1596', *International History Review*, 24(4) (2002), 757–82.

A Dragon's Head and a Serpent's Tail: Ming China and the first great East Asian war, 1592–1598 (Norman: University of Oklahoma Press, 2009).

Taliaferro, J. W., 'State building for future wars: Neoclassical realism and the resource-extractive state', *Security Studies*, 15(3) (2006), 464–95.

Tambiah, S. J., 'What did Bernier actually say? Profiling the Mughal Empire', *Contributions to Indian Sociology*, 32(2) (1998), 361–86.

Teng, S.-Y., 'Chinese influence on the Western examination system: Introduction', *Harvard Journal of Asiatic Studies*, 7(4) (1943), 267–312.

Teschke, B., *The Myth of 1648: Class, geopolitics, and the making of modern international relations* (London: Verso, 2003).

Tilly, C., *Coercion, Capital and European States, AD 990–1992* (New York: Wiley-Blackwell, 1992).

'How empires end' in K. Barkey and M. von Hagen (eds.), *After Empire: Multiethnic societies and nation-building* (Boulder: Westview Press, 1997), pp. 1–11.

Todorov, T., *The Conquest of America: The question of the other* (Norman: University of Oklahoma Press, 1984).

Travers, R., 'Imperial revolutions and global repercussions: South Asia and the world, c.1750–1850' in D. Armitage and S. Subrahmanyam (eds.), *The Age of Revolution in Global Context, c. 1760–1840* (London: Palgrave Macmillan, 2010), pp. 144–66.

Trocki, C., *Opium, Empire and the Global Political Economy: A study of the Asian opium trade, 1750–1950* (London: Routledge, 1999).

Truschke, A., 'Dangerous debates: Jain responses to theological challenges at the Mughal court', *Modern Asian Studies*, 49(5) (2015), 1311–44.

Aurangzeb: The man and the myth (Gurgaon: Penguin Random House India, 2017).

Turchin, P., 'A theory of formation for large empires', *Journal of Global History*, 4 (2) (2009), 191–217.

Veer, P. van der, *Imperial Encounters: Religion and modernity in India and Britain* (Princeton: Princeton University Press, 2001).

Ven, H. van de, *Breaking with the Past: The maritime customs service and the global origins of modernity in China* (New York: Columbia University Press, 2014).

Vigneswaran, D., 'A corrupt international society: How Britain was duped into its first imperial conquest' in S. Suzuki, Y. Zhang and J. Quirk (eds.), *International Orders in the Early Modern World: Before the rise of the West* (London: Routledge, 2013), pp. 94–117.

Vink, M. P. M., 'Images and ideologies of Dutch-South Asian contact: Cross-cultural encounters between the Nayaka state of Madurai and the Dutch East India Company in the seventeenth century', *Itinerario*, 21(2) (1997), 81–123.

'From port-city to world-system: Spatial constructs of Dutch Indian Ocean studies, 1500–1800', *Itinerario*, 28(2) (2004), 45–116.

Encounters on the Opposite Coast: The Dutch East India Company and the Nayaka state of Madurai in the seventeenth century (Leiden: Brill, 2015).

Vivekanandran, J., *Interrogating International Relations: India's strategic practice and the return of history* (London: Routledge, 2011).

Wade, G., 'Engaging the south: Ming China and Southeast Asia in the fifteenth century', *Journal of the Economic and Social History of the Orient*, 51(4) (2008), 578–638.

Wagoner, P. B., '"Sultan among Hindu kings": Dress, titles, and the Islamicization of Hindu culture at Vijayanagara', *Journal of Asian Studies*, 55(4) (1996), 851–80.

Wakeman, F., *The Great Enterprise*, 2 vols., I: *The Manchu reconstruction of imperial order in seventeenth-century China* (Berkeley: University of California Press, 1985).

Waley-Cohen, J., 'Religion, war, and empire-building in eighteenth-century China', *International History Review*, 20(2) (1998), 336–52.

'Changing spaces of empire in eighteenth century China' in N. di Cosmo and D. J. Wyatt (eds.), *Political Frontiers, Ethnic Boundaries and Human Geographies in Chinese History* (London: Routledge Curzon, 2003), pp. 324–50.

The Culture of War in China: Empire and the military under the Qing Dynasty (London: I. B. Tauris, 2006).

Wallerstein, I., *The Capitalist World-Economy: Essays by Immanuel Wallerstein* (Cambridge: Cambridge University press, 1979).

Wang, L., 'From masterly brokers to compliant protégées: The frontier governance system and the rise of ethnic confrontation in China-Inner Mongolia, 1900–1930', *American Journal of Sociology*, 120(6) (2015), 1641–89.

Wang, Y., 'Claiming centrality in the Chinese world: Manchu–Chosŏn relations and the making of the Qing's "Zhonghou" identity, 1616–1643', *Chinese Historical Review*, 22(2) (2015), 95–119.

Wang, Z., *Never Forget National Humiliation: Historical memory in Chinese politics and foreign relations* (New York: Columbia University Press, 2012).

Ward, K., *Networks of Empire: Forced migration in the Dutch East India Company* (Cambridge: Cambridge University Press, 2009).

Watson, B., 'Fortifications and the "idea" of force in early English East India Company relations with India', *Past and Present*, 88 (1980), 70–87.

Weber, M., *Political Writings* (Cambridge: Cambridge University Press, 1994).

Webster, A., *Gentleman Capitalists: British imperialism in Southeast Asia, 1770–1890* (London: I. B. Tauris, 1998).

Wight, M., *Systems of States* (Leicester: Leicester University Press, 1977).

Willerslev, R. and Ulturgasheva, O., 'The sable frontier: The Siberian fur trade as montage', *Cambridge Journal of Anthropology*, 26(2) (2006–2007), 79–100.

Wills, J. E. Jr, 'Introduction' in J. E. Wills Jr (ed.), *China and Maritime Europe, 1500–1800: Trade, settlement, diplomacy, and missions* (Cambridge: Cambridge University Press, 2010), pp. 1–23.

'Maritime Europe and the Ming' in J. E. Wills Jr (ed.), *China and Maritime Europe, 1500–1800: Trade, settlement, diplomacy, and missions* (Cambridge: Cambridge University Press, 2010), pp. 24–77.

Wilson, J. E., 'Early colonial India beyond empire', *Historical Journal*, 50(4) (2007), 951–70.

The Domination of Strangers: Modern governance in Eastern India, 1780–1835 (London: Palgrave Macmillan, 2008).

Winius, G. D., *The Fatal History of Portuguese Ceylon: Transition to Dutch rule* (Cambridge, MA: Harvard University Press, 1971).

Wolters, O. W., *History, Culture, and Region in Southeast Asian Perspectives* (Singapore: SEAP Publications, 1999).

Wong, R. B., *China Transformed: Historical change and the limits of the European experience* (Ithaca: Cornell University Press, 1997).

Woodside, A., 'The Ch'ien-lung Reign' in W. J. Peterson (ed.), *The Cambridge History of China*, 15 vols., IX: *The Ch'ing Empire to 1800*, Pt I (Cambridge: Cambridge University Press, 2002), pp. 230–309.

Wright, M. C., *The Last Stand of Chinese Conservatism: The T'ung-Chih Restoration, 1862–1874* (Stanford: Stanford University Press, 1962).

Yazdani, K., 'Foreign relations and semi-modernization during the reigns of Haidar Ali and Tipu Sultan', *British Journal of Middle Eastern Studies*, 45(3) (2018), 394–409.

Yoon, S.-H., 'Repertoires of power: Early Qing–Chosŏn relations (1626–1644)', *Chinese Historical Review*, 21(2) (2014), 97–120.

Zarakol, A., (ed.), *Hierarchies in World Politics* (Cambridge: Cambridge University Press, 2017).

'The Ottomans and diversity', in A. Phillips and C. Reus-Smit (eds.), *Culture and Order in World Politics* (Cambridge: Cambridge University Press, 2020), pp. 49–70.

Zelin, M., 'The Yung-Cheng reign' in W. J. Peterson (ed.), *The Cambridge History of China*, 15 vols., IX: *The Ch'ing Empire to 1800*, Pt I (Cambridge: Cambridge University Press, 2002), pp. 183–229.

Zhang, W., *The China Wave: Rise of a civilizational state* (Hackensack: World Century Publishing Corporation, 2012).

Index

CPSIA information can be obtained
at www.ICGtesting.com
Printed in the USA
BVHW051702051021
618210BV00008B/28